So You Want To Be
A Christian Counsellor

Elvira Burkwood

ISBN: 978-0-9954397-0-2

Order this book online at www.prayercounsel.com

TABLE OF CONTENTS

INTRODUCTION

We are told that both the reading and writing of books have therapeutic value. I trust that opening this publication will truly draw you into the intriguing world of relating and connecting to people in a meaningful and purposeful manner. I pray, from the bottom of my heart, that it will serve to bring you, the reader, closer to your Father God.

Putting this manual together has proven quite therapeutic for me, and I am trusting that it will serve to leave a legacy of my time here on earth. After all, what is the use of collecting a lifetime of experiences without leaving a record of the value of those experiences? Some of my most valuable have involved sharing the life stories of others, through both lay ministry and in my professional capacity as a Christian counsellor.

In my opinion, counselling is one of the most satisfying, purposeful and fulfilling occupations possible. Prayer ministry is definitely one of the most exciting and challenging forms of counselling. The best part has been the privilege of personally working alongside the world's greatest expert in counselling.

This person has proven to be always available. His expertise is limitless; because he has experienced everything. He is the most knowledgeable teacher, an expert guide and the wisest of mentors. He never makes a mistake, never tires, never gives up, exudes love and patience, and possesses incredible people skills. He cares just as much about me as the counsellor, as he does for my clients. As my supervisor, he provides everything possible to help me to get the job done. How exciting is it to be under the ultimate personal trainer and the perfect role model!

Who would not want to observe the most famous healer in history – moulding, restoring, pruning and bringing back to life damaged souls and spirits? For those who have never experienced watching the Holy Spirit at work in this way, it is hard to express the wonder of it – both the natural and the supernatural 'highs'.

To me, counselling under the Holy Spirit's supervision is like working directly under the outflow of God's love. It has meant that my own spiritual hunger has been consistently satisfied. I am drawn daily to the Heavenly Father, which connects me personally to the redeemer, Jesus Christ. As I encourage others to draw closer to Him, I become part of that drawing and reap the benefits from seeing yet another side to Him. The rewards far outweigh the difficulties.

Admittedly, it is easy to get tired with the challenges that this type of ministry affords, but recalling the rewards is more than enough to revive the passion when all seems heavy going. There are the good times – the deeply satisfying experiences in counselling. There is that sudden recognition that there is valid hope; there is no need for that particular person to feel they need to walk alone any longer, or for that dark memory to be relived. The pain has gone. The comfort has come. There is deliverance from the pit of despair for one more lost and hurting spirit. Revelation penetrates to a troubled soul and the balm of forgiveness is applied on a deep, deep wound.

How amazing it has been to see individuals with light in their eyes for the first time and to sense peace lightly descending like a warm blanket. Cleansing tears are shared as a tense body and an aching soul are released from a lifetime of guilt and shame. How fulfilling it is to turn the key to free a caged heart, to offer a confident hand and to coax a sufferer into the sunlight.

Through the healing process: relationships are revived and restored, families are learning to love unselfishly, and the abandoned are being placed in supportive comforting arms. This is what it is about – this wonderful calling.

All these experiences are imprinted indelibly on the memory and filed away as treasured ministry keepsakes. To be part of this, sometimes brings incredible joy. At the very least, it causes one to feel – yes, there is a God and all is well with the world. Our Redeemer lives!

Yes, I have concentrated on the joys here, because the following will give you the impression that this type of ministry is one very difficult path to tread (and so it is). If you take part in it you will surely share the depths of human despair and experience personal suffering. Perhaps it will be tempting to give up – many times over. From someone who has been there, I encourage you to persevere, as you will find it well worth the hope of hearing *'well done, my good and faithful servant'* at the end of your walk.

With that said, I hope you enjoy reading the contents of this manuscript as much as we (the team involved) have had the pleasure in putting it together for you. For the beginners, I pray that this handbook serves to give you a taste of what will be involved if you feel you could have a calling in this area. God bless you in your endeavours as 'a people helper', in any area of ministry you eventually choose. May you experience the tangible presence of the divine *Paraclete* on your spiritual journey.

ACKNOWLEDGMENTS

I have revealed my own personal testimonies within this text prayerfully and purposefully. I sincerely hope that glory to God has been given, as it is truly his handiwork recorded, not mine, nor the co-workers who have laboured with me to present his healing ways.

Thanks go to all who have come alongside and shared their own precious life stories with me over the years. To my clients and friends, be assured that your confidences have not been betrayed in order to format this manual. Instead, I have taken delight in scripting some fictitious casework, which I hope proves both insightful and entertaining to the reader (especially to my spiritual son 'R' who waited so patiently for the promised first copy to come to print).

Special, special thanks to my beloved husband of more than 40 years who has supported me in all aspects of this manual coming about (in particular for the perpetual proofreading of my never ending alterations). My deep gratitude goes to our son, for all his sacrificial time and his expertise with 'tweaking' the graphics, and to our dear daughter-in-law for supporting him in this. Thank you to our precious daughter for the enjoyable times we spent when she took over from my weary hands and eyes to finish that final, final, final draft (half-way through).

Indeed my gratitude goes out to all our friends, relatives and colleagues who contributed support and encouragement to push us over the finishing line. We did it!!!!! What a team!

The Author,

Elvira Burkwood

DEDICATION

To The Author and Finisher of Our Faith

JESUS CHRIST

And to His dedicated workers who are ministering to:

The sick of heart,
The despairing,
The lean of spirit;
And confused in mind,
The outcasts,
The rejected ones,
The broken and lost in their way,
Those who cannot hear His voice;
Because they fear Him or hate Him,
Those who have heard His voice;
Yet have turned away to seek personal pleasures.

HOW TO USE THIS HANDBOOK

This textbook exists to give a practical and general guide into the basic aspects of ministering to those who are of the Christian faith and have some knowledge of the foundations of the belief system. It is written from the perspective of one who does not claim to be an academic, or an expert in psychology or theology; but by an individual who is an experienced 'people helper'. Her main desire is to pass on knowledge experientially gathered, and to leave a legacy for future generations.

The main purpose of the teachings is to distribute the gospel message of redemption (according to the mandate of Isaiah 61) to a world in pain, and hungry for hope. Reconciliation to the father heart of God and the restoration of man is the ministry bias.

Now for both specific and general instructions on how to use this resource:

First of all, have you read the *introduction*? Secondly, have you familiarized yourself with the *table of contents* containing the *section headings*, *chapter headings* and general descriptions and location of the *images*? Have you located the *appendices*? Lastly, be aware that this volume contains a *glossary* of jargon pertaining to prayer techniques within Chapter 18.

Note that the graphics/images deserve special attention. Techniques illustrated graphically have been proven by repeated use successfully on the coal-face. These are more than decorative illustrations; they are supplied as specific resources for teaching purposes. Some will be repeatedly used by the counsellor directly from this handbook. Therefore the table of contents contains page references for easy location of the images along with a referencing number from 1-28 and a brief description of each image.

After explaining a concept to a client or student via a diagram from this publication you will often be asked for a copy. A set of images is also available for purchase in manual form as a separate resource, with the author's specific consent for reproduction. Please feel free to request individual images on-line to download and store in your counselling resources to print off when required (see boxed insert headed COPYRIGHT on the following page for contact details).

Areas which are shaded present the author's personal testimony as well as her experiences in the field. In this way there is an autobiographical essence and the publication has a point of interest for the general reader interested in self healing and personal development.

To effectively make use of the insight and knowledge contained in this handbook, the reader should keep in mind that it is not a comprehensive manual. This publication aims to cover the various issues the Christian counsellor encounters most frequently, and to provide a sprinkling of resources that are not readily available to the average person. Case studies are included in the form of fictitious client testimonials. Hopefully, they will prove interesting and informative and will whet the appetite for this intriguing ministry and calling.

A primary aim is to indicate the possibilities of how to go about offering help on a biblical basis as a first port of call, rather than relying too heavily on current secular therapies. This is not to discount the invaluable theories and systems contained in the therapies covered comprehensively by other textbooks and teaching institutions. The primary aim of this textbook however, is to cover the specialist practice of Christian counselling, based on the foundations of the Word of God as expounded in the Holy Scriptures of the Christian faith.

As a training manual, this publication needs to be read from cover to cover, in that the information is presented precept upon precept to study and acquire techniques for use in the practice of Christian counselling. However, it can be resourced for understanding of individual issues as a need arises.

Throughout the text you will be reminded of important points, or led to other resources available, by the following format of boxed inserts:

COPYRIGHT

To enable this ministry to operate financially, it is requested that you ethically respect copyright so that the author can continue to provide various avenues of assistance to those in need. Master copies of the resources found within this text are provided for client handout purposes (including graphic illustrations) in the companion ministry resource book: *'So You Want to be a Christian Counsellor – Resources Handbook'* – www.prayercounsel.com.

Apart from the companion handbook, special individual resources are available for purchase for counselling or teaching purposes, this includes permission to reproduce. If you have any questions or special requests, please contact the author via the following contact details:

Elvira Burkwood,
Email: elvie@prayercounsel.com

IMPORTANT: It is wise not to dismiss these boxed presentations (example shown above) as you could miss crucial and relevant information.

Workbooks and teacher manuals can be produced for group study purposes as the need arises. The focus on application of Christian ministry techniques, and experiential learning of counselling skills, makes the teachings very suitable for group learning or supervised practice. Generally, the teaching of techniques from this resource is best suited to small class tutorials, along with facilitators and peer group supervision. In this way the full benefit can be gained from the exercises, testimonials and casework through discussion and feedback.

The book is divided into five sections with the individual chapters having introductory remarks and a synopsis of topics in order to make referencing easier. Whenever a key word, phrase or topic is introduced, it will often be in *italics* for a similar purpose, that is, easier referencing for teaching and study purposes. As previously mentioned, there is a glossary attached to the prayer techniques (Section V). Further notes about the author's experience are included in Appendix I: *Ministering to Children and Families.*

The reader is encouraged to be open to Holy Spirit guidance for referencing from the handbook. Random dipping into the text is discouraged; whereas making the effort to read contextually is recommended. Presentation of the text accommodates those who are not familiar with the jargon used in church circles or in the counselling profession. Some theology and professional jargon has been included by necessity – particularly to support those areas where extra study is encouraged. It is strongly recommended that the bible verses (in both graphic illustrations and text) be studied for their contextual relevance.

The text is categorized into topics so that it can also be used as a practising counsellor's resource, as well as a personal development tool. To access appropriate topics, it is necessary to skim the table of contents according to the need. For example, when dealing with someone suffering from depression due to an intimidating boss at work, initially look under the relevant emotion in the table of contents, and then self-assess the relevant links to the presenting problem. For example, *Depression* is the topic heading of Chapter 7 in Section #2, *Dealing with Feelings.* Then, search and study how to handle conflict in Chapter 10, *Victims* in Chapter 11 under *Relationships* in Section #3. Then perhaps reference the *Unforgiveness Assessment* from Chapter 12 under the heading *Forgiveness.*

It should be further emphasised here that this handbook needs concentrated study as a whole. Each chapter is deliberately sequenced in order to build on the information presented in the previous chapters. Spiritually, the content is delivered precept upon precept. So it is advised not to give in to the temptation to take a preliminary perusal of the book (if you have purchased it for serious study) by picking out topics of interest. Overall, it aims to offer a solid foundation of relevant information and practical guidance to all – from the potential Christian counsellor and the novice student – right through to experienced ministers of religion and seasoned professional counsellors.

SECTION ONE

Foundations & Practicalities

CHAPTER ONE

COUNSELLORS IN MINISTRY

Addresses a person who feels he or she has a calling to the ministry of Christian counselling and differentiates between a Christian counsellor and a counsellor who is a Christian. This chapter begins the teaching experience, and includes the following:

- Criteria checklist for self-assessment
- Description of the aspirations of an effective Christian counsellor
- Client perception and expectations of the counsellor who is effective
- Call for self-awareness as a spiritual healer
- Six character traits which can interfere with effective ministry
- Author's testimony and promotional leaflet
- Student exercise on *Client Issues*
- Initial teaching on the practicalities – *Learning our ABCs*

The space below is provided for your study notes on the chapter.

Study Notes

COUNSELLOR CRITERIA CHECKLIST

So you want to be a counsellor? Are you able to meet the following criteria?

- ❑ Be discipled, trained and mentored
- ❑ Be able to give undivided attention
- ❑ Have patience, perseverance and persistence
- ❑ Express unconditional love and respect
- ❑ Be open minded, flexible and adaptable to others' beliefs
- ❑ Be sure of your own values
- ❑ Have a personal belief system without being judgmental
- ❑ Be ethical and moral according to your own beliefs
- ❑ Have a sound doctrinal base and a personal relationship with God
- ❑ Display no prejudice or favouritism
- ❑ Keep confidences yet be open to exercising duty of care
- ❑ Be shockproof, or at least give the appearance of being shockproof
- ❑ Have a passion for the work of counselling
- ❑ Be mature enough not to be weighed down by another's problems
- ❑ Have a high sensitivity to the needs of others
- ❑ Have a thick skin when needed
- ❑ Sound confident but not a know-it-all
- ❑ Admit your mistakes and be teachable
- ❑ Be mentally and spiritually stable
- ❑ Present your home life as a positive testimony
- ❑ Be hospitable, polite, kind and gentle
- ❑ Dispense hope and encouragement no matter how you are feeling
- ❑ Forgive, or be in the process of forgiving to the best of your ability
- ❑ Be open to debriefing and seek counsel when necessary
- ❑ Feel fresh and alive after each session or encounter with a client
- ❑ Admit to being only one step ahead at times but still command respect
- ❑ Self-disclose appropriately without losing personal power
- ❑ Act in a professional manner while being a nurturer of self and others
- ❑ Be consistent, reliable, trustworthy, caring and compassionate
- ❑ Show friendship attributes, but with a professional emotional distancing
- ❑ Have boundaries set, yet still be flexible and adaptable
- ❑ Have the ability to be firm & decisive
- ❑ Show tough love when necessary
- ❑ Be there in essence, as well as physically, during crisis times
- ❑ Be tolerant of rudeness from those under pressure, those with differences of opinion and those who habitually cross boundaries
- ❑ Be open to, and accepting of, those with a difference either culturally, emotionally, intellectually and/or spiritually
- ❑ Relate to all ages, relatives, friends and opponents of clients
- ❑ Enable each person you deal with to feel important and valuable
- ❑ Lead a person to Christ when the opportunity arises

The preceding personal qualities and characteristics, although idealistic, are something to attain to. As a caring professional or volunteer in ministry, you can still make a significant difference in the lives of others whilst being a work in progress yourself. Here are some further aspirations:

POSITIVE PERCEPTIONS

To be effective in ministry as a Christian counsellor, you must know who you are 'in Christ' and have a clear sense of personal identity at any given time. You know what you want out of life, and who you want to become. You also have an idea of your potential, not only in work and ministry related activities, but for all aspects of your life.

You are content to be who you are at any time and excited about your journey of self-discovery. You possess a clear sense of your own value and self-worth. You are able to appreciate where you have come from and how you have grown as a person. You possess a clear sense of where you are going and who you are capable of becoming.

You are able to live in the present and to appreciate how the past has affected you to form who you are today. You accept the fact that there have been negative aspects of your past life and you acknowledge the associated regrets, but do not allow them to rule you.

You are willing to be a risk taker, a faith walker, who can make mistakes and admit these to yourself and to others. You are able to readily and sincerely apologise, making restitution where possible. You are always open to change and possess a willing heart to grow as a person; thereby being a model of self-awareness and growth to the people you are attempting to help.

For you instinctively realise that, if you model incongruent behaviour, low-risk activity, and hide your true nature and motivations, then the people you relate to as a helper will not risk opening up to you nor be willing to follow your directives for change. Instead, they will tend to model this deceitfulness and not reach their level of potential in Christ during the period of the ministry relationship.

CLIENT'S PERCEPTION OF THE COUNSELLOR

Instead, it is obvious that you are deeply involved in your work for the Lord and for mankind as a whole. You are indeed deriving meaning from it – from being a people helper and a servant of God. Yet it is clear that you can be a whole person apart from your works. You are able to be a human 'being' as well as a 'doer', because you feel valued as a child of God. You are valuable – apart from what you can do or how successfully you perform.

Your clients will benefit from seeing that you have realistic expectations of life. Therefore, they will feel that you will not be a hard taskmaster as you are not hard on yourself. It will be apparent that you derive power from a deep intimate relationship with Jesus Christ as your Saviour and Lord. Those you are attempting to help will have confidence that you are able to empower them to grow in the Lord also. You truly are both a therapeutic and spiritual role model.

You will be viewed as an authentic person who is willing to self-disclose for your own benefit as well as theirs; someone who will not hide behind a mask of professionalism. Instead, you disclose yourself as a real person who is honest and sincere and who appreciates differences in others. You will allow others to be individuals and not just a copy of your own ideas, values and behaviour. You are culturally sensitive to the unique differences that a person's environment, upbringing, race and gender bring to the counselling arena. You are open to, and tolerant of, ambiguity in situations or persons, and able to cope with the fact that individuals perceive in individual ways.

Your clients are able to see that you have a sincere interest in their welfare, as well as being aware of, and taking care of, your own needs. You will show that you are able to set clear and healthy boundaries; that you can say no whenever it is appropriate and yes to all that is good and fair to both parties.

They are aware that your life has perspective, is prioritised and well balanced; your dependence is on God the Father and not on man. Jesus Christ is your role model. The Holy Spirit is your counsellor and guide. You know who you are in Christ and sense your purpose, destiny and potential in Him. Your passion is in the area of spiritual healing.

SELF-AWARENESS

Counsellors as spiritual healers need to have an increasing level of self-awareness in order to consistently and effectively intervene, disciple, role model and mentor spiritually. To be a vessel for spiritual healing, you will need to seek help for personal wounds and unfinished business and to be aware of personal opinions, mindsets, values, ethics, or cultural differences which might impede a client's growth, self-discovery, healing and personal development.

Prayer ministers need to be acutely aware of personal conflicts and needs, and whether they are operating from a foundation of personal neediness or other motives that will be harmful, rather than healing. You will need to recognise that you will influence clients inadvertently, if not purposefully, with your personal philosophy on life and your unresolved issues. It is essential that you do not short-circuit the client's self-exploration nor take away their personal power. Clarification of our own values, needs, progress and conflicts will encourage positive self-expression and appropriate self-disclosure to others.

HELP FOR THE COUNSELLOR

In your role as the healer, you may need to participate in spiritual and personal growth activities such as, therapy, group work, inner healing ministry and deliverance sessions, in order to explore whether old wounds are being opened up via your ministry endeavours. If you are able to self-confront, you will become more effective in your ministry for Christ as you confront and challenge others.

This does not mean that you will have to wait to be perfect to be used by God. Honesty and authenticity (being real) is of the highest priority. You will often be just one step ahead of a client, but can still be led by the Holy Spirit in your role as a people helper. To every session you will present as an individual with unique qualities and life experiences. Realising and appropriately revealing your own sins, doubts and inadequacies will humble you in your walk and allow more compassion, tolerance and understanding of your fellow man.

You should be consciously aware that you need to guard against the following:

> ➢ being overly in need of being needed
> ➢ overly responsible
> ➢ performance motivated
> ➢ being a people pleaser & approval seeker
> ➢ needing to be seen as perfect
> ➢ lacking boundaries
> ➢ controlling & manipulative
> ➢ needing to feel superior
> ➢ possession of an independent spirit*

---

*An *independent spirit* in respect to not being willing to seek supervision, accountability or other assistance.

MOTIVES FOR ENTERING CHRISTIAN COUNSELLING

There are many special people who have genuine interest in learning the craft of counselling and who have the calling to pray for those in need of spiritual and emotional healing. However, there are certain character traits that are <u>not</u> classed as assets, or beneficial to this type of ministry, which could interfere with being an effective counsellor. You may have a mix of these flaws in your own character, or you could have a predominance of one or two. Some flaws may be alarmingly obvious to everyone else, so be willing to pray that the Holy Spirit will guide and convict you personally in areas where you may be in denial. It is hoped that you will <u>not</u> come under condemnation when these are revealed; instead, you will be willing to yield your flesh to die to these tendencies.

These characteristics or liabilities could be classified under: –

1. The Psychological Voyeur
2. The Spiritual Defiler
3. The Controller
4. The Rescuer
5. The Wounded Burden Bearer
6. The Haughty and Superior

1. THE PSYCHOLOGICAL VOYEUR

The word *voyeur* is not being used in its sexual context here, but for dramatic effect in the context of Christian counselling. The psychological voyeur in this sense is a person who takes perverse pleasure in knowing the intimate details of another party's life and viewing problems and inadequacies as something to digest with relish.

Only a cursory look at the array of magazines at a supermarket checkout will indicate what sells to the average consumer. Intimate details of celebrities are published inside the covers. Whether false, true or embellished, details of real people's lives are offered under sensational headlines. Very personal photographs are displayed on the front covers. While queuing to purchase basic goods, curiosity is piqued, and the temptation to purchase is there in order to digest the juicier details. Heads are shaken over the latest scandal, or an opinion is given on the ten worst or best-dressed women in the country.

As counsellors, there is also the natural temptation to look into our clients' intimate lives with curiosity. Be aware of this, and do take precautions to check the tendency, especially when you feel the urge to gossip or to 'share' something about 'someone'.

2. THE SPIRITUAL DEFILER

This terminology is used in both the natural and spiritual context. In the scriptures *defilement* describes when something is made foul, dirty, impure, or 'unclean'. When something is 'defiled' it is made unfit for ceremonial (or holy) use (Mal 1:12). In the prayer ministry the word is used to describe the process of intimately intruding into a vulnerable person's private life when they are under your care as a Christian counsellor. This fleshly characteristic, even in its minor form, takes both client and counsellor into dangerous territory. In its most serious form, it can be a type of spiritual or emotional molestation which may personally shame the victim, or be classed as *spiritual abuse*.

Those who are gifted in counselling will often hear from clients, *I have never told this to anyone else before but...* or, *you are the first person I have ever told that to!* As well as the sign that you are a good listener and an effective counsellor, it can also indicate that you may have overstepped personal boundaries to become too intimate and personally intrusive.

Heed this warning only when you begin to feel an unhealthy and excessive desire to ask intimate and unnecessary personal details of a person. Ask yourself if you are guilty of probing and betraying the trust of a client by overstepping the mark. Be aware of feeling irritated when someone does not want to share everything with you. Everyone has the right to privacy in his or her personal thoughts and beliefs and the need for a private world to retreat into.

3. THE CONTROLLER

Some people satisfy their innate need to *manipulate and control* by choosing to help and advise others. In this way they feel they have a legitimate right to be in a position of power. In a ministry position, they will derive pleasure in being the rudder of the client's ship. This is in opposition to a basic aim of counselling – to help empower the client to take charge of his or her own affairs.

Even the most ethical and discerning of counsellors can be deceived and manipulated into a *co-dependent relationship* with a client who feels the need to have someone 'take over' their life. This person will actually choose to be controlled because they feel incapable of making good choices, or are fearful of being accountable or responsible for personal poor choices. A counsellor does well to constantly reassess whether a client is willingly relinquishing personal power, or, whether he or she is actually robbing the client of the right to make choices and to learn from personal mistakes. Encouraging a client to give away personal freedom, or to take it forcibly, is unethical and dangerous.

When someone comes for ministry they are in some ways offering control to a certain degree. They are seeking advice and guidance, healing and other forms of directional help. Your position should always be to direct towards God-dependency and self-empowerment. When your clients are generally requiring too much help from you, then you will most likely have encouraged dependency, and you would be wise to question your own motives.

4. THE RESCUER OR SAVIOUR COMPLEX

Most counsellors harbour some degree of *rescuer mentality.* This is fine, as long as it is not based on fleshly motives and the client is genuinely in need of rescuing. However, Jesus Christ is our redeemer and no one has a right to take up this position in a person's life. The unhealthy rescuer mentality or *saviour complex* is evidenced when we feel driven to help each and every person within our orbit. Our thoughts are centred on diagnosis and fixing problems. Everyone is seen as potential client. Every social conversation becomes a deep and meaningful probe for release of a confidence. It is fine and needful to have a spirited passion for ministering and to put all our heart and energy into the work; but it is unhealthy to all concerned when it becomes a lifestyle.

Be warned again; ministry can become an addiction. There are the natural highs of success and the reputation and acclaim that come with it and wonderful to feel personally needed and appreciated, praised and thanked by your clients and their loved ones. But, watch out when the need becomes *approval addiction* and your major role is 'The Rescuer' and you become a 'super hero' in your own eyes.

Clues to this happening can be subtle. Examine your self-talk, general speech and thought patterns. See if the following examples ring true for you: –

> ➢ *I simply cannot let him down; he has been disappointed too often.*
> ➢ *There is no one else she will trust. She needs me to be there for her.*
> ➢ *I just couldn't refer them on, as there is no-one else who would be willing to spend so much time working with them as a couple.*
> ➢ *She has suffered too much to have to retell her story to someone else.*
> ➢ *I just wanted to protect her from making the same mistakes I did.*

5. THE WOUNDED BURDEN BEARER

The last example in the rescuer segment illustrates a counsellor personalising the client's pain. Helping to relieve another's pain sometimes becomes a form of self-medication; which might indicate that you are operating in the *wounded burden-bearer* role.

Past victims of abuse, particularly survivors of domestic violence or childhood sexual abuse can fall into the trap of feeling driven to rescue and protect. They can be drawn to becoming involved in helping those in similar situations to their own. The helper expresses the desire to use their personal experience rather than waste it; to protect others and to fight against injustices; to spare others from similar abuse.

Until you have achieved the spiritual maturity to handle what could trigger *unfinished business*, it is advisable to be selective in what cases you take on. Those with gaping unhealed wounds cannot minister effectively. Some organizations are now geared to recognise and reject these candidates. Unfortunately, unregulated voluntary helpers on the church scene, and even in Government agencies such as the child protection services, can cause deep distress in this area of operating in a wounded burden bearer role.

On the positive side, those with true empathy and compassion can come from the ranks of the survivors of abuse and can be most effective in prayer ministry and other caring situations. Those overcomers, who have passed through deep waters and have received comfort and healing, are the ones who can best administer similar comfort in Jesus' Name. God also promises only as many burdens as we can bear and that his yoke is easy and his burdens are light. If you are limping along ministry wise, feeling weak and heavy laden, then you are possibly carrying more than you are meant to carry. It is time to let go and to transfer your load, to reach out for help and personal healing for a season. It is time to rest in him.

However, realising you could be operating as an unhealed burden bearer is not an excuse to avoid or to discontinue ministry until you are perfectly healed and ready for action. Healing and restoration is a lifelong process. We live in a fallen world and no one escapes the enemy's attacks. Some wounds take longer to heal than others. During your personal healing process you can be powerfully used by the Holy Spirit to minister to those in need. Indeed, present suffering and overcoming may add a depth to your ministry which your clients may sense and will appreciate in you. After all, suffering was Jesus Christ's pathway on earth also.

6. THE HAUGHTY & SUPERIOR

There is no place for feeling superior in your position of ministry. You are foremost a people helper and a servant. There are some academics teaching psychology and some theologians preaching about prayer who have not experienced any real depth of suffering and on occasions are bereft of empathy. This is not to say that we should be proud of our personal suffering or participation in sharing the burdens and suffering of others, as this is simply part of the calling.

AUTHOR'S TESTIMONY

I have, more than once, asked God, 'Why did you make me with such a tender heart, and then call me to share the suffering of so many others?' Sometimes, it is more than I feel I can bear. He always answers in much the same way: 'You offered your life to me and this is what I chose to do with it. This is the path I chose for you; walk in it.'

I would personally find writing or teaching about the subject from only an academic viewpoint an impossible task. The more I unearth about the intricacies of human nature and the dealings of God, the less I feel I know or understand. The more I come face to face with the unconditional love of the Father towards mankind, the less haughty and superior do I feel over any degree of success or satisfaction I get from operating in this calling.

With God, we <u>can</u> achieve the impossible. Without him, we can do nothing. Please, do not be afraid to step out into ministry in a spirit of faith, even if you have recognised elements of these character flaws as personal. I have been guilty of the whole six! We are each a work in progress; clay in The Potter's hand. Experience the privilege of looking into the beautiful tearstained face of a child of God and you will find it all worthwhile.

You will not regret the choice you made to answer this call on your life.

WHY *CHRISTIAN* COUNSELLING?

Christian counselling a *holistic** approach to what the secular world describes as *the therapeutic process.* Therapeutics is the branch of medicine concerned with the treatment of disorders. To be *in therapy* or to be *undergoing therapy*, describes the process whereby practical measures are employed to cure or alleviate suffering. So perhaps we could best describe the form of counselling dealt with in this text as *spiritual therapy.*

There are many styles of prayer ministry involved in spiritual therapy. As a professional counsellor and therapist the author presents her own style and approach in a promotional leaflet to prospective clients. You may choose to use the following as a basis for composing your own leaflet.

> **holistic* **– the medical term for the consideration of the complete person in the treatment of disease**

SAMPLE PROMOTIONAL LEAFLET

HOPE COUNSELLING SERVICES*
A counselling service based on Christian principles
'Restoring hope to His people'

Every person needs support at some stage in life. You can find a listening ear and learn practical skills for coping with your distress or personal problems. You only have to reach out and ask. This is a ministry, not merely another business or service. It is steeped in prayer and reliant on the Holy Spirit's leading. Our mission is to restore hope to His people according to Isaiah 61 & Psalm 23.

WHO NEEDS COUNSELLING?

Some common problems which motivate a person to seek help are: –

- ➢ *Relationships – neighbours, workplace, marriage, friendships*
- ➢ *Grief following loss such as death or divorce*
- ➢ *Ill health, ageing, fear of the future*
- ➢ *Handling feelings such as depression, anxiety, anger*
- ➢ *Stress and emotional distress*
- ➢ *Addictions and disorders*
- ➢ *Self-esteem and identity issues*
- ➢ *Crisis situations and traumatic experiences*
- ➢ *Abuse and victimization*

> ➤ *Chronic pain or sadness*
> ➤ *Loneliness or feelings of not fitting in*
> ➤ *Parenting/parental problems*
> ➤ *Carer's needs – including burnout*
> ➤ *Spiritual needs*
> ➤ *Unemployment or forced retirement*
> ➤ *Failure in jobs, finances, love, reaching goals*
> ➤ *Dealing with disappointments*
> ➤ *Hopelessness, despair & suicide ideation*
> ➤ *Lack of communication or other skills for conflict resolution*
> ➤ *Help needed solving problems or making decisions*
> ➤ *Desire for personal change and growth*
> ➤ *Need for healing of memories*
> ➤ *Personal support, discipling and mentoring*
> ➤ *Referrals or direction to other resources*

The ministry of counselling is not to be taken lightly. It is a form of covenant or contract, as well as a service. It is a team effort, which involves you as the client, your helper the counsellor, and the Holy Spirit of God. Christian counselling, in particular, ministers to the whole person – body, soul and spirit.

As with any other healing service – whether it involves naturopathy, mental health, surgery, general medicine or even dentistry – the client or patient must become fully involved in the process to ensure full benefit from the treatment. Some clients might come out of desperation to have an aching tooth pulled (in the spiritual or emotional sense). Others seek to better understand God, others and self in a deeper way.

Counselling sessions average 2 hours for the initial assessment and consultation, then usually 1-2 hours per week for the following sessions. Fees are charged on an hourly basis. Referral can be given to specialists in fields pertaining to a client's needs – including spiritual needs.

When long term counselling and support is needed, a personality profile will most likely be done. Many other such resources are on offer to assist you. Because it is sometimes difficult for a client to attend in person, professional counselling is also available through telephone sessions and through letter writing and email.

It might also be helpful for you to know that other support is available to assist with practicalities, such as support during court appearances, interviews, and filling out forms.

At 'Hope Counselling Services', the style of counselling and ministry is adjusted to the client's personal requirements and can include inner healing, mentoring and cognitive behavioural therapy (CBT). The latter simply involves practical help to adjust your thinking and behaviour with the aim of positive change and personal growth.*

Inner healing involves deep ministry to the wounds inflicted during the course of your lifetime. Renewal of your mind to conform to the mind of Christ is involved in the process. Whatever the motive or circumstance which brings you to reach out for help in this form, you need to have confidence in the process. Then again, faith without action is dead. You must be willing to apply the lessons learnt – even to do some homework.

To benefit fully from the counselling process:

➢ Come when you are seriously ready to seek help and motivated for change.
➢ Come willing to be open to whatever counsel is given – even some gentle correction at times – but also be willing to question that direction, to take part in deciding what is best for you.
➢ Know that your help comes from God; that the counsellor is only a tool or vessel of God's tender concern for you personally.
➢ Be aware that it is a process, not a 'quick fix'.
➢ Be prepared to help yourself and to apply the remedies and suggestions given.
➢ Most importantly, pray for your counsellor before and after each session – for their whole being – for skill, wisdom, protection, physical and family needs. Pray that they will not be 'puffed up' over successes nor discouraged over any inability to assist.

COUNSELLOR'S EXPERIENCE AND CREDENTIALS

As well as secular credentials in professional counselling and training in associated aspects of ministry, your counsellor/therapist has spent over 30 years in pastoral care work, and in support of church leadership. Her passion for spiritual healing has led her to teaching the layperson how to minister to the wounded within the Body of Christ – especially via the prophetic gifting.

She has established a training school propagating prayer ministry skills and associated pastoral care. She has also written a vocational handbook, teaching manuals and resource books based on her coal face experiences. The vocational textbook provides valuable insights into the processes of general counselling, contains practical resources, and, describes various prayer ministry techniques.

The author has included the preceding promotional based on her own practice, however she has omitted her specific business name* for various reasons. All information to do with her credentials, experience and form of operation, is genuine. The author's testimonies, contained within this publication, are also authentic and autobiographical, whereas the content of client testimonials and casework are fictitious.

Practicalities of Counselling - LEARNING OUR ABCs

A Christian counsellor/minister has three general areas of responsibility, which can be loosely categorised as personal, practical and prayer responsibilities.

PERSONAL RESPONSIBILITIES

Personal responsibilities as practising prayer minister/counsellors can be categorized under three subject headings:

A for Availability
B for Boundaries
C for Caretaking

A FOR AVAILABILITY

1. Are you willing to be available to others to be used as a vessel of God? Sometimes this could mean being ready at a moment's notice, often working for long hours and, at times, with great inconvenience to yourself and your family.

2. Do you feel you have a divine calling on your life in this area? Do sense a direct challenge and direction from God to become available for ministry – beyond ordinary pastoral care or friendship?

3. Are you gifted and equipped for the calling; or at least willing to be trained to discover your potential?

4. Have you a personal support system? Do you have supportive spouse, parents, children, church, friends and mentors who will come alongside, encourage, support, guide and protect you? Most importantly, are you open to correction and advice from this support network?

5. Are you open to being shocked at times and yet still able to appear calm? Do you have the innate ability to act calmly and professionally on such occasions?

6. Is someone available to whom you could *debrief*, that is, discuss and work through personal thoughts and feelings following times of ministering? Do you have someone you respect and trust who will not be burdened by the process and would not try to encourage you to breach confidentiality?

7. Do you have the time available to follow through and to give quality attention to each person, taking into consideration you might need to deal with the family, friends and professional support network of your client?

8. Is there a suitable and private place available to operate where you can safely store and easily access confidential records?

9. Are you willing to make home visits, and are you prepared to visit a court hearing or a public service agency as an advocate? Would you be willing to accompany a client to a doctor's appointment or a group support meeting?

10. Do you understand what advocacy entails? Are you willing to speak up on a client's behalf and accept the responsibility and consequences of such an action?

11. Could you cope with such situations as an abusive spouse or runaway child coming to your family residence unannounced? Are you and your family capable of handling being taken advantage of, lied about, or threatened?

Have all these questions been enough to cause you to have second thoughts about being (or becoming) a counsellor? Of course the basic consideration will be whether there is call of God on your life in this direction. One final question: are you willing and available to lay down your own life (as it is now) to follow His purpose for you?

The very fact that you are reading this is an indication that He could be calling you and that you are considering making yourself available. If you are feeling overwhelmed at this prospect, remember the following:

> **He promises to equip us with all that is necessary to carry out all He has destined us to do. Do you believe this?**

B FOR BOUNDARY SETTING

One absolute necessity of the ministry is to know how to set boundaries. There will be the occasional intrusive phone call or visit to your home from a client. There could be the crisis in the middle of the night. There will be clients who unwittingly, or deliberately, test your boundaries. Will you trust God to give you the wisdom to deal with intrusions into your personal life? If you fail to maintain healthy boundaries, will you have the courage to learn by your mistakes and soldier on?

In and out of session times you may be called on to handle: being taken advantage of, abused, drained of energy and tried to the limit. Can you learn to graciously cut off a long one-sided discourse consisting of whining, blaming and general negativity? Will you recognise when you are out of your depth and possess the skills to protect your own needs? Will you be able to psychologically and emotionally let go in order to refer on a client to someone who could help?

Your emotional boundaries will be tested in many ways. Hurting people can be quite manipulative. For instance, you could be tempted into disclosing your personal life details. A little bit of self-disclosure (speaking about your personal problems and victories) can be like salt on a bland meal and it can be interesting to hear a personal testimony. Self–disclosure can also help to explain why you are taking a certain route or stance during ministry. However, you may be enticed against your better judgment into emotional involvement by a troubled client for a variety of reasons. As a counsellor you could be tempted and trapped into disclosing too much personal information to your own detriment for the following reasons:

NEGATIVE SELF-DISCLOSURE

➢ An unhealthy emotional bond is forming out of your own neediness

➢ You begin to see a client as a 'soul mate' or a potential friend and cultivate the relationship on an unprofessional level

➢ You feel too much compassion and empathy; you try to 'fix' a person

➢ A rescuer mentality or martyr complex is developing

➢ You might feel sexually attracted to a client

➢ You are being deceived and/or manipulated by the client

➢ Jezebel and Ahab spirits could be operating from either side

➢ Various demonic forces are welcomed into the situation because of fleshly weaknesses such as: pride, lack of self-worth or esteem, or the need for recognition, power or control

➢ Operating from unhealed wounds and unfinished business you feel the need to emotionally self-medicate

➢ Addicted to helping others you are receiving a high from the drama

➢ An inordinate sense of achievement and satisfaction is achieved from disclosing from the deeper levels of intimacy

Set boundaries to ensure your own personal care in emotional, physical and spiritual areas. Also, be sure to make provision for your own children, dependent parents and significant others. Even your pets and possessions will need spiritual protection and care. Pray anointed prayers for spiritual hedges, walls, towers and hiding places to be put in place for protection.

> *Call on the power and covering protection of the Blood of Jesus and the Word of God. Stay close to the Father in relationship and obedience.*

In a practical sense, your spouse, flatmate, boarder or adult children may need to field unnecessary phone calls or visits from clients to your home or place of ministry. You will probably learn to heavily depend on modern technology such as answering machines and mobile phones. Ideally you will acquire a trusted receptionist of your own, or have shared access and office space in a safe environment. At times your pastor, or even the police force, might be called in to deal with boundary setting on your behalf.

Never operate in a setting where you do not have access to help from outside sources. For instance, have a phone at your fingertips to dial emergency services. If you are put in the position of having to counsel a member of the opposite sex alone, then have your door discretely open to observation by trusted staff or family members. Have private and personal liability and professional insurance cover. Volunteers working for churches or charities are usually covered by corporate member insurance, but do not take this for granted – be sure to check if this is in place.

Lastly, remember that your family and leisure times need to be kept sacred. Holidays, sabbaticals, private study and personal development need to be time-managed so that ministering does not take over your entire life. The major one – your intimate times with God – should be first priority in your daily routine. Your rights to mix with friends, to take care of your health, to enjoy hobbies and participate in other leisure time activities or personal pursuits, need to be respected. Sometimes it will be necessary to briefly explain to a client causing you difficulties that you do have a life outside of the counselling room!

A preliminary course in office skills, time management or boundary setting is an asset. It is also wise to acquire an *accountability partner*. Ask a friend to check for signs of self-neglect or indications of life appearing overwhelming or out of balance. Unchecked, this could lead to *burnout* – a subject covered later in this text. Obtain the services of a professional clinical supervisor or a church administrator. Have a resource and referral system including: – retreat facilities and refuges, clinics and other professional services for yourself as well as for clients.

Practise what you preach! Take good care of yourself. He cares for you.

C FOR CARETAKING

Everyone takes care of someone. Make sure you take care of yourself by setting up a network of carers and resources and do not neglect maintaining your network. An extremely helpful resource tool is *the bike wheel* concept (Image 07 Chapter 5) which should be referred to on a quarterly basis each year. Have a personal plan and system to suit your lifestyle and personality needs. When you discover you are not looking after your own needs, and that things are getting too much for you, treat yourself with as much care as you would any client.

Make appointments for yourself in your ministry diary – for self-pampering, spiritual and professional development, stress management and life coaching. Cultivate some friends who are not at all interested in any form of counselling or people helping. Indulge in playful and creative activities with family and friends who enjoy sport, music, theatre or art, so that you are using both right and left hand sides of your brain and also consistently maintaining your social life. Most importantly, live a balanced lifestyle.

So that your clientele do not become too ministry dependent and a drain on you personally, assist each one to become self-motivated and God-dependent as soon a possible. Direct to the right tools outside of your session times – tapes, courses, books, ministries, or alternate or complementary carers. The Bible, prayer and a personal relationship with God are of utmost importance. If you discover that a client does not already have an intimate relationship with God the Father, as well as Jesus as Saviour and Lord, make it a top priority to help supply the spiritual resources to move them along in the right direction. Use the teaching tools supplied in this course to remove blockages (*How We View God,* Image 13, Chapter 13). Help to connect each person with the right church environment and pastoral care to meet their personality needs and style of worship.

Begin the counselling process with care, follow through with a caring attitude, and follow up with those caring little things such as handouts and courtesy phone calls. Never allow a client to leave a session feeling 'half-baked' or without the comfort needed. Do not abruptly finish the counselling process without some form of closure. If you find you need to refer on to protect your own needs – if the relationship is becoming too difficult for you personally – refer on. Make the changeover with wisdom and graciousness and remember that ethically the client remains your responsibility until placed in the care of another helper.

A client may indicate, either subtly or overtly, that they no longer want any further help from you. Even though you could feel that they are not ready to leave your care, you must respect their personal choice. Learn to know when to let go. It is still their personal responsibility to look after their own needs. Commend yourself on what you have achieved, rather than coming under condemnation over what you could not do for that particular individual.

> *Make a habit of surrendering all into God's care – including yourself, in your role as the carer. Your self-care should be first priority. He cares about you.*

PRACTICAL RESPONSIBILITIES

A for Accountability
B for Bookkeeping
C for Confidentiality

A FOR ACCOUNTABILTY

Accountability is first of all due to God. We all must be conscious of having a clean heart and clean hands before our Maker. You will need to be in a constant state of self-examination to remain in right relationship with him. The aim is to be a clear channel of the Father's love towards those you are helping.

In a practical sense, as counsellors you will need counselling, debriefing and supervision for accountability reasons. If you are privileged to have mentors, spiritual advisors, supervisors and trainers, then your 'cup runneth over'; you are truly blessed. Most carers are very busy people. Those who care for us will usually have a full program too. We need mentors who <u>have</u> the time to care for us. You will need to search for at least that one special trustworthy person who can mentor you spiritually – someone who is willing and able to enter into the role long term.

> *A mentor can be described as an adviser or guide. The Holy Spirit is our divine mentor, but there is safety in being accountable for your actions and attitudes to those who are also accountable to God.*

Choose wisely and carefully to whom you will divulge your weaknesses and problems. You will need to feel that you can be honest and open. You will need to surrender yourself to correction, without feeling that you are being judged or condemned. Choose advisors who are open to being corrected. Pray for protection from control and manipulation. You will need to be accountable to your pastor, who is responsible for keeping you safely in the fold. He or she should be able to organise a mentor and a prayer ministry supervisor you can trust to take care of your needs.

Last, but not least, ask the Lord to provide a group of intercessory prayer warriors and watchmen, to keep you on track and to act as armour bearers. Look for intercessors gifted in discernment and prophecy. They will also need to be accountable and responsible people who will not gossip or slander. To protect your clients' privacy, and for confidentiality reasons, supply as few details as possible when requesting intercession from your prayer warriors. Trust the Holy Spirit to guide the intercessors as to how to pray.

You could say for example, *I will be dealing today with a very difficult situation and need your intercessory back up* or, *I would appreciate your spiritual discernment regarding a person I am dealing with right now*. You do not need to give further details. Certainly do not mention names and <u>do not</u> encourage questions or personal involvement with the client, nor voice your private concerns. For example, *I am worried that Anna is going to beat Alex over the head with his hammer one day. You know them, what do you think? Do you think you could find out how bad the situation is for me?* , is not appropriate.

B FOR BOOKKEEPING

Bookkeeping includes keeping the following records:

a) A personal spiritual journal
b) A practical working diary
c) A library system to keep track of your books, tapes, videos etc
d) Confidential client files stored in a secure place.
e) A set of accounts to show what is coming in and going out.

In voluntary ministry there will be gifts occasionally towards your work, which will help greatly with the purchase of more resources and to cover out-of-pocket expenses. There are many incidental costs. If you are planning to go into professional counselling in the future, it is good to practise your bookkeeping in this manner while you are still a layperson or studying and training. Further note that an adequate filing system of records needs to be kept in order to satisfy your supervisor as well as to keep you personally organised.

> **Lay up spiritual treasures rather than temporal. Depend on God the Father to meet all your current and future needs. He will supply. He wants to be good to you.**

C FOR CONFIDENTIALITY

All personal files and notes relating to clients should be kept in a very safe place. This point cannot be emphasised too strongly. You will need to make arrangements with family members and/or a solicitor or executor for the destruction of journals and client records on your death. You will need to provide specific instructions in your will for the executor to gain access.

Keep a lockable filing cabinet with client records in a room apart from where you counsel and pray. This keeps records safe from prying eyes when you might need to leave the room during a session. A client has the ethical right to access their own records by requesting to look at their personal file, but not without your permission and they certainly do not have the right to look at anyone else's file. Try to return each file immediately to the cabinet when finished. Remember to lock the file and secret the key away.

Phones and answering services ideally should be located in a separate room also, as this prevents messages and conversations from being overheard. Family members, boarders and flatmates can be educated on taking messages in a polite and professional sounding manner and be instructed in matters of privacy. Teach those involved the difference between confidentiality and privacy and when it may be necessary to *breach confidentiality*. You can access different legal requirements for *mandatory (compulsory) reporting* applicable to your locality via the Internet. In Australia there are different laws for the various states and differing requirements for different professions, for example, under the law doctors differ from teachers.

One last comment, sometimes the need for unloading and debriefing becomes unbearable. Choose carefully to whom you do so. If you do not have a person to debrief with, your medical GP may be willing to serve as such. No client names should be mentioned when debriefing. Because this is a stress related issue, it can be classified under your own personal medical problem. At other times you could need practical professional advice and referrals; so it is wise to foster a professional relationship for your clients' needs as well as your own.

> **Remember that the Holy Spirit is a wonderful resource and stress reliever in the roles of the perfect comforter, counsellor and guide. Make time for his personal ministry to you.**

PRAYER RESPONSIBILITIES

This brings us to the last of the ABCs – prayer. We will use the following headings as memory triggers:

A for Activation by the Holy Spirit
B for Being a Barnabas
C for Correction and Comfort

A FOR ACTIVATION BY THE HOLY SPIRIT

Ideally all ministry prayer should be done according to the Holy Spirit's leading. The ability to speak in tongues (or spiritual language) in your private prayer times is invaluable in building up your 'inner man'. This form of prayer will also become an essential element to your ministry in seeking knowledge, discernment and wisdom on different matters. The benefits of praying in this manner are included further on in this text.

Praying in tongues during a session can be beneficial if it is something you are accustomed to; but it can sometimes be distracting, or offensive to others. Check if your client is amenable to this form of praying; do not assume that it will be acceptable.

Rote prayers (those expressed by routine repetition or a set format) are not the best type for use in ministry, as this could give the impression of insincerity and lack of depth in your prayer life. However, do keep a few powerful anointed prayers for subjects such as freemasonry, breaking curses and shattering strongholds. Where appropriate, you may like to ask the client to read these out loud during a session.

The subject of prayer is inexhaustible so it will only be touched on briefly in this text (see section on *Types of Prayer)*. There are many other excellent resources for further study.

> **Develop confidence in God honouring your willingness to serve him. He will lead you in your prayers. He will never withdraw support or friendship or give up on you. He will cover your mistakes when you put your trust in him.**

B FOR BEING A BARNABAS

B is for the role a counsellor has as an encourager via prayer ministry. Although scarcely mentioned in the scriptures, Barnabas nevertheless has become famous for his encouragement and practical support to the apostle Paul. He was one of those quiet achievers, who went about 'doing good'. He was probably a good prayer partner to Paul and a wonderful support to many others. This fellow was an excellent role model for the Christian counsellor. Not much public recognition is given to the more private type of ministry counselling entails (in comparison to the preachers and teachers) however the gratitude shown by clients and their loved ones is more than enough reward to most in the profession or ministry. When a client sees the counsellor is praying compassionately and consistently for them in their difficulties, it is one of the most encouraging things on earth.

There are those special clients too, who will continue to pray for the counsellor's workload well after they have benefited personally from the ministry. Much prayer is needed for the counsellor as the secrets which need to be held, and the confidences shared, can become a very heavy load. At least a client has a glimpse of this burden.

> *Even though it may seem so at times, you will not easily be forgotten nor cease to be appreciated for your ministry. Remember that we reap from what we have sown.*

C FOR CORRECTION AND COMFORT

The last category here includes both correction and comfort. The psalmist poetically declares that, though he walks through the valley of the shadow of death, he will fear no evil, for God is with him. He affirms, *your rod and your staff they comfort me* (Ps 23:4). In the Biblical context the word 'comfort' meant to console, to encourage, and to draw alongside. Our English word comfort is drawn from the Latin 'to strengthen much'. It means 'to ease, encourage, enspirit, or to enliven'.

> *Be sure to seek counsel for your own personal issues and 'unfinished business'. The best kind of comfort is that administered by the counsellor who has received healing and comfort personally.*

In Biblical times the shepherd's tools of trade were the rod and the staff. They were used for specific tasks. The staff was the stick the shepherd used to beat down the bushes where snakes and reptiles abounded and into which the sheep strayed. Spiritually speaking, counsellors use God given authority to drive away 'serpents' at times, in the form of deliverance ministry or via intercessory prayers. The staff was also used as an aid to climb hills. The counsellor can be likened to a staff at times – someone to lean on in the hard times.

The rod was used to keep count of the sheep and for correction purposes. God reports that he will cause his people to 'pass under the rod' (Ezk 20:37). This could have culturally referred to the custom of shepherds, who let their sheep pass under a rod in order to number them and to see whether they were in good condition. The term also stands for the *rod of affliction*, as the means by which God disciplined his people (Job 9:34; Heb 12:6, 7). Further application is the rod with the bronze serpent, which was raised up in the wilderness by Moses as a symbol of healing. In modern times this is still assigned to our medical doctors as an insignia.

The *rod of correction* can be used to discipline, meaning 'to train'. We are instructed that, if we do not correct (or use the rod) then we do not love our children; *'he that spares the rod hates his son'* (Prv 13:4). Further on is the much quoted 'spare the rod and spoil the child' (Prv 13:24). That is, we weaken the child's character by giving in to whatever the child desires. We make of that child something less valuable, beautiful or useful to society if correction is not applied when necessary. Your client is a child of God and needs to be treated with reverence in a similar manner to a beloved family member.

As a spiritual counsellor you may need to take up your spiritual rod or staff in order to issue Godly challenges for growth and healing. However, remember that you are hearing and perceiving only a tiny segment of the client's life story. When you make use of the spiritual rod or staff, whether it be for comfort, healing or corrective purposes, you are neither to act as a policeman nor as a judge. Holy Spirit conviction is needed. Making judgments about a person's heart, conduct or opinions is allowable scripturally in three circumstances only:

a) matters pertaining to self
b) spirits operating in and through others
c) fruits of those spirits produced in self or others

IN CONCLUSION

To conclude this segment on responsibilities, it should be stated that counselling is a *contractual operation* where there are also expectations on the client, as well as the Christian counsellor. The following, based on the author's promotional brochure mentioned earlier, could be issued as a client handout. Feel free to adapt this to suit your own needs.

Client Handout: RESPONSIBILITIES OF THE CLIENT

Dear Client,

The ministry of counselling is not to be taken lightly. It is a form of covenant and contract, as well as a service. A recipient of Christian counselling needs to be motivated spiritually and serious about obtaining and receiving help. Punctuality and politeness are required, whether the ministry is being operated on a voluntary basis or as a professional service. You should be aware that costs are involved in time, energy, finances and other resources.

This ministry is a team effort which involves the client, the counsellor/s and the Holy Spirit. Ministry is to the whole person – body, soul and spirit. The goal is basically as follows: to seek a better understanding of self and to restore or deepen your relationship to God and to others. Spiritual and emotional 'eyes of the heart' will need to be opened in order to relate to God the Father.

Sometimes, it is necessary to feel in order to heal and it is your personal responsibility to face the emotions which could surface during the process. You will be given loving guidance in this matter.

We are essentially feeling creatures. God made us in his image - and God is love. He longs for us to love him back freely – without blockages. It is the client's responsibility to learn to lean on the heavenly Father for healing and for personal growth, rather than solely on the counsellor (who is present as a facilitator of the client's process of learning to love God more fully).

In order to reach these goals, there needs to be a willingness to learn, to repent, to renounce, to forgive, and to generally act on the revelation and truths received. Co-operation with the Holy Spirit is crucial. Honesty is needed on your side as well as on your prayer minister's part. Prayer commitment on both sides will also help the process enormously. The client is encouraged to pray for the counsellor before and after each session – for their whole being – for skill, wisdom, protection, physical needs and for their loved ones.

Just as the counsellor is expected to treat the client's problems in a confidential manner, the client should be cautioned to remember not to speak personally or critically about the ministry to others. This could undermine your restoration process and could damage the reputation of the ministry, hence the ability to assist others. If you find that the counselling methods or any other resources used, do not meet your personal needs, then you should feel free to ask for a referral to another ministry or agency.

Your Counsellor

CHAPTER TWO

ROLES & COMMUNICATION

This chapter introduces the basic roles of a Christian counsellor as he or she ministers to the different parts that go to make up man. The difference between secular counselling and Christian counselling will be clarified through this teaching and communication skills will be emphasized. This second chapter contains:

- Descriptions of the parts of man (including graphic illustrations)
- Advice on dealing with difficult cases & handling personal issues
- Teaching Discourse: *Roles of the Christian Counsellor*
- Practicalities of Counselling: *Communication*
- Sample scenarios of *Crossed Boundary Situations* (exercise included)

Study Notes

THE ROLES OF A CHRISTIAN COUNSELLOR

The difference is enormous between secular counselling and counselling in conjunction with prayer ministry. In all types of Christian counselling, we are dealing with the person holistically in the true sense of the word. We are ministering to the whole person – to the different *parts of man* – body, soul and spirit. When prayer ministry is combined with counselling, we are more directly relating to the Father, Son, and Holy Spirit and interacting with these three divine persons along with the client.

To further clarify, prayer ministry type counselling is a more experientially spiritual process, rather than a cognitive and emotional one. The latter is usually covered by pastoral type prayer at the beginning and end of a session. This text is aimed more at interpreting the prayer ministry type of counselling with some emphasis on what is called *inner healing*. However, it also covers the pastoral type counselling, which can be administered by the average layperson using the spiritual principles and prayer techniques presented.

> **N.B. Key words are introduced to the text via italics for teaching and study purposes. Space is provided under each chapter outline for the reader to make study notes. Do not ignore these boxed inserts as helpful information will be missed.**

INTRODUCTION TO CHRISTIAN COUNSELLING/MINISTRY

There are 10 *basic roles* we play as Christian counsellors/ministers. To introduce and prepare you for learning about the principles administered through these roles, the *makeup of mankind* needs to be understood.

THE PARTS OF MAN

We, as individuals, are made up of three distinct parts – body, soul and spirit. We may further dissect the soul into three parts. The soul consists of the will, the mind and the emotions. As prayer ministers, we will be particularly dealing with feelings, or the emotional side of man.

IMAGE 01a

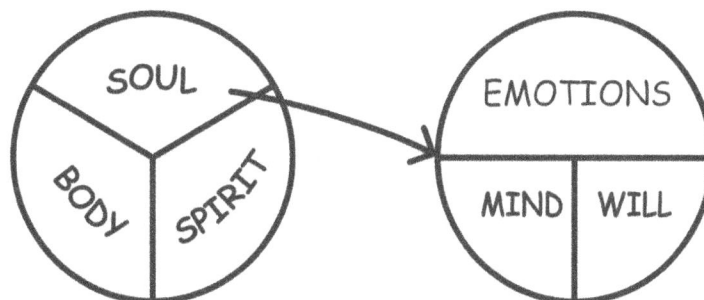

In a way, we could be described as spiritual *heart doctors*. The soul could also be divided into three parts in a different way. As such, it could be depicted as looking somewhat like the cross-section of an egg. The inner part, or the yolk, could be described as our *basic nature*. We will refer to it as our *true identity/real self*. This is how our Maker created us to be and is generally viewed as our *personality*, which in psychological terms covers the distinctive characteristics that make an individual unique.

IMAGE 02b

True Identity
(Real Self)

Acquired Personality
(Unnatural Self)

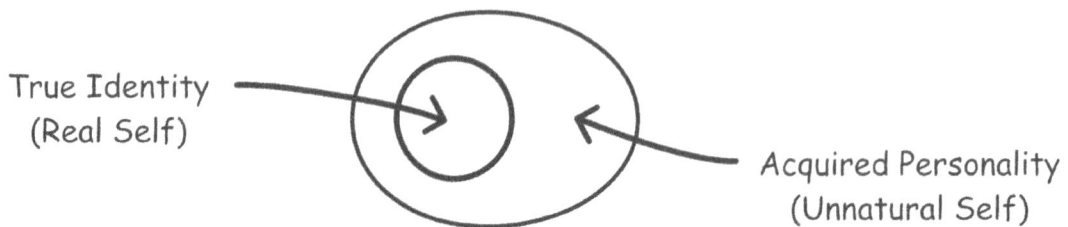

The second part, represented by the white of the egg, can be described as our *unnatural self* (in the sense of *affected* or *forced*) as opposed to our basic nature or real self. This is where we have deviated from our true identity to become the person we are today – the *persona* or personality we adopt and present to others. We tend to live behind *masks* and act out *roles* in order to adapt and fit into society.

This *acquired personality* has been created by the impact of the environment, our circumstances and from our relationships with others living in this fallen world. This involves how far we have fallen and wandered from our true and original God-given nature due to mankind's sinful nature. This is the basic 'stuff' a Christian counsellor is called upon to deal with. However, more about that further on in the text.

God, being Love, planned that we love and be loved. Living in this sinful world, our hearts have experienced damage along the way. A shell has formed cementing us into what we appear to be in the form of our acquired personalities or unnatural selves. This *outer shell* can be looked at as *scar tissue* built up on the *wounds* to our damaged soul.

Inevitable damage has taken place in our formative years as a child – the first seven years from conception. This is generally accepted, in both Christian and secular circles, as the time period when our acquired personality is basically formed. We will normally present this scar tissue to the world for the rest of our lives unless some intervention is made. From the egg illustration, the scar tissue is seen as a hard outer shell. Inner healing can only be achieved by cracking the shell open to get at the soft inner parts to begin the *restoration* work.

IMAGE 03c

True Identity
(Real Self)

Outer Shell/Mask
(Wounds and Scars)

Acquired Personality
(Unnatural Self)

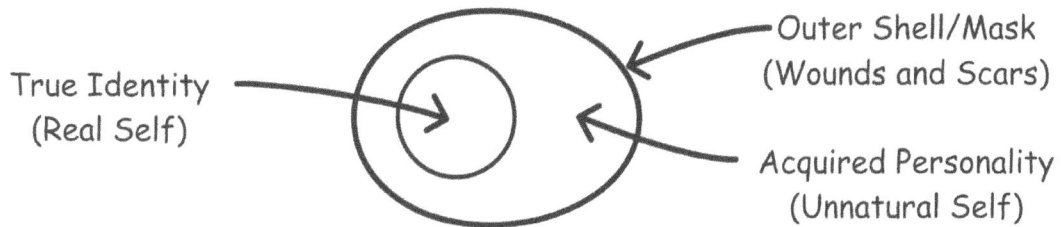

Restoration work often involves the Christian prayer minister assisting the client to touch base again with *the true self* – the person God intended them to be. It can be a process of *reconciliation* of our heart with God's heart, and, on occasions, it will be a prodigal son type experience. With the Holy Spirit's guidance, the counsellor can do a great deal to help a person reconnect with their true identity. The client needs to ready and willing to do so. This type of ministry entails *inner healing* of the *damaged child* (within).

More will be covered on this topic later in Section V containing *Prayer Ministry Techniques.* For now, we are concentrating on introducing our roles by explaining the makeup of Man (1 Thes 5:23; Heb 4:12; Ps 139:13-16, 23).

INSTRUCTIONS FOR USE OF IMAGE: The Parts of Man

The following image is a compilation of the concepts previously illustrated. To briefly describe and introduce the work of *ministering to man's soul*, use the following illustration only after becoming thoroughly familiar with the previous three images. Begin at the bottom of the diagram and work upwards

IMAGE 04

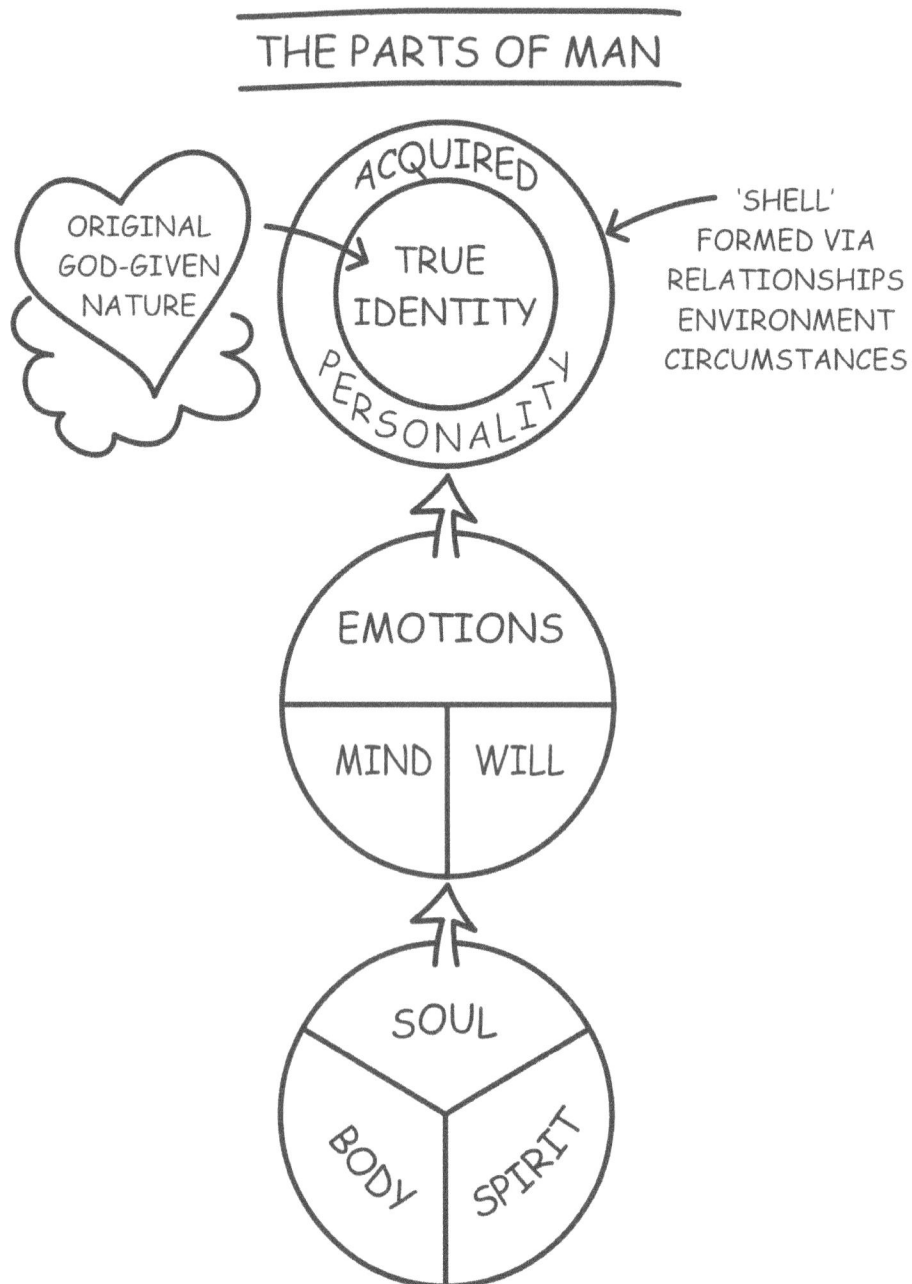

THE PARTS OF MAN

ORIGINAL GOD-GIVEN NATURE

ACQUIRED

TRUE IDENTITY

PERSONALITY

'SHELL' FORMED VIA RELATIONSHIPS ENVIRONMENT CIRCUMSTANCES

EMOTIONS

MIND | WILL

SOUL

BODY | SPIRIT

RECONNECTION WITH OUR TRUE IDENTITY

A person may come to a time in life when they feel they are *lost*. That is, they sense that their true identity or nature has somehow evaporated, or is hiding away. This may involve feeling, *captive, numb, fragmented or shattered, torn apart*, or, the person may feel he or she is searching for a part of the self. There is accompanying confusion and pain and an inability to cope with life in the same way as was possible in the past.

If many *knockdowns* and *knockbacks* have been experienced in life, the cumulative affect can be devastating. The wounds, perhaps arriving one after the other, have left no time for healing in between. This can be described as *rapid fire wounding*. Associated feelings of hopelessness and despair about ever getting on top of things again could exist.

These conditions can bring clients presenting serious problems such as: –

> - deep depression
> - chronic fatigue
> - burnout
> - mental and physical breakdown
> - serious relationship conflicts
> - isolation
> - personality disorders
> - suicidal thoughts (ideation)
> - psychosis

THE HARD CASES

With these more serious symptoms, we must be conscious of operating within our own personal ministry limits and natural capabilities. However, please do not discard the client to fend for his or her self. Networking with other carers is advised. Get supervision. Ask for prayer support. Seek medical support. Then, if you are not feeling confident and peaceful, by all means refer on in a respectful manner, explaining your procedure and leaving your client feeling truly cared for.

With this being said, we cannot abdicate all the caring responsibilities to secular psychologists, psychiatrists and medical practitioners. Some clients will have exhausted these avenues. They may be at the stage the woman with the issue of blood was when she touched the edge of Jesus' robe.

A troubled individual may be classed in the secular world as being mentally disturbed, or as having a chronic or terminal illness, but this does not exclude them from seeking emotional and spiritual support from a brother or sister in Christ. Even the professionals acknowledge that the layperson, friends and family, are often the very best allied resources for patients and clients. With teamwork, the church as a family can be very effective as *change agents*.

Even as a beginner in prayer ministry, you will be able to handle many issues you did not think possible. Some serious ones may be beyond your experience and natural abilities, but nothing is impossible to God. Stand firm in confidence that you are 'in Christ'.

COUNSELLOR'S PERSONAL NEEDS

As you study and practise counselling, you will most likely uncover a few personal problems and issues. However, guard against becoming a *spiritual hypochondriac* by being overly introspective. If you rely on the Holy Spirit to uncover only the issues <u>he</u> wants to deal with currently in your spiritual walk, you will not become confused or overwhelmed. If you should realise that you are in serious need of ministry or professional counselling, seek guidance from your pastor/minister/spiritual mentor as your first port of call.

Take heart, as Christians, we are forever in a learning process and are being cleansed. No matter how mature we are considered, we all have personal healing needs. At the very least, you should be able to use some of the concepts presented in this text for your own personal development.

CONCLUDING ADVICE

This section will conclude with some advice inspired from the book of Job. Recall that Job's comforters spent seven days and nights in silence before offering their opinions about his misfortunes. From experience, as a Christian counsellor of many years, please heed the following points:

> ➢ wait on the power of the anointing of the Holy Spirit
> ➢ it is not all about you – do not strive
> ➢ avoid talk for the sake of talking
> ➢ be a Barnabas rather than a Job's comforter

Most importantly, assure the sufferer of the presence of a caring God in their life. After all, your companionship will be withdrawn when the ministry finishes. His companionship is eternal. You will have achieved all that you have set out to do if you have succeeded in helping the client to become aware of our heavenly Father as the ultimate resource.

Counsellor Resource: THE 10 BASIC ROLES OF A CHRISTIAN COUNSELLOR

Key words and terms in this text are highlighted by *italics* when initially introduced into a teaching. The person being ministered to is called *the client*. The reason for seeking counsel is referred to as *the presenting problem*. Goals and strategies will come under headings of various *roles*.

1. FIRST AID OFFICER

The initial contact with a client is usually for first aid treatment of their presenting problem or *current issue*. Be conscious that this could be the first time this person in pain has found an empathetic, listening ear. A *faith connection* needs to be made. This person has come to you because they are wounded, in that they have soulish or spiritual *wounding/s* which need first aid attention.

Your goal is to begin building *a trust relationship* on the basis of the client's faith in you to help with their presenting problems. This cry for help might cover deeper underlying wounds. The quality of this initial treatment could determine the success of all future counselling sessions. Do not waste this opportunity to minister by making the following common mistakes: asking too many questions; talking over the person; talking down to them.

2. DETECTIVE

Basically, your aim is to <u>really</u> listen to your client to locate the root problem/s. Your challenge here is to treat every presenting problem as an important clue to tracking to the main *issues*. Even apparent trivia, such as the inability to make a decision or a complaint that life seems boring, might mask deep underlying pain. The client will not be ready to disclose the deeper problems until a relationship of trust is built between you.

Your role switches from first aid officer attending to present injuries, to that of a detective who looks for clues in the form of *fruits*. Do not forget to record your clues. Everything is relevant. Note taking is a very important aspect of this ministry.

3. GARDENER

Recall that Jesus was a great one for using parables associated with gardening. Your third role relates to cause and effect, with the objective of finding the *fruit to root pattern*. A diseased tree produces damaged or *spoiled fruit*. As the gardener, you are looking for the reason for such poor produce. Ask yourself whether the presenting problems are symptoms of disease, poisons in the soil, bad seed, or poor grafting. Is there a pattern of failed crops or scarcely any fruit happening here? The analogies are endless (refer to Chapter 19)

4. DAMAGE ASSESSOR

Our next role is to assess the consequences of 'eating bad fruit'. Damaged emotions need healing and those *poor in spirit* need restoration. This damage occurred from early childhood onwards, so there is much to be assessed. We locate the damage: the unnatural soulish nature was being formed and took root in sin (represented by *the poisoned soil*) beginning at conception. Our usual assessment is that there is a need to integrate the healed *inner child* with the healed whole person at their present stage of life. The goal is *reconciliation with the father* heart of God and a sense of true God-given identity. The process involves *opening the eyes of the heart*.

5. HEART SPECIALIST

The organ of the heart in our culture symbolises our emotions or feelings. As specialists in ministering to damaged emotions we act here as spiritual *doctors of the heart*. We indicate here, by the use of the term 'opening the eyes of our heart', that we are basically emotional beings who connect spirit to spirit with our Creator. We are made in his image, in that we are spiritual beings who resemble our heavenly Father who <u>is</u> Love.

We need to receive revelation from our God of why we feel the way we do and why our *damaged emotions* have been left unhealed. (This is why we cannot handle the problems as they present themselves today). Sometimes, in order to heal, we must be willing to face the pain of the past and to deal with it.

6. SURGEON

The next crucial step could involve *spiritual surgery* to reveal the underlying *lies* and deception causing the pain. Many factors could be involved in creating 'tumours' which need to be removed and the healing balm of God's truths applied. Everything you present to a client as a spiritual truth should be confirmable by the scriptures.

Everything that comes out of your mouth needs to be in accordance with what the Holy Spirit would have you say in your sensitive role as *surgeon to the soul.* The truth needs to be handled rightly in order to set the sufferer free from deception. No further damage should be inflicted if the delicate surgery is handled with God-given wisdom.

Having the truth revealed via divine surgery sets a person free to find their true identity in Christ. Then there is the need to learn how to live in the truth by *'walking the walk and talking the talk'* (Chapters 15 & 16).

7. TEACHER

The main teacher/counsellor emphasis is on the importance of the *renewal of the mind* – according to Godly precepts and principles. If the client has been under deception and believed lies, they will most probably have lived and acted in accordance to the lies. These behaviours have become an integral part of their life walk and have contributed to the scar tissue surrounding the soul. The ugly scar tissue is melted away by the power of the re-learning process. A new way of thinking, feeling and acting allows God-given beauty and strengths to emerge, as well as a child-like ability to enjoy life during this process of learning and healing.

8. RESOURCE OFFICER

In order to remain an *overcomer* it is necessary to have the resources to enable this new life style to flourish, e.g. a network of carers, fellowship, purposeful employment, service to the community, personal and spiritual development aids. As the counsellor and current resource person, always try to send a client home with some homework assignments in hand.

By choosing the right resources to match the learning style, something really valuable can be offered, rather than confusing material that will prove to be a struggle, or will be set aside without being used at all. At least suggest how to acquire what is needed. Check whether the material being offered is being genuinely studied and digested and place primary emphasis on the Word of God.

9. DISCIPLER

Disciplining is the next stage. To become a disciple is to become a follower of Jesus, not the prayer minister's dependent. The goal is for the client to become *God dependent* rather than a people pleaser or approval addict. A direct one-on-one relationship with God the Father is needed and a personal relationship with Jesus Christ is essential.

The ultimate aim of being discipled is to become rightly related to God and rightly related to oneself. A person can then *enter into God's rest*. External conflict and stress are diminished because the internal stress or *inner conflict* has been relieved. As God's created beings we also need to see ourselves rightly as his perfect creation as well as being able to perceive God as he truly is,. To be healed emotionally is to come to a place of rest and childlike trust in his goodness towards us.

10. PERSONAL TRAINER

Lastly, direct your client to find a balance in all areas of his or her life – to be able to appreciate their unique personality needs. This should take into account the sinful nature of course; but also the growth available through inner healing and the freedom to access the truth and power to overcome future problems. Our lofty aim is to help our client's whole being – the body, soul and spirit – to be in *divine order,* that is, to be in agreement and *in alignment* with God's holy will.

The body and soul should be in subjection to the born again spirit. The spirit of man needs to be under submission to the Lord Jesus Christ in order to be in alignment and in harmony with the Creator.

IMAGE 05   **HOUSE IN DIVINE ORDER**

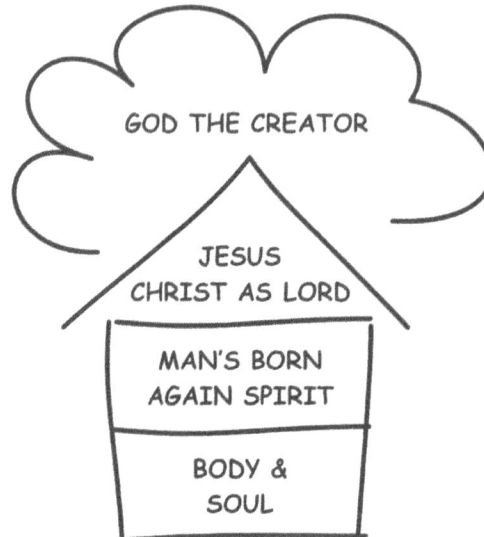

GOD THE CREATOR

JESUS CHRIST AS LORD

MAN'S BORN AGAIN SPIRIT

BODY & SOUL

Practicalities of Counselling: GOOD COUNSELLOR COMMUNICATION

As a counsellor your goal is to be a good two-way communicator but, compared to the average type of conversation, you are operating within a very unnatural setting. Your job is to allow the client to think that you have nothing else to do except ask questions of them and to listen with extraordinary concentration to all their responses. At the same time, as a spiritual counsellor, you are conducting a conversation with the Holy Spirit – your counsellor and guide. You are also sorting through your own ideas, values, opinions and reactions and deciding what is appropriate to disclose. At times, it is quite a juggling act, but very exciting and worthwhile.

For *therapy* such as Christian counselling which is *person centred*, you will need to show your client that you are indeed a person in your own right, with personal values, views, needs and wants. You need to be aware that, if you choose to *self-disclose* (reveal personal information) you will have much greater impact than the average person with whom your client communicates.

CLIENT ASSESSMENT OF PRACTITIONER

The information you choose to share will provide the framework for a client assessment involving thoughts such as:

What kind of relationship can I have with you?
Can I feel I can be honest and open in the process?
Will you understand me (show empathy and be sympathetic)?
Can you be of practical help to me?
Will I be wasting my time and money coming to you?
Will you have the spiritual value and input that I expect and require?

SELF-DISCLOSURE

As the counsellor it is your choice to share or not to share any of your private life or personal views with a client. You can choose to remain professionally distant. Keep in mind, however, that complete *non-disclosure* could have a profound affect in that it could appear as a personal rejection. It could appear that you are not interested enough in the client (as a person) to share your story. Not sharing your self could leave a client feeling:

➢ inferior
➢ frustrated
➢ uncared for
➢ a 'project' (rather than a person)

On the other hand, appropriate self-disclosure by the counsellor reveals:

➢ personal interest
➢ encouragement and empathetic listening
➢ willingness to relate

For the novice counsellor, it is sometimes very confusing as to what is appropriate. It is good to remember that counselling in a formal session is basically to promote self-disclosure <u>by the person with the problems</u>. Your work involves interviewing and encouraging the client to get past the clichés, facts and opinions of the 'small talk' (basic communication) and on to *deep communication* involving both the heart and mind and, of the spirit.

APPROPRIATE SELF-DISCLOSURE

Examples of appropriate self-disclosure on the basic level are (counsellor speaking):

a) When I am jumped in a queue I feel annoyed too.
b) I can understand how frustrated you feel when your wife jumps in and answers questions for you. My older brother used to do that to me!

Outside of counselling, it is rare that the average person self-discloses deeply. It is rare in basic communications to reveal more to a person than they are willing to reveal to you. In good conversation, speaking about self is usually composed of an equal exchange, reciprocal in disclosure and interaction. This deepens as trust builds and interest increases. This is especially so with women's thought processes – *you share something about yourself, then, I will share something.* This usually involves sharing something of equivalent value according to the depth of relationship.

However, within a counselling session, the aim is to enable the client to feel free to reveal as deeply as they are comfortable with, and to receive the feeling of being listened to wholeheartedly, and heard by the counsellor. Foremost, it is your position to listen to your client's thoughts and opinions (rather than to offer your own) but it is permissible and acceptable to self-disclose from your side in order to facilitate client self-disclosure. The best criteria for how much personally disclosure is appropriate, is to use the comparison to food seasoning. Just as you would add salt to a meal – disclose very sparingly to bring out the flavour.

A counsellor's basic premise (especially a Christian counsellor) should be, '*it is not about me*'. The sessions are a client's rare opportunity to completely bypass the usual conventions of conversation; to skip the small talk, honestly express feelings and to have some release from whatever suffering they are experiencing. Most clients do not want to hear about you and your problems. Hearing that they are not the only one in the world with a particular problem or set of circumstances might be of comfort, but a client is basically 'in session' on a self-indulgence quest, not on a friendship basis.

Give your client the freedom to talk and to relate their story, rather than to meet your needs to talk, to preach, to dispense advice or to be heard. On the other hand, they need to leave your office feeling they have not been speaking to a store dummy! So, having said all this, good communication rules still apply.

Counsellor Resource: GOOD COUNSELLOR COMMUNICATION

1. Give full and undivided attention
2. Communicate a calm and respectful attitude

3. Clearly express what you want to say

4. Make eye contact without staring intrusively.

5. Use receptive body language and open, nonverbal communication

6. Know when to stop and start speaking and how to stop and start listening

7. Know how to handle pauses and times of silence

8. Listen actively; respond actively, using single words and short phrases and sentences such *hmm, yes*, and *I understand*

9. Respond appropriately and be sincere – e.g. chattering nervously when someone is expressing pain is not appropriate

10. Display empathy by attempting to feel what the other person is feeling and to see the world through their eyes (this is not about your own perceptions; it is about the client's perceptions)

11. Be sympathetic without encouraging self-pity and be compassionate

12. Use your common sense when dealing with a client's emotional reasoning

13. Speak honestly and openly; but not bluntly or aggressively

14. Be straightforward rather than 'beating about the bush' or hinting

15. Attempt to understand the true meaning of what is being said

16. Clarify and request feedback: *am I right in saying/understanding/thinking that …?*

17. Ask open-ended questions to stimulate conversation, rather than closed questions that require a 'yes' or 'no' answer

18. Listen fully without interrupting or finishing sentences for the speaker

19. Prior to responding, attempt to understand the motives and the meaning of the situation from the speaker's perspective (by trying to understand the thoughts that have motivated the behaviours and created or stimulated the feelings)

20. Always show respect by acknowledging the feelings of others

21. Look out for the deeper issues behind what is being said, such as unexpressed fear, shame or guilt (and make allowances for such)

22. Verbally express God's unconditional love and express words of affirmation

23. Be aware of giving a voice to the Holy Spirit by allowing him to express Himself through you, and also to you through the other person

24. Portray optimism and confidence to the listener via your speech patterns

25. Replace *should* with *could* and *must* with, for example, *you might prefer to…* or, *it would probably be in your best interests to…*

26. Talk about choices and options (the pros and the cons) rather than about demands or expectations. Explain that positive choices will result in positive consequences – e.g. *if we keep God's laws then we can expect to be blessed.*

27. Be prepared to repeat your message without appearing irritated or frustrated (especially when offering choices and presenting consequences)

28. Discuss or impart knowledge; rather than preach or teach (it is all in the delivery and loving presentation)

29. Keep your composure when frustrated or opposed by focusing on your listening; rather than defending and justifying.

30. Listen for client frustrations and worries and confirm your understanding.

31. Use phrases and questions to calm and diffuse volatile emotions, e.g. *that is very interesting, why do you say that?* Or, *could you explain why you believe that to be true?*

SPECIAL NOTE ON COMMUNICATING AS CHRISTIANS

A special note here about style of communication. Christians, in general, use a peculiar vernacular, which can sometimes appear to be *jargon* (this would include using 'King James English'). At times, this can be quite offensive to the unchurched and intimidating to the new Christian. So, make allowances and be aware of this in your counselling and prayer ministry relationships.

For instance, it is wise not to use jargon such as, *'let's just leave it to the Lord'* or *'I will intercede for you'* and preferably use a conversational style in prayer. Get into the habit of speaking as casually and simply as possible at all times. For instance, try not to punctuate with *'just'*, *'praise the Lord'*, or *'Heavenly Father'** and do try to keep other such favourite phrases to a minimum – especially in your prayer times.

Having said this, there is a place for the use of scriptures as *confession of the spoken Word of God* (an example of more jargon) and other methods of prayer using scriptural terms. Refer to the sections on the subjects of *speaking in tongues, deliverance* and on *intercession.* Be wise in your use of these specialized methods of prayer as they may seem strange or offensive – sometimes even frightening, to some clients.

WARNING: * Regarding the use of the title 'Heavenly Father': Be cautious when praying for those who you know or suspect to have been victims of incest or other forms of traumatic abuse. Those who have suffered in this way may have a different perception of God as a father figure to the average person. Until you have processed some degree of healing, simply use 'God' or perhaps 'Lord God' when addressing him.

Practicalities of Counselling: APPROPRIATE PHRASES & QUESTIONS

COMMUNICATION OPENERS

Unsuitable opening phrases: *How can I help you*? *What is your problem?*

More appropriate phrases are:
What has brought you in to see me today?
What would you like to talk about during this session?

We have a whole hour to talk. Where would you like to begin?

When the person seems confused:
You seem to have a lot on your mind. Where would you like to start?
What is the thing that is of most concern to you at this time?

When the client is reluctant to start:
I have the feeling that it is difficult for you to have come in to see me. Perhaps you are not sure where to begin. Please, take your time.

When someone is resistant to receiving counsel:
I sense that you don't really want to be here.
I am wondering how you feel about being sent here.
It must have been hard having to come in to see me.

TRUST BUILDERS (ALONG THE WAY)

I appreciate that this must be very painful to talk about.
Thank you for sharing your concerns honestly and so clearly.
I admire your courage in sharing so much with me.
I trust you to let me know if I am asking too much of you.
I see it is not easy to revisit those precious times. Thank you for sharing with me.
Thank you for being open and frank in telling me how you feel about being here.

CHECKING PHRASES (CLARIFYING AND KEEPING IT FLOWING)

Would I be right in thinking that…?
I think I understand what you mean… but I would like to recap to be sure…
From what I can see… you seem to be saying….
Am I hearing you correctly in that you are feeling…?
I'm not quite clear what you mean… Perhaps you could give an example….
I'm getting a bit confused about… How can I understand further?
I'm trying to get a clear picture of your situation. Would you mind going over what you just said in a slightly different way?
Would you mind summarizing from the point when…?
Perhaps you could elaborate on that.
What else is causing you difficulties?
What do you think may be causing this?

CONFRONTATION/CHALLENGES*

I can appreciate how you … but have you thought about …?
As I understand it you seem to be … however, have you decided yet whether…?
On the one hand you are saying… but on the other hand you are (doing)…
So you feel that … but your mind seems to be saying to you …
How do you think you could put these two together?

It appears that you have mixed feelings about ...

MAKING RECOMMENDATIONS

May I suggest that you could...?
Do you think there would be some benefits in...?
Perhaps you could...?
How would you feel about trying to...?
Would it be feasible or possible to...?
How about starting with/attempting to/ making a beginning by...?

FEEDBACK ENCOURAGERS

How do you feel about that?
What do you think about this?
Does that sound close?
What does that mean to you?
How does this all sound to you?
What stands out most to you about what we have discussed today?
What did you learn that you consider to most valuable?
What will you be taking away from our session today?

CLOSURES

I am so glad we had this opportunity to talk today.
I will be looking forward to another productive session with you next week.
Well, that was fruitful. Shall we make it the same time for next week?
Our sessions seem to be coming to an end. I will miss our visits.

---

*SPECIAL NOTE ON CONFRONTATION

Confrontation or challenging in the counselling sense does not mean, as in the literal sense; a fight or an argument. You are looking at *mixed messages* and incongruous statements coming from your client, where you are feeling that what your client is saying and doing 'just doesn't add up'. In order to progress it is sometimes necessary to *confront* and to issue a challenge to facilitate change.

Most importantly, confrontation rests on effective listening skills. Then using *minimum encouragers*, it is your job to assist the client to make sense of incongruity (inappropriateness) and ambivalence (conflicting emotions). In a non-judgmental manner, your aim is to offer a *supportive challenge* to examine the situation more closely. You are to identify and point out mixed messages and help empower your client to work through and resolve their personal conflicts. As a *change agent,* allow the client to make sense of your comments in their own way, by offering appropriate phrases and questions to facilitate the confrontation.

To facilitate change:

a) Seek guidance and discernment through close personal communication with the Holy Spirit prior to confrontation.

b) Encourage client communication to pick up on key words giving clues to incongruity and ambivalence

c) Restate mixed messages in your own words to assist identification. Your words say, but your actions indicate. *You say you love him; but you state that you will not communicate your feelings to him. You continue to pursue him even though you say you hate him.*

d) Mediate inner conflict non-judgmentally. Reflect client feelings beginning with, *you feel, I sense, it appears to me that.*

e) Paraphrase using starters such as, *so you..., sounds like..., it looks like... So you feel as if he is avoiding you. It looks like he is avoiding you.*

f) Use feedback encouragers such as, *how does this all sound to you/ does this make sense to you?*

g) Be careful not to push the point. Remember that silences from your side can allow reflection on the client's part and can help avoid resistance to change.

h) Investigate attitudes, thoughts, feelings, motivation, and drive strength, then move on to making recommendations using the appropriate phrases or questions.

Practicalities of Counselling: ENCOURAGING TWO-WAY COMMUNICATION

1. OPEN ENDED QUESTIONS

Opened ended questions are preferable to closed questions, which usually result in a yes or no answer. For example, you would ask, *in what way would you like your life to be different right now?* Rather than, *would you prefer your life to be different?*

2. SILENCES AND PAUSES

Use silence and pauses in the conversation to advantage to allow both client and counsellor to collect thoughts; shift gears or to take control of emotions. The managing of silence takes practice (as do all counselling skills). This is where prayer ministry can be appropriately used by introducing with; *let us take a moment to pause for silent prayer ...*

3. AFFIRMING STATEMENTS

In the ministry of encouragement, a key tool is the use of affirming statements that clearly state one's support or agreement. Use these judiciously for the best effect. Also, do not confuse lavish praise with affirmations. Instead, encourage self-assessment. You would affirm by saying, *you have obviously handled that situation very well this time and don't you agree that you have come a long way in the last few days?* Rather than, *you have conquered all your trials incredibly well!*

4. BRIDGE & PROMPT PHRASES

These types of comments are sometimes not more than one word couched as a question or an exclamation to encourage further communication. With the right emphasis or inflection, they prove very useful for listening actively and keeping the conversation flowing.

> *Meaning?*
> *Tell me more about…*
> *So you said?*
> *For example?*
> *So then what I'd like to know is…*
> *And then you…?*
> *Really! Really?*

5. MINIMUM/MINIMAL ENCOURAGERS

Encouragers include body language such as head nods, stroking the chin, leaning forward and mirroring, and phrases such as: *I agree, definitely, absolutely, that is understandable, very interesting,* and, *do go on… (See point 12).*

6. SELF-DISCLOSURE

This type of communication is not on a friendship level; rather, it is used for disclosing something of a personal nature to enhance the counselling process. Use self-disclosure wisely and sparingly to deepen connectivity and to give glory to God. For example, *there was a time in my mid teens when I felt that there was no hope and I simply did not want to go on. But, just at that point, God showed me…*

7. USE OF CLIENT'S NAME

This can also serve as a form of affirmation and should not be overused. It is a form of building esteem and enables the client to feel that they are a person, not just 'a case' or a project. To overuse a person's name gives the impression of fawning or even arrogance and condescension.

If you are using a title (*e.g. Miss/Sir/Rev*) make sure it is age and culturally appropriate. For example, as a young woman in the position of counsellor, you would not call an elderly man by his Christian name without asking permission, and you would not include terms of endearment such as *sweetie* or *love.*

ACKNOWLEDGEMENT

This is a powerful tool for empathizing or to assist a client to express feelings without fear of judgmental responses. For example, *I can see that you feel strongly about this*, or, *you seem to have a deep understanding of the conflict this is causing you. You felt as if you could have punched him in the face* (sample of restating). The original statement was: *I wanted to punch him in the face!*

You can also acknowledge by reflecting feelings e.g. *you do not feel up to going today.* (This can be used for volatile clients to good effect).

8. EMPATHY, SYMPATHY & REFLECTING FEELINGS

Sympathy: *that callous remark must have really hurt.*
Empathy: *I would have felt angry under those circumstances too.*
Reflection: *you feel that this has gone on far too long.*

9. EYE CONTACT

Eye contact is considered polite and friendly in most cultures, but be conscious of cultures where it is not appropriate. It is encouraged in counselling as it usually serves to promote trust and to display interest. However, in times of extreme emotion, it can be uncomfortable for both parties. If you have trouble with looking directly into someone's eyes for any reason, use note taking to divert your gaze, or make use of drawing illustrations for a break from the intensity of long periods of concentrated active listening. If acceptable to the client, make use of a whiteboard or other visual aid to direct focus away from your faces.

10. USE OF PEN & PAPER

There are so many ways these simple tools can be used to encourage communication and to provide necessary information. Illustrate with drawings and write your key points to achieve maximum impact of your message. Record the key points that the client is making then make use of these for *active listening* (see point #14). Others include: filling out a client details form, tests, charts, surveys and assessments (e.g. personality profiles); use of notepads for client as well as counsellor; use of the pen/pencil as a pointer to emphasize a remark or to maintain eye contact.

11. BODY LANGUAGE

> ➢ mirroring (copying client's posture) to show connection and empathy
> ➢ stroking chin to show you are thinking about the problem
> ➢ leaning forward to show your wholehearted interest
> ➢ making notes to show you mean business
> ➢ eye contact to display undivided attention

> ➢ use of the pen or open palm to maintain client's concentration
> ➢ use of head nods and shakes, clicking tongue & saying *uh ha, hmm, etc*

12. USE OF PARABLES, OBJECTS, MUSIC, DRAMA, ART, IMAGERY & PLAY

Creative resources are useful to encourage discussion on meanings of concepts or practical applications of such, and can be used to communicate and process thoughts and feelings in a meaningful way, e.g. *The Prodigal Son.* Creative ministry is particularly helpful to communicate effectively with children or traumatised clients, e.g. sand play using figurines.

13. ACTIVE LISTENING

Active listening is the mainstay of counsellor communication with the use of: clarifying, confirming, summarising, praying, restating, paraphrasing, drawing out, etc. Your client needs to feel listened to, heard and understood; as this is the essence of encouraging two-way communication.

14. DEVELOPING THE STORY

The client needs to tell enough of their life story to enable the counsellor to draw from it and to collect enough information to work with. The story sometimes needs developing, e.g. *let me get this clear; it was back in your childhood that you first began having this nightmare. Can you describe what it was like for you back then in comparison to how it is for you now?*

15. SLOWING DOWN THE STORY

Most stories are told from an emotional viewpoint and sometimes this will cross the barriers of average conversation in tone and speed. The counsellor might feel they are being 'talked at' rather than 'communicated with' and they might need to take charge to change course. For example: –

Can we pause for a moment and just take a few deep breathes? Could you repeat that last part by including more details? I am having trouble sorting out where you were and to whom you were speaking.

16. ENCOURAGE FEEDBACK

Encourage feedback for clarification and to assess progression. For example, *how do you react/feel about this? Does that sound close? What does that mean to you when I say...?* Remember, it is important to you as a person as well as 'the counsellor', to know that you too are being heard and understood. Feedback is not just to benefit the progression of a session.

PRAYER

The act of prayer is a constant reminder that God is the third (very active) participant in the session. Points to remember about prayer: –

> ➢ encourage the client to pray (as much as he/she is comfortable with)
> ➢ invite to actively listen to God, and to express what is being 'heard'
> ➢ role model prayer as a visible sign of dependence on God
> ➢ paraphrase client needs during the closing prayer (as an outward sign that he/she has been heard and understood)
> ➢ encourage praise and worship as well as petitions and venting of feelings
> ➢ express blessings as a spokesperson for our loving Father God

Practicalities of Counselling: CROSSED BOUNDARY SITUATIONS

As a counsellor you will inevitably be placed in difficult situations where personal and professional boundaries will be violated, whether through ignorance or on purpose. The following are a few examples of such situations accompanied with suggestions on how to handle them. It is strongly advised that you find a supervisor or mentor to process the difficulties you will encounter.

SCENARIO #1

You have met someone at a church social. On learning that you are a Christian counsellor, this person draws you aside and begins to pour out their troubles to you.

Sample of a reply: *'that's terrible; you are really having a hard time of it. Sounds like you need to make an appointment to process everything that is happening to you. I have an hour to spare next week. Would Friday be OK? How about 2pm at the church office? Goodness, look at the time now. I must be off'.*

SCENARIO #2

A friend of a client meets you in the supermarket in your lunchtime. She is thanking you for how much your ministry has meant to her friend. She adds, *'and now that I have caught up with you, I wonder if you would mind giving me a bit of advice about the trouble I am having with my caseworker when I complain that my disability pension often arrives late?'*

Reply: *'I am sorry you are having trouble. That must be frustrating. You know, I have a service where, for the standard hourly rate, I can compose a letter of advocacy for you to present to your caseworker. Would you like to see me in say, half an hour, at the counselling centre to make up a draft? Then you could come in to pick it up... say Wednesday 10am? I will only issue your invoice when you are happy with the final copy'.*

SCENARIO #3

A client has been coming to your practice for several weeks and has agreed by contract to make payments of $... per session. (A Government agency has been subsidising your professional fee because you are a registered provider). At the close of the fourth session, she says she has lost her job and can no longer afford the $... In fact, she says she is sorry but she cannot pay you today.

Reply: *'that must be so disappointing for you. I will pray for you that you will find an even better job. You know, to have saved this embarrassment to both of us, the receptionist could have made alternate arrangements with you if you had explained ahead of time. I know just the person who can help you until you are able to afford the fees again. Annie Baker does some prayer ministry on a voluntary basis at the Long Lakes Church. Would you like her contact number? Our office will help you today by invoicing you for the amount you owe us and we will allow one month for payment'.*

Counsellor Exercise: *A client of longstanding wants you to make a home visit on a Saturday at great inconvenience to you. She has broken her leg and cannot come in. Her husband refuses to bring her to your office even though he will be home on that particular day. How would you handle this situation?*

CHAPTER THREE

OFFICE PROCEDURES

Begin with an exercise for the aspiring counsellor relating to client issues. This highly practical chapter spells out in detail how to use various forms and systems within a counselling practice. Sample documents are given and even a resource checklist to set up an office is included.

- Counsellor exercise – presenting problems (Client Issues list)
- How to fill out and use a Client Details Form to encourage disclosure
- Checklist to be used following initial consultation to assess needs
- Referral practicalities
- Office systems (samples of documents included)

Study Notes

CLIENT

ISSUES

Abandonment	Divorce	Pregnancy-inability
Abortion	Dogmatism	Pregnancy-unwanted
Abuse – emotional	Doubts	Prejudices
Abuse – mental	Dream interpretation	Pride
Abuse – physical	Drug abuse	Procrastination
Abuse – spiritual	Drug dependency	Prophecy
Abuse- professional	Eating disorders	Racism
Abuse- sexual	Emotional disorders	Rebellion
Addictions	Engagement	Reconciliation
Adoption	Failure	Refugees
Adultery	Failure to thrive	Rejection
Ageing	False religions	Relationships
Agnosticism	Family problems	Resentment
Anger	Fears	Self-absorption
Anxiety	Finances	Self-abuse
Arbitration	Fragmented spirit	Self-acceptance
Astrology	Friendships	Self-centredness
Authority issues	Frigidity	Self-control
Backsliding	Goals	Self-esteem
Bad habits	Guilt	Self-pity
Behavioural problems	Handicaps	Self-rejection
Bitterness	Hardened heart	Self-sabotage
Blame	Health problems	Self-worth
Boredom	Homosexuality	Separation
Boundaries	Hypnotism	Sexual deviance
Breakdown – physical	Impotency	Sexual problems
Breakdown- emotional	Incest	Shame
Breakdown –mental	Indecision	Sibling conflicts
Broken spirit	Infirmity	Singles
Bullying	Isolation	Slumbering spirit
Burdens	Jezebel spirit	Social
Burnout	Job loss	Spiritual disorders
Business problems	Learning problems	Spiritual giftings
Cancer	Life choices	Spiritual wounds
Carers	Loneliness	Stress
Chronic fatigue	Loss of identity	Strongholds
Co-dependency	Magic	Suicide
Cognitive problems	Marriage	Terminal illness
Commitment	Memories	Truancy
Communication problems	Menopause	Trust – inability to
Compulsions	Mental disorders	Unacceptance
Condemnation	Migrants	Unbelief – in God
Conflict	Missing persons	Unemployment
Confusion	Motivation – lack of	Unforgiveness
Criminal activity	Negative fruit in life	Vandalism
Crisis handling	Negative patterns	Victim mentality
Cults	Negativity	Victimisation
Curses	New Age practices	Violence
Debt	Nightmares	Vision interpretation
Deception	Numbness	Witchcraft
Delinquency	Obsessions	Workplace problems
Demonic oppression	Occult involvement	
Demonic possession	Overload	
Depression	Over-reactions	
Desertion	Overwork	
Despair	Parental inversion	
Disappointment	Parenting	
Discouragement	Parents – problems with	
Disillusionment	Perfectionism	
Disputes	Post-traumatic stress	

> *Choose 5 issues you would be most capable of handling and 5 issues you would be least capable of handling at this particular stage. This should help you to ascertain where your present capabilities lie and to realize areas in which you might like to study or specialize.*

Date of initial contact:

CLIENT DETAILS

Church Affiliation: Y / N

NAME: _____

Yr Born Again: _____

ADDRESS:

Water Baptism: _____

Spirit Baptised: _____

CONTACT DETAILS:

Birth Date:
Occupation:
Next of Kin:

REFERRED BY: _____

PREVIOUS MINISTRY: _____
courses/seminars,
.mentoring,   _____
deliverance,
pastoral care, etc.   _____

PREVIOUS PROFESSIONAL/LAY COUNSELLING DETAILS

psychologist,   _____
/psychiatrist,
any other counsellor.   _____

MEDICAL PROBLEMS: _____

chronic fatigue, depression,   _____
diabetes, heart problems,
epilepsy, severe allergies   _____
high blood pressure
_____

MEDICATIONS: _____

FAMILY HISTORY OF ADDICTIONS / GENERATIONAL PROBLEMS:

alcoholism, drug abuse,
suicide, depression,   _____
chronic illness
abuse, anger, anxiety, etc   _____

SPIRITUAL GIFTINGS:		**PREFERRED LEARNING STYLE:**	
Dreams	Prophecy	One on one	Tapes
Discernment	Visions	Lectures	Books
Words of	Journaling	Groups	Hands on
Knowledge		Videos	Other

PRESENTING PROBLEMS: _____
_____
_____

CLIENT'S GOAL (in own words):   _____
_____

SESSION DATES: _____ _____ _____ _____ _____ _____ _____ _____

Practicalities of Counselling: FILLING OUT A CLIENT DETAILS FORM

This is your first step in learning about OFFICE PROCEDURE

The *Client Details Form* consists of three segments separated by double lines. You will be repeatedly using this valuable format if you go into counselling or prayer ministry in a more formal way. This resource will give you a good platform to begin with and a structured sense of where you are heading with the average 6-12 sessions per client. Even if you do not enter counselling formally, it is still helpful to use the form as an exercise with family and friends to acquire an idea of what is involved in Christian counselling.

> Permission is given here to make a photocopy of the *Client Details Form* in order to hold it beside your text instructions to enable you to follow the directions more easily. Otherwise, please respect copyright. Master copies of resources found within this publication are provided for your use in the companion book: 'So You Want To Be A Christian Counsellor – Resources Handbook' – (www.prayercounsel.com).

Make sure you, or the person who makes and confirms the appointment, forewarns your client that an initial consultation will last from 1.5-2 hours, one hour of which will be used for filling out an *assessment form* with the counsellor. In formal counselling, your promotional brochure should be issued prior to the first visit to inform the potential client of your ministry style and experience. A sample brochure has been included in this text.

IMPORTANT: Be careful to explain clearly from the outset that this is a consultation to assess whether you can be of any help, and if not, then you will do your utmost to refer them to someone else. This is also their opportunity to assess you, as to whether your style of ministry will be compatible to their personality type and needs.

SEGMENT ONE

Begin to follow the photocopied form from the **top left hand corner.**

Initial Contact Date

This is the date your client first came on to the scene. For the sake of this exercise, and all others, we will call anyone you are helping a *client*. This date of contact could be, say, anything from when a friend introduces you to a stranger with a problem or to when someone formally makes contact with you to make an appointment for ministry or counselling.

As you begin filling out the details form, confirm with the client your date of *first contact* and record it at the top of the sheet. Then **move to the bottom of the form** to the heading *session dates* to record a second date – the date of the actual first appointment – the *initial consultation* session date.

Begin the session by saying that you, as the counsellor, will be filling out a form as you will need some details for your records and it will also prove helpful to clarify the reasons they are coming to you. Now might be the appropriate time to issue your *Privacy & Confidentiality Document*, especially if there appears to be a reticence about supplying personal details. This document will explain the difference between private matters and those to do with confidentiality. It will give your client an idea of your *duty of care responsibilities.* A sample copy is included in this text.

Now, **moving down the left hand side** of segment one, record the following:

Name and Address of Client

Be sure to ask for permission to make contact at the given address. Prompt for privacy issues by asking if there might be anyone at that address who might open personal mail, either with permission, or by accident. If it sounds like there could be a problem, ask if you could make contact in any other way. If the place of employment is supplied, ask if this will cause a problem for the employer. Those under stress sometimes do not think of this possibility.

At this initial stage, you are tactfully trying to ascertain whether there could be a domestic violence issue (or a similar problem). This may influence your decision as to whether you presently feel capable of handling such a case. Now is the time to attempt to find out – <u>before</u> you become embroiled in a complicated or dangerous situation.

Contact Phone Number/s

The same privacy issues apply to phone numbers. Ask if it is acceptable to phone (especially if it is a work number). If they have personal concerns, perhaps they would prefer to be contacted in writing through a post office box facility, or by telephone via a third party. Once again, a troubled client might not even think of this aspect.

Attempt to record more than one contact number if possible: mobile, work, home and perhaps a close friend or relative. In our changeable society phone numbers are transient – especially with mobile services. Sometimes it is vital to acquire a stable contact number or address for the next of kin (or perhaps a pastoral carer or family doctor) when you are concerned over a client '*at risk*'. There is also the possibility that you might need to pursue a client for non-payment of fees.

Do not disclose the above concerns here. Simply indicate that you might have to make a change to the appointment time. Note that there is provision to record *next of kin* on the right hand side of the form. This is where you might have a second opportunity to record these details.

Birth Date, Occupation and Next of Kin

Move to right hand side top part of the page. To help the potential client to relax it is beneficial to make conversational patter; however, be careful not to allow him or her to start speaking about issues at this point. Gently take charge of the session by emphasizing that you need to focus on the current task, that is, to get as much detail down as possible before the actual presenting problem is discussed. Explain that, if you allow discussion at this stage, you might not acquire the vital information you need to carry on further sessions.

Record names of children, spouse or significant others on the back of the form or in your notebook. Explain how you will need to have some idea now of significant people in their life story, so that you will not become confused during future discussions. You can indicate here that you may need to draw up a family tree (genogram) at a later date for various reasons.

Church Affiliation & Related Questions

As you have made it clear that you are a Christian counsellor they should be coming with the expectation that they will be receiving spiritual help (see sample promotional brochure).This will be your initial opportunity to find out whether you are dealing with a professing Christian and you should also gain some idea of their spiritual maturity and worship style. The questions in this segment are for the purpose of obtaining a general idea of the level of their spiritual commitment.

Having already asked their date of birth, now ask the year they were *spiritually reborn*. Most will be familiar with the term 'born again', which seems to remain in use in church circles. Without appearing intrusive, you are also seeking to discover whether they are affiliated with a church <u>at present</u>. You will lead into this through requesting which denomination they were born into, and in what year they were 'born again'. If this seems a 'touchy' subject, leave the spiritual assessment to a future session. If they appear co-operative, then move on to the baptism sections.

Water baptism might indicate a certain level of dedication and whether they have formally committed to Jesus Christ as lord of their life (as well as saviour). Being knowledgeable about *Holy Spirit baptism* indicates that they are familiar with the Pentecostal or charismatic giftings and the associated forms of worship. Through this questioning you can work towards adapting your ministry and conversational style to meet specific needs.

> NOTE: there are different kinds of jargon with various shades of meanings for similar words spoken by the different kinds of Christians from various denominations. For example, there is a world of difference between the Catholic/Episcopalian/High Church of England's traditional forms of worship compared to a Pentecostal service. These can be classed as cultural differences and can significantly impact the counselling process. Remember here that your own values and differences may be expressed if asked for, but judgments should not be made.

We come to the close of the first segment. We should have a great deal of information to work with, and by now you will experience how important *The Client Details Form* becomes with this style of counselling. Be warned that your client could be getting a little edgy here if you have not explained your system and procedures adequately. They could become anxious that their presenting problems will not be covered at all. Gently remind them that you have forewarned at the time of booking to allow <u>at least</u> 1.5 hours for the initial consultation. Reassure them that it is important to get the next section out of the way to be able to properly attend to their needs.

SEGMENT TWO

This section begins on **the left hand side** with the words 'referred by'.

Referral Details

Clients will come from a variety of avenues through *word of mouth referral*: through another client, a friend, a family member, or, via another professional such as a pastor, counsellor or health care worker *referring on*. Community welfare agencies, medical practices, schools, courts, churches and other ministries can refer. Alternately, you could have met your client directly and started chatting about personal concerns. This is classed as a *direct contact*.

Previous Ministry

It is important to know from the outset whether your client has experienced any ministry in the past. Examples are suggested on the form to guide you. You are looking for unhelpful (even abusive) past experiences, as well as positive and satisfactory ministry. (Be careful not to express judgments). If you feel it is appropriate, ask whether the client's pastor has given his or her blessing to seeking spiritual help outside his personal care. Perhaps substantial advice or guidance has already been given by a pastor or other spiritual mentor but this has not been sufficient or helpful in the client's opinion.

Previous ministry could include: personal or spiritual development courses, group therapy, marriage relationship retreats, pastoral counselling or some form of mentoring. If deliverance ministry has been applied, you will need to ascertain the degree of freedom the client is now experiencing. You may not feel capable or confident in assisting someone who has experienced the deeper problems and is still struggling to overcome.

Professional Counselling/Lay

Examples under this heading are given primarily to ascertain whether a medical health care professional has been involved. It is important to make this aspect clear. Prescribed medication could be masking problems and/or be interfering with thinking processes and moods e.g. anti-depressants or drugs administered for psychosis. You will need the wisdom to refer on before you are in too deep. The next section will help somewhat to determine this.

Medical Problems

Most clients are relatively comfortable in discussing physical problems and medications with a counsellor. As a spiritual counsellor, you are dealing mainly with emotions and matters of a spiritual nature; but you will also need to examine *thinking processes*. Extreme anxiety, deep depression and other serious psychological or psychiatric problems could complicate and impede ministry. Physical ailments such as diabetes, heart problems, high blood pressure, chronic fatigue, severe stress and even asthma or allergies could interfere with the counselling process. You could ask here, *are there any physical or other problems which might interfere with our sessions?*

Medications

By recording current medications, you are able to determine whether there is a cause for concern for your personal welfare. Some clients may not know (or be able to explain) the reason they are taking a particular medication. You should have a current prescribed medications dictionary on hand, or you can do a search on the internet for those approved drugs presently dispensed in your country. Be aware that various drugs are prescribed for more than the obvious reasons. For example, antidepressants are sometimes used for correcting disturbed sleep patterns or insomnia.

By now your client could feel comfortable enough to divulge whether there has been past experimentation or regular use of illicit or prescription drugs. Assurance should be offered that there is no need to divulge any information that would cause discomfort. Make clear that *duty of care* responsibilities could come into play and refer again to the difference between privacy and confidentiality*.

---

*Mandatory breaching of confidentiality and duty of care issues are explained briefly under *Office Procedures:* Section 1 Chapter 3 – for Australian conditions only. Be sure to check with your own local legislation, professional and ethical requirements.

Family History of Addictions or Generational Problems

Next is the important section for the family history record. Prompt by making use of the examples given under this heading and advise that this category will probably be dealt with in more depth later on. (We will learn how to record a family genogram further on in the text). For now, explain that you would like to have an idea of significant others involved in the client's life story and that this helps to alleviate confusion on your part.

SEGMENT THREE

By now the client could be frustrated or 'champing at the bit' to get problems off his or her chest. You could feel that you have covered a fair bit of ground in hearing the story anyway. If the client is expressing impatience, or too much discomfort, go immediately to the end of the form to record the presenting problem/s and goals.

At this time, if you feel confident that you will be taking this particular person on formally as your client, you could choose to start hearing presenting problems in depth now. Or, you can offer to leave the filling out of this section to the beginning of the next session. However, it is best to emphasize how beneficial it is to have all the information gathered at this point in order to begin your counselling contract. If they agree, continue on to the next section.

Spiritual Gifts & Preferred Learning Styles

The first section of this segment can be described as 'the fun part', because this is where you can choose to be a bit more informal and light-hearted. Here you will get to know your client more personally by understanding both their *spiritual and practical learning styles*. This is where you begin to interact in a more casual way. It is also the entry into the actual ministry process.

On the form, you will see **five basic giftings,** which are options for spiritual forms of communication:

1. dreams
2. visions
3. words of knowledge
4. discernment
5. prophecy

You could say here, *so that I can speak to you on a common level of understanding, do you operate in any special spiritual giftings?* If they seem unsure of what you mean, rephrase and ask about character traits rather than spiritual gifts/giftings. You could say something like, *do you have any special talents such as being specially gifted in communicating or teaching others, understanding people or of having compassion or empathy? Do you just seem to know things? Are you a sensitive type of person?'* Explain that you would like to communicate in their preferred 'gifting language'.

The following is only a brief description of the use of these giftings within the counsellor and client context. The various giftings will be dealt with in more depth further on in this text (Chapter 4, *Tools of the Trade).*

A client might bring *dreams or visions* to a session to discuss with you. The 'language' of dreams during sleep, and the interpretation of such, is a serious subject and should not be treated as a 'plaything'. First pray openly for discernment as to whether the dreams are of a spiritual nature or of the natural variety. Interpretation of dreams and visions is a very useful gift to cultivate for prayer ministry. Remember, we receive not because we ask not! Visions, in this sense, are classified simply as images experienced while awake. Dreams can be described as visions while asleep. One can also experience a vision within a dream. Do not attempt interpretation of either if you are not confident in this gifting.

Receiving *words of knowledge* and having *spiritual discernment* are classed as separate giftings. A word of knowledge can be in the form of a single word, a scripture, a simple phrase, or a sensing that something is *'of God'*. As a spiritual counsellor, you could be experiencing insight into a person's motives or discerning a spiritual force or power that is affecting the person/s concerned. Seek wisdom on this.

We are exhorted in the scriptures to covet the *gift of prophecy* but we are also warned about how and when to use this gifting. You would do well to study the subject further from the word of God and to come under the teaching of those experienced in the field. Some prayer ministers are quite adept at dealing with the prophetic word; others might occasionally hear *a message* from God in the form of that 'still small voice' or an inner sensing.

Preferred Learning Style

Move along to **the right hand side** of this segment. Discuss with the client how everybody learns best in their own personal style. Explain that you would like to communicate on common ground in this area (as with the spiritual giftings). Sample questioning ideas can be extracted from the following:

Can you assist the learning process by offering resources in between sessions, such as books or audio visual aids? Do they learn best by visual means such as videos, so that they are hearing and seeing at the same time? Can they concentrate more by listening to a cassette or CD/DVD quietly within their own private space? Would they be open to completing homework? Do they enjoy books? How do they read – studiously or skimming through? Do they love the Bible and study it constantly? Do they like attending lectures or seminars and sermons; attending courses and breaking into small groups for discussion; learning from home group participation? Do they like to participate in role-plays or other hands-on learning activities? Do they need to learn by actually doing something, or by watching someone else doing it? Ask if they relate and learn best on a one-on-one basis and do they respond better to tutoring or mentoring rather than group learning?

Presenting Problem/s

At last we arrive at the important part – the section where the client will probably begin to express their concerns. However, you must continue to regulate any anxiousness on the client's part to 'dump' intense feelings on you at this stage. Instead, guide them to be succinct by emphasizing that you require a defining description of what has caused them to seek help – so that the summary will fit into the space provided (2.5 lines). Then quickly move on to the next heading.

Client's Goal

The client needs to find their own words to express their personal goal/goals for counselling. You might prompt by saying, '*to record your goal, think about what you would like to have achieved in, say, a month's time. You will want both of us to look back at this record to see if we are each satisfied you have reached it.*' Explain that you are going to record their thoughts verbatim and point out clearly that the defined space you have available is 1.5 lines.

CLOSING THE SESSION

If you are unsure as to whether you are able to assist this particular client, simply ask if they mind that you take a couple of minutes to make some notes while they help themselves to a drink of water. Use this break to privately fill out the *Checklist Following Initial Consultation* form (following). In this manner, an assessment is completed prior to making another appointment time, or before suggesting referral alternatives.

Allow for an opportunity to pray out loud together to close the session.

Counsellor Checklist: FOLLOWING INITIAL CONSULTATION

CLIENT: ....DATE:................

1. To what degree is the client motivated?   HIGH/LOW/MOD

2. Am I able to personally minister to this person as a client?   YES/NO

3. If so, can I call on another person to co-counsel with me?   YES/NO

Name:

4. What type of help would be suitable for this client?

    ❑ Long term mentoring
    ❑ Inner healing type prayer ministry
    ❑ Crisis counselling
    ❑ Behavioural modification/renewal of the mind techniques
    ❑ Pastoral care – long/short term
    ❑ Relationship counselling
    ❑ Other

5. Are the client's needs critical?   YES/NO

6. The client shows signs/symptoms of: –

    ❑ Severe stress
    ❑ Burnout/chronic fatigue
    ❑ Psychosis (disturbed & out of touch with reality)
    ❑ Depression
    ❑ Suicidal low/mod/high
    ❑ Obsession
    ❑ Addiction
    ❑ Grief/Loss

7. Have I client consent to confer with colleagues? YES/NO

    ❑ Counsellor
    ❑ Supervisor
    ❑ Psychologist
    ❑ Psychiatrist
    ❑ Social Worker
    ❑ Self-Help Group
    ❑ Pastoral Carer
    ❑ Home Cell Group
    ❑ Deliverance Minister
    ❑ Resource Centre

8. Is the client in need of referral for specialist help? YES/NO

    ❑ Legal Aid
    ❑ Financial Advisor
    ❑ Social/Family Services
    ❑ Naturopath/Dietician
    ❑ Counsellor/Therapist
    ❑ Spiritual Advisor/Mentor
    ❑ Mental Health Worker
    ❑ Youth/Social Worker
    ❑ Refuge/Support Group
    ❑ General Medical Practitioner
    ❑ Psychologist/Psychiatrist
    ❑ Other

Practicalities: SETTING UP THE OFFICE – RESOURCES CHECKLIST

- ❑ Accounting software/books
- ❑ Answering service facility
- ❑ Appointments diary
- ❑ Assessment forms for disorders
- ❑ Bibles, commentaries and concordance
- ❑ Business cards
- ❑ Cashbox
- ❑ Computer system
- ❑ Diary for personal journaling
- ❑ Dictionaries, including dictionary of psychology
- ❑ Directory of community services
- ❑ Email facilities
- ❑ Fan and heater or air conditioner
- ❑ Files & lockable filing cabinet
- ❑ Frames for certificates
- ❑ Furniture
- ❑ Occult checklist
- ❑ Phone & fax machine
- ❑ Photocopier
- ❑ Plants, pictures or other décor accessories
- ❑ Play therapy equipment/other visual aids
- ❑ Prescription medications & illicit drugs manuals
- ❑ Promotional leaflets & stands
- ❑ Receipt book
- ❑ Referral resources
- ❑ Refrigerator
- ❑ Resource library
- ❑ Stationery
- ❑ Tape recorder or other recording device
- ❑ Tea/coffee making equipment
- ❑ Toys & books for waiting room
- ❑ Water jug or cooler & glasses
- ❑ White/chalk board

You will .need to have a documentation system in place if you are planning to operate in a formal way. The following pages contain sample documents and brochures to use as a guide in setting up your own system. These forms are not legal documents. The author does not accept responsibility for these samples being used as such. It is suggested that you seek legal and business advice for any documents that you use as well as for your insurance and accounting requirements.

Practicalities of Counselling: REFERRALS to AGENCIES/INDIVIDUALS

Regarding referrals, all information collected needs to be subject to client/counsellor confidentiality agreements and should take into consideration mandatory (compulsory) reporting requirements (See *Privacy & Confidentiality Document*). Other agencies or persons might require the following information from you as the referrer.

IMPORTANT: A client's prior permission and approval should be sought when providing a written or verbal report to a third party or agency.

EXAMPLES OF INFORMATION REQUIRED

    a) Legal
    b) Medical
    c) Specialist Therapist
    d) Spiritual

a) legal

> - Are there any current or possible future litigation problems?
> - Has there been breach of confidentiality issues? For example, *the client has admitted to current involvement in criminal activity and is at risk of harming someone/self and reports have been made to the local police station as well as the mental health assessment team.*

b) medical

> - Is the client potentially abusive (to self or others)? Is there a possibility of physical violence?
> - Is there suspicion of past/present abuse?
> - Are there present indications or history of psychotic behaviour or an existing personality disorder?
> - Is there a life-threatening or terminal illness involved? Is the client infectious?
> - Does the client have an addiction problem?
> - Is there suicidal ideation present? Have there been previous attempts to self-harm? Do you personally consider your client to be of suicide intent and to what extent are they experiencing suicidal ideation?

c) specialist therapist

> - What information do you have permission to disclose?
> - Are other professionals or carers involved?

> ➢ What intervention measures have already been applied? What has worked and what has failed? Has the client been co-operative?

d) **spiritual**

> ➢ Does the client have a professed religion?
> ➢ Has a 'crisis of faith' been disclosed?
> ➢ Have there been signs of any activity that might endanger another person's life or safety (or their own life) e.g. a death wish, cult activity, ritual abuse or witchcraft?
> ➢ Have they experienced deliverance ministry?
> ➢ Do they have present church affiliation and/or pastoral care?

SAMPLE REFERRAL LETTER FORMAT

Name of Counselling Service
Business Address

Date

Dear Sir/Ms/Dr/…

I am referring my client…………………………for your consideration of his/her needs. His /her presenting problem is …

Further particulars are…

Please feel free to contact me within office hours 8am – 4.30pm Mondays to Thursdays on Ph #……………or on Fridays on Mobile #…………………

Yours Faithfully,

Counsellor's Name
Qualification/Position

CLIENT RIGHTS
Sample Brochure Only (Australian)

Dear Client,

The three basic rights of a client in a therapeutic relationship are: -

      informed consent
      right to referral
      rights of minors

Informed consent is the right of the client to know what you are consenting to when entering into the relationship. This information leaflet has been prepared for you, as *informed consent* involves education in the counsellor's responsibilities towards you and what your responsibilities are as a client.

Sometimes a formal a *consent form* will be issued where the extent of confidentiality is provided, such as: duty of care clause, the difference between privacy and confidentiality, whether colleagues will be consulted and the ethos of the organization is explained.

More often, details are presented within the promotional leaflet where the therapist's style of assistance is described and the extent of service to you and to those associated with you is explained. The therapist/counsellor's specific fields of interest, background and, qualifications are often included.

Informed consent is elicited either by written means (including a signature), or verbally, but the client has the right to ask for particulars before signing or verbally consenting to a counselling contract –

- the therapist's experience in dealing with specific types of problems
- academic qualifications, including any specialised training such as: deliverance ministry, marriage guidance or group therapy
- personal or group insurance in the event of malpractice, or public liability cover
- accreditation or membership in a professional health organization

Asking questions indicates you are a shrewd 'consumer' and a willing participant in the therapeutic relationship. This honesty will build trust and allows participation in setting co-operative goal setting.

The client has a right to enough informed consent (right from the initial consultation, through to the end of the process) regarding such issues as degree of confidentiality, fees and the length of the service. In other words, you will need enough information to participate actively. However, there should be a balance struck, whereby the practitioner gives just enough information as to not overwhelm, but to ethically fulfil the spirit of the consent.

Length of Service and Referrals:

There is a right to terminate the process, from either side or the rights of referral. You may feel that the assistance is not to your personal liking, or you may prefer a second opinion and perspective, or another style of therapy. However, you remain the ethical responsibility of the original therapist until you see the next therapist.

Rights of Minors

Degree of confidentiality should be mentioned: minors have the right (in some states of Australia) to seek counselling (to *self-refer*) without parental knowledge or consent. This has been allowed legally because a child might not seek help otherwise, such as in cases of substance abuse, child abuse, abortion consideration, sexually transmitted disease concerns, or birth control needs.

With Compliments from your Counsellor

Sample CONFIDENTIALITY & PRIVACY DOCUMENT (*Australian*)

This information is presented to you, as a valued client of our services, regarding your right to privacy and our policy regarding confidentiality. If you have not already received a brochure regarding our services and general policies, please ask for a copy to be forwarded to you.

Confidentiality, in the context of a counselling setting, is aligned with privacy issues. In law and ethics, *privacy* usually means limited access to information about you. In your general life, whenever you share your private concerns with a friend, you assume, or hope, that your friend can be trusted not to tell other people. You should be able to hold even greater trust in a professional counsellor, that he or she will not divulge your personal affairs to a third party.

A person must give up some personal privacy to establish *confidentiality*. On entering the counselling process, you may expect to share a lot of your personal information and history and your associated thoughts and feelings. You will probably need to do this in order to procure the help that you need. In exchange for loss of privacy, you will no doubt expect promised confidentiality. You will receive this from our services under the following conditions.

The general parameters of counselling are, that unless the client asks for, or authorises disclosure, it is unethical to disclose confidences. However, other public societal needs counteract or limit the individual's rights.

LIMITED CONFIDENTIALITY: DUTY OF CARE & DISCLOSURE

All information you provide to our counselling services will be on a voluntary basis and will remain within our practice. However, the law requires health professionals to report to third parties under certain circumstances. In Australia, your rights as an individual are protected under *The Privacy Act*. This provides protection for you as a private citizen and as a client of our services. It is expected that any private information we obtain from you will not be disclosed outside the counselling service to a third party without your consent (with the exceptions outlined below). This is termed *'informed consent'*. For instance, we may ask you whether we can contact another professional for advice on your behalf.

MANDATORY REPORTING

When a person is classified as *at risk (of harm)*, there is both a legal and moral duty (of care) to divulge certain private information. Private pertains to being not public or widely known. There is a difference between privacy and confidentiality. Confidentiality may be breached on private (secret) matters for the sake of the general public or for an individual's safety. Say, for example, someone is threatening to take the lives of others (e.g. terrorism) or their own life (suicide ideation). Disclosure of information may be necessary because it is *mandatory* to do so. That is, it can be a compulsory *duty of care* to *report* such information.

The general guidelines **in Australia** are as follows:

> ➢ *when there is a clear risk to your safety or that of others*
> ➢ *where it is legally required of a counsellor to provide a file or information, or to attend court as a witness*
> ➢ *where there has to be mandatory (compulsive) disclosure of information such as reporting of child abuse*

As professionals, counsellors may be ethically and legally required to report. However, there is a moral responsibility to speak to the client about this disclosure prior to the reporting when possible. This may be done verbally. As the client you could also be formally asked to sign an *Informed Consent Document*. This allows for breaches of confidentiality to be limited (in your best interests) – see sample document below.

INFORMED CONSENT

I hereby give permission for .... of ABC Counselling Services to disclose personal information for the sake of interventions on my behalf. I acknowledge that these disclosures may be mandatory, or might be for: consultation purposes, finding resources, or to make relevant referrals. This consent is to enable access to suitable co-ordinated support for myself.

SAMPLE DOCUMENT ONLY (Do not sign).

Signed..…dated....................

Signature of Counsellor..…dated....................

Acknowledgement Document

I understand that *ABC Counselling Services* may need to consult and/or debrief, and, in the course of this, may need to disclose confidential information regarding my casework to other professional or paraprofessional workers. I also acknowledge the duty of care and mandatory reporting needs as stated in the *Confidentiality & Privacy Document* issued to me today.

Signed...dated........................

BREACH OF CONFIDENTIALITY DOCUMENT

Sample Only

Note from the Author

All counsellors please note that you have a duty of care to report cases according to the legal requirements of your local area and a duty to keep abreast of the relevant ethical standards of those associations, agencies and churches to which you belong. It is your own personal, ethical, legal and moral responsibility to keep informed of current requirements and standards and to adhere to them.

Dear Client,

Please sign and date both copies then hand the one below in to the office. You may retain the copy attached to your *Confidentiality & Privacy Document* for your personal reference.

OFFICE COPY

Acknowledgement Document

I understand that …………………………*of*…………………… *Counselling* may need to consult and/or debrief, and in the course of this, may need to disclose confidential information regarding my casework to other professional or paraprofessional workers. I also acknowledge the duty of care and mandatory reporting needs, as stated in the **Confidentiality & Privacy Document** issued.

Signed…………………………………………dated……………………

CLIENT:

INFORMED CONSENT/AUTHORITY TO DISCLOSE DOCUMENT

Sample Only

INFORMED CONSENT DOCUMENT

I, ………………………………………………………………… (please print)

hereby give permission for ………………………of …………………………….
to disclose personal information for the sake of interventions on my behalf.
I acknowledge that these disclosures may be mandatory, or that they may be
used for consultation purposes with other professionals and to make relevant
referrals. I am of the understanding that any disclosure will be used to find
suitable co-ordinated support for myself and will be used in my best interests.

Signed……………………………………………………………….dated…………

Signature of Counsellor…………………………………………...dated…………

ADVOCACY AUTHORIZATION DOCUMENT

Sample Only

ADVOCACY DOCUMENT

I,.. *(please print)*

give permission for…………………….………….of……………………………..

as my advocate, to speak on my behalf

with……………………………………………………………………………………

regarding……………………………………………………………………………

Signature…………………………………………….date………………

RELEASE OF INFORMATION DOCUMENT

Sample Only

AUTHORITY TO RELEASE INFORMATION DOCUMENT

I/we…………………………………………………………………………………

hereby authorize ……………………of ……………………….....................

to release personal information

to…………………………………………………………………………………

Signature(s) of Client(s)………………………………………….date………..

Signature of Counsellor………………………………………….date………..

CONCLUSION OF CONTRACT LETTER

Sample Only

Greetings from *ABC Counselling Services*

Dear Client,

This is to confirm that our counselling contract has come to a close. It has been an honour for us to be involved in helping you with your needs. Thank you for your openness and trust in sharing just this small part of your spiritual journey with us.

I, and all those associated with our services, will continue to think of you and pray for your future walk with God. Please remember that our door is always open to you if you have need of our help again, or even just to catch up to say hello and to let us know how you are going.

It has been a privilege to get to know you. As you have learnt, each one of our clients is very precious to us. We would be grateful if you would use the enclosed envelope to describe your experiences of our services for the benefit of others who are considering counselling.

> You might like to do this as a testimonial or a simple bit of feedback for us. Please endorse with your signature if you are agreeable to your testimony being used verbally as a teaching aid or as part of a written publication to promote our service. Be assured that it will only be used if endorsed personally by you.

Also remember that your confidentiality will continue to be maintained at all times, unless that is, any information you have disclosed comes under reportable categories ethically or legally in the future.

Yours in His Service,

Your Counsellor

CHAPTER FOUR

TOOLS OF THE TRADE – GIFTINGS

There are so many spiritual and natural resources to aid the counselling ministry. This chapter acknowledges the natural, but emphasises the use of the spiritual. It further explains the difference in operating under the anointing of God in comparison to secular counselling. This chapter includes:

- A graphic visual aid to explain the tools of 'the trade'
- Explaining the difference between spiritual gifts and natural talents
- The first of many client stories/testimonials to illustrate the ministry
- Teachings on the major giftings in the practice of prayer ministry
- The four main aspects of prayer are introduced from 'the toolbox'

Study Notes

Practicalities of Counselling: SPIRITUAL GIFTINGS

To be a Christian counsellor, it is useful to understand and to be able to explain the difference between: –

- a)   Natural Talents
- b)   Fruits of the Spirit
- c)   Spiritual Disciplines
- d)   Holy Spirit Giftings

a) *Talents* can be described as *natural God-given abilities* e.g. when one is gifted in music, or a talented artist, or good at sporting activities. Our natural talents can be used for God's glory as well as for our own fulfilment and the benefit of others.

b) *Fruits* are an indicator of *spiritual maturity and character* development. These come from putting to death our human (fleshly) nature and its natural desires, allowing the spirit of God to produce in us the nine fruits of the spirit: (Gal 5:16-26). We are instructed to bear fruit so that we will be known by our fruits (Matt 3:8; Matt 7:16). That is, we can be recognisable as belonging to Christ Jesus and his lordship over us, according to how we live our lives.

c) *Disciplines* are practices, which serve to *develop character* and enable us to please him by being fruitful in good works and knowledge of him (Col 1:10). Practical disciplines can be: service, bible study, worship, journaling, fasting, prayer, and waiting on, or communing with, God (meditation). These help us to grow in faith. Disciplines help us to control our fleshly desires and to relate to God in an increasingly more intimate way.

d*) Giftings* of a spiritual or supernatural nature (in comparison to a natural gift or talent) are activities using gifts given by the Holy Spirit to glorify God and to edify others (Rom 12). To *edify* in the spiritual sense can mean to inform or instruct in order to encourage and strengthen a person in their faith and moral values. (1Cor 12-14). The purpose of gifts given to the Church is to further the kingdom of God and to unify and build up the Body of Christ. There are as many gifts or services to the Church as there are needs in the church.

Loving/Graciousness	Administration	Organising/Planning
Mercy/Compassion	Faith/Signs/Wonders	Maintenance/Building
Prophecy/Knowledge	Healings/Miracles	Spiritual Restoration
Prayer/Intercession	Praying in Tongues	Counselling
Service/Helps/Care	Dreams/Visions	Mentoring/Advocacy
Exhortation/Encouragement	Visionary	Pastoral Care
Peacemaking/Unity	Preaching/Teaching	Sharing/Generosity
Wisdom/Discernment	Deliverance	Leadership/Discipleship
Material Stewardship	Spiritual Warfare	Gatekeeper
Business Operation	Pioneering	Watchman
Hospitality	Creative Ideas	Worshiper
Evangelism	Dance/Art/Music	Prophesying
Facilitation	Catering/Cleaning	Writing, etc.

There are specific *tools of trade* used for operating prayer ministry type counselling. This graphic representation of the different tools and weapons used will give the reader an idea of the diversity of resources we have at our disposal as Christian counsellors. The *toolbox* represents our *prayer closet*. You will note the lid is closed. This is our private time with the Lord, occupied by *praying in the spirit* as much as possible. By praying in the spirit, we receive the understanding to pray according to God's will.

IMAGE 06

TOOLS OF THE TRADE

18. Guidance / Light to Path
20. Power of the Anointing
22. Signs Wonders Miracles
"AND.... ABOVE ALL"
17. Keys of Truths
19. Authority of
21. Jesus Name
23. Love
15. Sword of the Spirit
16. Axe to the Roots
Prayer Closet
4. Wisdom and Understanding
3. Fellowship
Creative Gifts
1. Intercession
5. The Word
14. Natural Talents
2. Personal Communion
Journal (Rhema)
Revelation
12. Visions
9. Discipling Preaching Teaching
7. Cross
6. Prophecy Testimony
13. Knowledge Discernment
11. Dreams
10. Parables Shepherd
8. Blood Water

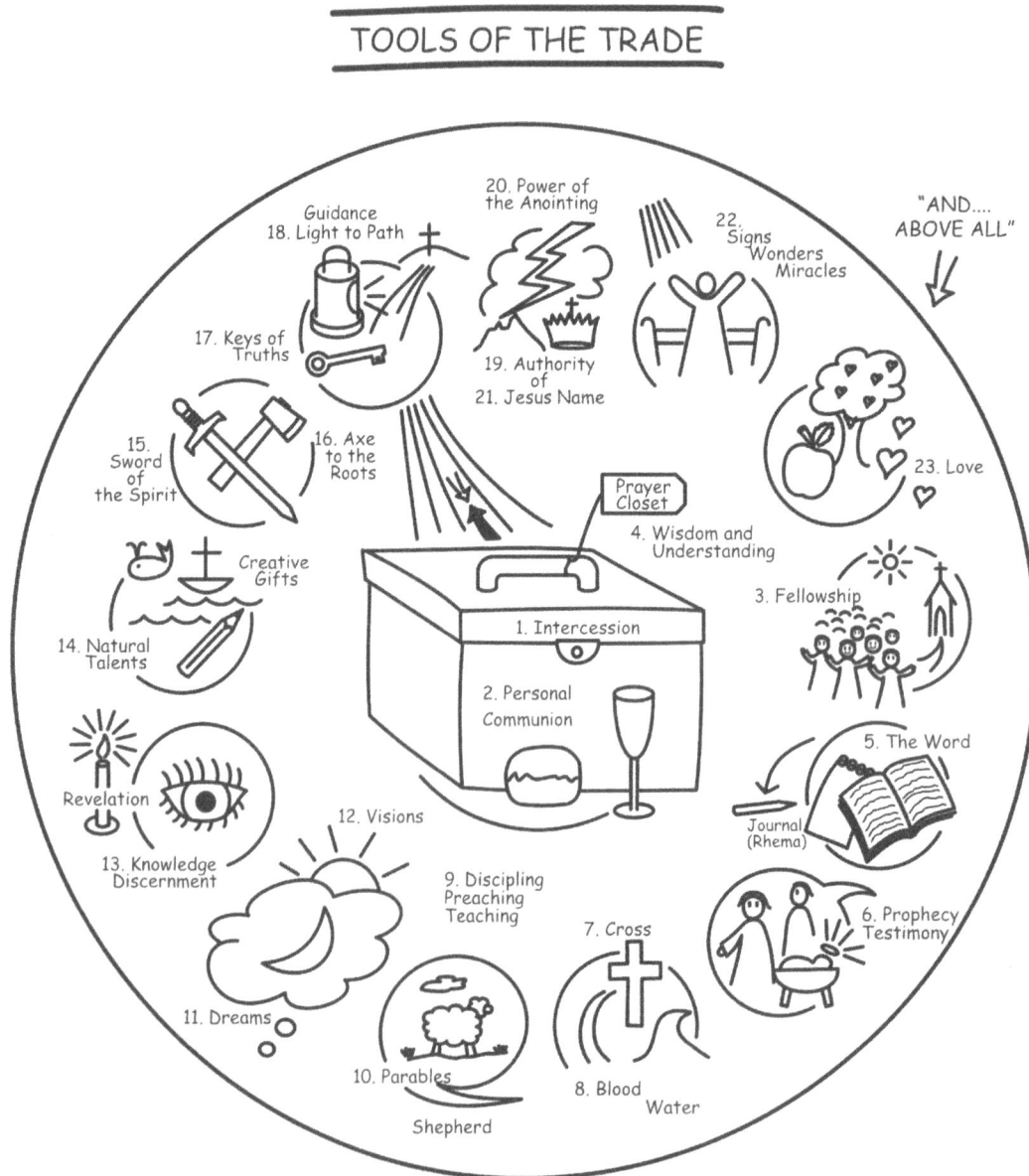

INSTRUCTIONS FOR VIEWING TOOLS OF THE TRADE GRAPHIC

Move through the numbering from 1 to 23 matching the brief explanation of each resource available to us in our trade. Start at the lid of the toolbox **intercession**[1] (petition prayer on behalf of others) which is a primary tool for ministry. As Jesus did, we should aim to say only what the Father would have us say and only what Jesus would do and say. This is our ideal. We will fail, we will fall, we will make mistakes, but we aspire to following in Jesus' footsteps. Jesus prays to the Father for us intensely and intimately (Jn 17).

Also in the centre, and to the foreground of the toolbox, are the elements *of the bread and the wine*; further representing our **personal communion**[2] *(spiritual union)* with our heavenly Father. Remembering how Jesus has reconciled us with the Father, we commune with him via public corporate worship – **fellowship**[3] – as well as in private worship. As we fellowship with our brothers and sisters, we remind ourselves that we are all part of the one body of Christ – not independent members, but interdependent with all believers (Rom 12:4,5).

While in our prayer closet, we access our tools and seek **wisdom and understanding**[4] through praying and listening for his messages to us. **The Word**[5] is represented here by the open *Bible and the notepad* into which we record our thoughts. We are open to revelation and daily *manna* (spiritual nourishment) from both the *rhema* (living word) and *logos* (the scriptures). Becoming conscious of what God is saying to us personally, we record as the rhema word and confirm this with the logos (written) Word of God.

This brings us to **prophecy and testimony**[6] (that is, our spoken words). We witness via *prophetic words* (messages of divine truths revealing the will of God) and our spoken *testimonies*. By the Blood of the Lamb and the words of our mouths, the listeners are, saved, healed, restored, renewed, blessed and sanctified. Constantly, we are bringing our clients back to **the cross**[7] to confess, repent and to receive forgiveness. This cleansing occurs via the Blood and the washing of his Word, portrayed as the *rivers of living* **water** *and the shed* **blood**[8] alongside the cross.

Next come **discipling, preaching and teaching**[9] in order to shepherd our 'lost lambs' into a right relationship with the Father. To shepherd, we use **parables**[10]**, dreams**[11] **and visions**[12] as well as *prophecies* (personal messages from God). It is via the dreams, visions and prophecies that our spiritual eyes receive **revelation, knowledge and discernment.**[13] Possessing **creative gifts and natural talents**[14] as well as *spiritual giftings,* we use all we have to get the message across to those in bondage, the hurt and wounded, the troubled, the grieved and the lost.

To the confused and those under deception, we use the **sword of the Spirit**[15] to *separate truth from error.* We cut off the lies believed, taking **an axe**[16] right down to the deepest roots of *core beliefs* to sever harmful generational connections. We will also cut, break, deliver, bind and loose from all *curses, bondages and oppression*, finding the **keys of truths**[17] that unlock prisons and provide **guidance**[18] via the light of God's Word. Using our Christ-bought **authority**[19] (crown) and **anointed power**[20] (lightning), in **His Name**[21] we will do **signs, wonders and miracles**[22] just as Jesus promised.

Lastly, refer to the apple tree at the top right hand side of the graphic representation. Love has its position above all else, for, apart from having all the spiritual giftings and natural talents, unless we have **love**[23], then we are just 'noisemakers' (1Cor 13:1). When we manifest the fruit of love in its various forms: love for God, love for ourselves and love for our neighbours, we are well equipped to do the job. Although our natural love is good, always remember that all tools are supplied and covered by the supernatural love of the Father. Without him, we can do nothing of lasting value.

CLIENT TESTIMONIAL: The Prophet

I'll never forget the day I met God through a real live prophet. I had been going to this therapist guy for over eight weeks. My car had been in the shop most of that time 'cause I couldn't afford to get it out as well as pay this guy. So I'd rock up, usually on time (because my mum drove me there). I'd been feelin' a real loser having me mum taxi a big guy like me everywhere. But there's no way she's gonna let me drive her precious car since I smashed mine up. That last smash made me figure I had to do something about my head.

I started going because this fellow, Jordan, advertised he was a cognitive behavioural therapist in the weekly newspaper. I was curious and suspicious at the same time, because the advertorial had him saying that he was 'a practising Christian', and to me, the two didn't go together – Christianity and psychology. I mean! I'm a guy who has done a bit of psych at Uni.

No, somehow they seemed oceans apart. It was like two different religions that clashed – the humanism and the like. I'd dropped out of Uni half way through my second year trying to do my B.Ed. I'd gotten so depressed over not keeping up with the others. I knew I wasn't dumb, but my mind just seemed in a fog. It always has been.

I don't seem to have it up there for some reason. Even though I'd really like to be a teacher, and there's a big demand for males in primary schools, I've ended up just going from one dead-end job to another, 'cause of my mind playing dumb. I couldn't even find my own way around high school or a class timetable without a mate to keep me on time and show me which room I should be in. It was even worse at Uni.

I'd been going along to a church youth group when I was around 16. So that's say… about, I think, 7 years ago. No, I tell a lie, it was 8 years back because it was when I had my first girlfriend. That's why I went along because she went to church. So I was 15.

I'd become a Christian, but like the high school and the Uni, I never really got anywhere with it. I couldn't understand the Bible and, when the other guys argued back and forth about doctrine it went completely over my head – my head with the fog in it.

So, as I was saying, the first time I rocked up to the counselling I explained this all to this guy Jordan. He seemed the real thing and kinda understood what I was on about. He seemed to know things about me that even I didn't know and things I did know that nobody else knew (if you know what I mean). He seemed to look inside my head and see things even at the first visit.

After a few sessions of this, I asked him how he knew these things about me and he explained that he wasn't a magician or a psychic or anything like that. He said he was what they call 'operating in the spiritual giftings'. He explained that he was particularly interested in getting prophetic messages or 'words' as he called them. I figure now that it was like The Man Upstairs was telling Jordan things about people so that he could help them.

I said that these spiritual giftings seemed pretty cool. I asked him if God told him anything about me. He said yes, that he felt that God had told him that something pretty bad had happened to me when I was a kid and that was what had caused my thinking problems.

He hinted about what it was. Man was I shocked that he knew! Because it was pretty embarrassing and still shook me up when I thought about it. So I changed the subject to how I really wanted a good job. I asked him if he could get my head working so I could be a teacher or something.

But when I came back the next week he brought up what had happened to me as a kid again. At the end of our session he tells me he has another message from God about it. He said he had had a 'word of encouragement' for me and asked if I wanted to hear it. Well of course, who doesn't want to be encouraged? So I said, 'Yeah man, go ahead'. He said, 'So do you want to read it?' He had written it down and he gave it to me. This was my first one.

Every week from then on he had another one waiting for me. He said they were called 'personal prophecies' by the people who went to his church. Sometimes, they were in a letter from God to me and sometimes he would just start speaking out what he thought God was saying to me in the middle of the session. I'd say, 'Man... that's spot on! Other times, he told me what he thought God had been telling him about me during the week when he was praying for me. He prays a lot.

And you know what? I think the first one was right too. I've got it here in my wallet. It's getting a bit worn out. I'll have to make a copy. It's got the Bible verses to go with it and everything. Do you want to read it? Here it is. I am really starting to think straighter already. I have an interview for a new job downtown in half an hour. So you'll have to hurry and read that because I want it back. It means a lot to me.

Jordan says, when I get a bit more help for what went wrong when I was a kid, he'll teach me how to hear 'words' from God for myself. Hey, maybe I can be a prophet too? That'd be cool...

All characters and cases are fictitious representations and any similarities to real persons or casework are purely coincidental.

INTRODUCING PROPHECY & JOURNALING

(Jer 1 & Isa 6)The following is a message from God recorded (as received) by the author. According to the scriptures, we are to desire the spiritual gift of prophesying (1Cor 14:1-5). Using this gifting, we are able to edify, exhort and to comfort the Body of Christ, his Bride the Church. God continues to guide his people in this way. However, it is essential to remember that modern day prophecy must be in line with the written word of Almighty God (confirmed by the scriptures). With this in mind the following modern message was received accompanied by the passage Deut 32:1-47. The correct terminology places it as *a prophetic word* in the form of a *general prophecy*.

'How Foolish is Man!' (Deut 32:6)

'I came as Creator; not to destroy. It was not my will that man should perish. I ordained from the beginning a home for man which would enable him to live in peace and in companionship with me.

'But man chose to come adrift from me, and to thwart my principles that were in place for his protection (v5). In doing this, <u>he</u> became the destroyer, the spoiler of my works, and he has lived to benefit himself, not to please the one who has made him (v15-18).

'This has been so from the beginning and will be to the end. This is why I will establish a new beginning, a new home for those who would choose to adhere to my principles and come under my protection (v36).

'My Son was the key to the Kingdom, the entrance to my spirit realm, where life is lived to the full and my orders are carried out; and where obedience is the sustenance of life and my words are the pivot of all that exists (v46,47).'

There are those in the Body of Christ who have the *calling of a prophet*. However, it is also possible for the average Christian to learn how to receive messages from God, for personal edification and for the encouragement of others. To those who seek to minister via counselling, it is a gift to be *coveted* (desired and sought after) and to be used skilfully as a *gifting* (spiritual activity) for the glory of God.

Many Christians feel that it is important to record their personal thoughts and feelings when communing with the Father. This *journaling* is often a step towards learning to operate in the spiritual gifting of prophesying. As we talk to God in this way, expectant on an answer in childlike trust, we can begin to experience the delight of our heavenly Father dialoguing with us. (See Isa 6 for an example of a prophet journaling).

COMMUNICATING WITH GOD VIA JOURNALING

The following *word* (message from God) is an example of a *'personal prophecy'* or *'a personal word'* from God. The author received this 'word' while *waiting* on God (to hear from him) and *meditating on* (spending time to think deeply about his ways and thoughts) God's *logos word* (the written scriptures) and his *rhema word* (the 'living' word which becomes personal and real to the receiver).

THE FATHER'S HEART

God speaking:

'The attention you pay me, my daughter, is a joy to me and I would have you come to me more often. Bring from your storehouse the offerings you have to give to me'.

Author speaking:

'Lord, the offering I have is my gratitude towards you. I know that we, as your people, have broken all your rules – the rules you have set up to remain true to yourself and laws you have set in place because of who you are – your perfect self.

'I know that, when you set these laws in place on our creation, you could foresee that we would let you down, that we would not be true to you. You even set yourself up to have your heart broken by us. Why did you do that Lord?'

God speaking:

'Because, my little one, I wanted you to love me as I love you. Why does a parent risk his heart to a child who may in turn reject or disgrace him? Why does a father yearn for offspring? Why does he risk his heart to this child?

'It is my nature to give of myself in the hope that I will receive. And I <u>do</u> receive. I receive much from those who worship me in spirit and in truth – who worship me for who I am. Who love my laws and seek to please me – to desire to know me as I truly am'.

Associated scriptures for confirmation: Ps 40:6-10; Ps 42:1-2

To practise the skill of journaling, you will need to be open to experiencing the spiritual disciplines such as: worship, waiting on God, focusing on Jesus Christ, meditating on his Word, listening for his still small voice and 'hearing' his messages.

AUTHOR'S EXPERIENCE

My personal experience with communicating with God began from my habit of keeping a journal or diary. This natural inclination served to keep me in contact with my own thoughts and self-talk processes. In this way I recorded my feelings and voiced my opinions on life.

So, when I became a Christian, I naturally (perhaps naively) progressed to include in my jottings, my personal 'conversations' with God. This took my beliefs, ideas, values and questions centring on the meaning of life to a new level. I was to discover that, not only was I talking to God, but that my amazing creator and saviour seemed to be answering my questions and revealing his thoughts, beliefs and values to me in return! I found I was actually having a written dialogue with God!

This communing with him became the mainstay of my spiritual walk, so much so that I would personally include journaling as a type of spiritual discipline (Hab 2:1 & 2, Ps 46:10, Heb 10:19-22, Heb 12:2). To substantiate this further, the scriptures do record men dialoguing with God via written means (Jer 11)*. For example, God Almighty instructs Jeremiah to record everything he had been told, and this must have entailed writing, as it was dictated to a scribe (or secretary) by the prophet (Jer 36).

Note also another prophet, Isaiah's, self-discipline in tuning his spiritual ear to hear God's voice and his faithfulness in relaying God's messages to the people – no matter how harsh the message. The first verses of the book of Isaiah introduce these scriptures as containing the messages revealed, received and <u>recorded</u>, of the prophet's dialogue with God.

Although the prophets of old needed to receive a calling and ordination (Isa 6:6-13) believers today are in the post crucifixion position. We are able to freely enter the Father's throne room to directly commune with our God because of our Saviour's sacrifice. What a privilege!

---

*For practical resources on journaling under the anointing access *Communion with God Ministries* www.cwgministries.org Mark & Patti Virkler.

Counsellor Resource: PROPHESYING

The use of prophecy within Christian counselling is a subject in itself and enough to fill another book. It involves hearing the heart of God and, sometimes, becoming a messenger or conduit for God's word to a client.

DEFINITION

A summary of the definition taken from several Greek lexicons brought the following meanings to light.

Prophesying: -

- ➢ Speaking under inspiration
- ➢ Publicly expounding (unfolding truth)
- ➢ Revealing the will and mind of God
- ➢ Revealing the counsels and ways of God
- ➢ Flowing forth (in a gifting)

AUTHOR'S LEARNING EXPERIENCE

To those interested parties who ask me how to operate in the prophetic gifting, or how I 'hear' from God in order to prophesy, I say that it all began by my personal desire to know God via a childlike form of questioning. What is he really like? How do I please him? What does he think and feel? What does he think of me? How does he do what he does? And so on.

Then it progressed into hearing God's voice answering me. By this, I mean that his thoughts seemed to be intruding into my thoughts and I was 'hearing' answers to those questions for myself. So I began writing down (journaling) what I thought I was hearing from God the Father and his beloved Son Jesus Christ. Fortunately, I was in a church which revered the Bible as God's written word to his people, so sometimes I cautiously shared my thoughts with others to confirm if what I was hearing was scriptural.

Looking privately at the relevant scriptures, I appeared to be on safe ground – especially when the Bible clearly states that all should desire the gift of prophesying (ICor14:1). When I noticed this for the first time as a young Christian, I coveted the gift for myself. However, I was in a conventional church where the charismatic giftings as we value and use them today, were not overtly operating. I was told that word 'prophesy' in this context meant preaching sermons from the pulpit based on the scriptures.

I did not accept this as a complete answer and began a quest to know the true meaning of what I was coveting. I began to know God for who he really is and I began to taste and experience some more of his beautiful aspects; this was because he was actually telling me about himself! I grew from coveting a gift, to knowing more of the Giver through the gifting.

Today, to those who ask me about hearing God's voice and having it flow forth in a gifting, I say the following: that it all began by wanting to know God as he truly is – his will, his mind and his ways. I explain that I personally did not want to simply accept what fallible human beings make of him, and this included my own perceptions of him. I wanted to know the one true God.

Then to those who really show an interest in knowing more about this aspect of relating to him through dialoguing, I might go on to ask, 'are you prepared to pay the price?' If so, then I interpret this as meaning that these are the ones who are already dying to self and who truly desire to hear God's voice.

I attempt to explain along the lines that we should consider it normal that God would want to speak to his people personally. I reason that Moses spoke to God as a friend; even arguing with him – as did Jonah, Jeremiah, and Job. And God spoke back to these all too human examples of mankind. I argue: then why should he not talk to us today when Jesus has given us direct access to the throne of God?

I like to use the analogy that we need to tune in spiritually, as we would tune into the frequency of a radio station. We also need to develop our communication skills so that it becomes <u>a normal part</u> of our spiritual walk to hear the voice of God. The following is the teaching I have compiled from my experiences.

SKILLS DEVELOPMENT FOR DIALOGUING WITH GOD

To develop the skills we need to be:

    a) an open vessel
    b) a clean vessel
    c) a clear channel

a) An open vessel

The best possible example is that of Mary, mother of Jesus when the angel told her about her great commission in life. She was informed by an angel that she was actually to conceive God's own Son in human form in her own body! Mary was to be responsible for bearing and delivering into the world its Saviour. She would be nurturing him into manhood. And her reply was, '*let it be so*'. She was literally an open vessel. We must admire this young girl's unconditional surrender to a message delivered from God.

What a struggle we have. We say that it is too hard, impossible, or that we simply do not want to do what we are being asked to do. But Mary '*pondered on it*' the Bible reports, and allowed God to have his way. It was a decision made without reservation; with no questions asked. She received the Living Word into her own body and received him into the world for our salvation. She was the ultimate messenger – a prophet in her own unique way.

b) A clean vessel

After the initial desire was planted in me to prophesy, I began to understand that it literally meant that I was to be a *message carrier* for God; however, I was not a Mary. I had to be willing to be cleaned up in order to become a vessel, a receptacle for his words. I needed humbling.

This is where the suffering came in. The process known as *dying to the flesh* came into operation. We are instructed to strive to be perfected. As a young Christian hearing this, I was bewildered at the thought that I had to be perfect. Later on in my walk, I discovered that *perfecting ourselves* and *working out our salvation* were analogous terms for accepting that we would never feel good enough, clean enough, nor perfect enough.

Via his amazing grace we come to understand, with spiritual eyes and ears, that *our righteousness* (or right standing or acceptability) has already been achieved through the perfect sacrifice made by Jesus Christ. We are right with God. We are now perfect in God the Father's eyes because he looks on us via his perfect son; he sees Jesus when he looks at us – an amazing concept!

So, what do we do after we express our willingness to become receptacles, carriers and deliverers of God's messages? As Mary did on hearing from the angel that she would carry the saviour of the world, we simply say, 'let it be so' and let the work begin. We have offered ourselves as *living sacrifices* and have virtually asked to be cleansed. We will need clean hands as well as a clean heart.

Year after year, daily, hourly, we look inside to our personal spirits. We are working out (processing) the salvation, which has already been purchased and gained for us. We see where we are currently failing to be a clean vessel by asking the Holy Spirit to convict us. We acknowledge that Jesus died on the cross to cover our particular failings and sins. We repent, renounce, ask for forgiveness, receive it, make restitution where necessary, and then get back on with the job. He fills our clean vessels with his *living words*.

c) A clear channel

We are like blocked drains. As an inquisitive young girl I used to watch my father use a sink plunger. This tool reminded me of giant versions of the rubber arrows we'd lick and fire at the fridge door. When too many food scraps were put down the kitchen sink, our dad used to grab that big plunger. Grumbling and swearing he would perform the rite of pushing and sucking and brushing my peering face aside. Then 'blob' the magic sound happened. We had a clear channel – an unblocked pipe.

In the days of plumbing with septics and grease traps, this was a primitive tool, but it (usually) worked. It worked as long as dad got to things before they became serious. If we just added one more little scrap down the kitchen sink –thinking one more wouldn't matter – then there was trouble with a capital T. There would be the switching off the water at the main. The Big Wrench had to be found. Then there would be the dreaded Opening of the Pipes.

I am sure everyone knows what I mean when I make the comparison with this to the sin in our lives. How can rivers of living water and springs of life flow with blocked drains? We need to unblock and wash our hands of anything that is not of God. Personal prophecy can be a means to this end.

As Christian counsellors, we may be revealing something that would otherwise be hidden, neglected or unknown. In Paul's writings, the words 'prophecy' and 'revelation' are used interchangeably (1Cor 14:26, 30). When a prophecy is declared, people should either feel that they have had a touch from God or that they have personally touched him (Rev 19:10). *'The testimony of Jesus is the spirit of prophecy'.* I understand this to mean that the revelation of Jesus and his character is testified to by prophetic utterances.

So how are we to use this gifting as a tool so that we may be vessels of honour in his service? How are we to reveal him to others so that they may have a touch from God, which will heal a wound or change an attitude?

ACTIVATION

The spirit of the prophet is subject to the prophet's own control (1Cor 14:32). We need to have the courage to open our mouths and speak out the message. Faith and courage are needed. More so, a simple trust in God to cover our mistakes and to allay our fears is required. The words, *'the Word of the Lord came to me'* are liberally scattered throughout the Old Testament. God is still speaking to us and through us today. Revise again the various aspects of prophecy as mentioned at the beginning of this chapter.

RECEPTION

A prophecy can begin to come in the form of a single word such as *come, give* or *now*, or a common combination of words such as *fear not* or *peace be with you*. It may be an idea or concept such as restoration of a lost child to the Father's heart. To use the lost child illustration: you might receive this message (or idea) in your session preparation time with accompanying scriptures and perhaps a word of knowledge or discernment as to why the client is 'lost'.

Alternately, God may choose to reveal the name only of a specific client during normal prayer time and expect you to enquire after a message for that particular person. There are a myriad of ways to receive a communication via the Holy Spirit of God.

He wants us to use whatever we have, whether phrases, ideas, scriptures, images, feelings, or a vague 'sense' to begin with. We may choose to open our mouths and exercise our faith during the actual prayer ministry, or we can journal prior to the session, writing down what we feel is the message until it begins to flow. Whether we present the message requires wisdom and discernment.

PRESENTATION

Presentation of 'a word' from God is an important factor. We must be mindful of a client's vulnerable position. We need to be extremely sensitive in the work we are doing. Better to present a message for example, by saying, *I feel that the Lord is saying that he will be restoring what the locusts have eaten*, rather than, *the Lord says that your bank account will be filling up from Monday onwards*. Make sure to work within the limits of the client's understanding and unique personality needs.

Sometimes, the Lord will privately provide you with personal understanding of a situation or a particular need. Do not be rush into directly delivering this message to your client as a prophetic word from God. It is wise to wait until the need arises during a session. Then, working the message into your general conversation, deliver it with the leading of the Holy Spirit, preferably accompanied by confirming scriptures.

If the message you have received seems to be directly speaking to the client, use discretion as to whether you speak it out or present it in writing. It will usually take years of practice to acquire the confidence for direct presentation during Christian counselling. If you do make a written presentation, encourage the client to have it judged by their pastor or spiritual mentor, as to whether it lines up with scripture and is suitable for personal edification. Acquire the help and supervision of those more experienced in this area. Learn by asking permission to observe others in its operation, or take a course in prophetic ministry and practise on other learners within a safe environment. Be assured of the blessings to everyone concerned.

Practicalities of Counselling: USE OF PROPHECY IN PRAYER MINISTRY

The ability to prophesy is a valuable asset to the ministering counsellor. The apostle Paul encouraged all Christians generally to seek this gifting and it was obviously in common use by the church leadership of the day (1Cor 14:1, Acts 13:2). Messages can be received and delivered in two basic ways during Christian counselling: –

a) Messages to the counsellor regarding a client usually occur either, during preparatory prayer, or can directly follow the session as a spiritual form of debriefing.

b) Messages directed to the client in the form of personal prophecy during, or at any time in between, sessions.

PROPHETIC WORD#1

Received by the counsellor *prior* to a session and recorded in *written form*. Here, God is speaking to the counsellor and giving the counsellor instructions as to how to act as a messenger on his behalf.

> God the Father speaking:
>
> *'My daughter has expressed to you her feelings of dryness in her walk with me. I am pleased with her willingness to open up her ways and heart to me. Tell her that she is not to be fearful that she is offending me. Tell her, I love my children despite their faults and weaknesses and that I do not expect them to understand my ways completely at any given time. Assure her that my love is unconditional and accepting at all stages of her growth. Tell her I am well pleased with her efforts to seek my will'.*

In a sense, this type of message is directional, as specific instruction as to what to tell the client is given. This also fits into the exhortation category of prophesying and seems relatively safe to deliver. However, always act cautiously regarding delivering a message, as already mentioned, it does take a great deal of experience and confidence in prophetic ministry to incorporate this gifting into a formal counselling setting.

If you are not yet confident in this gifting, or are in doubt of the authenticity or content, do not deliver immediately. Place the message aside in the client's personal file until you are able to seek some spiritual input from a mentor experienced in such matters, especially if it appears to be a directional or correctional word. Do remember to factor in confidentiality requirements.

You could wonder whether to pass on a message as it stands, or if it could be for your private knowledge in order to assist with the counselling process. The best form of delivery is to wait on the subject matter of the word to be introduced by the client. The client then can be asked whether they have an understanding of the giftings and are open to receiving a message in the form of a written prophecy. The word is then read to the client and discussed along with the appropriate scriptures. In my experience, the client will then generally request a copy, which is a sign that they feel the content is personally applicable and beneficial.

If there seems to be some opposition or doubt in the client's mind, do not offer a copy of a recorded prophecy. You may suggest that the client *seek the Lord* personally on the matter, or perhaps that they present their perception of the content for the consideration of those in leadership over them. Express that you do not consider yourself as infallible and assure them of your willingness to discuss the matter further. Advise of your openness to correction by those under Christ's authority within the church.

PROPHETIC WORD #2

Received as a direct spoken word from God via the counsellor and delivered spontaneously and directly to the client during a taped session.

> *'Heed my voice my child when I call to you in song and music. You have not yet entered into this way I have of communing with my people and now is the time to enter in. I have messages of my love and tenderness towards my children and I have chosen the voice of music to communicate this.*
>
> *'Even though you have not yet been led in this direction my daughter, nor feel you have the natural talent in this area, I will open this way to you now of singing praises to my name'.*

Similar guidelines expressed for the first example apply to the second. However, in this scenario permission has been given to tape the session and the spoken prophecy has been recorded. The benefits are as follows:

a)   If you are misquoted you have proof of what was actually said.
b)   You have the original spoken word to study for your own benefit and for your ministry records.
c)   The client can acquire a taped or a written copy, which can be of great personal value.

PROPHETIC WORD #3

This form of word is addressed to the client personally via a mediator (the counsellor) making use of his or her prophetic gifting.

'Yes my child, I will help you in this area. I will train you further to respect your own needs and to revel in the limitations I have set for you.

'Yes, there are those of your brothers and sisters who have taken my word for something it is not. They are the ones who would bring everyone up to the standards, which they have set. This is not my will. Everyone has been created to be the one I have made them to be – to be a reflection of my glory.

'Yes, there is a difference in each of you. There are many differences. Just as I have created the creatures of this world in such diversity, I have made my children to be varied in outlook and in temperament, as well as in their physical aspects. Yet, there are still the ones who challenge me on this, on my creativity. They would have you all of like mind and of uniformity.

'This is not my will and my way! Instead, I would have each one respect your differences and to see and understand that each of you only reflects another aspect of your Heavenly Father to be appreciated and revered.

'So my child, when you are tempted to alter the way I have made you, think again. In this, you are trying to alter your very nature. This is in rebellion to me and against my will. And I know my child that your will is to please me, above all else.

'So now that you are no longer ignorant in this area, do not trespass against me – accept yourself. Respect the traits within you and your own way of doing things. Do not try to emulate anyone else's way of doing things.

'I am happy with the way I have made you. I want you to be happy with yourself, my child, my creation'.

This third example is one in which God is directly communicating to the client during a prayer time. The subject matter, in this instance, concerns the client's lack of self-confidence. The client has been in the habit of trying to conform to everyone else's way of doing things and has been passive in her own spiritual walk.

This particular counselling session was centred on the subject of having confidence in God's leading, and involved the client's issues stemming from her lack of self-esteem. At the close of the session, the client prayed, '*Lord, help me to take pleasure in how you have made me'*, which indicates that the message was understood and received.

Although the above appears as a correctional word, it fits the general criteria of encouragement and exhortation delivered by an experienced counsellor with accompanying scriptures. For the less confident or experienced, expressing the general content and sense of the message rather than as a formal direct prophecy could be the safest method. For example, the counsellor could say, *I feel that God could be saying to you that you need to honour and respect the way he has made you.'*

> **The samples cited are based on the author's actual experiences on hearing personal words addressed to her. These 'words' have been slightly adjusted (with reverence) to fit the context and to suit the teaching in this text.**

AUTHOR'S TESTIMONY

Many more examples and instructions could be cited for the use of this exciting and treasured gifting. The joys and benefits of delivering prophetic messages to others as a Christian counsellor far outweigh the possible negative aspects.

Personally, I have had very few negative experiences. My only regrets are that the excitement of exercising the gifting has made me appear at times to be a little 'painful' and self-righteous to my friends and loved ones. In my enthusiasm, I am still often heard saying that God said this and that to me, rather than couching it in a more mature or discreet manner. My apologies to everyone concerned!

Seriously, I have lent heavily on God's grace to cover my mistakes in my attempts to learn and certainly hope that I have steadily matured in the practice of this gifting. I strongly encourage all who have the desire and leading, to step out in faith in this area. After all, the scriptures instruct that we desire this specific gift and that we are to use it in love for the building up of the Body of Christ (the Church). When we also consider how it adds depth to our love and understanding of him, it is a very important gift to covet.

Rom 12:6, 1Cor 14:3-6, 1Cor 13:9,10

Counsellor Resource: THE GIFT OF PRAYER

TYPES OF PRAYER

This text will only be covering four aspects of prayer as there are many excellent resource books, which deal with the subject. The first aspect covered will be the use of praying in tongues, the second will be the importance of intercessory prayer, and the third covers reasons for encouraging the client to pray. The final one is about praying in agreement and is in the form of a testimony by the author, which mainly consists of a prophetic word.

a)   tongues
b)   intercession
c)   client
d)   agreement

AUTHOR'S EXPERIENCE

In my intensive ministry style, I allocate at least half an hour of personal time in prayer for each client prior to each session. This does not include follow up prayer and intercessory prayer at other times. I mention this, as it is very different to a secular operation where clients are seen 'back to back' on the hour. Consider the time factor for prayer as well as Bible study if you are planning to enter this ministry. Personally, I am only able to deal with two clients daily in this fashion as a full on prayer session may extend into two or three hours.

Disclaimer: The author notes here the diversity of theological stances in regard to the following topic of *tongues*. She makes no claims to be an expert on theology and advises the reader to research the related biblical passages for his or her self. This article has been based on her own personal research, opinions and conclusions.

a) Praying In Tongues (1Cor, chapters 12-14)

There are several reasons for speaking in a (spiritual) prayer tongue other than our own natural language. This scripture says that whoever speaks in a tongue does not speak to men but to God. It is a direct communication to him – spirit to spirit – and occurs when we surrender our will to God. Thereby, we are placing ourselves purposefully in the divine flow of God's spirit, where we speak mysteries beyond human understanding.

Speaking in tongues as a gifting is, in my opinion, an essential key to entering in to the realm of the spirit. Jesus said that, when the Spirit of truth comes, he will guide you into all truth (Jn 16:13). When speaking in a spiritual language or *a tongue*, we can access the mind of the Spirit (the mind of Christ) to gain wisdom that is pure and true. We can connect to an infallible guide, the Holy Spirit himself, to understand *the mysteries* of God.

As we contact the physical realm with our bodies and the mental and emotional realm with our minds, we use our <u>wills and spirits to contact the spiritual realm</u> to converse with the Spirit of truth. The Spirit himself bears witness (affirms as the truth) with our spirit, that we are children of God (Rom 8:16). This verse does not say he bears witness with our hearts or minds; it states that he guarantees and affirms spirit to spirit.

THE MYSTERIES

We are warned to be good stewards of *the mysteries*; to seek spiritual wisdom and to avoid worldly wisdom (1Cor 2:6-16, 1Cor 3:18-20,1Cor 4:1-5). The *mystery of salvation* and redemption is only apparent to those who have experienced it. Through our willingness to surrender and accept the gift of salvation, our spirits, which have been dead in sin, are reborn. Consequently, we become spiritually alive – and more connected to the things of the spiritual realm.

When we pray in the spirit, our spirits pray under the inspiration of the Holy Spirit. Paul apparently received his wonderful revelations of the mysteries of God through speaking in tongues 'more than any' (1Cor 14:18-19). To support this statement: as it is apparent that he received more revelation than any other in his time, it appears that praying in tongues could be the vehicle for achieving this.

The Spirit searches all things, *the deep things of God.* Praying in a tongue provides us with divine revelation as to how to minister to the depths of the spirits of our clients. We are also *edifying ourselves* in the process. At times, we can have the privilege of becoming amazingly aware of what only God the Father could know about a client. Jesus demonstrated this with his meeting with the woman at the well (when he had discernment beyond his limited earthly capacity).

THE ANOINTING

This method of praying can become *an exciting tool* for the counsellor. If we walk in the Spirit we will not fulfil the lust of the flesh (Gal 5:16). Therefore, by using this gift, we will minister more *under the anointing* of God as our Lord did, rather than our own natural thoughts and ways. The Word says that the natural man, who depends on the mind alone, does not receive the things of the Spirit of God for they are foolishness to him. Through the power of speaking in tongues, we can *flow in the spirit*, rather than the wisdom of man, and be spiritually discerning in our dealings with our clients.

DIVERSITY

The Bible speaks of a diversity or variety of tongues. There are tongues as received on the day of Pentecost (Acts 2) where all (the believers) were able to 'talk in other languages'. There was the other occasion cited when the Gentiles received the gift of the Holy Spirit and the Jewish preachers were amazed to hear them (also) 'speaking in strange tongues' in worship (Acts 10:44-48). There is the gift of tongues and interpretation of such for use in corporate fellowship which we are not to forbid (with provisos) (1Cor 12:10; 13:5-6; 14:20-23, 39). There is the gift of tongues used for personal edification and communication with him one on one (1Cor 14:2-4). This gift is received in like manner to receiving our salvation; as a *free gift* which is received by faith and this is said to accompany *the baptism in the Holy Spirit* (Acts 10:44-48; Acts 19:1-6).

Tongues can also be a gifting (or *spiritual activity)* in the service of God. As we use 'tongues' as a gifting we are being channels through which the Holy Spirit of God may talk to others. Note that there is a difference between operating in the *gift of a spiritual language* and the *gifting of tongues*. You are encouraged to search the scriptures on the differences in tongues and baptisms for yourself (from the Books of Acts and 1Corinthians).

> **Suggested reading: Dave Roberson's ideas and teachings in *'Walk of the Spirit – The Walk of Power – The Vital Role of Praying in Tongues' – 1999 (disclaimer applies).*

A SPIRITUAL LANGUAGE

The Holy Spirit intercedes for us and reveals the concerns on our hearts and in our minds to God the Father. We can be channels of *intercession* for ourselves and for others in tongues of deep intercessional 'groanings' (Rom 8:26).

When we start speaking in the language of the spirit, it is a *matter of obedience* and *faith*, because it seems a foolish thing to do in the natural. Therefore, the more we surrender our natural minds and tongues to speak in this manner, the more we develop our faith, which pleases God. It also pleases the Father to hear us speak this way, simply because we are speaking to him directly as his spiritual children in his 'natural' language. This alone should be reason enough to desire to speak in tongues.

SANCTIFICATION & EDIFICATION

The practice also has a *sanctifying* (cleansing to make holy) action because we are leaving our minds out of the process. Then, his Spirit is able to speak to our spirits directly with his pure word. Talking *in the spirit* is resting from our own thoughts, so that we are then able to receive God's wisdom to impart to others, or to ourselves, from *the mind of Christ*.

In doing so we *access wisdom* for our present needs and plant seeds for the future, which are able to take root and grow when watered by the Word of God. The benefit is more fully realised when we are mature and capable of handling them rightly. We are able to *edify*, or build ourselves up, because our spirits are taught truths which the Holy Spirit can *bring to our remembrance* when needed.

WARFARE

His language is powerful. After all, his Word created the worlds and gave us life (Heb 11:3). By speaking in the spirit (or tongues) as well as verbalizing (confessing) the scriptures, we are available as warriors to bring down human strongholds; warfare against principalities and powers (demonic forces) and to stand firm in our faith.

There is also the spontaneous gift of the *diversity of tongues* as *a sign to the unbeliever* as occurred on the Day of Pentecost previously mentioned, where language barriers are completely overridden by the Holy Spirit (1Cor 14:22, Acts 2:4-11). A believer may be able to preach, teach, testify and counsel, in an earthly language unknown to the speaker himself.

INTERPRETATION

Then finally, there are tongues for interpretation, manifested during some church assemblies as a gift to the church (1Cor 14:5). Exercising of the gift should be accompanied by an *interpretation* (of meaning and content) by either the speaker or a listener in the congregation.

Basically, it is useful to remember that tongues for interpretation and tongues as a sign to the unbeliever are normally for use in public; tongues for personal edification are for private use. The tongues exercised by a Christian counsellor are usually for intercession or for private devotional benefit. Note that, for warfare and deliverance ministry today, the use of tongues is commonplace.

b) Intercessory Prayer

Paul mentions that supplication, prayers, intercessions and giving of thanks are four separate *disciplines* to be exercised in praying (1Tim 2). We will concentrate here on *intercessory prayer,* as it can be an integral part of the ministry of Christian counselling. The dictionary meaning of intercede is 'to go in between', but, spiritually speaking, there is far more to it than this.

Intercession is used when there is a gap (a distancing) between a person and God and the person in prayer speaks to God on behalf of that person. An intercessor identifies with the person and may understand and even experience (carry the burden of) the physical and emotional pain for a time. See the passionate and sincere example of Paul the apostle (Rom 9:3).

AUTHOR'S EXPERIENCE

Intercession can be exercised for someone unknown to the person praying, or for some unknown situation, to bring about a change or a solution according to the will of God. My husband and I woke simultaneously one night with the same vision of a stranger. In describing our vision within a dream to each other we agreed that he appeared to be a missionary on his sickbed. We simply prayed for his recovery using intercessory tongues – then went peacefully back to sleep. A short time later, we had a guest speaker at our church who turned out to be that very missionary who was indeed in great need of prayer on the night that we were called to do so.

On another occasion, I had a day vision of an American man around sixty years of age dressed casually in a tan suede jacket and a red checked flannelette shirt. He was in the cockpit of a light aircraft unsuccessfully trying to turn the motor over. I had the impression he was particularly frustrated because he had to get going to do some work for God. I was led to pray in agreement with my husband that this American be given a new plane. I sensed his name to be Stan and that he is possibly a business man.

UNITY IN PRAYER

The Holy Spirit may call a group of people, known, or unknown to each other and *empower* them *to pray in unity* and with the tongues of deep intercessional groanings (Rom 8:26). This call can be for their own or another's life, a family, a church, a city, a country or an ethnic group and may be accompanied by visions, dreams, discernment or supernatural knowledge and *manifestations* (symbolically acting out of the situation). Jeremiah and Hosea are prophetic examples of symbolic intercession via the use of role-playing.

There may be a heartfelt crying out to God, which is often more than just supplication (humble pleas) and can involve *spiritual warfare*. It may involve a great depth to prayer – deep calling to deep (Heb 5:7). A person interceding may actually experience or identify with God's thoughts and heart on a given situation or on behalf of a person or group.

SACRIFICIAL

Intercession can be a *sacrificial position* taken, as a human representative before God in a *particular situation* for a *specific cause* (such as 'the starving millions', or political prisoners). See where Abraham intercedes or *advocates* for Sodom and Gomorrah (Gen 18:20-33, 19:29). Modern representatives can be cited as Martin Luther, Martin Luther King and Mother Theresa.

Sacrifice can be in the way of allotting time and giving up comforts, fasting from personal needs, or relinquishing personal feelings or ideas. Moses depicts the seriousness of an intercessory position (Deut 9:12-29). He was a man willing to forgo his own salvation for his people.

WATCHMEN

From a *watchman* position (Isa 62:6-7, Ezk 22:29-31) the intercessor is sometimes required to *warn* and sometimes attains to a *place of authority* in the situation via faith in the power and goodness of Almighty God. It is this position of power and faith before God, which releases change and gives glory to himself. Commitment and loyalty to both God and man is required. For example, Esther was a woman who fully committed her life in every aspect, spoke up to one in authority, and found favour with both man and God for the sake of his chosen people.

LEADERS

Those in leadership positions may be called to remind God of his promises to his people both day and night and to '*give Him no rest*' (Isa 62, Rom 8:34, Heb 7:25-27). Intercession can involve an ongoing commitment to remain true in the position until it is resolved or God releases you from the responsibility. Jesus is the ultimate example of this as he remains interceding on our behalf beyond the Cross (Isa 53).

THE PERFECT EXAMPLE

Jesus made the ultimate sacrifice for us in intercession by coming down to earth and identifying with mankind fully, bearing all our sins. An intercessor's calling can involve matters of life and death. Unfortunately, there are few willing to stand in the gap as obedient, humble servants to mankind and to God (Phil 2:1-11). It is indeed a sacrificial role but, it receives its own reward.

In summary, regarding the ministry of counselling, the role of intercessor can be either, a **specific calling** on a Christian counsellor, or, a **transitory responsibility** incorporated into Christian counselling.

> **Recommended reading on prophetic ministry: '*Calling All Intercessors*', M. & A. Wales, Oracle Publications, 1984 (disclaimer applies).**

c) Client Prayers

A formal counselling session may develop into prayer ministry as such. For instance, the whole content may become a Holy Spirit led healing journey back into the past, or perhaps the opportunity for a formal deliverance. But a great part of spirit-filled counselling involves bringing the client to the point of being able to heal in depth via prayer ministry. An important aspect of the process is to encourage a client to be interactive in direct prayer to God.

Surely he loves to hear us audibly give ourselves to him in prayer! We are his precious children and a relationship without communication is dry indeed. Many clients will be 'silent pray-ers'. They have not been in the habit of praying out loud, or could be too sensitive as to what you, the so-called 'expert' prayer, will think of their attempts. It is your job as a Christian counsellor to encourage overt participation. There is great power in a person opening their heart to God in this way. Very exciting things happen, including absolute breakthroughs. This is especially so in the area of *self-eviction of internal ruling spirits* (Chapter 20).

Listening to a client's prayer content and style also has the added benefit of seeing where the heart lies. However, be wise in this type of assessment, as a simple prayer expressed in a few, faltering words, can hold more honesty and sincerity than the most biblically correct, poetic flow. Just as some people are good speakers, some are fluent in prayer, either from much practice, natural talent or from a gifting in that area. There will of course be those who are out to impress like the Pharisees. You will not always be able to discern the difference. So, be careful of a critical or judgmental spirit in yourself.

Most importantly, do not force a person to pray. Just explain the need for participation and gently encourage because of the following factors:–

> ➢ it pleases God to hear his children speak to Him
> ➢ there is strength in agreement
> ➢ there is power in the spoken word
> ➢ this could result in a breakthrough (and has done so for others)
> ➢ there are many benefits to sharing burdens openly
> ➢ there is a command from God for confession and renouncement of sins
> ➢ there are blessings which follow
> ➢ active participation aids the recovery process

d) Prayers of Agreement *(Matt 18:18-19)*

Prayer has power when done in agreement according to his will. Even after all these years of using the various forms of prayer and coming to the firm conclusion that there is such power in this privilege, the Lord continues to emphasize the power of prayer in my life daily. Prayer changes things. Prayer changes people (Acts 5:38-39) from both without and within. Christian counselling without the focus of settling on specific points to agree upon, and follow through in prayer, is a pointless exercise.

AUTHOR'S TESTIMONY

The following is another excerpt from my personal journal in the form of a personal prophecy received soon after Christmas Day 2007 when I was feeling an increased need to pray with others:

'My daughter, it is significant that you come to me at this time with thoughts of widening your horizons in prayers of agreement.

I have foreordained my people for peace and unity. Conflict in the Body is not of me. This is why there is lack of power in those who seek to do my will. The enemy has done a work in isolating and propounding the message that independence is strength and that conflict is necessary to produce progress and change; whereas my message is that dependence on me and my laws promote goodwill and peace.

Indeed, there is power in agreement as it is necessary to produce change. This is the message I would have preached as the days grow short. my will be done on earth as it is done in heaven. This is the power of agreement with me and my will, which will bring unity and a fresh anointing for the days ahead.

Pray my daughter that there will be unity and peace between those of your family and other loved ones. Enmity is not of me. Unity is of me. This is the message – pure and simple. Strength is needed for the time ahead. Strength may be found in agreement'.

CHAPTER FIVE

THE CARER'S NEEDS

Here we will focus on a certain type of person called to counsel others in need – the *burden bearer*. This chapter concentrates on strengthening the minister for ministry and provides practical advice on caring for the carer in order to prevent burnout. The stressors of successful ministry are concentrated on. Warnings are issued against using unhealthy coping mechanisms in your practice.

- Testimonial of an experienced 'on the field' counsellor
- Defining negative burden bearing types
- Striving – self-assessment resource
- Support networks – *The Bike Wheel Model*
- The stress of success – physical & behavioural signs
- Burnout inventory & resources

Study Notes

COUNSELLOR TESTIMONIAL: Burden Bearing

It has been very hard to come to a place of peace recently. I realise now that I have been dealing with the accumulated grief associated with the ministry work of nearly 20 years. As chaplain to the terminally ill in a large public hospital, I am well aware that I need to process the vicarious sorrow that comes my way. I need to do this in order to keep my head above water – so that I do not sink under the load when my personal losses and problems come along.

Even with all my strategies and safeguards in place, it has been particularly difficult to find time to process my personal pain since my wife of forty years succumbed to cancer. My Becky died three months ago, after a valiant battle lasting two long years. At her request, I have chosen to carry on with my work here at the hospital; but, it has been oh so hard. It has taken all my strength not to succumb to this overwhelming feeling of unreality, which has taken over my waking hours. I know the stages of grief and the processing of losses. I know the research and the counselling techniques, but it has not helped my own heart to have this knowledge in my head.

I miss her so much. While she was with me, I somehow found the daily strength to minister. Now, on my journey without her, I am still daily accompanied by so many other grieving souls. In my line of work, I look into the eyes of those ones who are riddled with pain – spiritually, physically and emotionally – some who beg because they are not ready to die and some who are dead to life already.

It seems God has given me this … one might call it 'a gift'. I have a passion to share the load of others who suffer. I felt that God Almighty told me, as a young theological student, that my calling was to minister to the dying. He promised me that I would be one who would never become desensitised to another's pain – as some do; that I would not succumb to 'compassion fatigue' as some now care to name the apathy and hardening that sets on some in the caring profession.

Bleary eyed, this morning, I reluctantly stepped aside at the bedside of a crippled woman with motor neurone disease when her regular doctor arrived, with cheerful countenance, on his ritual rounds. He may spend a few moments checking her chart and will then move on to the next ailment.

As for me, I continue to linger, listening to her heart's cry. She is concerned that there will be no-one to care for her frail father when she leaves this earth. She grieves the loss of her little dog she has had to put down and her beautiful garden which is going to ruin. She begs me to call on her disabled, institutionalised daughter, who has lost her only visitor.

> *Yes this gift of empathy sometimes proves too much to bear. Then I remember my Lord. I see that what I do in love is but a drop in the ocean compared to His compassionate outreach to mankind. I visualize the Saviour's loving arms around my dear Rebecca during her last days here. I take great comfort in the thought that they are encircling her still, though mine are empty...*
>
> *With these thoughts of my beloved, I return to an empty house. This evening I recommit myself. I will continue my work until it is also my time to go... Home.*

Except where the author recounts her personal testimony, all characters in this text are fictitious representations and any similarities to real persons or cases are purely coincidental.

BURDEN BEARERS

Many caring individuals who enter into Christian counselling are *burden bearers.* Summarized, this is a person who displays a natural sensitivity to others' needs or, a supernatural awareness of others' suffering. Even though easily burdened by others' problems, this type of carer usually cannot resist the need to become intimately involved with another's pain (in comparison to praying for others and 'helping out' in a practical pastoral sense).

As an *intercessor* and/or Christian counsellor, it is important to evaluate whether you have too many of the negative characteristics associated with being a burden bearer to be able to handle these roles in a ministry situation. The resources following should enable you to recognise and monitor your own needs – particularly in times of stress during ministry. In order to be a *positive burden bearer*, you will need to be conscious of the privilege it is to be equipped to help others with your giftings, but at the same time, be consciously aware of the danger of *compassion fatigue* and *burnout.*

You are aiming to be a clean vessel and positive channel of the anointing power of God. If you are a burden bearer, then you are more than likely overly sensitive to your own problems and inadequacies. However, remember that in your weakness he can be your strength. There is such power in this realisation! He promises that his yoke is easy and his burden is light; that we are to come to him and he will give us rest (Matt 11: 28-30). If we are yoked to Jesus, then he is the one bearing the load for us. He <u>is</u> our strength in this (1Jn 5:3).

We can then picture ourselves as the passenger on a two seater bicycle 'going along for the ride'! If the journey is far too difficult in our call to 'bear one another's burdens' (Gal 6:2) then we are possibly doing all the work – simply because he also promises that he will not give us more (suffering) than we can bear. The more natural attributes or spiritual giftings you have, the more danger you are in of operating without dependence on the Holy Spirit (Jn 6:63). If you are carrying more than your share of the load, while purported to be 'yoked to Jesus Christ', then you are possibly striving in your own good works and natural talents, rather than ministering under the anointing to the best of your God-given ability. If this is the case, then it is a matter of surrendering your own fleshly desires and strengths to him. Remember to allow him to deal with both weaknesses and strengths before they deal with you.

Client Handout: NEGATIVE CHARACTERISTICS OF BURDEN BEARERS

CHECKLIST

PHYSICAL
- ❑ Unexplained aches and pains
- ❑ Chronic illness
- ❑ Easily fatigued and stress prone
- ❑ Chest pains or pressure, heart palpitations, migraines
- ❑ Open to infirmity, hypochondria and somatic disorder (focus on what might, or could be, wrong)

EMOTIONAL
- ❑ Sulky, and a grudge bearer
- ❑ Negative focus emotionally
- ❑ Inability to deal with strong feelings
- ❑ Angry outbursts or 'black' moods
- ❑ Prone to melancholy, fluctuating moods and depression
- ❑ Unexplained mood swings and depressive episodes
- ❑ Sensitive to own, as well as other people's moods – unable to differentiate
- ❑ Enjoys creating drama, then unable to handle the consequences

PSYCHOLOGICAL
- ❑ easily confused and indecisive
- ❑ anxiety prone
- ❑ obsessive thoughts, fears and phobias
- ❑ irrational, foggy or scatter-brained
- ❑ can be easily cognitively over-stimulated and sensory overloaded
- ❑ prone to excesses (e.g. dramatic expression in speech)
- ❑ constant struggle to keep balanced and to think rationally and logically
- ❑ attracted to lie based belief systems and values

BEHAVIOURAL
- ❑ compulsions
- ❑ self-critical
- ❑ guilt driven
- ❑ performance orientation
- ❑ overly self-defensive and defensive of others being hurt

- ❑ addiction prone, especially to approval
- ❑ shy, timid, too tender or sensitive, vulnerable, irritable, defensive
- ❑ reactive and easily hurt (grudges, sulking and emotional withdrawal)
- ❑ prone to shame and self-condemnation
- ❑ slave to duty and doing the right thing
- ❑ overly reactive
- ❑ suppressive of strong emotions

RELATIONAL
- ❑ identified 'patient' in the family
- ❑ overly critical and judgmental
- ❑ tendency to parent parents or siblings
- ❑ overly empathetic
- ❑ self-blames for others' shortcomings
- ❑ unpredictable and inconsistent (can switch from dominating and bossy to submissive and self-depreciative)
- ❑ manipulative to acquire dependence or dependencies, or for self-defence
- ❑ trigger reactions in others purposefully
- ❑ role player – enabler, rescuer, co-dependent, a substitute mate
- ❑ needs someone to focus on or rescue to alleviate own pain

SPIRITUAL
- ❑ may over-spiritualize, be dramatic or too passionate
- ❑ may become spiritually proud or proud of natural abilities
- ❑ so spiritually minded that you are 'no earthly good'
- ❑ out of touch with reality e.g. obsessive fasting or church attendance
- ❑ religious, or attracted to the unconventional e.g. cults/alternate religions/witchcraft and occult activities
- ❑ tempted to dabble in mind reading or other psychic activities
- ❑ tempted to use ESP or counterfeit giftings instead of spiritual charismata
- ❑ psychic experiences may confuse and alarm or be found attractive
- ❑ discerns evil or demonic activity and either worries, is frightened or it proves overly attractive
- ❑ prone to forming negative soul ties (close unhealthy spiritual bonds)
- ❑ spiritual hypersensitivity can cause overload
- ❑ self-depreciation (may feel cannot take up god's time, with own needs)
- ❑ blame god for woes of world and for own or others' problems
- ❑ self-reject (becoming opposite to what god intended)

SOCIAL
- ❑ hatred of hypocrisy, nit-picker, crusader, soap-boxer, a nag, a loner, reclusive, antisocial, introverted (*circle relevant traits*)
- ❑ unable to cope with crowds
- ❑ need a lot of time out from social interactions
- ❑ likes a special friend to devote attention to or makes everyone into a 'needy' friend

❏ excessive concern over the disabled, disadvantaged and 'starving millions'
❏ poverty mentality, fear of waste or extravagance impedes socialisation
❏ a social reject as a result of being judgmental and critical
❏ tends to isolate and feel different (looked at as 'not quite with it' or 'weird')
❏ hides true feelings and identity and acts out unnatural roles in an attempt to conform

WORK & MINISTRY
❏ highly empathetic – can be overly burdened with others' problems
❏ carries burdens unnecessarily
❏ easily offended and overly sensitive to criticism
❏ intuitive rather than practical
❏ overly excitable and dramatic
❏ expects too much of self
❏ performance orientated, easily overloaded and prone to burnout
❏ does not work well in a team situation
❏ overly people oriented, therefore does not get tasks done efficiently
❏ over-performs to meet others' needs
❏ perpetual peacemaker, or one who habitually acquiesces
❏ approval addiction impedes initiative and drive – delaying promotion
❏ buries talents, becoming a non-achiever
❏ constantly makes excuses for not fulfilling dreams
❏ people pleaser and non-confrontational
❏ overly submissive and ingratiating
❏ physically and emotionally retreats from any sign of conflict
❏ picks up others' tensions and does not trust others to God (*saviour complex* or a *martyr spirit*)

> *If you have more than a dozen of the work and ministry problems and characteristics listed, then you may need to take steps to seek help from an objective source in order to operate in any ministry involving caring for people with serious problems.*

Practicalities: HELP FOR BURDEN BEARERS IN MINISTRY POSITIONS

This resource is also available in client handout form.

IDENTIFICATION OF NEEDS

Identify as a *burden bearer* through personal evaluation. Administer a personality profile to identify major personal needs which contribute to stress, for instance: social, achievement, security or recognition needs which are not being met. Administer a *spiritual assessment* to evaluate current position.

Study negative burden bearer characteristics (refer to previous resource). Ask the Lord to assist you to appreciate the positive aspects of this gifting. Pray for protection from the temptation to carry *false burdens*. Pray for relief from any present emotional weight of experiencing *vicarious* (second hand) *pain* and unnecessary suffering. Identify and release yourself from *false burdens* and *false guilt*. Study the difference between guilt and shame (Chapter 14, Images 15&16).

PERSONAL HEALING

If personal burdens are not shifting in a particular ministry situation, then consider a personal need for healing in that area (e.g. childhood abuse or domestic violence). Become accountable for personal burdens. Seek help to deal with buried childhood hurts and present emotional pain via inner healing and cleansing prayer. Break residual soul ties from the past. Deal with present negative relationships, making sure you concentrate on the forgiveness aspects.

DEALING WITH FEELINGS

Study methods of communicating feelings to clarify and validate intellectually what is being sensed emotionally, e.g. use journaling to develop personal intimacy with God. Debrief with God the Father and share moods with him e.g. communicating via writing, music or artwork, or just talking out loud to him. Practise the practical aspects of disentangling from burdens and consciously releasing them over to him, e.g. symbolically 'lift off' burdens before retiring at night. Learn how to separate soul issues from the spiritual through the use of speaking in tongues and other spiritual disciplines.

SELF-CARE

Seek a mentor or supervisor's assistance for accountability regarding self-care. Join a prayer group of peers where members minister to each other and respect confidentiality. Appreciate that 'holidays' are allowed from burden bearing. Find involvement in a variety of activities – hobbies, clubs, sports, studies and an exercise regime. Remember that it is possible to be multi-tasking while interceding, so that there is a balance in lifestyle activities (e.g. work, play or exercise while praying in the spirit). Maintaining a good balance of social activities and introverted periods daily is important.

IMPORTANT: Use the cognitive resources within this text to develop rationality and logic to complement your 'gut instincts', strong feelings and spirituality.

Counsellor Resource: NEGATIVE PERFORMANCE CHARACTERISTICS

This resource is also available in client handout form.

As well as negative burden bearing characteristics (see resources in this section) there are common *striving* behavioural traits, which impede the functioning of counsellors and prayer ministers: *perfectionism, performance orientation, approval addiction, people pleasing, workaholism and overachieving.*

Counsellor Exercise: Use the following checklist for self-assessment. Think carefully about the samples of typical speech and thought patterns. Do you recognize any of your favourites? Complete the sentences and, using the list, match your personal characteristics to the checklist.

CHECKLIST

- ❑ I feel I must earn my place in God's kingdom. *I always strive to please God by…*
- ❑ I feel I must do the right thing by everyone in order to be loved. *If I let them down then I couldn't live with myself.*
- ❑ I have a reward system. *Got to do this, before I can relax.*
- ❑ I am prone to martyrdom. *I am doing the best I can!'*
- ❑ I am overly defensive. *I was only trying to do the right thing!*
- ❑ I strive to do good things but they seem to backfire or go unnoticed. *I was just trying to do something nice/my best.*
- ❑ I feel I must perform to earn God's love. *God will not be happy with me if I don't…*
- ❑ I find self-approval and acceptance hard. *I just need to try harder at…*
- ❑ I need approval from others. *If I just…maybe he will see that I am…*
- ❑ I strive for self-acceptance. *I am not happy with the way I am. I need to… If I could just…*
- ❑ I feel the need to earn love and support. *I figure if you do something nice/well, then…*
- ❑ The standards I set myself are very high. *I don't care what others expect of me I want to… I like to do things my way.*
- ❑ I need to succeed and to be the best at everything I do. *Trying my best is not good enough. I must…*
- ❑ I cannot afford to fail or to make mistakes. *I couldn't live with myself if… I am going to keep going until I get it right.*
- ❑ I have to be doing something to feel my life has purpose. *I would not feel that my life had any value if I couldn't…*
- ❑ I cannot see Jesus as a friend. *I see Him as…*
- ❑ Other problems …

OTHER CHARACTERISTICS

Other problems include: *self-righteousness, being judgmental, critical, dogmatic, driven to succeed, lone wolf syndrome, a friend to everyone, self-appointed problems, domineering, self-effacing, overly high self-expectations, approval seeking, perfectionism and over-achieving.* If you have recognised any of these characteristics as problem areas in your life, then know that you will not receive rest or peace until you have acknowledged that you are a sinner in need of grace.

If life seems *dominated by works* and you are striving for approval from God or man (including self) you will never enjoy the rest of the righteous. Any work that seeks to qualify you, or is done to earn acceptance, is not 'of grace' (Eph 2:8, Gal 2:16, 21).

RESOLUTION (Rom 12:9)

Recognize these character traits, attitudes and behaviours as part of mankind's sinful nature. Ask God to reveal your *sin-nature* to you (not just your sins). Follow through on Holy Spirit conviction to repent of, and renounce, specific sins within your specific problem areas. Realise that He is your righteousness. Nothing you can do, short of repentance and acceptance of his free gift of salvation, will make you any more acceptable.

Receive forgiveness from God and set yourself free from the habits, which have formerly ruled you. Rise up and make a choice for a God honouring lifestyle. Redemption from these sinful habits comes from co-operating with the Holy Spirit for positive change. Make a choice for change. Pray for protection from the temptation to return to old ways.

Acknowledge Jesus Christ as your friend as well as Saviour. Lay down your own high (and false) expectations of yourself. Ask the Father for a revelation. Ask him to reveal his Self to you. Ask how he sees you, and what he expects of you.

STEPS TO HEALING (Rom 6:11, Rom 7:18-25)

Recognise foundational experiences from the past, which are still affecting you to this day. Consider that your *inner child* could be in need of healing. Seek counsel and prayer ministry. This should enable you to: –

a)   See the driving forces behind your behaviours.
b)   Assume responsibility for past choices and mistakes.
c)   Confess attitudes, which sowed the original seed.
d)   Lay the entire matter on the altar.
e)   Take full responsibility – no excuses.
f)   Submit to him without explanation or defence.
g)   Realise that we are not capable of changing our own hearts by any act of will or by our own strength or power.
h)   Invite the Holy Spirit to sanctify (cleanse) and transform so that you are able to live by grace and not by works.
i)   Allow Jesus Christ to be Lord of your life.

The grace of our Lord Jesus Christ be with you (1Cor 16:23).

CARING FOR CARERS

A common misconception of what it means to minister involves the *others first, and me last* syndrome. As counsellors, our priorities are usually in a mixed order, consisting of God, work, church, family, friends – with 'me the carer' usually tacked on the end of the list. However, Jesus' command to *love your neighbour as your self* implies that you will need to take care of yourself, just as carefully as you would a client. What you might be taking to mean, *'don't be selfish'* actually turns out to be, *'do not be a martyr'*. To be completely selfless is to be disrespectful to our Creator as well as our selves. It actually means we place little value or worth on ourselves as his creation.

From this perspective, the actual order needs to be the following: God, self, family and then others (which includes work, church and ministry). Take the example of a breastfeeding mother. She will learn that, if she does not take steps to feed and nurture her self, she will not produce enough milk for the baby. And for another example: if one wants to provide for the family then, one has to be rested and fit enough to turn up for work and to function in your daily tasks.

This can be a revelation to some, accompanied by the thought, *oh, is this where I have been going wrong?* Obviously, if we are going to be nurturers in the caring profession, we need to have a network of carers in place to look after our personal needs. This is essential in order to prevent burnout – to remain in this ministry for as long as possible – in order to help as many as possible. We should not have to run completely out of internal resources before we learn the lesson about needing external resources.

No, you cannot do all the care work alone as a counsellor. Yes, you are teaching others to be God dependent. However, you are also responsible for showing clients how to find other resources for support. Some of the loneliest people are lonely simply because they do not know how to reach out for human companionship and support.

IMAGE 07 the **bike wheel graphic** is to instruct clients about resources and support networks. This resource is essential for personal use, as well as for a counselling tool, because most carers do not take good care of their own needs. It is advisable that you use it on a regular basis to keep check whether both your professional and your personal resources are in place. A resource missing, counts as a spoke in the wheel missing. The missing spokes need replacing in order to strengthen the wheel for use. Obviously, you do not necessarily require the entire 24 resources suggested at any one time, but you will be able to assess your personal needs with experience.

Counsellor Resource: SUPPORT NETWORKS

IMAGE 07

PERSONAL RESOURCES
FOR SELF CARE

ME

HOW MANY SPOKES ARE
THERE IN MY WHEEL?

GOD   OTHERS

Put God first, and then lean
on others for support in my life.

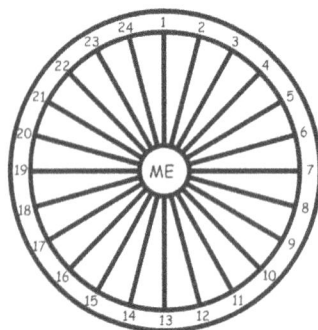

1	Prayer Partner
2	Pastoral Care
3	Spiritual Mentor
4	Church Base
5	Home Group
6	Counsellor
7	Health Professionals
8	Lifestyle Coach
9	Financial Advisor
10	Career Mentor
11	Professional Network
12	Best Friends
13	Social Friends
14	Work Mates
15	Family
16	Spouse
17	Confidant/e
18	Pets
19	Creative Hobbies
20	Sporting Activities
21	Cultural Activities
22	Travelling Companions
23	Club Associates
24	Alone Time

This resource is also available in client handout form.

INSTRUCTIONS FOR USE OF THE BIKE WHEEL MODEL

The bike rider illustrates the concept of balance. The front wheel represents God's support for you personally. The back wheel represents your personal carers and any other resources which keep you functioning and sane. We steer and direct from the front by trusting in God and we sit comfortably on the seat of our supporters to make the ride a smooth one.

The client/counsellor is to draw his or her personal bike wheel. Next they are to draw spokes within the wheel. Against each spoke they are to name a person, place, or activity, which could be classed as a personal resource in their lives at present. The legend will provide suggestions. Note that it is surprising how we can think that we have more resources in place than we actually have. Point out that those with sufficient spokes to strengthen the wheel usually live a pretty comfortable and balanced kind of existence. Their life journey is smoother and they will not prove a complete burden on any one person. In times of crisis they will have more than one option. It is suggested that a new wheel be drawn up at least three monthly.

Practicalities of Counselling: THE STRESS OF SUCCESS

There are certain positive aspects to experiencing stress and pressure. We have all used *positive stressors* to stretch us into moving on to the next level. For example, a stressful exam or interview qualifies us for our next career move, or perhaps we have made an effort to widen our social network in order to have more opportunities to evangelise.

There are the satisfying times in life when all is running smoothly. There are the exciting moments when we feel the outcome has been particularly good: in that our dreams are fulfilled, goals are reached and new levels of achievement are realized. We feel that we have succeeded. Personal expectations are met, as well as receiving approval from others in our fields of endeavour. We could even feel the Lord is saying, '*well done, my good and faithful servant*'.

Then there are the *negative stressors* in life such as the struggles of building a business, career or ministry and our efforts to avoid failure. In essence, the busier and more success we experience in our God-given calling, the happier we should become. However, we sometimes forget to factor in the consequences of success, which will lead to more demands on our time, our energy and our health. Our *resiliency* (ability to bounce back when faced with adversity) is open to weakening if we do not have all our self-care resources and skills in place and operating.

In the field of counselling, you will be called upon to cope with periods of relentless pressures, whether vicariously as you share your clients' stories, or through your personal stressors with workload, relationships and *inner conflicts*. When you are successfully ministering to so many in such an intense way, it is important to take regular inventory of signs that could indicate that you are becoming dangerously close to being on overload. You <u>could</u> be experiencing the *stress of success*.

PHYSIOLOGICAL (Physical) SYMPTOMS OF SUCCESS STRESS

- ❏ increased heart rate/missing beats
- ❏ muscular tension
- ❏ shortness of breath
- ❏ headaches
- ❏ cold extremities
- ❏ excessive perspiration
- ❏ eyesight impairment
- ❏ chronic fatigue/hyperactivity
- ❏ sensitive to light/noise
- ❏ co-ordination clumsy
- ❏ physical agitation
- ❏ sleeping difficulties
- ❏ immune system breakdown

PSYCHOLOGICAL SYMPTOMS OF SUCCESS STRESS

COGNITIVE
- ❑ decreased and/or impaired mental performance
- ❑ unable to concentrate or focus
- ❑ short term memory loss
- ❑ inability to rationalize
- ❑ losing touch with reality
- ❑ forgetfulness e.g. double booking or not turning up to meetings; not recalling names or faces

EMOTIONAL & ATTITUDINAL
- ❑ irritable and short tempered
- ❑ helplessness (internal stressor) e.g. can't voice problems, loss of hope
- ❑ lack of humour
- ❑ easily frustrated
- ❑ angry and arrogant
- ❑ unco-operative
- ❑ unable to relax
- ❑ more aggressive and impatient e.g. *'I'll do it myself; they'll do it my way or else'*

BEHAVIOURAL
- ❑ doing less and taking longer to do it
- ❑ mental capability diminished so no longer multi-tasking
- ❑ periods of over-activity and appearing flustered and unkempt
- ❑ fussiness and unusual attention to fine detail e.g. obsessive compulsions
- ❑ abusive and complaining; irritable, snappy and nit-picking
- ❑ sleeping a lot more (or a lot less)
- ❑ missing meals or eating while working
- ❑ working outside office hours and taking work home
- ❑ expressions such as, *'I can't cope'*; *'it's all too much/too hard'*, or, *'I've had enough'*.

> **If you have checked a dozen or more points on this list then you would be wise to enlist help. Refer to the sections on *Burnout Prevention* and *Help for the Negative Burden Bearer* in this text. This checklist is also available as a client handout.**

COPING MECHANISMS

Of course our *coping mechanisms* will depend on our *personality type.* Basically, there will be two major ways a person might attempt to handle the negative symptoms caused by an abundance of positive stressors – denial and/or isolating.

When *in denial* regarding the above symptoms, behaviours could be:

- ❑ not seeking help
- ❑ resents suggestions
- ❑ displays irrational thinking
- ❑ blames others
- ❑ defensive

When *isolating* because of success stress, behaviours could be:

- ❑ distant/ uncommunicative
- ❑ intense focus on one particular area of work interest
- ❑ pushing friends and family away
- ❑ reducing external stimuli (e.g. refusing social invitations)
- ❑ inordinate requirement for peace and quiet
- ❑ non-communicative with God (e.g. not praying or worshipping)
- ❑ aspiring to a 'sea change'
- ❑ resources no longer accessible or acceptable (e.g. no time for gym, not networking, refusing spiritual counsel, expressing that friends do not care)

> **If you have checked off more than 6 points it is time to seek help. Recheck on a consistent basis (say fortnightly) to assess for an increase or decrease in symptoms.**

COMBATING STRESS

(Matt 11:28) Jesus said that everyone who is 'heavy laden' should come to him to seek rest. He has already given us the keys to handling the stress of success by example. Our answers lie in studying Jesus' example as he travelled his personal ministry path here on earth. Not only did our Saviour handle the ultimate adversity of the crucifixion experience (the ultimate victory) but, he dealt successfully with the masses, as well as his intimate relationships with family, friends and disciples.

Serving God involves carrying the fruit of our labours. Jesus said we are to learn from him and we will find rest for our souls, because *his yoke is easy and his burden is light.* It is our responsibility to put on his guiding yoke, which includes his attitude to life – so that we do not step outside of obedience to God in our service to mankind.

When our minds and bodies are at peace, we are more capable of carrying heavier loads of stressful activities and can work harder and more efficiently. More likely we tend to be carriers of *heavy burdens,* when we take on extra responsibilities and try working too hard outside of our *grace zones.* We are then classed as being on *overload* and possibly heading towards *burnout,*

Counsellor Resource: GRACE & SAFETY ZONES

In your mission as prayer warrior and spiritual healer, the answer to combating stress is to stay connected with your Lord and Saviour and stay within his will for your life on a day by day basis. Also focus on your overall vision and calling by working in the corner of the vineyard where he has placed you. It is important to keep in mind your personal mission statement so make sure you have one to clarify your goals. Consider the following aspects of ministering within your own personal *safety zones:*

a) Check for propensity for performance orientation and people pleasing (see *Checklist for Negative Performance Characteristics*) and seek counsel if you have the need.

b) Ask God if you are taking on burdens that have not been divinely assigned to you (see section on *Burden Bearers).*

c) Refer to resources in this text on prevention and treatment of burnout (see next section: *Burnout in Carers).*

d) Prioritise all areas of your work life; delegate only where you are able to release to others without causing yourself further stress.

e) Be firm in establishing the boundaries necessary to release you from any unhealthy alliances and further pressure.

f) Give permission for the Holy Spirit to prune anything from your life that is not 'of Him'.

g) Seek to understand yourself by habitually keeping a personal journal to express your feelings and to keep life in perspective (see section on *Dialoguing with God*).

h) Accept with grace the things you cannot change; focus on seeking to change the things you are able to change within your safety zones.

i) Work towards establishing an atmosphere of peace in your workplace and home life (see section on *Conflict*).

j) Seek to cultivate and appreciate simplicity.

k) Daily savour the small comforting rituals, which you find relaxing, and take care of your personal health needs.

l) Set comfortable personal goals and put adequate self-care resources in place (see *The Bike Wheel Model* Image 07).

m) Reopen lines of communication with family and friends who are positive influences on your life.

n) Find time to spend alone with the Father, remembering that he wants to take care of you.

o) Invite the Holy Spirit's presence into all areas of your life and enter into his rest and peace within your personal safety zone – through his mercy and grace.

Practicalities of Counselling: BURNOUT IN CARERS

DEFINITIONS OF BURNOUT

1. *to become inoperative as a result of heat or friction*
2. *to cease functioning as a result of the exhaustion of the fuel supply*
3. *to become exhausted through overwork*

The objective of this resource is to explore the causes, prevention and treatment of burnout in relation to a person who is a giver, caretaker or negative burden bearer.

The condition of burnout results from a continuing and irrecoverable depletion of the physical and emotional resources, which enable a giver to keep giving. Resiliency has been weakened. The ability to adapt in the face of adversity or challenges has been seriously diminished. To describe it simply: it is as if the giver has run out of fuel and the engine has stopped.

Burnout happens to givers who have too little consciousness of (or concern for) personal needs. The giver does not do what is necessary to replenish depleted resources and has run out of any reserves. Complete fatigue, mental and physical breakdown can occur. Once experienced, the condition can reoccur, even when it appears a full recovery was previously achieved.

The signs and contributing factors to breakdown need to be recognized well in advance, especially if this is a reoccurring problem. This resource should serve as a warning to those in the caring field, who may be susceptible to the condition but have not yet succumbed. It should aid in ministry to sufferers, as well as give personal survival techniques to those ministering. The main objective is to help break destructive life patterns through practical and biblical means.

CONTRIBUTING FACTORS

> ➤ overwork or overachieving
> ➤ performance orientation (perform/work in order to feel self-worth)
> ➤ approval addiction (need to please everyone, all of the time)
> ➤ unresolved hurts and conflicts, and woundings (see next section)
> ➤ all types of tension – circumstantial or personal (including ill-health)
> ➤ overload of frustrations, disappointments, grief and loss issues
> ➤ repressed anger, resentment, bitterness, pride (as sins not dealt with)
> ➤ an independent spirit, loneliness and lack of a support network

WOUNDINGS

Burnout can occur through *woundings* (damaged emotions). Wounding, in this sense, is 'an emotional condition resulting from the hurtful acts of others'. Other painful circumstances such as a physical accident, death of a loved one, or loss of a job can add to the *wounds* (*offences*) caused by others. When life's hurts and tragedies come too quickly in close succession, recovery between episodes becomes impossible. This is called '*rapid fire wounding*'.

Of course, counsellors are more susceptible to being wounded than the average person, as they are constantly dealing with the extra burdens of other's problems and cares. Also, they are more likely to be personally attacked by clients (and those in relationship to clients) because hurting people tend to hurt others.

DEPRESSION

Rapid fire wounding creates ongoing stress, which may lead to depression. Depression can lead to a total loss of the ability to function. It can result in the person living in a state of utter hopelessness as a reality. Thus, burnout must be taken very seriously when coupled with depression. It can lead to despair, lack of hope and to suicide ideation.

SUICIDE

A person with serious *suicide ideation* can be described as being like a horse with blinkers on, intent on going in one direction only. There is no ambivalence present. The person who once cared for others has no thought for self, let alone the consequences to others of their self-destruction. What others may see as a selfish act could be the end result of a chronic and severe case of burnout – the 'acting out' to escape the pain.

Leading up to severe or chronic depression, the burnout sufferer still experiences hope. However, when burnout develops into the depressed state, hope can diminish to the point of total despair. Even the three most common feelings of frustration, anger and anxiety are unable to surface. Fear leaves; numbness *and apathy* towards life set in.

However, if caught in time, the following symptoms and signs are nearly all curable through rest and refuelling. Medical help should be sought <u>before</u> the advanced stages occur. Recognition of the symptoms is vital. A psychologist can assist by administering a *personality profile* to give valuable insights as to why a client has succumbed, or whether there are personality traits that would contribute to *susceptibility* to burnout. Understanding of one's inherent nature often helps to avoid relapses.

GENERAL SIGNS OF BURNOUT
- ❏ nerves raw – overly sensitive, emotionally vulnerable, jumpy
- ❏ sudden impulses to weep over small things
- ❏ crying uncontrollably for long periods
- ❏ despair; despondency, confusion

- ❑ irritability or irrational anger – even hatred
- ❑ fear and anxiety; obsessive thoughts
- ❑ decline in sex drive and creativity
- ❑ work affected – over activity or inability to work effectively
- ❑ inability to minister or be ministered to
- ❑ inability to relax (re-create)
- ❑ sleep patterns disrupted and not refreshing
- ❑ inability to focus mentally
- ❑ withdrawal from activities and companionship
- ❑ general illness
- ❑ general feeling of sadness
- ❑ feelings of being betrayed by God
- ❑ loss of faith and personal spirituality

PHYSICAL SIGNS:
- ❑ headaches
- ❑ sleep disorders
- ❑ weight loss
- ❑ nervous tension
- ❑ stiffness and muscular aches and pains
- ❑ chronic fatigue or other chronic illness
- ❑ digestive upsets including colitis and ulcers
- ❑ susceptibility to viruses, infections and allergies
- ❑ hormonal fluctuations & imbalances
- ❑ nutritional depletion, eating disorders, etc

CANDIDATES:
- ➢ disability workers
- ➢ carers of the elderly and handicapped
- ➢ teachers
- ➢ mothers and childcare workers
- ➢ doctors and nursing staff
- ➢ church workers and missionaries
- ➢ intercessors and burden bearers
- ➢ community welfare workers and counsellors
- ➢ perfectionists
- ➢ workaholics and the performance oriented
- ➢ overachievers

IMPORTANT: When the final stage is reached 'wounded warriors' can no longer initiate or sustain their own recovery. They are to be carried; not exhorted. They need to be loved; not instructed. There is no quick fix! Following are some useful tips for those ministering to the sufferer.

Practicalities of Counselling: MINISTRY TO SUFFERERS OF BURNOUT

a) Intercede in prayer from a distance and pray directly only if asked to.

b) Do not insist that they participate in corporate worship or prayer.

c) Respect personal and physical boundaries (privacy and touch).

d) No deliverance ministry or in-depth counselling/healing should be undertaken at this time.

e) If delivering prophetic words, write out and deliver at an appropriate time and place, and allow time for digestion of the content.

f) Listen with a sympathetic ear and be courteous, not patronizing.

g) Avoid discussion of ministry or business matters with the sufferer.

h) Discuss their condition with key carers only and squash any gossip.

i) Do not talk about time management; instead, help to prioritize duties.

j) Do not talk delegation of responsibilities; instead help supply carers.

k) Give the sufferer space and solitude but remain on hand.

l) Love unreservedly in ways that demand no response.

m) When ready for it, encourage to participate in things formerly enjoyed.

n) Administer hope and belief in their ability to recover at all times.

o) Assist to preserve the outward appearance of strength before those they are responsible to and for, e.g. pastors to congregation, mothers to children, husband to wife.

p) <u>Do not</u> counsel to praise God in all things (or use other such clichés or platitudes). Speak directly, kindly, simply and sincerely rather than play the role of a Job's comforter,

Practicalities of Counselling: A SUFFERER'S SURVIVAL TIPS

Choose to do what is objectively right even if you do not feel like it. Exercise, spend time with your family (church family as well), get outdoors, etc. Feed your spirit in ways that don't require much energy -- tapes, music, creative hobbies, gentle outdoor activity, visit art galleries, exhibits. Watch light-hearted or inspiring movies (choose comedies above everything else).

Find a safe environment in which to share feelings regularly – an objective friend or counsellor. Do not associate at all with wounders or anyone for duty's sake. Remember that those closest can often wound the most. Try coffee once a week with a carefree, patient friend, and for the men, something like fishing with a trusted mate.

Your spouse or your best friend knows you best. Listen to their advice about your general welfare – when they think you should rest or what you should eat and do. However educate not to nag or pressure; show them this resource material. Insist on help in the way you want help; not the way others think you should be helped.

Lean on protective friends and family members: children or neighbours who will answer the phone and shield you from unwanted calls; friends who will do your errands without fussing, those who will protect you with grace and tactfulness from prying eyes and wagging tongues. Accept hugs and quiet companionship – as much as you can get – whenever you feel up to it.

Accept physical help with your workload. Even the simplest of tasks may tax your strength. Tell yourself that this is temporary and that you are blessing the helper by allowing them to help. This is an ideal opportunity to learn to receive unconditionally. You have sown, so it is now your turn now to receive and to reap the harvest from all the giving. And you are not to add up and keep score over how you will repay the giver when you are well again!

Get help with your diet and let someone cook for you as much as possible (someone who knows about good nutrition and eating habits). Your turn for some nurturing for a change!

Do not feel guilty about your temporary lack of attendance at church or reduced private prayer time. God will never leave you nor forsake you. Ask for an intercessory group of friends or church members to pray just for you on a regular basis to see you through. When you can not praise God, be honest about it – to yourself and to others. Remember the psalms. Find the appropriate ones and recite them as your personal prayers (Ps 35:1-8, 58:6-7, 69:22-29, 109:1, 6-20).

Remember that you are allowed to get angry – once in a while! Acknowledge that your own strength got you into this trouble in the first place. Accept your current weakness and the end loss of your own fleshly strength. Receive God's strength to go on.

KEY SCRIPTURES (related to a carer's burnout)

The Lord sent His word and healed them (Ps 107: 17-22).
Return to God's ways and rest in Him (Isa 30:15).
Come and I will give you rest (Matt 11: 28-29).
He heals the broken-hearted (Ps 147: 3).
Create a clean heart in me (Ps 51: 10).
I will give you a new heart (Ezk 36: 26).
The Lord is my strength (Ps 28: 7).

Practicalities: BURNOUT REOCCURRENCE PREVENTION STRATEGIES

a) Teach others to respect your personal boundaries.

b) Be wary of your tendency to over commit yourself.

c) Learn to say no without feeling guilt and condemnation.

d) Take time to nurture yourself and to be spiritual and childlike.

e) Establish ways to respond to violation of your alone times.

f) Develop detachment and release skills, which allow you to stop, let go and move away from others' problems.

g) Rest completely from your usual duties one day in seven.

h) Take annual holidays free of all duties and commitments.

i) Hobbies are crucial and should bring both fulfilment and relaxation.

j) Have some fun according to your own personality type.

k) Establish healthy diet, relaxation habits and regular sleep patterns.

l) Meditate (be still) as well as being active in prayer.

m) Surrender to God for inner healing for your emotions.

n) Seek ways to be shown how to break old destructive life patterns.

o) Make it a daily discipline (practice) to renew your mind with His Word.

p) Establish a network of discreet and understanding carers.

q) Fill out your self-care wheel on a monthly basis (see resource *Care for the Carer: Bike Wheel Graphic*).

SECTION TWO

Dealing with Feelings

CHAPTER SIX

FEELINGS AS MESSENGERS

This chapter will serve as a prelude to resources covering the basic emotions most frequently expressed as troublesome – depression, anxiety and anger. It introduces ways of dealing with emotional overreactions and gives a preview of the healing methods used in restoration ministry.

- The process of recovery as described by a client
- Emotional intelligence – maturity assessment
- Expression of personal feelings safely as a counsellor
- Dealing with troublesome *messenger* feelings
- Use of overreactions to achieve personal healing

Study Notes

CLIENT TESTIMONIAL: The Road to Recovery

I cannot imagine how I would have got through all the garbage following my divorce unless I had stuck with the counselling. I really had to work hard at trying to understand how to deal with my feelings and to accept myself where I was at. I realise now that things that happened to me in my childhood actually stunted my emotional growth.

When I started getting prayer ministry, I guess I expected that God would just fix me up; that I would get over all the hurts and that I would forgive and forget and just get on with my life as a single mum. How could anyone have been so naïve!

Last night I sat down and realised I was finally getting somewhere. I wrote the following piece for my, oh so patient, Christian counsellor. If she likes it, I hope she might give it out to some of her clients.

HONOURING THE PROCESS OF RECOVERY

Healing, or recovery, is a process. It is not a quick fix and it will not be a miraculous, instantaneous happening. It requires work and it takes co-operation. You must work to understand and to accept yourself. You probably took a long time to get into this mess. God will work along with you for as long as it takes to get you out. You not only need to understand godly principles; but you must apply the principles. He will treat you as a unique individual; therefore, you should respect your own individuality. YOU are YOU.

Do not expect perfection from yourself. Be patient with yourself... just as he is. He will never give up on you. He understands you perfectly. He will complete the good work he started in you. Be childlike, but not childish. Realise recovery can be frightening. Whenever you face a new issue, visualize placing your hand in the Father's hand. He can be trusted implicitly. He will walk with you, matching your every step... resting along with you when need be. He will never hurry nor push you, or leave you to do it alone.

Do not be afraid of your feelings... You must feel to heal. Open the eyes of your heart and allow God, your Heavenly Father, to walk you through the healing process. Jesus your Redeemer will be covering your back. The Holy Spirit will be guiding you where to walk. Respect the process (2Cor 3:18). You <u>WILL</u> make it.

Except where the author recounts her personal testimony, all characters and cases are fictitious representations and any similarities to real persons or cases are non-intentional and purely coincidental.

INTRODUCTION TO HEALING METHODS

(Jer 29:10-24) As counsellors, we often see people at vulnerable and unstable periods emotionally. If we could describe a client as emotionally stable, we would probably be judging on the degree of control the client has over emotions at the time we are personally dealing with them. However, to consider whether a person is an emotionally mature individual over the long term, we would be making an assessment on their general ability to achieve the following:

EMOTIONAL WISDOM & MATURITY FACTORS CHECKLIST*

- ❏ able to manage anxiety, depression and anger
- ❏ control impulses and have the capacity to delay gratification
- ❏ deal with disappointment and frustration
- ❏ recognise and withstand stress (or use it to advantage)
- ❏ maintain balance and deal with overreactions
- ❏ handle the emotions connected with change and move on effectively
- ❏ understand the power of emotions and accurately label them
- ❏ not allow feelings to rule life in general (especially decision making)
- ❏ make wise decisions and follow through
- ❏ recognise triggers to unexpected deep-felt emotional responses
- ❏ accept personal responsibility to manage their own life
- ❏ be healthily self-aware and know what is important to self
- ❏ be spiritually aware and in relationship to God
- ❏ possess interpersonal skills – especially empathy
- ❏ have social competence (including flowing with others' moods and understanding non-verbal communication)
- ❏ feel connected to, respected by and valued by others
- ❏ readily recognise feelings and deal with them appropriately
- ❏ deal with personal and relational conflict
- ❏ self-reflect, understand, manage and value personality traits and behavioural tendencies
- ❏ not need the approval of others to feel capable or motivated
- ❏ possess an aura of well-being, relaxation, contentment, optimism, peace, good humour, self-confidence and self-acceptance

---

This checklist is also available as a *Client Handout*. Please respect copyright. Resources found within this publication are reproduced in the companion book: 'So You Want To Be A Christian Counsellor – Resources Handbook' – (www.prayercounsel.com).

Emotional wisdom or intelligence can be cultivated. The less emotionally resourceful and resilient are usually those who feel the need for approval from the counsellor in order to reach maturity. Direction towards becoming God-dependent, rather than ministry-dependent, is required. You can start a client on the road to emotional maturity by assisting to first recognise, then to express, the more troublesome feelings appropriately. The following segment offers resources on dealing with feelings. This will serve as an introduction to healing and *restoration of the soul and spirit.*

Counsellor Resource: SAFE EXPRESSION OF PERSONAL FEELINGS

PERSONAL HELP FOR THE COUNSELLOR

Just as you might stub your toe and feel physical pain, you may react to any hurtful situation in the course of ministering, with a range of emotions. These may include anger, sorrow, disappointment, jealousy, dissatisfaction, guilt, anxiety, regret, and frustration. It is not wrong to have strong feelings. It is what we do with the particular emotion, which counts – particularly the negative and intense kind. Here are some points to consider when dealing with the distressing types of situations encountered by those in the caring industry.

Recognise your personal feelings as well as your clientele's problem areas. Be aware that an obvious feeling such as anger may be only a *secondary emotion* to primary feelings of fear or shame. Learn to *label emotions* correctly and to take ownership. Acknowledge that your emotions are neither right nor wrong in themselves, just reactions in a given situation. Be aware and assess yourself for *overreactions*. These can be very pointed messengers to you that you have *unfinished business* to deal with from the past, or that something is affecting you at present.

Question yourself as to whether you are dealing with your *messenger feelings* wisely. Once you receive the message and have realised these feelings could be negative and destructive to you, or to other persons, then dispose of them appropriately. It is no use bottling or suppressing emotions as this will result in self-damage. For example, frustration and disappointment constantly unexpressed could develop into *depression* and perhaps lead to *burnout*.

At the right time, and to the right person, it should be *appropriate and safe* to express feelings outwardly so that they will not become inwardly destructive. This is where another counsellor, therapist, clinical supervisor, mentor, pastoral carer or a trusted friend or spouse can be a support.

However, remember that it is not right to practise *dumping* your feelings under the guise of debriefing – even on suitable persons. This is especially so when it may be at an inopportune time, or without requesting permission to do so. And, of course, it is <u>not</u> appropriate to disclose personal problems and associated feelings to your clients.

When you have found a suitable and willing listener, then it is also irresponsible to keep rehearsing the same scenario and the associated feelings. This will only serve to damage the hearer as well as yourself. It is an indicator that there could be underlying unforgiveness, resentment and bitterness, which may have its *root in revenge* (or a desire to punish). Deal with *underlying attitudes and beliefs*. This being said, do not condemn yourself for having negative or strong feelings. Deposit these with your Maker as only He has broad enough shoulders to bear them.

Do not despise nor repress tears or expressions of *righteous anger*, as they have their usefulness. Just because you are in a responsible position and must reserve expression of your true feelings at times, it does not mean that you cannot have your turn at letting off some steam or showing empathy and concern – particularly when a gross injustice has been committed towards one of your precious flock. After all, Jesus did! So let your emotions do the work they were intended to do; then let go when they are of no further constructive use to you.

Client Handout: DEALING WITH FEELINGS

1. Recognise feelings as they occur. Ask the counsellor for help to label feelings correctly and to sort as *primary or secondary* emotions.
2. Allow yourself to feel. Emotions are important 'messengers' to you; listen to what they are saying.
3. Take responsibility for your personal feelings; acknowledge them as your own; then, deal with them in an appropriate manner.

The following points should help you to do the assignment set below:

> ➢ feelings as messengers, sent to inform us of the heart's condition
> ➢ acknowledge the message, then deal with the associated feelings
> ➢ learn to communicate feelings to relevant persons appropriately
> ➢ do not store, repress or suppress, as you will be the one who will suffer
> ➢ do not 'dump' on others; your feelings are your own responsibility
> ➢ blaming or punishing someone for the way <u>you</u> are feeling is not fair
> ➢ do not store up resentment and hurt, as it can lead to bitterness
> ➢ respect others when they communicate <u>their</u> feelings to you
> ➢ try not to guess what others are feeling; request clarification

- be tolerant when others discharge feelings, but do not take ownership
- allow tears to serve their purpose (release tension or to express grief)
- do not condemn yourself, or judge others, for having strong feelings
- let no strong feeling go unexamined
- do not downplay emotions, as they must not be underestimated
- focus on the problem causing the emotion and compare the strength of the feeling in relation to the problem
- welcome an overreaction as a sign that there is a problem to work on
- locate secondary associated feelings, correctly label, and deal with them appropriately
- deal with underlying attitudes and beliefs*
- do not be afraid to ask for help from your counsellor

Please respect copyright. Master copies of resources found within this publication are provided for your use in the companion book: 'So You Want To Be A Christian Counsellor – Resources Handbook' - www.prayercounsel.com.

This following resource is also available as a *Client Handout*.

Attitudes, intentions, beliefs and ensuing actions can be sinful; but feelings are morally neutral. For example: *I hate that person and I believe I have the right to take back what she stole from me – and I am going to do it,* is not acceptable, whereas, *what that person has done to me makes me feel as if I want to take revenge,* is morally neutral. Although we often cannot control our initial emotional reactions, we can control the negative and destructive <u>use</u> of emotions by making a choice as to how we will respond in a situation.

Counsellor Exercise: On Dealing With Feelings

Examine a strong feeling that has troubled you recently.

Using the questions as a guide, write a summary of your findings in the space provided below.

a) *Would you describe this feeling as a 'negative emotion'? Why?*

b) *Trace back to the thought process, which has created the feeling. Record your thoughts along the pathway they have taken.*

c) *Link the thoughts and the feelings together. Would this be classed as an overreaction; if so, why?*

d) *Could this overreaction be harmful or destructive to you or to someone else? If so, are you going to dwell on it, thereby giving it more power? Are you going to feed it and make it grow?*

e) *Which keys from the Word of God will allow the Holy Spirit to help you to take control of your thoughts and to release your feelings safely?*

Counsellor Resource: Discourse on OVERREACTIONS

Prayer ministers and counsellors are primarily *'doctors' of the heart*. We deal with damaged souls in the main part – healing and repairing, restoring and reconciling, preaching the Word so that it is applied. Emotions can be fickle and confusing, mysterious and disturbing. These are either reactions or responses. Love, for example, can be a reactive emotion yet it can also be a matter of will and of free choice – a response. We choose to love; therefore, we feel love. It can be a stimulus-response effect. The choice activates the feeling. Love can be a matter of will, as can any other emotion. It is important to remember that our thoughts produce our feelings. For example: –

My wife left me for another man a year ago and now she tells me she wants to come back. My initial reaction was one of outrage. I had lost all my love for her. After much soul searching, I have made a choice to forgive her. She is my wife and I want to love her again. I hope the feelings (of love) will come back.

LOSING CONTROL

There are the occasions when we no longer feel we have any choice. We see that our emotions are taking over our ability to choose and thoughts are out of control. Anxious, obsessive thoughts turn into panic attacks and mental disorders. Hate turns into uncontrollable rage, leading to murderous thoughts of revenge. Grief turns into deep despair and suicide ideation. Serious overreactions threaten to ruin our lives. We feel very far from the ideal of the 'perfect Christian'.

Sometimes, *mediation* (an intervention or change agent) is necessary to prevent our feelings from leading us into deep waters. We are instructed by the scriptures to 'captivate our thoughts' – to take control of our thoughts and feelings so that they come into alignment with the will of God (as with the previous example of the man with the unfaithful wife).

The truth of the Word of God, as revealed to mankind in the scriptures, is *the mediator* that affects positive change in a person's life. It is the counsellor's responsibility to witness to the truth of this and to minister the truth to damaged souls and troubled spirits. Once the client has personal knowledge of the truth, they can then be encouraged to exercise personal faith and spiritual muscles to regain anointed spirit-control over troublesome emotions.

MINISTERING TO THE HEART

It is so important to minister to the heart because this is usually where the damage lies. The heart is the physical organ that symbolises our emotions. Thoughts produce feelings, but emotions often overwhelm our ability to think logically or to respond with sound reasoning. Feelings often produce reactions rather than considered responses. This is where our spirit needs to take dominion over the damaged soul by using the Word of God to declare the truth in the matter. For example: –

The facts are, having been abandoned by my parents at birth, I still feel wounded and rejected; but the truth is, that my Father God loves me unconditionally and His word says that He will never leave me nor forsake me.

A feeling is neither bad nor good in itself. Emotions are neither morally right nor morally wrong. They are a reaction or a response to a stimulus. If the stimulus is based on a false belief (that is, something that does not line up with the Word of God) then the thoughts associated with it can be classed as *a lie.* If we react or respond based on a lie, then we are programmed into living a lie – living without God's protective covering (Prv 19:5).

COMING INTO ALIGNMENT

We need to align our thoughts, feelings, and responses to the truth and wisdom contained in God's word, rather than on emotions, experiences, intuition and false securities (1Cor 2). God cannot lie (Titus1:2). Real security lies in spiritual resources outside man-made ones – those that cannot change or diverge from the truth (1Cor 3:18-20, Prv14:12). There is no compromise. The two edged sword of God – the Word of God – cuts and divides truth from error and makes known the condition of our hearts (Heb 4:12).

We are expected to live self-controlled righteous lives – living proactively rather than reactively (refer to the book of Titus). Feelings should not control our lives. Our spirits should be ruling our emotions – based on the truth. Our spirits should be searching our minds for the toxic thoughts and false beliefs that are producing destructive overreactions. Our born again spirits should be taking command and ruling in any situation; *taking every thought captive to the mind of Christ* (2Cor 10:4-5) so that we are strong and rooted and grounded in love for God and in unity with each other (refer to the book of Ephesians).

There is no benefit in teaching about anger management or dealing with depression and anxiety without using the Word of God as the infallible guide as to how we are to live our lives. In general, people balk at the use of the words 'lie' and 'liar' but, if we are not living according to God's ways, then we are living based on feelings rather than faith in the integrity of God – we are *living a lie.*

RESPONDING & TAKING COMMAND

A reaction based on feelings can be a protective measure and a form of self-defence. It is what we choose to do with a particular feeling that counts – our response to a situation needs to be according to God's laws and through spiritual discernment. A response from the soul can be either, good or bad, healthy or unhealthy, functional or dysfunctional. Therefore, we should examine our feelings with interest, either as they occur or after the event. A choice made – based on either the truth or a lie. – establishes what to do with the manifested emotion. Our objective is for our spirit to take command if the emotion tries to take over again.

For example: –

The fact is, that I am feeling depressed about not having a job; but the truth is, that my hope is in God's promise that He will provide for me in every way possible. Therefore, I am going to enjoy today by sewing a new outfit for my next interview.

PRACTICAL APPLICATION

The scriptures say that *'faith without works is dead'*. It is all very well teaching about being proactive in faith, but some clients will present with *immobilisation* as a reaction to certain problems. We can have three basic reactions/responses in a given situation – *flight, fight or freeze* (immobilisation). Picture a rabbit on the road at night caught in a car's headlights. Deliver this concept by asking the 'frozen' client, *are you going to be a bunny about this?* In other words, are you going to stand on the road to be run over, or are you going to make a choice and act upon it in a positive way? This illustrates that there is just as much danger in denying our emotions healthy expression (by internalising, suppressing and remaining frozen) as there is in giving full vent to them.

At the scene of the rabbit and the oncoming car, the animal's fear creates immobilisation, which results in the bunny's painful demise. On the other hand, the rabbit's fear might elicit the opposite – a positive effect. The fear response can mobilise the animal to move off the road and out of danger. This is the response to concentrate on now – being proactive in seeking help when faced with emotions that are in danger of getting out of control.

OVERREACTIONS AS SIGNPOSTS TO HEALING

In the following segment, we will be looking at the effects of overreactions or those feelings which cannot be ignored or denied and cannot be classed as normal. The dictionary defines feelings as 'emotional reactions'. Overreactions are quite beneficial to counsellors as they can serve as indicators for deeper *inner healing type ministry* needs. The deeper and more intense the feeling, the clearer it can serve as a signpost directing us to what underlies the overreaction. Prayer ministry releases the sufferer into freedom.

Just as physical pain is a warning of physical danger, emotional pain is a warning that something is amiss. For instance, we might accidentally put our hand on a hotplate and the physical *reaction* of the pain experienced should lead us to a response. We should respond by immediately taking our hand off the heat – the source of the pain. We then need to administer care to the burn in order for it to heal.

In like manner, we can recognise the pain of an emotional overreaction as an indication that the heart, placed on the 'hotplate', is in need of removing in order to minister to the emotional wounds. If we are in denial about the pain and immobilized for some reason, then we will remain on the heat and experience further damage. The bottom line is that we need to *feel to heal*. To continue to ignore or deny the emotional pain we are experiencing means we will continue to be vulnerable.

INTRODUCTION TO INNER HEALING TECHNIQUES

The following graphic illustration explains the process of healing and recovery for the damaged soul. It will also serve to introduce the powerful prayer technique presented fully in *Section 5 – The Healing Pool Method*. This method involves cleansing the client of the pain contained in memories of the past, by using signs of overreactions to locate lies (embedded in the soul at the time of damage).

THE ROAD TO RECOVERY

When a real or perceived offence takes place, it can elicit an overreaction. This distorted reaction may be highly recognizable to onlookers at the time, but, to the offended one, the strength of the reaction might seem quite normal and justifiable.

During the counselling process, new *offences* will often trigger pain in the still sensitive areas (*scar tissue*) formed from wounds inflicted in the past. This is a natural outcome – to have old wounds resurface and emotional reactions re-triggered. Your client is being taught during the counselling process to reach out to God for healing. He or she is being educated in recognising the need to *feel to heal.*

As we teach the client to become more in touch with their feelings (through allowing the Holy Spirit to *open the eyes of the heart)* he or she will begin to acknowledge particular *overreactions* in current situations, possibly linked to old wounds. This is an indication of the need to process yet another healing experience. With appropriate teaching, a client will begin to welcome strong feelings (in the present) as *signposts* on the road to recovery directing us back to co-operatively deal with the painful memories of past hurts.

Refer to IMAGE 08 *Overreactions as Signposts to Healing.*

Using the principle of welcoming overreactions as signposts to healing, we can travel on from healing place to healing place by following the signs erected on the Road to Recovery. Refer to accompanying graphic and text.

IMAGE 08

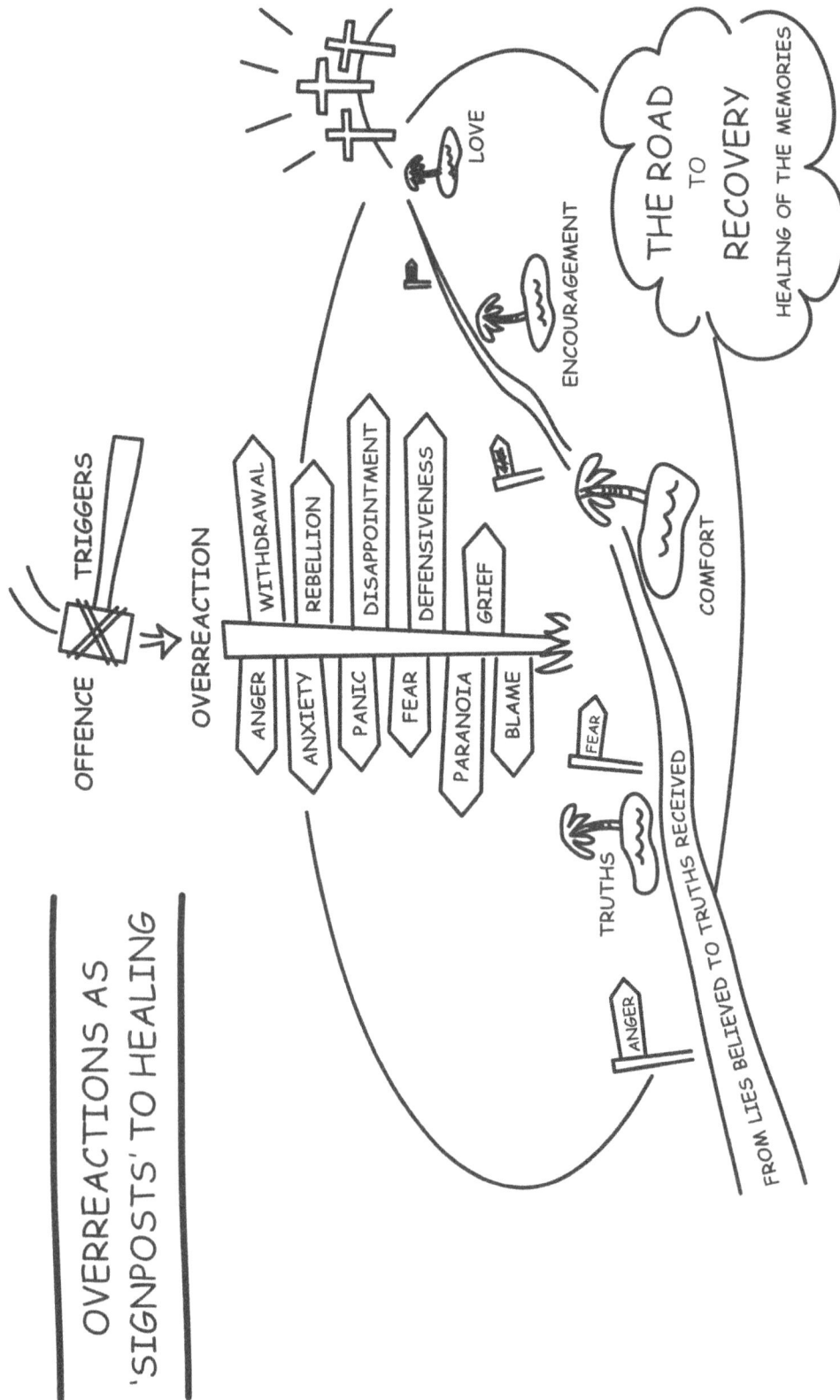

OVERREACTIONS AS 'SIGNPOSTS' TO HEALING

Client Handout: OVERREACTIONS AS SIGNPOSTS TO HEALING

Examine the feeling that is troubling you. Would you class it as an overreaction? If you are unsure, then try comparing the intensity of your feelings to an obvious example such as road rage. Rating a serious incident of road rage as a 10, on a scale of 1-10, how would you rate your feelings in your case in comparison? Can you relate to these other illustrations?

> A. **major disappointment** felt over some minor setback, such as the flu keeping you from an outing with friends
>
> B. **overly aggressive or defensive** on being criticised or corrected
>
> C. **explosive anger** over the slightest infringement of your rights, such as when someone jumps the queue or bumps into you
>
> D. **outright rebellion** when asked to say or do something; sometimes even doing the opposite
>
> E. **extremely anxious** in everyday situations such as driving or speaking up for yourself

Messenger emotions associated with overreactions are 'signposts' directing you to your healing place. Pause here to think of another personal example similar to those above. Record the last time this overreaction occurred and describe what you think triggered it.

Through this simple exercise, you will learn to welcome the triggers and the associated emotions such as rage, acute disappointment, overwhelming grief, paranoia, depression, jealousy, stubbornness, panic, escapism, and so on. These will be your signs pointing towards your next oasis of healing on your road to recovery.

Remember the **trigger** (perceived threat or offence) is probably not the real issue. An overreaction is likely to be the surface symptom of a deeper, underlying hurt (wound). Therefore, for this exercise, think only briefly about what has triggered your initial emotion and move on to deal with what underlies your reaction/response (the feelings). Are you willing to face the necessary pain in order to heal? Are you ready to feel to heal? If so, follow these specific steps:

1. Focus on the primary feeling associated with the incident.
2. Check for secondary feelings and label them.
3. Ask the Holy Spirit to reveal the root cause of the overreaction.
4. Deal with the root cause/s.

Practicalities of Counselling: CASEWORK ON INNER HEALING

CLIENT 'ANNIE'

Emotional damage can begin from a point where a lie embeds in a soul and assimilates into the spirit as a perceived 'truth'. Annie was sexually molested at the age of four. The adult Annie's *inner child* is still suffering debilitating shame over this violation. As a child, she believed that she had done something to deserve the offence and to attract the offender. This lie remains hidden into adulthood. The lie needs to be exposed and needs replacing with the truth because it is affecting her relationships with men in general and with her self-image and sense of worth.

Her presenting problem to the counselling is that she is extremely shy of men and sensitive to criticism from them. As all her workmates are men, this is proving a major obstacle to her career progression. Annie has blamed herself for myriads of problems for forty long years; her most recent incident being acute *embarrassment* over a minor accountancy discrepancy in the office in which she works. Recognised as an obvious overreaction, this indicates her need for inner healing ministry.

During the counselling process, through following the road to recovery from healing oasis to healing oasis, she receives truths to replace the lies located. The ponds represent the various prayer ministry sessions where she becomes increasingly open to receiving the comfort, encouragement and love she has longed for. However, it is only by stopping to examine specific overreactions, such as the embarrassment over a minor mistake, that she has been able to gradually process and achieve full recovery. She has acknowledged her real problem – that she has been deceived into believing the *shame based lie* that <u>she</u> is a mistake and that she is the problem.

Consequently, Annie has turned to the Cross and received by faith the amazing grace offered to her and goes on to overcome her shyness and fear of criticism.

> **Except where the author recounts her personal testimony, all characters in this text are fictitious representations and any similarities to real cases or persons are purely coincidental and non-intentional.**

SELF-HELP HEALING METHODS

DEALING WITH FEELINGS

Prayer ministry experience within the counselling setting can enable a client to step into self-help methods at home. The author now relates a very personal experience achieved after many years of practice in this 'skill'. The prayer ministry technique below makes use of *The Healing Pool Method* as described in Chapter 19 under *Cleansing Techniques*.

(Isa 35:10) AUTHOR'S TESTIMONY (for background to healing episode).

Much of my childhood memories centre on poverty and emotional neglect. There was also the major lack of spiritual input, which would have done much to compensate for the material blessings that were missing. I was born in 1950 in post war Australia. This placed me square in the middle of the baby boomer era. Our generation looked forward to a future of promise and hope. On leaving high school we expected a university education if we wanted it, a marriage partner, a career rather than 'just a job', and a car to enjoy getting about with our friends to the beach or 'the pictures' (movies). It was a happy period in history.

However, I was trying to picture my childhood home one night. It was not a happy home. I am a grandmother now and I was musing on the differences my grandchildren are experiencing to what my family life was like as a child growing up in the 50's and 60's.

Our family of four lived in a fibro house – one like the grandkids draw. Our little home was protected with a pitched galvanized iron roof. It was virtually a box with two windows (wooden frames) out front, another on one side, two on the other side, and one at the back. We had a few steps leading up to a slab of cement serving as 'the porch' (patio) for the front entry. The house was set up on brick piers in a flood prone area without drainage. It was on a 60ft frontage sandy block surrounded by areas of wildflowers, swamp, sea, sand and bush. Our street, ostentatiously called an avenue, was a dirt track.

One memorable year when it flooded, we boated to the main road to catch the school bus on a wooden raft perched haphazardly on kerosene tins. We never had a car so the dirt track didn't bother us. My father did not have a driving licence, even if we could have afforded a vehicle, as he was near blind from a cricket ball accident as a boy.

Our house furnishings didn't amount to much... A couple of campers' kerosene burners served as a stove and hotplates. We had an ice chest to refrigerate the food and a smelly kerosene heater to keep us warm in winter. There was no shower, except when the rainwater tank overflowed. An electric copper provided hot water for baths and boiling up clothes and hankies to disinfect them. We shared bath water out of sheer necessity, one kid in after the other. The cleanest one washed first, as we only had a small water tank for the entire household needs.

It was the dream of every Australian post war citizen to own his or her own home. Even someone at the bottom of the working class scale like my dad held on to this hope. My paternal grandfather had had his farm repossessed by the bank in the previous generation, so our father would not take on a mortgage as such. Instead, our home loan was on 'a gentleman's agreement' with the owner-builder who came for a social visit every now and then to collect the payments. These were made in cash!

To earn those precious house payments my father bicycled to the station before dawn to travel two hours via steam train to work. He always arrived home after dark when my brother and I were fast asleep. My father worked as a spray painter of industrial machinery. This menial work was far below his capabilities and completely outside his interests, which were in literature, fine art, politics and current affairs in general. The struggling days of the trade union labour movement for fair hours and pay, produced for him mostly six days per week on the factory floor (including much sought after overtime) and two and a half hours travel either way on bike and steam train. He was fifteen years locked into the same job to purchase our house.

I thought it ironic that my father found a trade to support our family as a spray painter when, at times, he could barely see for cataracts and glaucoma in his one functional eye. He had lost sight completely in the other eye from a displaced his retina at the age of thirteen. There was not the medical ability to repair it back then, nor the finances to access medical help anyway. Neither was there a blind disability pension for him, as there would be for him today.

He had no veterans' rights either, as his blindness had precluded him from military service. His wartime legacy was the memory of receiving chicken feathers in the mail. These symbols were sent by the women on the home front aimed to shame the men they personally judged too cowardly to volunteer for active service. Apparently, his disability was not obvious to them, as he was a working family man.

My brother and I mostly spent our school holidays at our grandmother's in the city – two hours travel with our mother by train. Our biggest school holiday treat was lunch with our maternal grandmother at Coles cafeteria in the city. Our father spent his annual holidays painting (as usual) and repairing the house, and weeding the strawberry patch. It was not much of a life for our intelligent well-read father. My sensitive child heart went out to him daily. My burden bearing characteristics were honed right from early childhood.

Sometimes, when tucked in bed in a sleepy half-aware state, I would feel his end of day beard and gentle kiss on my forehead. My brother and I didn't see much of our dad. Sunday afternoon he caught up on his own sleep. It was really only breakfast and lunch once a week spent as a family around the table. Sunday morning I was sent off to Sunday school because 'it might do her some good'. My brother attended once and deemed it uninteresting so he requested that he might never have to go again. This was fine with both of my parents. They had 'no interest in religion'. I continued to go because I enjoyed dressing up in my cousins hand me downs. It also served to assuage my all-pervasive guilt feelings.

This childhood legacy left me feeling that I never really knew my dad. Obviously I can see now that the physical absence and lack of intimacy with my father left me with deep emotional scars. It did much to shape my view of God being distant and unavailable to meet my needs. We had a good moral upbringing but never any real spiritual input from either parent. God remained just as impersonal and unobtainable to me as my earthly father seemed to be.

THE STRAWBERRY PATCH HEALING

Current Situation*: Myself as a counsellor feeling a client's pain.*
Overreaction*: Too much empathy.*
The Healing Process Begins*: I recall the concept that I must 'feel to heal' (see teaching on Dealing with Feelings).*

I allow my feelings to be stirred up. I feel empathy and sorrow. I feel like my heart is huge, so big and tender it is about to burst. I feel pain, another's pain and I feel like it is my own pain and that there is nothing I can do about it. I feel helpless. So full of sorrow I cannot stand it. There is nothing I can do about this pain.

CHILDHOOD MEMORY:

I step back in time. I am about eight years old. Dad is in his strawberry patch. He is telling, no, ordering me, to weed it. I am saying to myself, 'I don't care about your stupid garden!'

I am feeling resentful. I am thinking that they are <u>his</u> strawberries. He grew them. He wanted to put them there. Why do I have to look after them? Then I feel guilty. He works hard all day. I should be doing this for him. I feel great guilt. I should want to do it. I am a failure as a daughter. I am lazy. I am no good.

My father is telling me this, because I won't help around the house. I am lazy and no good. I feel I really am. I don't want to do anything. I have shut down to stop the pain. I don't feel my own pain; but I still feel his. It is in my face. It follows me around, even in my dreams. I can never escape his anger, his frustration, and his unhappiness.

PROCESSING THOUGHTS FROM THE FRAMEWORK OF THE CHILD

He will never be happy; so I am never to be happy. When will it end? I tell myself, it will end by pretending that I am not alive; that I am dead and buried. I just want to make my father happy. I am a failure because I can't. So I don't want to live. Life is too hard. Everyone around me is unhappy. Dad makes them so. Why can't he be different? Why can't we talk together? The only times he talks to me is when he is unhappy with me, or worried over me because I am sick. He makes me sick. Then, when I am sick, he worries over me and lets me off from working around the house.

But the guilt doesn't stop. I am still guilty because I know I am making myself ill to escape his sharp tongue. Being ill has made his tongue gentle, but it has caused him more pain because he is worried over mum, himself and me now. Now we are all sick – except for my brother. Somehow, he escapes the pain. He just lives his life and all this pain of our mother being sick all the time. Our mum and dad unhappy, and me being utterly miserable, just goes over his head.

It makes me so jealous that he can do that. I am so weak because I can't do it. I feel guilty because I know jealousy is so bad. It makes me do bad things to my brother. Just like dad punishes me, I take it out on my brother because he is happy and I am jealous of that. He has no right to be happy!

LIES BELIEVED AS A CHILD

I am responsible for everyone's unhappiness, including my own. I have no right to enjoy life unless everyone around me is happy. I am a failure at this. I have not fulfilled my purpose for being here. So I have no right to be alive. I should never have been born because I am too weak to do what is expected of me. There is no one to help me so I may as well give up on life. I have no right to be happy if I can't make others happy.

PRESENTING FEELING/S

I feel utterly miserable. I recognise resentment and jealousy in me.

ASSOCIATED UNDERLYING FEELINGS

Guilt when I feel happy; comfortable when I am unhappy.

BELIEFS AND ATTITUDES

It is what I am used to and what I deserve (to constantly feel guilty and unhappy).

PROCESSING TRUTHS

Looking to Jesus for my personal truths based on what He says to my inner child in the present. He, Jesus, says to me as this child of the past: 'I made you to be happy. I want you to be happy. You have my permission to be happy. Go ahead and just play with your dolls. You don't have to weed the strawberry patch; because I am the boss and I say so!'

The author is then able to affirm these truths to her 'inner child' in the present in the following way and to receive healing and comfort.

THE TRUTH

The truth is that there is a higher authority than my dad or anyone else and I am to listen to Him, not to them. He says I am allowed to be happy. So I will be happy. I choose to be happy that I am alive and have a life to enjoy now.

(See further instruction on Inner Healing Techniques in Section V).

CHAPTER SEVEN

DEALING WITH DEPRESSION

Chapter 7 presents a brief but practical covering of this complicated emotion. An explanation is given to the layman to help evaluate whether depression is to be dealt with as a natural reaction to common stressors, or whether it has progressed to becoming a psychological disorder of the soul. Refer also to chapters covering *Renewing the Mind* and to the Appendix on *Suicide*.

- Casework – includes both client and counsellor testimony
- Clinical disorder versus reactive depression
- Practical evaluation
- Supports available

Study Notes

CLIENT TESTIMONIAL: Mad at the World

I don't know whether I can take this counselling thing any longer. I need to have a reason to keep going back. I don't seem to be getting anywhere even though my counsellor says she's really pleased with my progress.

How much more can a bloke take of fronting up each week to rehearse all my problems about how I don't get on with my boss, or my wife – or my kids for that matter! No one seems to understand that, when I say that I hate my job, I really mean it! I've been doing it for 25 years. It is hard yakka and I get nowhere; but I'm stuck with it because of the mortgage. For the sake of the kids I can't pack it in.

It is taking me longer and longer to get my butt out of bed on weekdays, and, on weekends, I just don't get up at all. What's the use when I have nothing to look forward to? I don't even want to play golf any more. The yard is a wreck and I can't afford to pay someone to mow it for me.

I just want out of the whole lot – the marriage thing, the holding down a job, and ... well, I just want to climb up the highest mountain and drop off of it. Trouble is: I don't have the energy to climb out of bed. Ironical isn't it?

You know, I wanted to be a climber when I was a kid. I was going to climb Everest! Yeah, me, the biggest loser on the block, and I thought I could have dreams and achieve something with my life.

Now this counsellor woman has me going to the quack and he's put me on these pills. He says I am depressed! I'm not depressed! I'm mad at the world and I'm mad at The Big Guy up there. This God doesn't seem to care or even know I exist. The woman – the counsellor from my wife's church – tells me her God loves me; that, if I open the door just a crack, then the Big Fellow can come in and help me. So I tell her, 'I don't believe it. No one has ever given me a break and I don't expect things to change now'.

Like these happy pills; they were supposed to get me moving and out playing golf with my old mates. She said to give 'em three weeks to start doing their work. I've taken them for over a month now (well... that is...when I think of it, I take them). And I don't see the slightest change. I just get madder – at my wife for telling me I have to go to this shrink, at the shrink for telling me to go for the pills (I'm a druggie now!) and I am mad at myself for listening to them.

Following this fictitious testimonial is the counsellor's discussion of this fictitious case with a protégé who is learning how to Christian counsel. This would-be counsellor is a social or community welfare trained young person and is mid-way through a pastoral care course. The trainee sat in on two sessions as an observer, but was not there for the initial consultation. The client has (surprisingly) given him permission to do so. The client's reasoning was that it made no difference to him. He stated that, if this young bloke wanted to help people, then he might learn something from the mess he is in, and maybe have a better life than he (the client) has had.

The Counsellor Speaking:

I had not seen the client's wife for over a year. She had been under contract with me for several months as a client referred to me by a mutual friend. When she arrived at my office for a follow up session, I was pleasantly surprised at her joyfulness. She reported that she was personally doing very well and delivered the details of her progress. She said that her husband was the one who needed the help currently.

She asked me if I would consider counselling her non-Christian husband. She felt that he was suffering from chronic fatigue or depression. I reminded her of the type of counsellor I was. I am a Christian, professionally ministering to church people, rather than a professional counsellor who happens to be a Christian. With that understanding in mind, I asked her if she would like to hear my spiritual views on depression. She consented. Before I offered them I asked her to describe her husband's condition.

Her husband, it seems, was always feeling sorry for himself. She described how he seemed unaware of his negativity. It had become a habit with him. She felt that he was personally responsible for his deterioration because he was unwilling to help himself.

I offered my opinion based on my experience as a counsellor. I conceded that Christians and non-believers alike do tend to fall into self-pity and self-indulgence, which accompanies depression. It was one of those things where one wonders which comes first – the chicken or the egg.

Certainly, in my professional experience, most depressed people appear to be self-centred. It seems to come hand in hand with the malaise (that is the milder feelings of depression). I described how it is easier to treat Christians because they are more open to understanding that self-pity can be part of our sinful nature. When I point this out, they are less likely to take offence than a non-believer would. I also point out that self-pity and self-centredness need to be repented of, and renouncement made. They can ask God for forgiveness and receive it.

With work, the client can self-release from the carnal habitual ways via the application of Biblical affirmations and reprogramming with scriptural truths. A spirit of praise and optimism eventually displaces self-indulgence.

For a variety of reasons, some people lose faith in anyone helping them, let alone God. From my spiritual experience, I have seen that a depression prone person's view of God is usually a negative one – whether believer or non-believer. To the sufferer, God can appear to be too big to care, or the opposite: too small and impotent to do anything about their woes. He can be perceived as anything from punishing and vindictive, to apathetic, or a killjoy to say the least. Even a mature believer will hold some of these childish views.

I warned her that, even if her husband embraced the Christian faith and accepted the gift of salvation, it could be a long road ahead for all concerned. From her description, it seemed he had already given over to faulty and irrational ways of thinking and acting. He would surely need to widen or alter his perception of what God's nature is like. He would need to adjust his thinking patterns accordingly before he is restored by faith to health. He would need to renew his mind to the mind of Christ.

A true personal relationship with The True God comes without preconceived ideas interfering with reconciliation with Him and the healing process. Repentance from self-centredness is generally necessary before the healing will truly begin. I promised to do what I could to bring her husband closer to a truer perception of God (that is, if she could get him along to see me). She said she would try.

To close our session, I asked her to describe her husband's personality. She said he was intrinsically a whiner and possessed a passive nature, but that he could get quite angry. I also stressed that self-condemnation and an oversensitive conscience can accompany a depressive nature. In bringing a person to repentance, the counsellor needs a great deal of sensitivity and a gentle spirit must be in operation. Otherwise, the counsellor's words will only serve to strengthen the underlying anger and other negatively expressed feelings. The depression might worsen and could eventually tip the person over the edge.

I asked her whether he was seeking medical help and had he ever taken antidepressants or any other prescription or non-prescription drugs. I also asked if he had experienced suicidal ideation. Apparently, he had sought medical help but had not stuck to the instructions given. As far as the idea of suicide, she exclaimed that surely she would know if he were seriously ill enough to be thinking about that. This question obviously shocked her. I explained that I would be asking him directly about this on his initial

consultation, as we needed to know where we stood. She voiced her concerns
about 'giving him ideas'. I assured her that would not be the case and immediately handed her a leaflet explaining my approach.

At this point of the mentoring of my protégé, I explained a few things of a spiritual nature to him – as he wanted to enter the arena of prayer ministry. I explained to him that we, as Christian counsellors, needed to know, from the beginning, whether a depressed person is on medication. This is one reason why I use the medical section on my client details form during initial consultation and assessment. I emphasized that in no way was I an adversary to the medical profession. We each had a corner of the vineyard. Sometimes I needed to visit their corner for my own practical needs, as well as conferring for professional reasons.

I told him that it does help to keep up with current research on the possible side effects of prescription drugs or illicit drug use when you are counselling someone with symptoms of depression. Would the drugs affect the ability to reason? The heart and the spirit have to be reached, along with the cognitive faculties. Will something physical stand in the way of that? Sometimes, the mood-altering effects of medication will mask or hide from the counsellor such things as grief and loss issues, the habit of projection (blaming others) or self-condemnation problems. There can also be deep roots of self-rejection and shame issues. Depressive symptoms can result from anger turned inwards. I let my protégé know that any emotions are welcomed in my own style of counselling as signposts to healing – especially overreactions.

I described myself as a 'spiritual heart doctor'. If medication is masking the signs, it is hard going. Anger needs to be exposed and dealt with. Ways of looking at, and handling emotions associated with the anger, need to be learnt and applied by the client. Anger is often an accompanying emotion to such feelings as disappointment, grief, frustration and rejection. Most counsellors agree that fear or hurt are the primary emotions and anger is a secondary reactionary feeling. Lies need to be exposed and truths applied. The roots of shame, rejection and self-hatred may need pulling out. Demonic forces may be hindering the healing. Deliverance ministry may be required.

My style of counselling, I said, also involves therapeutic techniques. My role can often be one of an educator to a person who is recovering from depression – educating into healthy, normal thinking patterns aligned to the Mind of Christ. I mentioned here that I often made spiritual adaptations of cognitive behavioural type techniques that I had learnt from my studies. However, I emphasized to my protégé that I was always careful to surrender myself to the anointing of the Holy Spirit when doing so.

> *For the chronically depressed, unwillingness to give up old habits is a major hurdle. This usually involves a long tedious program of re-education. I warned that he would also need to surrender himself to be a willing channel of God's deep love and patience. It is, indeed, a process of restoration and renewal. More complicated cases involving the mentally ill or demonically oppressed, can involve a team of carers for years. Encouragement and teaching of even the basic living skills for survival may be needed. This involves constant assurance of unconditional love.*
>
> *My protégé commented here that he had a heart for working with suicidal youth and survivors' support programs. I commended him for his aspirations and promised to give him further resources* from my files in this specialised area.*

Except where the author recounts her personal testimony, all characters and cases are fictitious representations and any similarities to real persons or cases are coincidental.

*See Appendix II for resources on suicide.

Counsellor Resource: DEPRESSION AS A MOOD DISORDER

> **Disclaimer: The author makes no claim to medical expertise or the qualifications to diagnose medical conditions. Information presented is issued to the layman (in layman's terms) from her personal experience and research. She accepts no personal responsibility for the use of misuse of this information. A government healthcare site can offer further resources and the most current information for research purposes.**

MOOD DISORDERS

We all experience changes in our state of mind and feelings described as *mood swings*. If others class us as being moody or temperamental, then we are usually giving out vibes, often described as sulky, sullen or gloomy, with a mix of more cheerful and happier periods. In the last generation, you were considered 'nervy' or 'moody'. Today, we have come a long way in understanding what we call 'disorders' and have various and complicated labels for these.

The clinical descriptions of mood disorders and personality disorders are as confusing as they are varied, and they have symptoms only identifiable to the trained eye. However, as Christian counsellors, you will definitely be dealing with those who are depressed and anxious, so it is wise to have a little background knowledge of these conditions.

Mood disorders are among the most common *psychological disorders*, and the risk of development is increasing worldwide. Symptoms of depression are increasing dramatically in our elderly population as well as diagnosed more often in the very young. Note that mood disorders in children are fundamentally similar to mood disorders in adults but require specialized treatment by those knowledgeable in child developmental stages.

> DISCLAIMER: This text is not intended as a means of disseminating medical advice. It contains references to other resources, which may provide related materials, treatments and information on depression. However, the content and practises of these parties are not the responsibility of the author.

TYPES OF CLINICAL DEPRESSION

The following depressive disorders are widely classified as *clinical depression* because they will usually require medical treatment and counselling.

> ➤ unipolar disorder
> ➤ bipolar disorder
> ➤ manic depression
> ➤ major depressive disorder
> ➤ dysthymic disorder

An individual who suffers from episodes of depression only, experiences *unipolar disorder*. An individual who alternates between depression (the down side) and mania (the euphoric high side) has a *bipolar disorder*. A manic-depressive state is when there is a mental disorder characterized by an alternation between extreme euphoria and deep depression (more than 'moodiness').

A person afflicted with this type of depression as a mental disorder is classed as a *manic depressive* who will require clinical medical attention. Mania, as a mental disorder, is characterized by 'great or violent excitement'; whereas, mania as an everyday display of emotion can be described as an enthusiasm for something – e.g. *he is a maniac when it comes to football*.

A less severe episode of mania that does not cause impairment in social or occupational functioning is a *hypomanic episode*. An episode of mania coupled with anxiety or depression at the same time is *dysphoric mania* or *a mixed episode*. The difference between the last two disorders *major depressive* and *dysthymic depression* or *dysthymia* is briefly touched on in the author's testimony at the end of this resource.

CAUSES

Approximately 20% of bereaved individuals experience pathological grief reaction, in which the normal grief response develops into a full-blown mood disorder. The incidence of suicide has been increasing in recent years, particularly amongst adolescents – for whom it is the third leading cause of death. A common contributing factor will be depression – either reactive or as a mood disorder.

Causes of disorders lie in a complex interaction of spiritual, biological, psychological, and social factors. From a biological perspective, researchers are particularly interested in the role of neurohormones. Psychological theories of depression focus on learned helplessness, generational role modelling and the depressive cognitive schemas, as well as interpersonal disruptions (relationships). Spiritual theories encompass generational curses resulting from personal and corporate sin, demonic oppression from involvement in freemasonry, witchcraft, idolatry and the occult; and interpersonal relationship problems (including man with God).

AUTHOR'S TESTIMONY

Dysthymic disorder interests me personally, as I believe I suffered from this form of depression as a child. It went undiagnosed and lasted well into my forties. The symptoms are somewhat milder than major depressive disorder (which has time-limited single or recurrent episodes) but they remain relatively unchanged over long periods.

As a child, I was always described as shy, nervy and moody – a loner. These days a young sufferer with similar symptoms to mine will undergo clinical treatment for depression and suicidal tendencies. However, my condition went unrecognised and untreated. I have never undergone any prolonged medical treatment for this condition to this day. Neither did my father who obviously was a sufferer.

The interesting thing is that I owe my great interest in spiritual counselling to the personal benefits of prayer ministry – mainly relating to the complex presenting problems associated with my chronic depression. Through the spirit-led application of the concepts based on Biblical principles presented in this text the Lord has graciously freed me to be the person I am today.

Footnote: To the many dedicated colleagues and friends who have contributed to my healing in this area, I send my love and gratitude out to you all. In particular, my deepest gratitude goes to my longsuffering husband for standing by his 'moody' girlfriend, then wife, in the early days.

TREATMENTS FOR MOOD DISORDERS

A variety of biological and psychological **clinical treatments** provide *short term effectiveness* for mood disorders. For those individuals who do not respond to antidepressant drugs and psychosocial treatments, a more dramatic physical treatment, electroconvulsive therapy (ECT) is applied for specific problems.

For *long term effectiveness,* there are **psychosocial treatments** such as cognitive therapy (CT) or Cognitive Behavioural Therapy (CBT), Rational Emotive Behavioural Therapy (REBT) and Interpersonal Therapy (IPT). These do seem effective in treating depressive disorders; however, relapse and recurrence of mood disorders are common in the long term. Treatment efforts must be made on maintenance to prevent relapse or recurrence.

When Christ (JC) sets us free we are free indeed! Experientially, the author has found that it is **spiritual treatment** which serves to *most effectively* release from bondages contributing to depression. This comes via restoration and deliverance ministry. Application of the Word of God, a closer walk with the Father, and establishing positive healing relationships within a Christian fellowship, serves to maintain the freedom. (2Tim 2:26, Jer 29:10-14, Ps 1:1-5)

Counsellor Resource: DEPRESSION AS A CLINICAL DISORDER

Depression is commonly assessed by the length of time the symptoms have been experienced without relief; this involves more than simply feeling pessimistic, down or gloomy. If you personally feel that your ministry to a client is not having the desired results spiritually, as the client remains unresponsive, unmotivated and incapable of making changes, then you should probably consider that depression has gone beyond normal reactive responses to circumstances. (See section on *Reactive Depression).*

If the client expresses that symptoms have lasted longer than two weeks and it is becoming harder to carry on normal daily tasks, then the following quiz (see *Client Handout: Self-Evaluation Quiz – Depression)* could be offered. This will create awareness that there could possibly be a mood disorder present; however classification as *clinical depression* needs evaluation professionally by the appropriate and qualified health practitioner.

This does not necessarily mean that prayer ministry or formal counselling needs to be totally discontinued. Perhaps more specialist help needs to complement your ministrations for a time. These days the medical profession is quite amenable to working alongside counsellors (sometimes referred to as *allied health professionals).* Remember it is not your business to diagnose a psychological disorder or a physical complaint. You are simply acting as a bridging agent for your client to gain access to further help.

If your client is not confident enough to speak up to his or her doctor, or, is anxious about going in alone for an appointment, it may be possible to brief a close friend or relative to take on the role of advocate. Probably the most expedient and effective way of operating is to use the formal structure of referrals as described in this text under *Office Procedure*. A busy medical practitioner will appreciate precise (and concise) information received via letters and forms. Do not suggest nor state a diagnosis; briefly report the main troubling symptoms (see *Sample Referral Letter*).

The general practitioner will then refer on to a psychologist or psychiatrist if necessary. Your client can keep you informed of the treatment and progress made. The doctor will not contact you as the referee due to patient confidentiality. However, prior to any advocacy, make sure you have your client sign suitable documentation (see *Informed Consent/Authority to Disclose Information/Advocacy Authorization*) so that you are able to freely and appropriately disclose any problems (such as suicide ideation) with the doctor if necessary (see your local governing requirements for *mandatory reporting* situations).

SPECIAL NOTE

The following is a quiz/test devised by the author for use in her own practice. It is not a clinical assessment. This set of questions is a tool to encourage a client to discuss personal emotional problems, particularly those associated with grief issues. This helps generally evaluate whether a client <u>could</u> be in need of help in the form of a more formal clinical assessment for depression and/or anxiety problems. It is also useful to issue again following clinical treatment to monitor a client's state during follow-up sessions with you.

Disclaimer: The author makes no claim to medical expertise or the qualifications to diagnose medical conditions. Information presented is issued to the layman (in layman's terms) from her personal experience and research. She accepts no personal responsibility for the use of misuse of this information.

Client Handout #1: SELF-EVALUATION QUIZ – DEPRESSION

Tick the boxes if you have continuously experienced any of the following symptoms OVER THE PAST 4 WEEKS. Where there are a variety of choices, tick the box and underline or highlight appropriate others.

- ❑ I have felt sad, flat, and empty, down or low most of the time.
- ❑ I have isolated myself physically and emotionally from most people and have stopped going out unless I have to.
- ❑ I feel irritated, edgy and agitated, especially when around those I love.

❑ I have lost interest and pleasure in the activities I usually enjoy.

❑ I have not been reading my Bible, going to church or praying.

❑ I have to force myself to work or remain at any task and finish it.

❑ I have difficulty concentrating, thinking clearly, or making decisions.

❑ I do not feel like eating/ I have been overeating.

❑ I have had trouble dropping off to sleep/have had trouble staying asleep/have been waking up too early/have been sleeping too much.

❑ I have been overactive, wound up, restless and cannot settle on anything or make decisions easily.

❑ I am speaking and moving slower (generally slowed down),

❑ I am constantly tired and lack the energy I used to have.

❑ I am constantly on the verge of tears/I have been crying a lot.

❑ I feel things are only going to get worse; that there is no hope.

❑ I have been feeling worthless, useless, embarrassed and ashamed.

❑ God seems far away from me and uninterested in my world and me.

❑ I have been looking back at past failures/having regrets/blaming me for everything.

❑ I feel guilty and ashamed of myself most of the time.

❑ I feel like giving up and running away from it all.

❑ I am thinking about death and having bad dreams and/or nightmares.

❑ I want to end it all; I have been contemplating suicide.

> **IMPORTANT: If you have ticked one or all of the last three factors, you should seek both medical and spiritual attention immediately. Be open and honest about how you feel and do not downplay any of your symptoms/concerns.**

If you have checked a total of five or more boxes you could possibly be experiencing some type of depression at this stage of your life. First, tell a close friend or family member that you are having problems coping with life in general. If you like, share your quiz results. If you are told to '*cheer up*', '*snap out of it*' or some trite phrase is offered such as '*surely it's not that bad*', speak to someone else who <u>will</u> take you seriously. The next thing you should do is to tell your doctor. Do not be fearful about taking the quiz along. Book a double appointment so that the doctor will have sufficient time to speak with you, do some tests, or compose referral documents.

Some serious medical conditions, and even medications, can cause similar symptoms to depression and can even produce depression/anxiety. If your doctor does not have the time or interest in treating you to your satisfaction, book another appointment. This time, take a friend, spouse or parent as your advocate. If this fails, then it could be time to seek the service of another health care professional (a 'second opinion').

Client Handout #2 REACTIVE DEPRESSION FROM STRESSORS

As indicated by the name, reactive type depression develops from reaction to circumstances, or social and environmental stressors. A depressed state is triggered by a sudden significant life event, such as losing a job, a relationship breakdown, the death of a significant other, or physical or emotional trauma. Depression can also result from ongoing stressors, which eventually take a toll from the cumulative effect. For example, various disappointments in life may serve to lower self-esteem, or constant frustrations may result in despair.

OVERLOAD REACTION

God designed our bodies to handle only so much stress. When we absorb as much as we can take, depression acts like an electrical circuit breaker. If we overload the mental, physical and emotional systems, we have a protective natural mechanism, which God has designed to force us to 'turn off' when we are faced with overload. This is to allow time to restore emotional energy in order to cope with stressful circumstances.

MEDICATION

Medication on a temporary basis will sometimes give a kick-start to the circuit again, but looking for slower and more natural ways to health can be a lot more beneficial in the long term. Natural means such as changes in lifestyle and thought processing, will serve to strengthen our cognitive, emotional and spiritual coping mechanisms for the future. Be aware that some medications such as sleeping tablets, sedatives and anti-depressants may cause serious side effects in some sensitive individuals, especially if the dosages and patient application are not monitored. As the patient, you must take an active role in co-operating and self-monitoring and this is acknowledged as difficult when you are in a depressed state.

BENEFITS OF THE CONDITION

A depressed state in reaction to special circumstances can be beneficial overall if understood and experienced spiritually as a positive life lesson. Perhaps for the first time, we are dealing with a certain problem in an honest, realistic way. Admitting things are out of control can draw us into deeper dependence on God and His power to help us overcome in a distressing situation. We are sometimes forced into soul-searching and into making some practical adjustments in lifestyle.

The state of reactive depression usually means we have come to the end of our own resources and are ready to seek some outside help. Positive introspection (rather than self-condemnation) should help us to come out the other side a better person. Physical and emotional rest, coupled with a break from current stressful circumstances, will allow for positive introspection. Possibilities are: – respite care, a spiritual retreat, a complete holiday from work, or simply some time alone with God to resolve say, unforgiveness or grief issues.

SYMPTOMS

Sometimes a break or time out will be forced upon us by ill health and the inability to continue with employment or other activities. This can be humbling and baffling to our once independent and resourceful selves. Disappointment, due to our expectations not being fulfilled, might produce an aura of sadness which often lingers and pervades. Perhaps abstractness and an emotional flatness might be observable to the onlooker. The sufferer could become steeped in self-pity or exude resentment and irritability. Anger can be a problem – either turned outwards or in on self. Some sufferers experience an inability to find pleasure in anything (*anhedonia*) and describe feeling empty and numb – as *'having a black hole inside'*. Other common descriptions are, *'a dark cloud over me'* or *'something dogging my steps'*.

SORROW VS GRIEF

Grief and *sorrow* are powerful forces. If these two emotions are not validated, real damage can ensue. Feelings need recognition and identification so that emotions are labelled correctly and distinguished one from the other. Sorrow, for instance, serves to release pain, so should not be dismissed or cast out, as you would a demon. Sorrow is a natural expression of regret, loss and hurt, and, if not denied or repressed, is of great benefit. Grief, however, is a poignant sense of loss, that can become deep and abiding if the wounds and pain are not faced and healed. Sorrow might come and go as a visitor would. However, grief welcomed as a 'visitor', might remain to take up residence and then mature into chronic *clinical depression.*

Reactive depression can also involve a process of grieving over a real or perceived loss. The standard stages of grief – initial shock, the denial, arguing with God over the unfairness, frustration, anger and fearfulness – could be experienced. Comfort, through connection with God and supportive others, is needed. Sometimes, deep grief might become a spiritual *stronghold* in a person. A *spirit of grief* can sometimes enter the vulnerable person in a chronically depressed condition, making its home as an *oppressive spirit*, which is difficult to fight or shake off,

When reactive depression does occur, it is wise to become proactive so that it does not become an accepted part of life. Even when we least feel like it, we need to make a choice not to allow this condition to develop any further than the allotted time it takes to do its work. With the right practical and spiritual support, most people can start feeling well again within a few weeks. Christian counselling coupled with cognitive therapy is highly recommended for the reactive type of depression. With prayer ministry, deeper needs can be recognised and met; wounds carefully revisited and healed. We might need to seek forgiveness for holding on to burdens. With therapy based on Biblical precepts, we can learn to walk in our blood-bought freedom.

Assistance is available for reactive type depression:

1. **Objective Counselling** Someone emotionally uninvolved and objective (whether lay or professional) who can listen, counsel and offer sound advice on coping with the situation as it stands e.g. financial advisor, relationship therapist or prayer minister.

2. **Trusted Friends** Choose those who will listen empathetically and stand by you to see you through this period without judgment. Be careful not to place all the responsibility on one friend only – a network of carers is advisable.

3. **Pastoral Support** Find suitable spiritual guidance and encouragement to be assured that this kind of problem is common to others and of a temporal nature. Many have found private comfort through prayer and the scriptures, alongside emotional and practical support (rather than being 'preached at').

4. **Prayer Ministry Practitioners** Roots and lies could be contributing to the depressed state. These specific troublemakers need to be located and dealt with (e.g. *'I am of no value any longer because I am unable to work'* or, *'the shame of my helplessness is too much to bear'*).

5. **Medical Professionals** Medical help should be sought for associated physical complaints (such as headaches, sleep disturbances and chronic tiredness) and needs to be combined with general health care counsel, for relaxation, nutritional advice and an exercise program. Antidepressants are prescribed only if the reactive depression remains long after the environmental or circumstantial stressors have been alleviated.

6. **Allied Health Professionals** Consult a therapist who can contribute different ideas and techniques to help alter stimulus and response affects; that is, someone who can show you how to respond in a constructive way, rather than reacting negatively to your circumstances. This will help strengthen you to cope with future stressful conditions.

Disclaimer: The author makes no claim to medical expertise or the qualifications to diagnose medical conditions. Information presented is issued to the layman (in layman's terms) from her personal experience and research. She accepts no personal responsibility for the use of misuse of this information. Government healthcare sites can offer further resources and the most current information for research purposes.

MENTAL HEALTH RESOURCE SITES:

Included below is a sampling of internet sites (Australian only) for your personal research purposes.

www.beyondblue.org.au
www.ybblue.com.au
www.headspace.org.au
www.bluepages.anu.edu.au
www.crufad.unsw.edu.au
www.infrapsych.com
www.moodgym.anu.edu.au
www.reachout.com.au
www.kidshelp.com.au
www.blackdoginstitute.org.au

CHAPTER EIGHT

DEALING WITH ANXIETY

Another complicated emotion is dealt with here in a practical manner. Varied aspects of anxiety such as, the thought life that stimulates tension, role modelling received from childhood, and the perplexing condition called panic disorder, are covered. The concentration is not so much on diagnosis but on helping to understand how to deal with vulnerable souls who are prone to worrying and fearfulness.

     Client testimonial of long term care using a variety of therapies
     How intrusive thoughts contribute to anxiety and panic disorders
     Practical help for the sufferer including self-help techniques
     Handling anxiety and other obsessions using drama & imagery
     Legacy of Fear testimony

Study Notes

CLIENT TESTIMONIAL: *The Angel Lady*

What's a girl to do when she's so self-conscious that she can't ever eat in public without worrying over whether she has food on her face? How normal is a person who is so scared of being with someone (anyone) – scared of what to say and do, what not to say or do and whether she can say anything at all – that she just wants to curl up and die?

That's what it was like for me most of my life; except, it got worse at 15 after my dad died. Then I just couldn't handle it anymore and I did think that the world was just too scary to cope with. I just wanted to die too.

Then this lady came along. I call her my Angel. It was like she was sent from God to reach out and touch me, right deep in my heart. She just came at the right time. I met her at church. I was sitting up the back where the light is always poor – my usual spot – with my back against the wall and right at the end of the aisle close to the door. It was the best spot in the whole place because, when I felt like I just couldn't breathe and my heart was pounding in my chest and I thought someone was going to notice how much I was sweating, then I knew I could escape. Mum knew she could find me behind the tree out the back after I had a panic attack. She always noticed - from her place out front with the other singers on the worship team. At least I had someone who noticed I was not there. No one else cared.

But this day, 2 years ago, just after my 16th birthday, God showed me He cared by sending me so kind a person. How many times I had sat wanting someone to ask me why I was alone! But then, I'd be worrying that someone would want to talk to me; and that I would make a fool of myself because I didn't know how to tell them what was worrying me. I just worry. Mum calls it 'ruminating'. I get a thought in my head and I go over and over it from all angles. Like when I thought 'I had hurt that nice girl Alison's' feelings when she showed me her painting. I lay awake for over two whole hours that Friday night thinking about what I said, and what I could and should have said to make it up to her. I woke up late morning still worrying over hurting her with the silly comment I made. I decided back then that perhaps I should just never answer anyone at all when they asked my opinion on anything.

But, I'm so glad I spoke back to the angel lady that day! I really believe I would be dead now if I hadn't. All she said was, 'Your name is Genevieve isn't it? Would you like me to pray for you?' I nodded and that was the start of it. She told me that she was a Christian counsellor and liked to pray for people. Said it was her passion or something.

She sat next to me in morning church service for six whole weeks in a row! Just sat next to me, smiling and nodding in that knowing way and always saying when she got up that she was praying for me. Then she invited me to come see her (with my Mum's permission of course) for proper prayer ministry. I was totally scared; my mother had to come with me for the first three sessions. After that, I was OK. I could hardly wait until each Wednesday because she taught me so much about myself and about my problem of always being afraid of everything and my habit of worrying. She used the words anxiety and panic disorders and she showed me I had something that could be treated with some techniques she had learnt from the counselling course she had done.

What she did in her studies was something called cognitive behavioural therapy. She said that it involves thinking and behaving properly. She explained how well this therapy works with Christians because we know about Jesus and about having our minds renewed by the Bible and the Holy Spirit. Basically, she said that I thought in a negative way and that this was causing all my fears and anxiety. She said she would help me to think differently. Then, I wouldn't be like a scared rabbit all the time. She drew this picture of a rabbit on the road and said that bunny was like me – too scared to get off the road when a car was coming. She asked if I wanted to be a bunny and that stuck in my head.

After praying over me to begin each session, she taught me stuff like that with diagrams and what she called 'teachings' God had showed her. She taught the lessons to me, because she said that she had tried them; they worked and that made her feel closer to God. She taught me practical things, like, when I felt I had a panic attack coming on; I was to notice my physical symptoms like the sweating and awful tight feeling in my chest. Then I could breathe in a certain way and tell myself certain things to calm myself down.

I was surprised to learn that everyone talks to themselves and that some people always think and talk negatively. She gave me examples of positive self-talk and little jokes I could make like, 'Genevieve, you are such a drama queen!' So I could make fun of myself in a nice way. She always makes me laugh during our sessions.

It's been two years since I first met her and I don't have to go so often now because, you see, I do have a life. On my 18th birthday, I met this cool guy Larry and he helps me heaps with putting into practice what I've learnt from Mrs Collins. Larry sees that she helped me to set goals for myself when I first started going there. He agrees with her that the Bible says that 'without a vision the people perish'. So, guess what my goal was? It was to have a boyfriend like Larry.

This seemed totally impossible to me back then. I was too shy and afraid to talk to anyone but my Mum and Mrs Collins. But I had to start with the small stuff – little goals first. It's called 'gradual desensitisation' or some such thing. I started very small by agreeing to face my fears of being with people. I began by practising talking to myself in the mirror as if I were a stranger. Then I promised

Mrs Collins that I would speak to five complete strangers on the street. All I had to do was smile and just say 'hi', but it was awful! I was petrified. But I did it, to please her.

I asked her what my mother meant when she said I was a 'ruminator' because it really hurt me when she said that ... I thought she meant that I was like a cow. Mrs C gave me this funny little smile and explained that it is 'the tendency to think a lot about feelings, rather than to do something practical about them'. She said that Mum probably meant that I dwell on how badly I am feeling and that she agreed with my mother that I over-analyse my own personality. And I do admit that I obsess over all the possible meanings and consequences of whatever is upsetting me. She called me a pessimist and I didn't like that either! I went straight home to look it up in the dictionary.

Then she had me learn not to generalize, catastrophize and all the other stuff – the stuff I used to worry with, before she let me loose into the world. She even went to the shops with me to start me off facing my fear of asking people for directions. It was kind' a fun when we both actually did get lost trying to get out of the plaza. She was like a little kid herself. We laughed and laughed all the way home.

It was no laughing matter though when we did 'The Big Prayer Session'. She saw in her spirit that I was actually troubled by this demonic thing that kept taunting me to keep me scared. I think she called it a 'mocking spirit'. I cried my eyes out with relief, because I saw that it wasn't all me that was causing my problems. I felt so much better after she prayed that one away! Then she prayed for my beautiful dad who died trying to save me from drowning in the surf that day. I had a lot of guilt and fear about that and I'd never told anyone, not even Mum, that I felt it was all my fault.

You know what? I saw Jesus with my spirit eyes that session, just like Mrs C. does. Jesus (who I know, knows everything) told me personally that it wasn't my fault and not to be afraid anymore. He looked so kind and comforting. I could have looked in his eyes forever.

I started to feel good about myself after the big prayer session and that's when I met Larry at the video store... but that's a long story. When I have more time, I'll have to tell you. I'm going to a huge concert tonight and I want to get right up front. So, I told Larry and all the others that we have to get there at least an hour early. No more dark corners near the exit signs for me!

Except where the author recounts her personal testimony, all characters and cases are fictitious representations and any similarities to real persons or cases are non-intentional and purely coincidental.

Client Handout #1: ANXIETY, FEARS & INTRUSIVE THOUGHTS

Intrusive thoughts (in the sense we will now be looking into) are the unwanted, involuntary thoughts accompanying fearful or anxious feelings. These thoughts and ideas are usually irrational and described as *faulty thinking* or *automatic negative thoughts*. They range from a fleeting intrusion, to unremitting obsession and can develop into panic attacks. Fear of further attacks might lead to *panic disorders*. If you are experiencing panic attacks or obsessive thought patterns, ask your counsellor for further resources.

Anxiety is a state of uneasiness or tension caused by fear of possible misfortune or danger. Like fear and pain, anxiety can be a natural protective mechanism to keep you primed and ready for action, for either a *fight or flight* response. Feeling anxious prepares you for what is ahead, which is not necessarily a bad thing as it may lead you to plan or rehearse for stressors so that you will not *freeze*. It may help you to avoid a shock or increase your *resilience* (ability to overcome) and *hardiness* (ability to withstand).

ANXIETY AS A DISORDER

When anxiety is not resolved, the suspected danger is constantly anticipated, rehearsed and 'worried over'. Worrying becomes habitual and stressful and may develop into an *anxiety disorder*. Faulty and irrational thinking patterns, physical sensations and *compulsive behaviours,* may accompany disorders.

- ❑ avoidance of feared places and situations
- ❑ obsessive compulsions (attempts to control and avoid danger)
- ❑ intrusive thoughts can become obsessive
- ❑ dependency on others in order to seek protection and reassurance
- ❑ excessive fears and timidity
- ❑ addictions – self-medication via drugs, sex, work, exercise, alcohol, shopping, talking, food, self-abuse, anger

10 STEPS TOWARDS RESOLUTION

1. **Face your fears.** Avoid avoidance. Satan wants to use your fear of fear to keep you captive. Resist Satan and he will flee from you. Learn everything there is to know about faith versus fear and a loving God who protects and cares for you (1 Pet 5:7). Use a Bible concordance and reference key words such as *anxious* and *fear*.

2. **Walk the walk of faith.** Do not wait for the anxiety to abate. Do things whilst afraid or anxious. Do not allow fear to immobilize you. Fight back! Be proactive. Become more objective – problem and solution focused rather than emotion focused. Research the problem as if it is happening to a friend. Imagine you are gathering resources in order to help your friend and playact what you would say.

3. **Understand the problem.** Learn everything there is to know about anxiety. Fear of the unknown is often the problem. Understand how anxiety affects your body. Resource government health sites online, then discuss your findings with your medical doctor, therapist or spiritual counsellor.

4. **Learn from overcomers.** Speak to others who have conquered their fears. Ask for practical pointers as to how to strengthen your resiliency. Personalise their stories to suit your own needs so that you will acquire an effective coping style of your own. Be sure to concentrate on their victories, rather than past sufferings; otherwise you will be further burdened with thoughts of what could happen to you!

5. **Choose a medical mentor.** Look for accessible, consistent medical support – a local family doctor who will listen to your concerns. Ideally, choose a GP or psychologist who will be at liberty to pray with you on request. If your anxiety is chronic and/or acute, get properly diagnosed and be supported medically by specialists in the mental health field.

6. **Seek specialist support.** Seek therapy to give you one-on-one support via a therapist-client relationship. Make sure it is someone who uses CBT (Cognitive Behavioural Therapy) techniques. Alternately, consult a REBT (Rational Emotive Behavioural Therapy) practitioner. If you cannot afford professional therapy, use an interactive website recommended by your doctor.

7. **Seek holistic healing.** Seek spiritual help alongside the emotional, cognitive and physical, and all areas will benefit. Your prime directive is to eliminate your faulty thinking habits. Every thought creates a mood. Every mood affects your bodily functions. If your body is suffering, then every other aspect of your life may be affected.

8. **Come into alignment.** Your spirit man should be in command of your soul, which comprises thoughts, emotions and choices. If your spirit is born again, then it has dominion rights over your body and soul. Your spirit is rightfully the master of your mind, moods and bodily functions.

9. **Get deliverance from fear.** Undergo prayer ministry to challenge and deal with the basic lies you have believed both spiritually and cognitively. Use a journal and worksheet to challenge your faulty thinking patterns. Ask God directly for insight as to how you are breaking His command to *'fear not'* and seek to understand why God's perfect love seems unavailable to you.

10. **Deal with the roots.** Seek spiritual support and inner healing for the root causes of your anxiety. Learn positive thoughts based on scriptures to displace the intrusive thoughts with truths such as: *God is love*; *his perfect love drives out all my fears* and *I cast (throw) all my cares onto him*. Use personal affirmations such as: *I trust in God to protect and care for me.*

Client Handout #2: PANIC ATTACKS

Be conscious that anxiety (like pain) is a ***natural biological response*** that serves a purpose to protect you, rather than to harm you. Accept panic as an overreaction - only a temporary aberration (brief lapse in control of one's thoughts or feelings).

Be aware of ***defensive physiological signs*** such as 'pins and needles' in toes and fingers, or claustrophobic feelings (including being 'smothered'), as normal biological symptoms generated by anxiety and fear. However, stop monitoring and focusing on the physical signs.

Use an ***objective approach*** – as if the symptoms are something happening to something material (a body) rather than the real you (your inner man or spirit). Take an interest and be curious; however, depersonalise the experience. Do not become emotionally involved in what is happening to the body.

Various self-help techniques can be learned to resist and eliminate panic attacks:

The best course of action is to develop ***physical control skills*** prior to an attack in order to deal rationally rather than emotively with an incident when it does occur. For example, slow your breathing down – 3 seconds to take air in and 3 seconds out. Use the second hand of a watch to monitor and try to practise 2-3 times per day. Learn how to relax parts of your body that retain tension, for instance, purposely tightening and then loosening jaw or shoulder muscles.

Learn the concepts of ***cognitive behavioural techniques***. Make rational thinking a habit. Using self-talk in order to keep in touch with reality; challenge your thoughts and feelings by rehearsing a possible scenario. For example: *So what! It's only anxiety; it's not going to kill me. I can deal with this. What is the worst thing that could happen to me? I could faint and then feel embarrassed afterwards. I can be fine with that. No big deal. If that actually does happen, it wouldn't be the end of the world for me.*

Ask questions to ***challenge self*** : –

a)   *Have I really used my faith and the scriptures?* Quote the relevant scriptures out aloud and apply them.
b)   *Have I underestimated my own ability to cope?* Recall times when you have coped in the past.
c)   *Have I asked someone for help?* God will supply all your needs including those capable of helping you. He also helps those who help themselves. Be proactive.
d)   *Why am I scared?* Take a reality check. Look for evidence as to why you should be anxious. Examine whether the things you have been fearful of in the past have actually come about.

Review past experiences and ask more questions: –

How many times has a panic attack actually taken place?
Am I making the problem larger by overanalysing?
Am I making progress yet not giving due attention to it?
When have the physical signs occurred and a panic attack did not follow?

Look at the possibility that your symptoms (physical signs of panic) are caused by something material, e.g. *I drank strong coffee, ate chilli while lying on my back on the couch, and then, I got up too quickly.*

Make a list of all the things that personally cause you anxiety – from the least to the worst. Set tasks to overcome the associated anxiety slowly (***graded exposure***). Be patient with yourself and do not be embarrassed or ashamed to reach for help when you need to. ***Journal your feelings*** for two whole weeks and ***strengthen yourself spiritually*** with the Word of God (Lk 12:1–31). You are meant to be free from anxiety and living life to the full.

Avoid artificial fixes such as burying yourself in work or using alcohol or pills. Rather, distract yourself with a spiritual or creative activity, which uses a different part of your brain.

Lastly, tap into your sense of humour. Laugh at yourself! Have some fun. ***Play with the physical sensations***, e.g. hyperventilate on purpose during non-worry periods. The purpose of playing with the symptoms is to render them harmless, to consider as trivia rather than perceived threats. You can spin or breathe fast, put your head between knees – then bob up. Do so until you become bored with the game.

DISCLAIMER: The preceding text is not intended as a means of disseminating medical advice. It contains references to resources, which provide related materials, treatments and information on anxiety. However, the content and practices of these parties are not the responsibility of the author.

Please respect copyright. Master copies of resources found within this publication are provided for your use in the companion book: 'So You Want To Be A Christian Counsellor – Resources Handbook' - www.prayercounsel.com.

Counsellor Resource: ANXIETY & PANIC AS DISORDERS

The following is a resource composed for the counsellor towards a better understanding of the extreme anxiety sufferers feel who experience panic as a disorder. Many of us have experienced circumstances when we have lost control; where we have had a critical period or episode when we are suddenly overwhelmed by terror or anxious thoughts and feelings. This overwhelming fear can be a once only experience for the average person – usually described as *being panic-stricken* or *feeling overwhelmed'*

Fear takes over and we cannot function normally, for example, when learning to drive, or during a job interview, or in the middle of a crucial exam. For the average person these are normal experiences, to endure and to overcome. For someone in the grip of anxiety in the form of a disorder, the position is reversed; the fear of becoming overwhelmed with fear is a 'normal' experience.

It is helpful to remember the following: *panic* becomes a disorder when episodes are more frequent and evolve into fearful anticipation of the next attack. The disorder involves '*fearing the fear*'.

CLIENT PREDISPOSITION & VULNERABILITY FACTORS

- ❏ inherited vulnerability to stress and tension
- ❏ learnt response and behaviour patterns
- ❏ negative caretakers as role models in life
- ❏ neuro-biologically overactive to daily events (overly 'body aware')
- ❏ very sensitive emotionally, shy and introverted
- ❏ faulty thinking patterns, belief systems and mindsets
- ❏ chemical imbalance (lack of serotonin)
- ❏ environmental factors such as long periods of stress
- ❏ rejection or unawareness of God's protective power

PRODUCT OF LEARNED BEHAVIOUR

These disorders have become learned (behaviours) via cues. For example, when anxious and fearful, a sufferer might regularly notice a change in heartbeat rate and sweaty palms prior to experiencing panic. This same person might notice their heart pounding when exercising and take this as an *internal cue* for a panic attack. This is a *conditioned response*; normal bodily functions are misconstrued by the mind as an emergency alarm.

Or, an *external cue* can be experienced. For example, a previous panic attack could have occurred at a supermarket; therefore, the sufferer could feel another might happen if he or she is to venture there again. There is a conditioned fear response whenever thoughts of the supermarket occur. Eventually, the thought of going anywhere at all induces anxiety and fear. This can lead to *agoraphobia* – an abnormal dread of open spaces, or claustrophobia – the fear of confined spaces, and so on.

Key Symptom: habitual reflexive response to familiar cues.
Solution: replace the destructive habitual response with verbal confession of God's goodness, loyalty and faithfulness.

> ➤ *No matter where I am, and whatever happens to me, God will look after me. God is not a man who lies or changes his mind (Heb 6:17-19, Num 23:19, Tit 1:1-3).*
> ➤ *He has promised to be there for me and he <u>will</u> be by my side wherever I go. Whatever comes up we will handle it together. God is on my side. My mind, my body and my emotions will be at peace whenever I think of him.*

CREATION OF A PANIC DISORDER

A sufferer's irrational thought processes could develop from, *'I just know something terrible is going to happen';* to examination of physical symptoms, *'I feel so hot and my heartbeat is racing faster and faster';* concluding with, *'I might have a heart attack and die!'* To the onlooker, this could seem an extreme reaction, but it is commonplace to a sufferer of panic attacks to believe the worst possible outcome. It is theorised that people with psychological vulnerability are those who interpret normal physical sensations as dangerous and are more open to developing panic disorder.

Focused anxiety creates the panic symptoms. Occasional unexpected panic attacks are common. They might occur during intense stress periods but most people will not develop undue anxiety over an attack. The average person will probably be alarmed initially but will eventually put it down to natural causes such as an argument, a bad day, or work overload. Generally, a person will get over it and get on with a normal life. However, a small percentage will be anxious over the prospect of future attacks. In these cases, the anxiety can lead to the development of a *panic disorder.*

Key Symptom: Quick interpretation of normal as dangerous.
Solution: Rational thinking based on spiritual concepts.

> ➤ *God has not given us the spirit of fear. He endows with power and love and a sound mind (2 Tim 1:7).*
> ➤ *If our minds are kept on the Lord, He promises to keep us in perfect peace – free from anxious thoughts (Isa 26:3).*
> ➤ *Bring every thought into alignment (obedience) to the mind of Christ (2Cor 10:5b). We are repeatedly told <u>not</u> to fear; but to trust.*
> ➤ *It is the supernatural peace of God that keeps us safe and free because of our faith* in what Jesus has done for us via the Cross (Phil 4:7).*

THE CYCLIC EFFECT

The same could be said of both panic and anxiety disorders, in that the person could misinterpret normal physical sensations such as bleary vision caused by strain or tiredness as a disease leading to loss of eyesight. The person worries. The choice to worry leads to actual stress related physical sensations such as sweating and heart palpitations. Extreme anxiety over the physical symptoms could lead to a panic attack, which leads to more anxiety over the possibility of further attacks. Thus, physical sensations, emotions and thoughts interact in a cyclic effect and escalate to become out of control.

Anxiety's natural purpose is to caution and to protect. Panic is a sudden overwhelming feeling of terror or anxiety. It is interesting to note that panic is believed to be biologically different from anxiety in that there are different locations in the brain responsible for anxiety and panic.

Key Symptom: Panic manifested as a biological response.
Solution: The force of *faith can counteract this response.

> ➢ *The victory is by means of our faith* in a God who keeps us safe (1Jn 5).*
> ➢ *We are to be still (at peace and calm) and know that He is in control (Ps 45:10a).*
> ➢ *Like the psalmist, we are to be ready to put our faith* and trust in the Lord so that we will never be confused (Ps 71:1).*
> ➢ *There is a promise that God is always faithful to make a way to escape from any common temptation to man (1Cor 10:13).*

---

*"Faith is not the product of reason; it is the product of the reborn human spirit. It is not the product of the mind but the product of the heart. Faith is a power force. It is a tangible force. It is a conductive force. It will move things. Faith will change things. Faith will change the human body. It will change the human mind. It will change the human heart. Faith will change circumstances ... every man that has been born again has had this faith put inside of him.' Kenneth Copeland, 'The Force of Faith' 1992

TREATMENTS FOR DISORDERS

a) **Application of Spiritual Concepts.** There is much to learn spiritually on the subjects of fear and anxiety. Work to overcome the fear of fear. Sound spiritual counselling is essential. For those experiencing more than an occasional panic attack, it is wise to seek help from a Christian mental health worker. Do not rely totally on medical or psychological treatment. Take a holistic approach. Basically these disorders can become disorders through disconnection with our Maker through spiritual immaturity and unresolved conflicts. Spiritual roots to the problem need to be found and treated spiritually.

b) **Medication.** 60% of those with panic disorder are free of panic if remaining medicated on tricyclics (antidepressants). However, be aware that there is serious addiction potential with the use of tranquillisers (called benzodiazepines). Anti-depressants are preferred, but the right type to suit the individual sufferer needs to be administered and monitored skilfully as there can be serious side effects from these in vulnerable metabolisms. This is also the case with medication used to help the anxious to sleep.

Note that sufferers treated with medication alone (without complementary forms of care) have high rates of relapse.

c) **Cognitive Behavioural Type Therapies (CBT)**. Coping skills need to be taught in order to modify conditioned responses so that panic attacks do not reoccur. Therapy is conducted with or without short-term medication. Learning personal skills to control and deal with panic attacks so that they do not become cyclic is the better approach. Panic attacks are considered more physical than cognitive. Note that it becomes a disorder when there is a cognitive and emotional focus on the next possible attack. Clinical trials show that 70%-90% of people who receive good mental health assistance remain free of panic attacks.

d) **Exposure Based Treatment**. This is where conditions are arranged for gradually facing feared situations in order to overcome avoidance. These conditions are combined with education in anxiety coping mechanisms – learned breathing styles, retraining of responses and relaxation techniques. Graded exposure is best applied as part of CBT.

e) **Panic Control Threat Treatment**. This is where mini attacks can be created in a clinical situation e.g. exercises are done to step up heart rate or the client is spun in a chair to cause dizziness. Cognitive therapy identifies basic attitudes and perceptions of fears; the previously learned behaviour is modified. There can be as much as an 80-100% success rate after 12 weekly sessions with treatment by an advanced skills therapist.

f) **Desensitisation through Graded Exposure**. This treatment is for specific object or situational fear type phobias e.g. to snakes, spiders or flying. Most sufferers tend to have multiple phobias of several types. Females outnumber males 4:1. Situational phobia is where people never experience panic attacks outside the context of the phobic object or situation. However, with panic disorder one can never relax as an attack could happen at any time – even during sleep. (Note that, if only passing fears exist that do not substantially interfere with lifestyle, then a condition is not classed as a phobia). *If we listen to (obey) God, we will live in safety and peace (Prv1:33). We will declare (in faith*) that we will not be afraid at night or by day of being attacked (Ps 91:5).*

DISCLAIMER: The preceding text is not intended as a means of disseminating medical advice. It contains references to resources, which provide related materials, treatments and information on anxiety. However, the content and practices of these parties are not the responsibility of the author.

COUNSELLING ONLINE

There may be circumstances where your client cannot physically come into your place of ministry due to their condition (such as anxiety) or circumstances (such as moving overseas). There is no need to refer on to another carer or to put therapy on hold. With the modern facilities available, such as emailing, telephone access and audiovisual means, a session can still be conducted. As long as the professional boundaries are set initially, and adhered to from both sides, emailing can be an especially effective method of counselling.

Rather than the expense of phone calls, home visits and the slow passage of ordinary postage, with emailing you have ready access to all your resources on file to be able to transfer through as attachments. You also have time to research or pray about particular issues before jumping in too readily. Even an anointed prayer, forwarded at a specific time at your own convenience, can be received at the Holy Spirit specified time needed by the client. It is another interesting way to minister. The following is a sample (fictitious) email: –

Dear Anxious Client,

I am so sorry you didn't feel up to coming in to see me for a session today. As you suggested, I am happy to continue your treatment via the internet. It will offer me the chance of teaching you in more detail what we have been discussing over the past two weeks.

As you are already in the middle of suffering from acute anxiety, you may find reading the attached handout only makes you feel worse. Even reading the words 'anxiety' and 'fear' could trigger more of your churning stomach and chest pains. Right now you will benefit more from therapy by being spoon-fed to get on top of the thing. Then, when you can think more rationally for yourself, you can use my suggested resources for management and prevention.

You expressed, 'I get anxious at the thought of feeling anxious and it develops into a vicious cycle'. This is so true. You have been like a little mouse caught on a treadmill, when all he needs to do is to jump off to escape. Let us plan how you can jump off. These thoughts and feelings do not have to belong to you. By retaining ownership of the anxious thoughts, you will remain on the treadmill. They are intruders robbing you of your peace and joy, and your right to live a normal life. It is, of course, natural to feel fear, because fear is a natural protective mechanism. However, you do not need to dwell on the associated destructive thoughts.

Did you know that fear can be an actual sinful choice, as fear indicates a lack of trust in God? Now don't start feeling bad that you are sinning and worried that you will be punished for it. We will discuss that when you come in for your next counselling session. We need to get to the roots of your fears and pull them out. God is good and He will show us how to do that by His Holy Spirit guidance.

That is why the scriptures say that 'perfect love casts out all fear'. If we trust in a good god, a god of love (who has our best interests at heart at all times), then we can give our cares over to Him, 'for He cares for us'. God is Love. He actually commands us to 'fear not' in many places in the Word, then He gives us the ability in Him to do so. He understands our natural tendency to worry; but He gives us the grace and strength to deal with it.

From the assessment we did of your symptoms, your condition appears to be developing into a generalised anxiety disorder. It is not my job to diagnose, but I can describe the condition in a way that suits your experience as a theatre director. Your symptoms are more than just the butterflies or the knots in the stomach a person experiences when having to make a speech, or when about to sit for an exam. Remember when you had that stage fright when you became frozen, and missed your cue to go on? Well, it is a little like that; but rather more like the feeling that you are perpetually on stage, constantly charged with adrenaline and not able to get off!

You report that you are now worrying about your general health, as you cannot switch your mind or your body off in order to relax at all now. You confess that you are turning away from God, not towards His loving arms. I will give you as many spiritual resources as possible to help alleviate your pain in this area. Do not give up the fight of faith. Perhaps your pastor can find you a prayer partner. As for your physical symptoms: it seems that your fight or flight responses are not turning off. It appears that your body has been affected by your fears.

Because you have described being constantly restless, hyper-alert and on edge all the time, it would be advisable that you seek attention from your doctor. You are having difficulty getting off to sleep and staying asleep. You are becoming easily tired at the simplest of tasks like making the bed. Even when you do get a good sleep, you say you do not feel refreshed. You have complained to me during sessions that you have constant muscle tension in your neck and shoulder areas. And I have noticed that you become irritable when I suggest I help you to learn relaxation techniques.

Anxiety becomes a disorder when it affects your quality of life. GAD, or generalised anxiety disorder, is diagnosed when you have worried excessively about two or more life situations for most days over a period of six months or so. Explain to your doctor that you feel you could need a referral to a psychologist for a formal assessment. This does not mean that you will have to stop coming to me as your Christian counsellor. We can all network together if we have your permission to do so.

You have made no real progress with your previous counsellors for coping with your divorce or your business problems. You claim that nothing has worked and this anxiety is beginning to affect your functioning at work and in social situations. Your relationships are obviously becoming strained and this puts you under a lot of stress. I know you love to socialize. Your anxiety seems to be turning into something that is all pervasive.

But I have confidence in you that you can still resist the temptation to give in to the thoughts and feelings that accompany all these physical and emotional symptoms. You can make a choice to get better by using the Word of God to replace all the anxiety-producing words you have been saying to yourself.

Controlling your worrying thoughts and overcoming the physical symptoms, which are a product of these thoughts, will conquer GAD. The Bible says that what is in your heart comes out of your mouth and that what you say has the power to affect your spirit and soul. The power of life and death is in the tongue. Did you know that you could word curse yourself? Therefore, you need to do the opposite. You need to bless yourself with your tongue. Hebrews 4:12 says that God's word is like a two-edged sword that separates what is of the spirit and what is of the soul.

During our next session, I will give you a selection of other relevant scripture passages on cards. I want you to place them around the house, learn them as you would a script and rehearse them out loud. Use your two-edged sword! For every anxious thought that comes into your mind I want you to 'take it captive to the mind of Christ'. Put it under the anointed power of the cross. Remember the power is in your tongue speaking out the Word of God to counteract your intrusive automatic negative thoughts. I will also give you a table for challenging and disputing the thoughts that come into your head.

The natural key is that every thought produces a mood. We want to produce moods of peace and calm, rest and strength, joy and trust. We want to increase faith – belief in The God who is able to keep safe those who believe in His ability to do so. Attached is a handout with some helpful and practical images you can use to take your thoughts captive. As an actor yourself, I know you will enjoy these.

God bless you and keep you. See you next Monday at my office at 10am.

Your Counsellor.

This illustration of a counselling technique is not meant to replace the advice of a health care professional. Refer to the disclaimer at the beginning of this section.

Counsellor Resources: DRAMA & IMAGERY FOR MANAGING ANXIETY

An adaption of this resource is available as a client handout in the companion – *Handbook of Resources* available from: www.prayercounsel.com.

Technique #1 ROADWORK SIGN

Instruct your client to imagine a worker holding up a sign at a road works site indicating for vehicles to stop. You, the therapist, then hold up your hand to indicate the stop signal whenever the client starts to repeat a concern already expressed. If the hand signal alone does not work, then hold up an actual stop sign in your other hand until the imagery of the traffic sign becomes automatically associated with the hand signal. Eventually, the hand signal alone should serve to deflect attention away from the anxiety (or other obsessive thinking patterns and associated feelings).

Having stopped and being caused to pause at the sign, your client can then work on dealing with the troubling thoughts, by choosing to displace them with alternate thoughts, thus producing more positive feelings e.g.

- a) Recalling how God has blessed them in some particular way.
- b) Thinking of a creative idea (not related to the problem).
- c) Verbal confession of an appropriate scripture.

Technique #2 TRAFFIC LIGHTS

Instruct your client to imagine a set of traffic lights and to remember that every thought produces a feeling. The red light directs the anxious person to distract from thinking the troubling thought by concentrating hard on the colour red. On the red light, the thought is addressed out loud, *Stop. No! I am not going there.* Orange represents a pause to look around for new thoughts to replace the old. Green is for '*go ahead*' to moving on in a different frame of mind, because the mood (anxious feeling) would have been changed (with the new thoughts) at the lights.

IMAGE 09

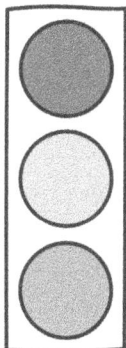

RED = STOP (BLANK OUT)

ORANGE = PAUSE (TO COLLECT NEW THOUGHTS)

GREEN = MOVE ON (TO A NEW LIFE)

Technique #3 CREEPY CRAWLIES

Instruct your client to:–

Picture your worries as little poisonous spiders (or biting ants) running all over you. Brush them off. Then stamp on each one, naming them as you go e.g. *Lack, I stamp you out in Jesus name. Disbelief, I break your power by the promises of His Word to me! Doubt, get out of my life, I don't want anything to do with you. Fear, I drive you out with trust in God's perfect love and care for me.*

Then raise your arms and cup your hands and ask for the individual blessings by saying out loud, *I receive peace/power/protection/love.* Then put your arms down and say, *Jesus, You* <u>are</u> *my peace (power/protector/ rock/safe place etc).*

AUTHOR'S TESTIMONY: Driving out the Legacy of Fear

One of the most debilitating emotions in my life has been fear.

We can give into fear until 'Fear' becomes our middle name. I was brought up on fear for my physical safety. Along with my breakfast cereal I was fed on fear. I was fearful about the neighbour down the road who might ask little girls into his place and might … Nothing however was ever really voiced or explained, and the insinuations were even more powerful in feeding the anxiety.

Even the simple pleasure of going to a community playground was poisoned for me. Don't swing too high; you might fall! Don't push that roundabout too fast; you'll get dizzy. Don't cross that road by yourself; you <u>will</u> *get run over… Even now, as I write this, I feel those old nightmares creeping up on me, and it takes willpower and faith to quench them.*

When I became a mother, I was determined that my children would not be ruled in the same way. I encouraged my son and daughter to conquer fear whenever it raised its ugly head. Unfortunately, I did not understand at the time about the existence of bondages and spiritual oppression being passed down through family lines. I did not know about deliverance and the power of prayers prayed with authority in agreement with others.

Still, I did the best I could at the time. I made a conscious decision that I would not pass my fears on to my little ones. It was a positive inner vow. I now know in hindsight that several of the women in my family line were victims of infirmity and unable to enjoy physical activity. Fear would have had a lot to do with that heritage. However, I was determined that <u>my</u> *children would live life to the full.*

My husband was brought up within a large family, with plenty of outlets in physical activity. His stories of his brothers and sisters and their daring exploits and mischief curled my hair. My own, and my brother's timidity, were such a contrast. I chose to encourage my children in my husband's heritage in that area. I decided that whatever they showed an interest in doing, I would not discourage. So, when the swing swung until it nearly did a full circle over the bar I laughed and clapped (underneath I quaked and nearly cracked). I promised myself that my children would never miss out on any activity that was wholesome and good, because of my fears.

Thanks to my husband's encouragement, our now adult children, have developed into normal healthy individuals. They have followed in his footsteps; in his adventurous spirit with his desire to try anything and everything at least once. As for myself, I am still somewhat bound by my upbringing in many ways. I wander around a theme park or carnival, carrying bags and jackets. I watch as others spin, race, climb or jump, on rides and contraptions far more inventive and dangerous looking than a simple swing. I was happy to have fun by watching others enjoy themselves.

Over the years, I am gradually doing things that are daring for me. I learnt that I needed to be patient with myself and to be content when my progress is slower than I would like. For instance, to get my driving licence and to actually take a car onto the road was an overwhelming challenge to me. Even after gaining my licence with much difficulty, it was seven long years before I ventured out on the roads alone.

The impetus for overcoming this fear of driving was when my husband had a suspected stroke down one side of his body and I could not even drive him a few kilometres down the road to the local hospital. He drove himself with one arm, while I sat in the passenger seat abusing myself inwardly for my cowardice. (It was a false alarm – just a compressed nerve.)

Challenged by that episode I made a deliberate choice to become a driver. This, I had to achieve, in stages, and alone, as I was fearful of anyone going out on the road with me lest they distract me in any way. I drove endlessly around a few streets locally and gradually widened the area covered over a long, long period, until eventually I felt confident and safe enough to travel from A to B.

Amazingly, the Holy Spirit was showing me what I recognize now as a do-it-yourself type of cognitive behavioural therapy. I would picture Jesus in the passenger seat beside me. This would quell the anxiety to a degree and then I would 'do it afraid' with him by my side. I was gradually desensitized to the feared task; facing my fears in stages, instead of avoiding the attempt altogether. Today I am a competent and safe driver, but only within set limits that I feel I can handle confidently.

Fear was only one of the many emotional challenges I faced with Jesus as a friend by my side. As with learning to drive, I made progress in healing of the emotions and mind renewal, through ministry from the Holy Spirit directly. This direct ministry was to become the basis of the concepts formed, and the principles used in my prayer ministry school and professional counselling practice.

So, this is how I would attempt to describe this emotional disability:

The temptation for fear comes as the seed. These seeds are planted in the fertile ground of ignorance of the Word and works of God, and they are watered and fertilised by more fear until they become a forest. You make your home in this forest until it becomes so dense and dark and overwhelming that even a little beam of sunlight finds it hard to shine in.

Then God finds a little patch where He comes shining in to plant the tiny mustard seed of faith in that area of your life. He starts to make a clearing for it to grow to full size. What results is a magnificent tree. This tree eventually shelters and sustains other life. The threatening forest is pushed further and further back by God to make room for more growth.

Praise him for his patience and his faithfulness to us.

CHAPTER NINE

DEALING WITH ANGER

As many practical resources as possible have been included in this chapter to enable the counsellor to define and understand this volatile emotion. It is one of the most misunderstood and socially unacceptable of feelings. However, if handled appropriately, anger can release and empower, rather than remain a cause for shame and condemnation.

- Counsellor casework exercise – *Client with Attitude*
- Discourse: anger defined and understood
- Counsellor resource – *Calming An Angry Client*
- Other practical resources on handling negative expression of feelings
- Client Testimonial – *Lessons Learnt*

Study Notes

CLIENT TESTIMONIAL – Client with Attitude

It's all very well you saying 'take every thought captive to the mind of Christ', but, when you've had the problems I've had with my mind running over and over on even the smallest of things, then you don't know what you are asking of me. Here I am a woman, not a foolish young girl anymore, and I still can't get it right.

You are a counsellor who has had a good education and who is so well organised. You can think straight. You have this job, which pays good money. You have all the help you need and want with the work you are in. You are a leader in the church and everyone respects and looks up to you. You look good and you have nice clothes and a man by your side, and you have a great family.

It is unfair of you to just pull out these catch phrases – even if they are from the scriptures – and expect me to apply them to my life! I haven't got a life! I haven't made it like you have. I need something practical to work with which will work for me. I am at the stage now when I think they are going to lock me up and throw away the key.

My biggest fear is that I am going to have one of my panic attacks in church and they will cart me off to some psych ward. I haven't anyone to explain to the doctors that I am not insane – well, not yet anyway. Although, my GP must think I am, because he insisted I see you when I mentioned voices. If I'm crazy then I've been that way since I was born.

I've just been like this all my life. I am not schizo! What I meant was that I hear voices, like myself talking to me about things. And I can't get away from me. I even talk to myself out loud. I can't shut myself up. I just can't stop thinking about everything – about being alone, about dying; about how I'm ever going to get a job; about what I should and should not eat because my stomach feels acidy and churning all the time; about why my head feels like it is about to explode; why no-one likes me and how I'll never have a boyfriend.

My mind just <u>won't</u> turn off. When people talk about having fun or feeling peaceful and relaxed, they make me so jealous. I say to myself that I would give an arm and a leg to know what it is like to go to a party, have just one or two drinks and to be like anyone else there – to be able to relax, join in like a normal person and to have fun telling jokes and all that stuff.

I'd like to be able to sit in church without feeling guilty that nothing is making any sense to me. I am wondering why on #@!/ earth I am there; because I am so worn out, I am #@!/# well sick with worry and afraid of what lies ahead for me. I hate my life. No, that's not right. I don't have a life. No, I hate myself. I wish I were someone else. I wish I could just go to sleep and not wake up.

I sit there on Sundays fidgeting and churning. I'm seeing everyone there singing their @#! little hearts out and nodding and taking notes on the sermon. Like they understand what the preacher is saying?! Yeah...well I don't! I wish someone would get that!

At a party or at church or even in a shopping plaza, I feel different to everyone else. I always have. And I hate it! I hate me...and...and I have had thoughts lately of how I am going to get rid of myself. Coming to you is my last ditch attempt before I do something @//#! about it.

People tell me to 'just relax' or 'take it to the Lord' when I am agitated. It just makes me feel like screaming at them, 'I would if someone would #@!! tell me how to!...

Except where the author recounts her personal testimony, all characters and cases are fictitious representations and any similarities to real persons or casework are non-intentional and purely co-incidental.

Counsellor Exercise for the *Client with Attitude*

As her counsellor, how would you personally deal with her, using as a reference the following questions?

1. *What would be the first thing you would say to her after hearing this speech?*
2. *How would it personally make you feel hearing all this?*
3. *What would you personally feel about this woman?*
4. *Would her use of profanity upset or faze you?*
5. *What boundaries has she set for you in asking for help?*
6. *In what form is she asking for your help?*
7. *Would you feel confident in how to begin helping her?*
8. *Would you need to refer this prospective client on to someone else immediately following this initial consultation? Or would you take her back for a second session? If so, why?*
9. *What boundaries would you set for her if she was willing to come back to see you as a client?*
10. *If you decided to enter a counselling contract with her, what paperwork do you feel you would need to fill out before you would begin your contract with her?*

11. Would there be a need to break confidentiality at the outset? Why or why not?

12. What personal, spiritual and professional resources do you feel you would need to cope with a client such as this?

13. What would your personal aims and counselling goals be in the counselling process?

14.   What would you do if you entered into the contract and then found that you were out of your depth?

UNDERSTANDING ANGER (Prv 25:28)

LIABILITY/ASSET

There is no one who has not experienced anger in one form or another. Depending on personality type, temperament and our inherited character traits, we can find anger as anything from a real problem to just an occasional disturbance. It becomes a problem when we use this emotion to control others in a negative way, or when anger controls us. On the other hand, it can be an asset when it motivates and drives us to affect positive change.

There is a great need to differentiate between the positive and negative aspects of anger and to take ownership and be accountable for the destructive use of anger. Driven by the thoughts of a violation of rights, this emotion can be used as *a defence mechanism* or *a coping mechanism*. Frustration is another troublesome emotion. Based on loss of control or lack of resources it is a close partner to irritability which can suddenly erupt into an angry outburst. Wielded as a weapon, anger is used to gain back a sense of power and control at the expense of others. When deliberately used to manipulate others to get what we want this can become a dangerous habit.

AS AN ADDICTIVE FORM OF ABUSE

Anger can become addictive physically as well as emotionally. A person can feel a fear-motivated need to self-defend. Lashing out in anger at the perceived attacker gives a sense of power and release. The angry person enjoys temporary control over another person. This can become habit forming. The secondary emotion of anger has overridden the deeper, primary feeling of fear. A physical high can be experienced. As the hormones override the fear, a positive shot of pleasurable excitement increases the desire to repeat the experience.

Watch a typical bully's face and body language when they are in action. There is usually visual evidence that pleasure is being derived from someone else's pain. This is a learnt experience – usually resulting from adapting to pain in the past. It can seed from the thought: *I'll get them before they get me*. Experiences of pain and fear are exchanged for a satisfying and pleasurable activity. The victim becomes the abuser.

VICTIMS

Active anger in the form of obvious abusive behaviour or verbal venting is easier to recognize and to correct than the passive type. When a counsellor deals with victims of abuse, they will mainly present with the *passive/aggressive traits* that favour displays of anger in a suppressed or simmering form. *Internalised anger* is the basic source of so many emotional, spiritual and physical problems for this personality type. For these clients, depression and ill health are the two most common symptoms presented. The underlying cause is anger – usually in the form of its counterparts, *resentment and bitterness.*

If this is pointed out during the counselling process, a passively angry type could become quite prickly and defensive, or could go the other way into throes of remorse and self-denigration. Sometimes, an old client will come back and describe how angry they had been with something said years ago when the counsellor had probably been *issuing a challenge or confronting.*

The purpose of the confrontation might have been to point out to the 'victim' their own destructive or negative role in a relationship or, a personal contribution to a health problem. Hearing this challenge was a source of *inner conflict* and an offence to the client at that time. However, anger over the perceived offence was not openly expressed. Sometimes, a client will simply terminate the counselling contract without saying a word, to return later having learnt the skills to safely express anger (the therapist or prayer minister has been 'forgiven').

So, be aware that passive types can be experts at hiding, suppressing or denying emotions. You might sense the subtle reactions and repressed feelings at the time you are confronting or challenging. At other times, you could experience just a coolness or slight withdrawal. Some people feel they have no right to feel anger at all towards anyone and will go to great lengths to hide natural reactions to real or perceived injustices.

HEALTHY/UNHEALTHY EXPRESSION

Sometimes, it is quite productive to stir up a person's *assertiveness* in order to create a natural (and healthy) *righteous anger.* Even Jesus had his moments! You may like to remind the client that our perfect Saviour knocked over the moneychangers' tables and called Pharisees 'whitewashed tombs' and 'vipers'. There is a time for righteous anger (Ex 32).

This can prove to be a big eye opener to some habitual victims and martyrs; anger is permitted! Sometimes, it is even appropriate to encourage a client to give self-permission <u>not</u> to forgive until they have felt <u>enough</u> anger. Be careful however as this might encourage a role change; as they may feel they now have a right to carry anger as a weapon and to use it as they please (Ps 37:7-11).

TARGETS OF ANGER

Anger needs a target. Basically, clients can be: –

> - angry at self
> - angry at others
> - angry at God
> - angry at the world

In some cases, these feelings have been so much a part of life that they are not readily recognised as destructive 'leading unto death' forms of anger, until they are specifically pointed out as *sinful attitudes, choices and behaviour* (Matt 5:21-25).

DEFINING ANGER

Dictionaries describe anger using the following expressions: *a feeling of great annoyance or antagonism as the result of some real or supposed grievance* or *a feeling of great displeasure, rage or wrath.*

Spiritually, anger harboured and not dealt with, can be classed as a form of *rebellion.* This can prove quite a *stronghold of denial.* Our *pride* does not allow us to concede that we have made a home for sinful attitudes and responses. It can seriously *isolate* us from both man and God (Ps 68:6). The Bible instructs us not to let our anger lead us into sin, *'be angry and sin not'* (Eph 4:26-27). We are allowed to express anger, but in a healthy and appropriate way.

Most people would define 'real' anger as the type when you feel very strongly wronged, as in *feeling a sense of injustice* and as being: *in a rage, boiling over, really irritated* or *greatly annoyed,* or as *being mad at a person to the extent of feeling hatred and violence towards them. Profanity* can be an outward sign that there is anger growing from the *root of rebellion.* If not checked via self-control, this root of rebellion could possibly fruit into violent acts. Rape is often considered a product of anger and control issues rather than a sexual issue. It can be a quest for power over another human being – the power being fuelled by anger, frustration, resentment, hatred and bitterness.

DIFFERENT FORMS OF ANGER

There are more subtle sinful forms of anger, which are harder to label, such as: *resentfulness, bitterness, self-pity, self-righteousness, over-sensitivity, vindictiveness, unforgiveness, frustration and fretfulness.* There are the sinful habits of bearing *grievances and grudges,* or the character traits of being a *grumbler, complainer or whiner.* If we have ever been accused of any of these things, perhaps we should look up the meanings in a dictionary and take a good look at ourselves. Are we personally trying to *punish* someone with our anger?

DIFFERENT CARRIERS & FAVOURED STYLES

An elderly gentleman was prone to being angry at the world in general, irritable, critical and cynical in nature. Although happily married, he confessed to being driven to distraction by his wife's patient and placid nature. He claimed that he would have given everything to enjoy a good fight every now and then, but the 'little woman' would not co-operate. This caused him a great deal of frustration because of his lack of control over his 'non cooperative' partner.

On the other hand, women are particularly adept at passive forms of punishing others. A woman's hidden anger will sometimes drive a spouse to the outwardly aggressive displays of anger, leaving the female victim's own contribution hidden, or at least less obvious. Domestic violence for instance can be a frightening product of a power play and of the different styles of anger interacting.

As ministers and 'people helpers' we need to examine our own favoured styles of showing anger. We might passively draw back from a client – sabotaging any progress made. We might lose patience, refuse assistance, reject the person outright, or defy attempts to reconcile following a disagreement. We could wallow in the felt injustices and wipe our hands of the responsibility, and refer on to another carer. Perhaps, in everyday relationships, we are in the habit of giving the silent treatment or withholding physical or emotional affection; so we subtly treat our clients in a similar manner.

> The above teaching is available in a client handout format. This also applies to the resource below, adapted under the title of *Calming an Angry Person*. They can be found in the companion resource handbook from Trafford Publishers.

Practicalities of Counselling: CALMING AN ANGRY CLIENT

The proverbs teach us how to handle 'wrath' which is the old-fashioned term for intense anger (Prv 14:29, 15:1). The following are techniques and ideas to calm an upset client who has become angry during a session.

1. **Remain calm** by responding rather than reacting (Prv 29:8). If you feel fearful or threatened and have lost your peace, reconnect quickly with the Holy Spirit and stay under the anointing power of God. Allow yourself to manifest the mind of Christ (Eph 4:29-32). Ask yourself what Jesus would do in this situation (Eph 5:1-2).

2. **Respond** in the temperament of a mature Christian, harnessing the fruits of the spirit (Prv 29:23, 25). Be confident in your ability to move in the spirit within the parameters of your giftings.

3. **Reduce the level of agitation** through peaceful interaction. Do not become defensive or respond harshly (Prv 29:22) Keeping your voice in low controlled tones, speak soothingly and with authority. Speak slowly and calmly, with a deliberate, positive manner in order to bring the reaction down to a manageable level for both sides.

4. **Manage personal emotions** as well as those coming from the other party, remembering that feelings can be contagious. Do not attack the person and do not retaliate with anger or attitude (Prv 29:11; Rom 12: 17-21).

5. **Do not mirror nor mimic** by adopting the facial expressions, body language or general aggressiveness of the angry person. Note that when we think of an angry person we naturally picture someone with a red face, cursing, yelling and gesturing. This is not always so. An angry person might manifest in a variety of ways, appearing calm on the surface. They might go silent, tense up, become cynical or sarcastic, begin to mumble, or to talk through clenched teeth. You could be tempted to respond in like manner (Jas 1:19-27).

6. **Acknowledge the speaker's emotion** in order to disarm the situation. Phrases such as, *you seem upset* or, *I see that you are feeling strongly about this*, might seem an obvious statement, but it could serve to prompt the person to realise just how upset they have become. Unaware of either expressed or subconscious feelings, this feedback might come as a surprise. Often just reflecting their feelings back as a statement is enough to produce a calming effect, for example, *you are angry with me for interrupting you*, in response to the client saying, '*Stop interrupting me!*'

7. **Label the emotion correctly** and use affirming words to convey understanding and acceptance. Look for underlying/secondary feelings. For example, *of course that situation would make anyone angry... what did you say then?* Or, *I don't blame you for feeling upset and embarrassed when you called in to find I had forgotten our appointment.*

8. **Apologise when called for**, whilst maintaining self-respect and dignity (Prv 28:13). If you are in the wrong, do not follow the apology with excuses or self-derogatory remarks about how stupid, or selfish you are. Instead, apologise with sincerity and feeling, remembering that this is a brother or sister in Christ (Jas 5:16). When you are obviously in the right, at least acknowledge that you are sorry to see the sufferer hurt and upset (Jas 4:5-6, 10) – *I am sorry you were hurt by that remark.*

9. **Refuse to become a scapegoat** for someone else's wrongdoings (Jas 4:7). You might have inadvertently triggered the client's unfinished business and the issues they have with someone else (see to *Wound Transference*). You could firmly say something like, '*I understand that you were ignored by your*

boss but you have my full attention here as my client. I am indeed listening to you and hearing what you are saying'.

10. **Use reflective listening and feedback** techniques. *So from your point of view, it seems that no-one ever takes any interest in your feelings. Am I right in feeling that you are concerned that all I want from you is your money and that I am not really concerned about you personally?*

11. **Separate the person from the problem.** Do not allow the other party's feelings to become a personal problem to you. In your mentoring role, assist them to self-manage emotions <u>before</u> they become a problem. Encourage the client to own (admit the problem) and empathetically assist to responsibly deal with it. Again, be sure to apologise for any personal responsibility on your part, for either provoking anger or retaliating in anger.

12. **Speak the truth respectfully**, and in a loving manner. If appropriate, allow the client to see how the misuse of anger against you personally has affected the counsellor/client therapeutic relationship. Express that one of the goals of a responsible counsellor is to encourage accountability for any negative or destructive use of anger. For example, *yelling and swearing at me is not going to help either of us to get anywhere with this session. I would like us both to speak calmly and respectfully to each other if we are to continue our association.*

13. **Negotiate and discuss strategies to prevent a reoccurrence.** *Next time you feel that I am overstepping the boundaries with you perhaps we could plan to have a signal? Perhaps you could say that you prefer we don't go there, or you might raise your hand in a stop sign gesture.* Be gracious. You might need to help the client save face and avoid embarrassment Ask for resolution ideas from the client. You are aiming for a win-win situation. If this fails to happen, do not feel that you are a failure as a counsellor. Any feeling expressed serves a purpose. Hand the present situation over to the Lord and recall the times you <u>have </u>succeeded.

> **IMPORTANT WARNING: Remember to have back-up and safety procedures in place in case of violence or hostility, whether it is expressed verbally, emotionally or physically. You do not have to accept or tolerate abuse from a client. You must also be aware of the possibility of dealing with demonic manifestations; so be positioned in a safe place, where you have both practical and spiritual support.**

Counsellor Resource: HANDLING TROUBLESOME EMOTIONS

THE BALLOON TECHNIQUE

Blow up a balloon to about three-quarters capacity. Seal the air off tightly with the fingers of your left hand. Squash the balloon with the right hand. Tell the client that the air inside the balloon represents the problem feeling. Explain that when he tries to manage this feeling by keeping it down inside, the emotion will tend to pop out in odd places at odd times. Demonstrate this by pressing the balloon in, causing it to bubble out in various places.

Describe how the bottled up feeling tries to escape but still remains in the sealed space (his body, represented by the not quite blown up balloon). Ask, *if you keep adding further air* (resentment, frustration, disappointment, hatred, anger) *bit by bit, what do you think will happen?* The client should reply that the balloon would burst. Continue to blow the balloon up as far as you can – increasing the tension.

But, before it bursts, let it go like a rocket to fly out of control across the room 'blowing raspberries' (expending the warm air). Now you could say, *you don't want that to happen to you either. It is not very dignified – flying off like that!*

Blow another balloon up, showing the client that the correct way to handle tension is to let off steam gradually in a controlled manner, as the tension is experienced. Let the balloon air out bit by bit to demonstrate. Instruct the client to find a safe outlet when anger or any other problem feelings begin to build up inside. In this manner the client will keep their 'balloon' (body, soul and spirit) deflated and relaxed.

If the client is ready to listen and to understand, you could say, *of course we need to find out the reasons why you are feeling this way. Maybe your choices (options) for handling these feelings right now in a safe manner could be to:*

WRITE IT OUT
TALK IT OUT
PRAY IT OUT
WALK IT OUT.

Explain that there are also plenty of other 'outs' or outlets to release built up tensions, such as: physical exercise, playing with pets, computer games, crosswords, watching or participating in sports, drama in the form of role-playing, creative hobbies, movies, reading, music and dance, massage or other relaxation techniques (like learning to breathe properly or counting backwards). The client may need to practise a variety of activities until personally effective ones are found, in order to avoid bursting one day from all the 'bad air' inside (suppressed emotions).

Client Handout #1: ANGER ASSESSMENT

Your reactions/responses to the following statements can be used as a basis for discussion during a session with your counsellor.

*Client Exercise: Circle the numbers of any responses that best describe how you personally feel at present. It is important that you answer as honestly as possible. Give your **spontaneous reaction**, not what you think should be your response. Simply circle if you agree, leave unmarked if you disagree.*

NAME ....   DATE:

1. My anger solves problems
2. My anger causes problems
3. I feel I have missed out on life
4. I am usually critical of others
5. Life is unfair most of the time
6. Some people have it in for me
7. I feel better when I pay someone back (take revenge)
8. I am usually the one who gets the raw deal
9. Most people let me down or disappoint me
10. People make me angrier than situations do
11. Placid people make me angry
12. I can not tolerate weak people
13. I get angrier with myself more so than at others
14. I often get angry with myself
15. I like things done my way, or not at all
16. Getting mad is the only way they will take any notice
17. It is best to get them before they get you
18. I am not an angry person. I just get angry
19. I am not angry with God – just church people
20. People say I am an angry person
21. I just like to let some steam off now and then
22. If I get angry with someone, then they deserve it!
23. I am not an angry person
24. Having to fill out this questionnaire has really 'ticked me off'!

Client Handout #2: NEGATIVE METHODS OF EXPRESSING ANGER

Tick your favoured ones – then write some positive alternatives to these.

- Act superior or arrogant
- Anxiety
- Activity – hide in (work/exercise/hobby)
- Avoidance
- Bicker
- Bitterness
- Blame others
- Blame self
- Blow up
- Break things
- Bully
- Cold shoulder
- Compromise
- Cruelty
- Defensive/guarded
- Denial
- Depression
- Distort the truth
- Emotionally distance
- Exaggerate
- Fight/spar
- Flyback/retort/retaliate
- Go on strike
- Generalise
- Glare
- Grudge
- Hate
- Harshness
- Hide
- Hostile
- Illness
- Indignant
- Intimidate
- Malice
- Mean
- Obsess
- Pedantic
- Personalize
- Petty
- physical attack

- Physically distance
- Pout
- Projection
- Punish
- Rage/hate
- Resentment
- Rebel
- Repress/push down
- Retreat inside
- Revenge/ pay back
- Run away
- Scapegoat
- Secretive
- Scold
- Scorn
- Self abuse
- Self–righteous
- Shame
- Silent treatment
- Slam doors
- Spend money
- Spit dummy
- Spiritualize
- Slack off
- Stew
- Stalk
- Sulk
- Take it out on third party
- Throw things
- Two-faced
- Vandalise
- Verbal abuse
- Vindictiveness
- Victimize self
- Victimize others
- Withdrawal
- Work harder
- Other:

Client Handout #3: SELF-MANAGEMENT TECHNIQUES FOR ANGER

These exercises can be done as homework and brought in as a basis for discussion with your counsellor.

Exercise #1 THINK IT OUT

- ❑ Do I know and admit it when I am angry?
- ❑ Why am I angry? Is this a part of my personality style?
- ❑ What type of anger is it?
- ❑ Is it masking other feelings such as hurt, resentment, shame, bitterness, disappointment or fear?
- ❑ Has it become a habitual stronghold with me? (Am I a chronically angry person?)
- ❑ Who am I angry with? (Am I angry with myself? With God?)
- ❑ Do I dwell on past hurts?
- ❑ Am I slow to forgive and do I find it hard to forget offences?
- ❑ Do I constantly rehearse what I would like to say to those who have wronged me?
- ❑ Am I often irritable or complaining?
- ❑ Do I need to look for reasons to stay angry?
- ❑ Do I feel no one is really listening to me?
- ❑ What benefits do I get out of holding on to these feelings?
- ❑ When am I most likely to be angry?
- ❑ What are the causes?
- ❑ What is my anger pattern?
- ❑ What are the physical sensations that accompany it?
- ❑ Am I trying to punish or control someone with my anger?
- ❑ Does the expression of my anger hurt others?
- ❑ Do I hurt myself with my anger?
- ❑ Am I misdirecting my anger onto the wrong person or thing?
- ❑ What is my style of anger?
- ❑ Do I use anger to confront people?
- ❑ Do I use anger to defend myself?
- ❑ Do I get what I want when I show anger?
- ❑ Do I repress anger?
- ❑ Do I give myself permission to be angry?
- ❑ Am I slow to express anger openly?
- ❑ Do I build up to a point when I explode?
- ❑ Do I pick fights in order to vent my anger?
- ❑ Am I afraid of other people's anger?

- ❑ Do I preserve (stuff it down) in order not to make a scene?
- ❑ Do I enjoy the excitement and drama of my anger?
- ❑ Do I enjoy the other party's reaction to it?
- ❑ Do I physically and emotionally experience a high through my anger (only to have a letdown experience in the aftermath)?
- ❑ Have I become addicted to anger?
- ❑ On a scale of 1-10, how guilty do I feel after I express anger?
- ❑ Do I really think that this is a problem with me?
- ❑ Do I want to change?

Exercise #2 TALK IT OUT

Now that you have thought about these questions, discuss what you have discovered about yourself with someone you can trust to be honest with you. If they know you well, start off by asking if they know when you are angry and how they know. Ask them if they think you have an *anger problem* and, if so, would they be willing to talk it out with you to see if you need some further help. Explain how you will need help to correctly identify and label your emotions and that perhaps your underlying feelings are actually disappointment, frustration, grief or hurt, which will need to be worked on in different ways.

Exercise #3 PRAY IT OUT

The scriptures have much to say on the subject of anger. Acquire a topical bible dictionary and a concordance to study the subject, or find a resource on-line. Look at both Old and New Testaments – particularly concentrating on the passages describing God the Creator's wrath and Jesus Christ our Saviour's righteous anger. Using these scriptures, pray through into freedom and peace. Ask the Holy Spirit to guide you in the future as to how to manage your feelings so that they will yield positive fruits in your life.

Bring your findings along to the next counselling session and ask for prayer. If you suspect that you could have a spirit of anger, hatred, rage, resentment, bitterness and so on troubling you, then seek deliverance.

Exercise #4 WALK IT OUT

Do something physical in the way of healthy exercise to relieve the stress of dealing with your feelings. Express your anger in a new way physically. For example, if you have been in the habit of slamming doors or faces, then go to the gym for a set of specific stress relieving exercises. Instead of obsessing over slights, go outdoors and do some physical activity that is creative so that your thought patterns are disrupted, or distracted.

If you have previously enjoyed the adrenalin rush when discharging your feelings, choose instead an adventure sporting activity to satisfy your needs. The aim is to retrain your brain and to alter your body chemistry. The main thing is to express your feelings according to your own style, but in a new way.

Make positive choices such as learning to watch for the physical signs of anger becoming out of your control. Remember that anger is a natural reaction, and usually secondary to frustration, pain, disappointment, grief etc. Deal with primary feelings by looking for the root causes. What do you do with anger when it does come? This is your choice. If you recognise it as the negative or destructive type, then you can choose to either exaggerate or extinguish the flame. (Refer to the following testimonial *Lessons Learnt*).

The following testimonial on *Anger* accompanies the preceding resource.

CLIENT TESTIMONIAL: Lessons Learnt

Being a young guy with anger problems, do I ignore my feelings? Do I allow my feelings to be in charge of my life? No, I have to say I have never ignored my feelings; but I have given in to self-pity, resentment and bitterness. I have learnt, through going for counselling, that these things are attitudes. I have learnt that attitudes are orientations towards things or people. I have learnt that I can change my attitudes by changing my beliefs.

Beliefs are anything that I accept as truth. I learnt that I could actually believe a lie and accept it as the truth. My feelings can confirm that the lie is a truth and make it into a mindset. So I must constantly be on guard as to what messages my feelings are sending to my brain and what my thoughts are telling my feelings to do. All very confusing and darned hard work!

Anyway, these days, I treat my feelings like friends, not enemies. Feelings, like anger, guilt and jealousy, I now treat as signposts to unresolved hurts, or as problems that just need working on. I now know that feelings are not negative in themselves. They are just feelings – something that happens when I react or respond to people, things or circumstances.

The best example I've been given is this: if I stub my toe I feel physical pain, but I can also feel things like annoyance or anger. I can tend to look for someone to take my feelings out on. And that someone is usually me! I blame and shame myself for being stupid! It comes out in some pretty foul language sometimes.

Anyway, as I just said, I now know that feelings are not negative in themselves – only what we do with them, can be negative or destructive. Like, with anger, I usually get defensive and grumble. Or I feel sorry for myself as the offended party or the victim. Even after I forgive, I hang onto a grudge for a while. You see, my attitude has come from the belief that I can punish people with my resentment and condemnation. I was amazed when I realised I was my own worst enemy.

It was explained to me that it is the Holy Spirit's job to convict people and God's work to deal with unrepentant sinners, not <u>my</u> job. I was helped to realise it only comes back on <u>me</u> when I try to do God's job – that it causes me problems and suffering. I had to ask Him to forgive me for that. Just a simple prayer did it. The funny thing is, since I began getting prayer ministry, God is allowing bigger and more dramatic offences and hurts to happen. Like, they are coming to me from left, right and centre. And they are major things – even persecution type stuff. But, man, am I learning a lot!

I am quickly learning to forgive, then to get on with dealing with my anger in a more positive way. I am becoming the master in charge of my feelings. As my counsellor says, 'you are expressing anger in an appropriate manner to the right people at the right times'. I am not letting 'It' rule my life any longer.

My sulking times are getting shorter. The attacks are coming faster on each other's heels, with each one even worse than the last. It's like having a set of sticks that I'm juggling – pretty well too, if I may say so. I am learning to deal with my root problems, not just the surface pattern of anger. Best of all, I am learning to apologise verbally – more often and more graciously. I am seeing when I am the one who commits the offence and I am learning to forgive from the heart, so that I am not holding on to grudges when people offend me. Great stuff!

My love for God's way of doing things is growing. I love the way His principles work – and they do work. I love His way of doing things now. I have stopped feeling resentful towards Him. In fact I can actually feel Him. (Now that's a positive feeling I want to hang on to). I feel that I am pleasing and blessing Him more. As a by-product, my self-esteem is soaring. I am seeing miracles happening in my relationships with others – especially with my dad.

Even though I am not nursing any feelings of outright anger right now, I do feel resentment over a small offence in relation to authority – I won't say 'who'. I feel someone is trying to control me. I am constantly being tempted to be angry with this person. I am confidently asking God that he 'lead me not into temptation' to sin. I do not want my anger to be taking control of me ever again.

I sure hope these lessons will not be necessary much longer – that they have served their purpose to make me strong in that area. I am working hard towards learning to go on automatic pilot in dealing with my feelings in a more positive way. I am letting Him fly my plane now. I'm sure glad I realised I needed help and, that I went for it!

IMAGE 10

ANGER IS (NOT) A CHOICE

IT IS A NATURAL REACTION

However . . . . what you <u>do</u> with anger <u>is</u> your choice

EXAGGERATE? ⟶ OR ⟶ EXTINGUISH?

SECTION THREE

Man in Conflict

CHAPTER TEN

VICTIM OR VICTOR

Most clients who enter prayer ministry will come from the position of victim in some way. Some who have been repeatedly wounded or abused, will need releasing from a victim mentality. Others will see themselves as victims without real cause. This chapter introduces the section by offering a variety of resources to free Christians to move into a true position of victory in Christ Jesus.

- Discourse on intimidation & bullying
- Jezebel & Ahab spirits in church and other ministry situations
- Abuse of the counsellor – wound transference – case study of Rose
- Special attention to adult survivors of childhood sexual abuse
- Reality issues checklist (for both intimidators and victims)

Study Notes

CLIENT TESTIMONIAL – Aunt Dee

It has always been on my mind that I wanted to be a Youth Worker. I don't really care whether it is with the church or with a Government agency. It can be as a pastor, or a social worker, a school chaplain or on the street as a cop. I don't care. I just want to make a difference with the kids – especially the misfits, the truants and the homeless. I want to see that they are protected from bullying and that they get justice when they are victimised.

Well, I have made a start in that direction. I've been to a bible college for two years and laid down a good foundation spiritually. I didn't manage to meet the girl of my dreams there, which I aimed to do by the time I was thirty, but I still have two years to go on that.

I've got my certificate for Yr 12 despite school being hell on earth for me up until Yr 10. I got to go to a good private school because my aunt sponsored me to go to a Christian one when she saw I was serious about what I wanted. Thank God she did, or I would never have what I have now – knowing Him as my personal Saviour.

I would have stayed a wimp, a reject and a misfit the way I was heading, if it hadn't been for mum's good old Aunt Dee. I have to admit I had a pretty rough time before Aunt Dee came into my life. I was always the victim of the class bully and his gang – even the girls. Then, when I dropped out of school, I was intimidated and treated lousy by any boss I had and was the butt of all my workmates' jokes. It was like it even carried on into the churches I used to go to as a teenager. I was looking for that love of my life and I thought a church youth group would be a good place to meet a nice girl. I was wrong.

It's like they heard me coming. The guys in the group would pick me straight off as the one to shoulder out. They'd smirk and dig one another in the ribs and tell the girls to watch out for me because I couldn't be trusted, or some other crap. I ended up getting paranoid and thought someone was tailing me from church to church.

The girls just seemed to back off of me – because of the wimp status I guess. I stopped fighting it. I was a loser. It's just that when you are knocked down so many times you just think, what's the use of setting yourself up like a bowling alley pin?

But, then Aunt Dee came into town after Uncle died and left her alone in a big house. She sold up and moved in with us because we were her only family. I was in my late teens and a total dropout. I spent most of my time in my room. I was nearly giving up on life. She was my great aunt, really – 80 and a widow (certainly not the girl of my dreams). I kind of liked her from the start because *she gave my dad cheek and made my mum laugh. Aunt Dee hadn't given up on life.*

She told us straight up she got 'saved' at 71 - in one of those old fashioned Pentecostal churches - and she said she had got 'into the Word'. She couldn't drive because they had taken her licence away because of her eyes. So, poor mum had to taxi her to church twice on Sundays, then bible study and ladies meetings weekdays. About six weeks into moving in with us, she decided she wanted to be a women's bible study leader herself in her own granny flat. Mum, the taxi driver was relieved to have a bit of time off, but then, a few weeks later, she said she 'had the Lord's call to be a prayer minister'. Then she wanted mum to take her to these courses to learn about counselling and praying. Then it was demons and deliverance for a while. After that, it was youth mentoring.

That's when she honed in on me. I'd pick her up from her current course to give mum a break and she'd be trying her latest counselling technique out on me – always sliced between two big slabs of 'The Word'. She knew her Bible. She said she had to make up for the lost time of her misspent youth.

Funny thing was... I began to really pick up on this stuff she was into. Somehow, with her little old lady ways (which, at first, I took to be just another form of control and bullying); things started getting better for me. I started to see what I wanted in life. I began to have some hope that I might achieve what I wanted, my 'vision' as she put it.

The turning point for me came when she started chattering on about this Jewish fellow named Nehemiah from the Old Testament times. God put it on his heart to leave his job, because he had to do something special for the Jews. He had 'A Vision'.

He had to get permission because he was virtually a slave to a foreign king at the time, but he got it easily because he had always been a good worker and served the king faithfully. But leaving his job was the easy part....

Aunt Dee told me about how this Nehemiah was intimidated from every side when he tried to fulfil the vision God gave him. His enemies were at him, and even his own people. He was bullied and harassed, laughed at and discouraged. And this was all over a city wall!

God had told him to rebuild the walls around the city of Jerusalem. They had been pulled down when the Babylonians, who utterly destroyed the city, took captive most of the Israelites who lived there. He was to gather them back together again to rebuild the protective walls and to then restore the ruined city.

When Aunt Dee told me a bit more of the history of the Jewish people, I began to see how this wall business was so important to them. It was important to God too because it sort of represented His protective wall of love around the people. He had especially chosen and loved these Jews, but, throughout their history, they were either taking Him for granted or outright rejecting His love and protection. This was why the protective wall came down and their enemies stepped all over them. They lost their homes and family life, their city and all their possessions. They virtually lost the freedom to live the life they wanted. They were bullied and their lives taken over – just like mine.

I began to see that each time I had tried to rebuild, forgiving and trying to trust people, they betrayed me, disappointed me, or just plain laughed at me. I ended up hating them all and hating myself for being such a loser. I was a misfit, had no friends, no job and nothing or no one to live for. All I had ended up with was an old lady for company. How desperate can you get?

So I began to look at the Bible story about Nehemiah and discussed with Aunt Dee why he was different to me. She said it was because he was a man acting under authority and told me to look at Psalm 27:11. God Almighty Himself had called him to do a job and he wasn't going to let anything or anyone stand in his way. As each new problem came up, he used the wisdom God gave him to counter the attack. He didn't back off, hide away or give in.

We worked out together that he seemed to have his own personal 'love wall' around him. Aunt Dee said he just knew God loved him and that was his protection and defence. He trusted God to help him to do the impossible against all odds. He had courage because he knew he had a big god. She said he could boldly say, 'The Lord is my helper, I will not fear. What can man do to me?'

She explained that, when we can achieve Nehemiah type faith and confidence, we can actually love our enemies and do good to those who try to hurt us. We cannot be intimidated or bullied. I remember that her face turned away a little as her eyes teared up. Then she turned back and faced me full on to say, 'That is why a widow, who was getting old and frail and going blind, is no longer afraid. She plans to live in confidence that God will protect and use her to the very end of her time here on earth!'

Next she lowered her eyes and asked if she could practise some old fashioned prayer on me. I was real quick to say, 'You sure can!'

Except where the author recounts her personal testimony, all characters and cases are fictitious representations and any similarities to real persons or cases are non-intentional and purely coincidental.

BULLYING & INTIMIDATION

A bully can be described as a person who hurts, persecutes, or intimidates someone less powerful, undermining the victim's confidence in the ability to protect and defend their personal rights. 'Intimidate' means *to subdue or influence by fear.* Long-term intimidation can create submissive and accommodating behaviours in the victim because he or she gradually loses a sense of personal identity and diminishes in coping mechanisms and the ability to set personal boundaries to counteract the abuse. The abused becomes complicit in the behavioural interactions and feels confused, anxious, belittled, hopeless, and isolated; as the bully grows in power and skill in controlling the game and manipulating his or her 'pawn'. To counteract bullying, the victim needs to learn the skills to lessen the impact of the fear inducing activity long enough to regain his or her personal confidence and personal power.

Not all bullies are aware of their problem, or will acknowledge it if and when they do become aware. Skilling a victim into victory is the answer in most counselling situations. On the premises that we train people how to treat us, and that we are more likely to continue in behaviour, which works for us, bullies will be bullies unless they are confronted, challenged with reasons to change, and deprived of their victim/pawn. On the same premises, victims will remain victimized until they have learnt the skills to become non-compliant and lose their victim mentality.

PROFILE OF A BULLY

Bullies have been historically classed as cowards and believed to have low self-esteem (which they attempt to boost at the expense of others). However, this is not necessarily so in all cases.

Intimidators are more likely to be arrogant people who have a strong sense of entitlement. They are angry people with unrealistic expectancies of what life owes them and feel their own needs are more important than the next person's. Therefore they are basically selfish and self-centred. Some will abuse privately and secretly, but usually, they will hold in orbit those who feed their ego. Those who circle or support the abusers are either doing so in order to avoid becoming the next target or being abandoned or rejected.

Bullies too have an inherent need for acceptance. They will sometimes express that they are picking on others in order to be popular, to gain attention or to make others laugh. One school bully was even heard to say that he *'had a reputation to uphold'* and that he *'needed to frighten kids into liking me'* and that *'it makes me feel good'*. Others express the need to be *'big and bad'* in order to feel powerful or safer. They display the *'I'll get them before they get me'* attitude. Some are being bullied and abased by those higher up the food chain. Therefore they are exacting revenge vicariously. It is easier to intimidate an employee for example, than to face the fact that you have a controlling wife who leads the family from the home base.

It is easier for a gang leader to terrorise the younger kids at school, than to report that his dad beats him up on a regular basis.

Once personally aware of the problem, bullies need help with discipline, boundaries, channelling aggression and developing the fruit of self-control. A bully needs to be confronted and his faulty beliefs challenged. Boundaries and personal accountability needs to be put in place, as would any perpetrator of a crime. If we are dealing with the abuser or intimidator, we need to work towards setting the prisoner free from the root causes of his or her need to operate in this manner.

Examples of intimidation a counsellor might come across:

1. **Small children** who are in the experimental stages of realising the power of intimidation and the enjoyment derived from bullying, or, those who are copying (without understanding) the behaviour of peers and older siblings (even experiences they have viewed via the media).

2. **School bullies** who need to victimize to elevate their own personal worth (or to diminish their feelings of fear and insecurity) or those who simply enjoy it. This can involve gang membership. A bully could be a victim of bullying by those in power over them e.g. a parent might be beating a child at home or a teacher could be victimizing a student.

3. **Gangs** of peer members, or families, or neighbours, who vie for power and turf rights, often resulting in physical violence and vandalism of property through revenge seeking and vendettas.

4. **Employers or supervisors** driven by the need to 'keep others in their place' or to extract or increase productivity and maximise profits. This can include unions or any other agency.

5. **Sociopaths and psychopaths,** who manipulate, control and persecute others to gain personal power or privileges (with no hint of conscience about doing so). This includes workplace bullies.

6. **Spouses or other family members** in abusive acts in various forms towards each other e.g. domestic violence, child molestation, sibling rivalry, negative parenting.

7. **Those with disability** who feel the need to regain power or maintain control in order to survive. For example, the intellectually or emotionally disabled, who abuse carers, siblings or spouse.

8. **Social groups** where ranks are closed to those unacceptable as participants. The unacceptable can include any party with 'a difference' e.g. race, disability, social or economic strata, religion, age, nationality. (Members are sometimes coerced into conformity; so they can also be classed as victims).

9. **Occult groups/religious cults/church hierarchies** where authority figures isolate threaten and coerce members into submission for personal power and monetary gain. Torture and sexual abuse is sometimes involved.

10. **Demonic oppression**, where principalities and powers are either in operation via a human vessel, or are directly involved in intimidating a person spiritually, or on a soul or physical level, e.g. spirits of infirmity, violence and insanity, delusion, witchcraft or, a Jezebel spirit.

11. **Spiritual abuse** by another person/s where a weaker vessel is intimidated into going against personal values or belief systems and/or is personally discriminated against, abused or taken advantage of in various forms. This can include both secular and Christian counselling and prayer ministry. (We need to be aware and free from these traits and sins in our own lives, in order to be effective tools for delivering others).

SPECIAL NOTE: ON COUNSELLING VICTIMS INTO VICTORS

In counselling, we are usually dealing with the victim. Sometimes a victim might not even realise that they are being victimised. After this is acknowledged and discussed, the primary objective is to raise the level of consciousness of their personal authority in Christ and the power of '*His perfect love, which casts out all fear*'. The secondary objective is to show that suffering for doing what is right is more honourable than resorting to retaliation and becoming an intimidator oneself (1 Pet 3:8-17). The third objective – the escape plan for the one being victimized – comes from a *no tolerance* stance (from both counsellor and client). Sometimes the only way out for a victim is assistance to find a physical escape. Pointers for emotional positioning for an escape are given here.

POSITIONING A VICTIM FOR ESCAPE

Educate your client in the following:

> ➤ Never say '*it's ok*' that you are being victimized
> ➤ You are important; your welfare and safety is important
> ➤ If necessary, temporarily harden your heart towards the other party (even if it is a significant other such as a child or spouse)
> ➤ Ask for God's help to escape the situation
> ➤ Seek wisdom from God for the timing and plan of escape
> ➤ Be willing to lean on God's provision of carers who are willing to intervene, rescue and provide for you
> ➤ Following escape, seek personal healing and strengthening so that you will not be put in the position again
> ➤ Ask your pastor/minister for resources on who you are 'in Christ'

Counsellor Resource: JEZEBEL & AHAB OPERATIVES

The Jezebel spirit manifests in several ways as far as the church is concerned. Since, as a Christian counsellor, you will be ministering to the members of the Body of Christ, it is well to safeguard yourself by having some knowledge of these operatives. You might also be called to deal with associated problems such as: –

a)   spiritually abused victims
b)   fallout from church divisions
c)   false doctrine repercussions
d)   cult and witchcraft victims
e)   infiltration of the church by the occult
f)   influence from charlatans, false prophets, healers and apostles
g)   personal influence or attack from the Jezebel spirit

In the Old Testament Queen Jezebel is seen as the rebellious manipulative wife of King Ahab. The spirit operating through this woman caused over 10 million Hebrews – all bar 7,000 faithful souls – to bow down to the idol Baal. Jezebel caused them to forsake their covenant with the one true God, to destroy the sacred altars, and to kill the prophets (1 Kings 19:14-18).

Last mentioned in Revelation, is another Jezebel of a similar spirit, whom the church tolerated and who called herself 'a prophetess'. She was teaching and leading the Lord's servants astray, so that they committed acts of immorality and sacrilege (Rev 2:20). From this latter example, some will readily associate the spirit as of the female gender, with a seductress type mentality and on assignment to bring down church leaders with sexual temptations to immorality.

While sexual perversity is a means of destroying reputations and ministries, immorality is not the real issue. Control is what this spirit seeks. A modern everyday example would be the woman who publicly humiliates her husband with her tongue. She dominates and controls by fear of public embarrassment through ridicule. But, be assured that this spirit uses whichever gender it chooses.

The same could be said of an abusive manipulative husband who dominates the wife and other family members under the '*I am the spiritual head of this house*' approach. The precious Word of God can be twisted by this spirit and used to serve its devious purposes within the church family also. Hell and damnation can be preached to elicit fear and servitude, or a consistent overemphasis might be placed on tithing and sacrificial giving in order to build a Babylonian type empire. The church might be built up in numbers, only to be brought down through divisiveness, corruption, or lack of finance. The joy of participation and of giving has been taken away.

However, a Jezebel spirit requires an Ahab in the form of a *co-dependent type relationship*. Sometimes, the Ahab can be a force in itself as a perpetuator of the abuse. A victim mentality can turn the Ahab from a submissive vessel to a servant who might enjoy 'the game' in the end and begin to think up his or her own innovations. These operatives will seek to manoeuvre into leadership positions – Jezebel especially as that of worship leader, prophet or teacher; even, in some cases, controlling the board of a church, the finance department or missions committee. In particular, those who are involved in intercessory groups, are most hated by demonic forces, and are used by the spirit infiltrators to cause strife and division within a church.

The Ahab spirit might use a spouse, a secretary or an unobtrusive servant, as the spy, the messenger, or the front person for the Jezebel contender. For example, a pastor's gentle wife might be sent to 'correct' a wayward parishioner on her husband's behalf. Or a church administrator might be called upon to demote an elder who is under suspicion based on unsubstantiated gossip.

These partners in crime particularly target the prophets/church leaders who call to repentance. Recall the fate of John the Baptist through the manipulative and vengeful Herodias. Jezebel might 'act out' as a prophet with *directional prophecies* aimed at controlling the lives of individuals; individuals who could prove a threat because of their significant giftings – in particular, discernment of demons and false doctrine. Many a *watchman** has been ejected from a ministry or church when attacked via subversive means through these spirits.

---

*Watchman: one assigned by the city as sentinel to guard and warn of the enemy's approach.

Be on guard in your role as a Christian counsellor for these traits of manipulation and control operating through you. The spirit could be upon yourself as well as come against you and your ministry. Make sure you are within a group of your peers who all feel free to minister to each other in a loving and corrective manner. Have that inner circle of friends, as did both Jesus and the Apostle Paul. You need others who will walk alongside, discern trouble, encourage and watch over you personally in your work.

Be under supervision, both clinically and spiritually, if possible. If you work within a secular agency in particular, do find a faithful shepherd and seek pastoral care, which will not breach your confidentiality and workplace responsibilities. If you work within the framework of a church structure, see that you are covered by the organizational insurance. If you are in private practice seek clinical supervision with ethical and legal accountability, and have appropriate insurance such as personal liability, public liability and business coverage. Most importantly, cover yourself with *the blood of Christ* daily.

Practicalities: ABUSE OF THE COUNSELLOR – WOUND TRANSFERENCE

As people helpers, we are open to abusive situations. As with all those in the helping profession, personal boundaries can become blurred. Particularly when it comes to a long-term caring situation, we can become too closely associated and vulnerable. We need to pray for protection for our ministry and wisdom to handle such cases. As prayer ministers, we are often privy to very personal details of a person's life, both past and present, and even entrusted by God with private knowledge through spiritual discernment. Therefore, we need to be conscious that we have a greater responsibility than the average person to show love, patience and tolerance, and to operate in wisdom when we have this knowledge.

In the natural, there can be times when we might feel we are being abused in the ministry situation. Much is expected of us. We can sometimes feel 'hard done by' when a client turns on us and suddenly vents feelings for no apparent reason. Harsh, critical words might be hurled towards us directly, even profanity and very personal and derogatory remarks. We can become aware that we are being criticised outside the practice in the form of gossip, personal slander or attacks on our ministry.

Within the practice it can show in subtle manipulative practices such as the usually punctual client turning up late for appointments, or 'forgetting' to do things, we have requested of them. This can indicate that we are being tested to see whether we will love unconditionally, now that we possess intimate secrets and the relationship is getting deeper. We are actually being tested to see if we are trustworthy.

We are specifically referring here to *wound transference,* the term used for personal attacks where the client can be punishing a counsellor for wounds inflicted on them by a third party. The client could be using the counsellor as a *whipping post* in anger and bitterness towards God or another authority figure. There can be involved unrealistic expectations – counting on the minister to be forgiving, all loving and accepting of bad behaviour.

They could see this as an opportunity to resolve some present conflicts (say with a spouse) or to clear some *unfinished business* from the past. We can be used as vehicles to meet the client's unmet needs, in that we are expected to relate to according to what their view of love is. If we are unaware of the danger, we could be successfully manipulated into bowing down to wants and demands.

For example, the client's father was unavailable to listen to childhood personal needs therefore the counsellor could be expected to do all the listening, and to be available on demand. Indicators of this can range from a subtle: *remember how I told you dad was never there for me,* to, *how dare you take holidays when I am going to end it all this weekend?!*

WOUND TRANSFERENCE CASE STUDY: ROSE

Example #1
Rose has been a timid child who has been wounded by the verbal abuse of her mother. Consequently, she has had nothing to do with her since she left her family home at 15 years of age.

As your prayer ministry client, Rose begins to appreciate your kindness and gentle way of relating to her during sessions. As the counselling progresses over a number of weeks, she is beginning to feel safe enough to start 'speaking her mind'. She is becoming more assertive towards you.

At first you welcome this new courageous side to Rose. Suddenly she seems to have a complete change of personality! She starts bickering with you within the session - even ringing you up outside of appointment times to object to some slight from you she feels she has experienced. You are shocked at her use of profanity over the phone. You receive your first 'hate mail' at your home address.

> *As an adult, Rose could be saying to you, the counsellor, what she would have liked to have said and done as a child to her abusive mother.*

Example #2
Same situation, but Rose is trying to meet her needs in a different way. She wants you to be 'the mother she never had'. She has warmed to your nurturing manner. She asks for special favours such as extra time with you for coffee, or perhaps a little walk together. She takes a special interest in your family photos on the desk and hints at being invited to your next family special event. She seeks you out and sits with you in church on Sunday mornings.

You gently state to her that, as her counsellor, you cannot ethically nor emotionally meet her personal needs in this way. She turns on you in rage and disappointment. She discontinues the ministry with you, making sure you know that she has sought and found someone 'more qualified' or 'more helpful'.

> *As an adult, Rose is still the 'little girl lost' looking for a family who will take her in. She has made an attempt to wound you through rejection, just as she has been wounded as a child by parental rejection.*

Counsellor Exercise: ROSE

  a) *Try to think of a third example of what Rose might do to transfer her wounds onto you as her prayer minister?*
  b) *What would you do in this (fictitious) third situation to resolve your problem? Support your plan of action from a biblical basis.*
  c) *How can Rose's wounds be healed?*

Counsellor Resource: PASSIVE/SUBMISSIVE CHECKLIST

If you check off more than half of these points you would do well to seek assertiveness training and personal development before embarking on a career/ ministry as a Christian counsellor. This is essential to enable you to function comfortably in relationships in your work and future ministry.

Are you a passive type and/or a submissive type?

- ❑ Do you struggle to say what you want and or need?
- ❑ Do you find it difficult to say no?
- ❑ Is it hard for you to speak up for yourself?
- ❑ Do you avoid expressing your own opinions?
- ❑ Do you go along with others just to keep the peace?
- ❑ Are you constantly apologising?
- ❑ Are you a people pleaser?
- ❑ Do you need to be liked by everyone?
- ❑ Do you seek approval for everything you do and think?
- ❑ Do you frequently back down without negotiating?
- ❑ Are you always a follower and never the leader?
- ❑ Do you avoid confrontation at all costs?
- ❑ Would you describe yourself as timid or shy?
- ❑ Are you afraid of expressed feelings – in yourself or in others?
- ❑ Do you often use phrases such as: *don't know/what do you want to do?/I will fit in with you/whatever you like/which one do you think...?'*

Also available are accompanying handouts for assertiveness training for passive/submissive types, including the topics *Setting Boundaries & How to Say No.*

Client Handout: REALITY ISSUES CHECKLIST

- ❑ I must have the approval of all the significant people in my life
- ❑ Everyone should like me
- ❑ I must be treated with complete fairness
- ❑ If people do not give me immediate attention, then they do not love me
- ❑ I cannot live/work alone
- ❑ I am nothing without a partner
- ❑ I must be responsible, dependable and needed by everyone
- ❑ I should always be appreciated and thanked for everything I do and say
- ❑ My happiness and welfare takes precedence over everything else
- ❑ Everyone should be interested in what interests me
- ❑ My anger needs to be immediately vented at all times
- ❑ All those who wrong me should be punished
- ❑ Every person should know what I think of them
- ❑ Everyone should know what I think
- ❑ Everyone should want to do what I want to do
- ❑ People should do what I want them to do
- ❑ Everyone must tell me the truth all of the time

Before continuing on with this list, take some time to reflect on how the points you have checked off are presently affecting your relationships. You might like to record your thoughts here. Discuss your insights with your counsellor at this point.

My thoughts:

- ❑ I can do what I please
- ❑ The world owes me
- ❑ Everything must be done perfectly and on time
- ❑ I must reach all my goals
- ❑ I must succeed in everything I do
- ❑ I am what I do
- ❑ I have no value as a human being unless I'm doing/achieving something
- ❑ I must earn God's love and approval
- ❑ Frustration is bad for me
- ❑ I must keep my cool at all times
- ❑ All my ideas are original
- ❑ I only have to do something when I want to
- ❑ I can only do one thing at a time
- ❑ I should be compensated for every effort I make
- ❑ My privacy is sacred.
- ❑ No one should challenge me
- ❑ I am doing the very best I can
- ❑ I must complete all 'to do' lists
- ❑ I should feel guilty when I want to do something for myself
- ❑ Others first and me last
- ❑ I must read every word and every thing
- ❑ I must answer every letter/phone call/text/email message
- ❑ I should be healthy at all times
- ❑ I must get 8 hours sleep every night

'Reality' is defined as the state of things as they are, or appear to be, rather than as one might wish then to be, the state of being real', Collins Dictionary. You might be surprised to learn that all of the above points are unrealistic. Your insistence on holding on to these ideas/values/restrictions/ideals, and attempting to live by them, is probably contributing to your life problems. This will need discussion with your counsellor/therapist.

CLIENT TESTIMONIAL – Glasshouse Orchid

You asked me the other day why I had never sought help for my childhood experiences before this. Well it is my 70th birthday next week and your question started me thinking. Yes, why haven't I before this? Why did I only start to go for counselling and prayer ministry two years ago? Why did I wait this long to rid myself of my demons (as my hubby calls them)?

I guess the bottom line is that I have never felt that I deserved to be happy, that there are people out there that have experienced far worse problems than me, and they seem to manage. It's been hard for me to admit that I have been hanging on to my pain because I haven't felt worthy of a better life than what I have had.

There were the little voices in my head that kept telling me that it was too late for me at 68 to learn anything, that 'you can't teach an old dog new tricks'. And who would want to help an old dog like me anyway?

Look at my Bassett hound Ruby. She is going on 14 now and she has just got into a routine of eating and sleeping and won't even go out for a walk with Jack now. Dear Jack, he's 85 next year and he just won't give in. Every morning at 5am, rain hail and shine, he'll be out there, whether Ruby and I want to go with him anymore or not.

I asked myself recently why, when Jack lost his first love Emily, then every other member of his family through cancer, why would he risk marrying me with all my health problems? And how, in God's name, did he survive the war seeing his best mates tortured and blown up? How can he always manage to enjoy his life? And here's me; I give up and take myself to bed at the slightest little knock back!

I asked Jack himself the other day. He just said in his typical easygoing way, 'I guess dear that some are hardier than others. It's like the difference between my best glasshouse orchids and those little daisies out there in the front garden. Some people, like the orchids, need a safe place and extra care to survive, and, when they don't get it you never get a good bloom out of them. Then there are others, like the daisies God just leaves to get on out in the sun and the rain and they do just fine.'

My dear Jack has been so good to me over the years. We married late, because, after Harold died and the other two rotters I called husbands left me, I found I still needed someone to look after me. He was the one that took me along to Minnie the church counsellor.

He said the doctors certainly weren't doing me any good and that he was sick of taking me to one after another of them. He reckoned it was time to face my demons. I think that he was worried about how I would survive after he's gone, him being so much older than me. I have been such a trial to him with my moods and my illnesses. It was the first time that he really took charge after five years of us being together. He said it was time for me to get some help for my emotions as well as my body.

Minnie, the counsellor, is so nice. I already knew her from church, but only to say a little about the weather at suppers and such. She always seemed so busy. Even though, at 65, she is nearly my age, she is always on the move, always chatting to one or the other and going on retreats and seminars. Her face has always intrigued me – it sort of shines. I have always envied her for her happy face.

Well, she taught this old dog some new tricks. At the very first visit, she gave me a label for all my complaints – Post Traumatic Stress, or PSTD. Jack got straight on to my grandson to look it up on the computer for us. Jack read about it. He just kept reading and nodding and saying, 'aha', 'ummm' and 'aah!'

So that was the beginning. I learnt that not all people who suffer trauma need treatment from a professional. Some hardy characters like Jack are blessed with the skills to survive and to move on. But some like me, we need to have support to even feel the pain, let alone face it and be able to find faith in ourselves (as well as in the good Lord).

What really helped me was when Minnie told me a bit about what she had been through as a kid, the poor little thing. With her, it was incest. With me, it was only a neighbour, but she said my pain was just as real as hers.

She told me, after the second session that, unless I was willing to learn the necessary skills and to get the prayer I needed, my life would always be miserable and that Jack would suffer along with me. That's what got me motivated to start. It was for my darling Jack. He deserves to have a happy wife. I may not be a daisy, but I want a shine on my face like Minnie. If God made me to be like one of His glasshouse orchids, then I want to look like one.

Practicalities of Counselling: SURVIVORS OF CHILDHOOD SEXUAL ABUSE

Counselling of *adult survivors* of childhood sexual abuse is *a specialist ministry*. You will not always be aware that a client is *a survivor* (someone who has suffered in the past in this way) until you are sometimes well underway in the counselling process. The same basic counselling techniques used in other cases can be used for those you suspect are victims of sexual abuse during their childhood, but with some very important provisos.

> IMPORTANT: Remember that we are dealing with only <u>suspected</u> historical abuse issues in this portion of the teaching. Be extremely careful not to cause further suffering by coercing or manipulating to purposefully uncover suspected abuse.

SPECIAL MINISTRY CONSIDERATIONS

When there is even the slightest hint that you could be dealing with an adult survivor of childhood sexual abuse, seek experienced support for both yourself and the client. Lean on those in supervision and authority over you. You should already have *informed consent* documentation from the client to do so, as well as acknowledgement that you are covering *duty of care* aspects (see section on *Privacy and Confidentiality*).

Privacy and boundary issues can be extremely sensitive issues in such cases. Secrecy could have been a major factor for your client's survival in the past. Coping and defence mechanisms such as denial, dissociation, and repression most probably have been set in place. Tread cautiously and even more respectfully than usual. On the other hand, the client might divulge too much too freely to you once he/she is liberated to do so – perhaps more than you are capable of handling.

There could be a spiritual stronghold of grief or of anger involved. Taking the person back to the point of entry of these often repressed emotions can afford deep healing, but it can also be risky business for both you and the client. Grief and anger can be so ingrained that it has become an integral part of the victim's personality and lifestyle. Sometimes the refusal to let go of it as a coping mechanism may manifest in some very unusual ways. Specialist deliverance ministry could be needed (see Mk 5:1–20).

If you have already been processing wounds via The Healing Pool Method (see Prayer Ministry Techniques) discontinue this method as it could fully stir up the associated feelings of the actual abuse. Stick to peripheral problems. For example, if the client says her current employer makes her feel trapped or claustrophobic, you might have sufficient reason (from other clues or disclosures) to suspect that this is related to childhood abuse. However, do not lead her back into recalling these *past traumatic experiences*.

Instead, allow the Holy Spirit to help her to express and vent her present feelings – where she is dealing with her boss yelling at her. Deeper ministry can be accomplished at a later stage, after the abuse has been confirmed, and by those experienced in these matters. Be careful not to implant any *false memories* by making any suggestions – particularly by the use of symbols, or putting words into the client's mouth, or by placing ideas into his or her head.

Do not minister out of your depth. Seek supervision from colleagues and refer on for specialist care at the earliest possible opportunity. Ethically, the client remains your responsibility until under the care of another party. Seek spiritual support for yourself during the transition. Very carefully, make the handover with lots of loving supportive care. You could offer to write referrals with the client's input, or, to act as a personal advocate with the specialist where appropriate.

However, be prepared that God may choose to use you to minister up to a certain stage of healing with the client. Seek God on this, and remain available, rather than stepping in too quickly to refer on. This could add to the client's stress in having to build another trust relationship with a new counsellor, particularly for those who are dealing with self-harming issues.

Make sure that there is a trusted carer available for the client to debrief with directly following Christian counselling sessions. A support person could be a pastor, a home group leader, a friend, a family member or a medical doctor. Do not liaison with your client's carer unless the client is fully aware of your connection and communication with the third party.

During significant healing sessions make adequate notes for your own private use. These are to help you recall what was said and also serves as an ethical check on yourself and your methods. Take into consideration that you could be subpoenaed by the courts and made to submit your records as evidence if the perpetuator is eventually brought to trial.

AUTHOR'S MINISTRY EXPERIENCE

Teachings on counselling *adult survivors of childhood sexual abuse* are usually pretty academic. It is possibly a lot easier to write and to research the subject, than to actually have to deal with the issues in reality. Prayer ministry and counselling are fraught with pitfalls and challenges on this subject. Personally, it has always been the most difficult issue I have had to handle, but also the one most satisfying for me to deal with on a coalface basis. I hope that the following few observations will help other carers who are reaching out to those living with the legacy of abuse.

The counselling process can be painfully slow and time consuming in these cases and can involve psychiatric problems (including self-harming and suicidal ideation).

It is my belief that this does not exclude any individual's right to emotional and spiritual care, as long as it is in conjunction with physical and psychological treatments and there is a good support network in place for both the client and counsellor.

I noticed quite early as a prayer minister that clients were coming to me who had proven too difficult and time consuming for other health care practitioners and church leaders. I welcomed them into my office somewhat naively, and without reserve, simply because I felt I did not have to lean on my own understanding – as the Holy Spirit was my major source of guidance. I firmly believed Jesus would take over as The Counsellor when I needed him, and he always proved faithful.

So, when clients would come to me saying that they were desperate to find the help they needed, I would quietly and confidently say, *that's OK. Let us see what God is going to do for you now. I am in the business of restoring hope to his people; I just know he is going to use me to give you some hope back. He would not have sent you to me otherwise.*

I would inevitably find out that those considered to be in the 'too hard basket' were victims of sexual abuse – usually beginning back in early childhood. Abuse might have occurred on more than one occasion, and by more than one abuser. I would bide my time, knowing that I was in for a long haul, because I had to wait for them to trust me enough to reveal what had happened in the past. I learnt that it would be in the client's own timing and in their own way.

There were those who told me early in the counselling relationship that they had been raped or molested. They would say things like, *but I have had prayer for that and I have forgiven .... or, but I am all over that. That is not really what I am here for...actually I am having problems with my job/children/husband/ church.*

We would work on the presenting problems: the lack of career direction, inappropriate behaviour around men, problems with disciplining the children, the inability to fit in at church meetings and all the rest. However, we would often end up going around in circles. Some progress with cognitive therapy and inner healing would take place, but when one problem was resolved a similar one would appear in another area.

The trust relationship would slowly be established over the weeks. I would then be able to gently reintroduce the topic of the abuse. By then, the counselling process would be stirring up old issues. This would sometimes manifest in dreams, flashbacks and troubling memories of old wounds and this would indicate to me that the Holy Spirit was graciously and very gently doing His work.

If I felt comfortable that the groundwork for trust had been laid, then I knew from experience that the latent issues would emerge. It could be compared to being introduced to a shy child who hides behind a mother's skirts. You find that if you continue to talk to the mother, while still acknowledging the child with a fleeting smile, then the child will communicate when ready.

A client might say, *do you think I could be having problems at work with my boss because my dad yelled at me like he does?* I would then ask for a recent example of the boss verbally abusing her and how it currently reminds her of her father. Gently we would allow the emotions to come to the fore by prompting: *how did you feel when your boss said that? Now, if it is OK with you, can we revisit a specific incident from the past when your dad yelled at you? How did that make you feel? Do you remember?* Eventually we would get to foundational problem and then work from there.

Client Handout #1: CHILDHOOD FAMILY HOME WORKSHEET

Take a moment to ask the Holy Spirit to reveal to you all the ways the *kingdom of darkness* was operating in your family home as you grew up. As you go through the counselling process, you will probably discover more issues. **Concentrate only on what is being revealed to you personally at this time.** List your current revelations below, e.g. abuse (specify type), perfectionism, harsh discipline, criticism, intimidation, lust, fear, anger, abandonment, rejection, neglect, addictions, selfishness, scapegoating, mental cruelty, violence etc.

FAMILY ISSUES

Sometimes, the sin of another against us can cause *bondages* in our souls: self-rejection, anger, lack of forgiveness, bitterness, shame, self-hatred, loneliness, isolation, timidity, anxiety, and so on. Ask the Holy Spirit whether there is any bondage operating in your life, **now**, that you feel has its root cause in the sin or the actions of family members against you. Describe whatever comes to mind below.

PERSONAL BONDAGES

If you want to share your thoughts with your counsellor please do so; otherwise, take it to the Lord as a matter of prayer for your release and healing. However, if you decide to deal with it privately, make sure that you deal with any personal issues that are your own responsibility, e.g. unforgiveness.

Client Handout #2: PROCESSING PAST ABUSE

CLIENT'S NAME:
DATE:

STEP 1 TALK ABOUT THE ABUSE to a safe person other than your counsellor, e.g. trusted friend, mentor, or spiritual advisor

STEP 2 SUMMARISE YOUR PAST EXPERIENCES (Use extra sheets of paper if you need to).

STEP 3 IDENTIFY PRESENT FEELINGS: I feel: anxious, grief, resentful, bitter, angry, hatred/rage, disillusioned, disappointed, relieved, comforted, peaceful, victorious…

STEP 4   LIST PAST UNHEALTHY WAYS OF MEETING YOUR NEEDS

addiction, self-pity, depression, shutting down, anger, aggression, overreactions, co-dependence, overwork, manipulation, control, revenge

STEP 5   CHOOSE HEALTHIER WAYS TO MEET YOUR NEEDS

List your options then bring this worksheet to your next session for further discussion with your counsellor (*1Pet:14-19*)

CHAPTER ELEVEN

CONFLICT IN RELATIONSHIPS

Man in conflict with man basically covers communication skills and conflict resolution. It describes a little of how relationship problems take seed in the first place, and how we reap different types of conflict from different types of seed sown. This chapter leads into one of the major issues brought into the counselling arena – marriage conflict – followed by the topic of forgiveness, which is the central theme of Christian living and relating.

- Introduction to conflict and forgiveness
- Sowing and reaping in relationships via judgments, inner vows, etc
- Resources for resolving conflict including communication guidelines

---

Study Notes

INTRODUCTION TO CONFLICT & FORGIVENESS

Counselling often involves conflict *mediation and resolution*, even if it is ministry solely to the conflicts within an individual (*inner conflicts*). The message to your clients will basically be to:

> ➤ operate in a spirit of forgiveness
> ➤ attack the problem not the person
> ➤ deal with the feelings involved and move on into freedom

Be prepared to spend some time with clients on unforgiveness issues. Daily, make sure your own heart is clean in this area (Ps 51). You cannot afford to hold on to a grudge whilst teaching others about biblical principles (Rom 2:21, Tit 2:7, Jas 3:1).

UNFORGIVENESS

An assessment test to locate issues of unforgiveness is included as a standard resource because some of your practice will involve drawing your clients to come out of denial in this area.

> a) Some will flatly refuse to forgive.
> b) Others will state that they are willing to forgive but vow never to forget.
> c) Some will feel that they have already forgiven; but need to be prompted into deeper levels of forgiveness.

Unforgiveness can be classed as an *attitude* accompanied by a feeling. This is created by a responsive choice not to forgive based on a judgment. Basically, it is helpful to remember that unforgiveness is a *response* not a reaction. You will not be able to help any of these individuals to proactively establish harmonious relationships until the issues of judgments and unforgiveness are thoroughly dealt with (see *Relationships – Sowing & Reaping Table*).

God makes a response to forgive us for our personal sins <u>after</u> we have forgiven others for offences against us (Lk 6:37; Matt 6:14-15). He makes the startling statement that, until we do forgive others, he refuses to forgive the wrongs we have done. Obviously, we are not able to move on in freedom and victory in our relationships until our conflicts are processed and resolved by forgiving.

Unforgiveness issues underlie a very large part of presenting problems involving bitterness, resentment and anger. Yet, sometimes, we feel that we somehow have a right to collect and hold onto feelings, which cause so much harm to ourselves and to others. The anointing will not be coming through in your ministry if this is so. Be particularly careful about your attitude towards the abusers of the clients with whom you are dealing. We need to understand anger in particular in order to develop the skills to handle it appropriately when dealing with some pretty hard cases. The word 'appropriately' here, means in a mature and God honouring manner (see *Dealing with Feelings* section).

The scriptures need to be our yardstick. Harmonious and peaceful relationships are the goal. God sees our hearts, the hypocrisy and the games we play with each other. He sees where we are harbouring resentment and bitterness, and how we are repressing anger, hostility and hatred, rather than allowing it to be exposed and dealt with. He views our emotional baggage for what it is and warns us for instance that, 'the devil comes in the door' and wreaks havoc if we hold on to our anger (Eph 4:26-27).

EMOTIONAL BAGGAGE

This is why the complicated emotion of anger has been given particular attention in this text. Earlier, there was very little written and taught on handling anger due to fashionable humanistic views. Mankind embraced 'being a law unto ourselves' and some felt that we had the right to free expression no matter who was hurt. It was felt that, as we were basically all good at heart, 'everything would sort itself out in the end'.

Underlying unforgiveness issues were not justly acknowledged. Therefore, the secular world had no real answers, because *bitter roots* were never exposed. We have reaped the consequences with an angry aggressive new social order where emotions poison bodies and souls. We are medicating emotions in children, rather than teaching respect, values and self-discipline. The *spirit of unforgiveness* has taken hold and is being passed down to our offspring as a *societal curse*.

GODLY RESOURCES

The Body of Christ has counteracted this trend with some excellent Christian books on managing emotions, such as Dr Don Colbert's *Deadly Emotions,* Thomas Nelson, 2003 and Joyce Meyer's simple and practical teachings on emotions, conflict and the pursuit of peace. There are still many fine books on forgiveness on the shelves. There is a new emphasis on learning to forgive self as well as others, and on moving on in order to leave the past behind so that the present and the future can be enjoyed to the full.

The following text will cover a token assortment of resources to offer your clients. It is suggested that you collect and keep a good list of books and recordings to recommend. As a counsellor/prayer minister, you will learn that there is never sufficient time to cover all you would like to within a session. Homework assignments and directional reading will be necessary. Always remind yourself that the Holy Spirit is at work in between. Each time a client comes through your door, a changed person enters (to the one who left the previous session).

Client Handout #1: RELATIONSHIP CONFLICT

'*A house divided against itself will fall*', whether it be a partnership, a family, a business, a community, a church, a ministry or a nation. Strife and conflict create division, and division leaves us vulnerable to attack (Matt 12:25-32).

Conflict usually involves the emotion of anger. Never resort to physical violence. This includes scratching, pinching, shoving and slapping and throwing things at a person, as well as the more obvious forms of abuse like punches or attacks with a weapon. Communicating anger appropriately is a skill, which can be learnt. Outbursts of anger are non-productive and verbal abuse such as name-calling and profanity are completely unacceptable.

Angrily *stonewalling* and *freezing people out* are also not productive ways of dealing with conflict. These, and other passive methods, such as *retreating into your cave* or giving the other party *the silent treatment* are called *passive/aggressive behaviours*. You are still operating in a retaliatory style in the process of communicating your feelings. Ask your counsellor for the resource: *Guidelines for Good Communication* for better alternatives.

The right kind of communication is important. Think about your normal *language style* and your negative *body language* when engaged in conflict. Do you: scream, screech, mumble, grumble, harass, nag, manipulate, intimidate, generalize, denigrate, swear, lie, exaggerate, defend or attack, take revenge, jump to conclusions or judge? Do you punish with words, gestures or actions? Do you bear grudges and reflect this in your speech and body language?

Failure to communicate well indicates that you do not value the relationship or respect the other party. Not communicating at all is unfair. The offender has the intrinsic right to be allowed to know what they have done to offend you. When informed they may be able to clear up a misunderstanding or to make amends. Remember it is often better to have a relationship where you are working towards resolving a conflict, rather than no relationship at all. The heartache of loss and loneliness can be excruciating (Gen 2:18).

Aim for respectful forms of communication. Speak the truth in love with the aim of healing and reconciliation, rather than to exact revenge (Eph 4:15). Remember that forgiveness means surrendering your 'right' to hurt someone else for hurting you. Forgiveness works because it breaks the cycle of retaliation. Are you holding on to a grudge? Ask your counsellor for a copy of the *Unforgiveness Self-Assessment* and take the test.

Listen to the other party's point of view <u>carefully</u>. This means from the positional basis of caring for the other party. Be tolerant on hearing another person's opinion and what <u>they</u> perceive as the truth. Truth has many different viewpoints and perceptions; but truth is still the truth. Remember that, if you insist on holding on to any belief other than the truth, then you are *under deception*. Ask God's opinion on the matter and be sure that there are no blockages in the form of pride or stubbornness, which will prevent you from hearing his answer. Pray for wisdom, wisdom and more wisdom to be able to use the knowledge and insight you receive.

Look for the facts, and avoid blowing findings out of proportion based on feelings. Do not expose the facts purely to use as weapon, nor choose those who will side with you. Be gracious and merciful, treating others as you would have them treat you. Heed the warning about hypocrisy and judging others, that is, take the plank out of your own eye first (Matt 7: 1-5).

Love others as you love yourself (Matt 22: 34-40). Do you love and respect your self? (Be sure to think carefully about this point). Are you using conflict to abuse and punish yourself because you think you deserve no better than havoc and bad relationships? If this question has troubled you, then you possibly need to acknowledge that you could have low self-esteem and shame issues. Remember that shame and anger turned inwards can lead to physical and mental illness.

Investigate whether you have reality issues. (Ask your counsellor for the handout *Reality Checklist*). Are you living in an unreal fantasy world? Are you addicted to love/hate type relationships where you experience a 'high' from the emotional conflict? Do you experience a feeling of significance from the drama of fighting and making up? Are you hooked on the excitement of a good fight?

Avoid being the victim. Do you receive a reward out of playing the victim? Do you like to control others to prevent others from controlling or manipulating you? Do you suspect you have an Ahab or Jezebel type nature? Do you enjoy controlling or being controlled? Could you be in victim/intimidator or co-dependency type relationship? All of these issues are quite common; so don't be shocked over your all-too-human nature. Do something about it!

Learn about *conflict resolution,* which is a satisfying and exciting skill to acquire. You can begin by being open and honest within the counselling relationship. Learning to form a trust relationship with your therapist or Christian counsellor is the first step towards forming good relationships in everyday life.

Client Handout #2 SOWING & REAPING IN RELATIONSHIPS

In nature, the root is an underground structure, which carries nourishment to the plant for growth. As human beings we also derive nourishment from our habitual ways (root structures) in our relationships. Just as a plant's roots are hidden from view, our habitual way of relating (for the most part) is hidden. These habits can be in the form of *judgments or negative expectancies* and can have tremendous power to do harm. This is why the roots are described as *bitter and defiling* (Heb 12:15). Poisons, rather than nourishment, are drawn up from the soil bed of relationships, defiling (making dirty or polluting) self and others.

Roots of bitterness produce fruits of bitterness. In this sense, we are personally accountable to God for bitter or spoiled fruits. As with natural laws, spiritual laws have been put in place, so that like reaps like; in this case, death or life to relationships. If we plant a radish seed, then we will not reap a watermelon; plant hate, rejection and shame and we will not harvest a loving, caring relationship. We might be surprised to learn that perhaps our divorce had its roots in unforgiveness towards a parent or a sibling, or that a judgment on an anointed man of God is defiling our ministry.

The Collins dictionary defines 'bitter' as *'showing or caused by strong unrelenting hostility or resentment'*. We have personally defied or rebelled against God's immutable (unchangeable) laws, which tell us to love one another (this includes forgiving deeply and fully). Unforgiveness, for example, causes relationship conflicts and, sometimes, physical and mental ill health. Many illnesses can be seeded by sinful interactions and maintained by the negative use of emotions. Issues of the spirit are manifested in the realm of the soul. Mental, emotional and physical restoration will at times follow repentance and the act of forgiving and being forgiven.

During ministry, patterns of rejection, loss and abandonment in a client's life history are studied and described as *'bad fruit'*. This ministry often centres on unresolved conflict between husbands and wives, parents and children, brothers and sisters. Relationship conflict can manifest in mood disorders and chronic stress related illness. <u>This is not to say that all illness and tragedy is a direct result of bitter roots</u>. However, many physical and mental health problems decrease once spiritual healing methods have been applied. Perhaps this is the reason a *miracle healing* of the body is sometimes not maintained, as the old bitter root system has not been exposed and dealt with and the 'poisons' are still active.

Elijah House Ministries **have some very powerful and solid teachings similar to the information presented in this resource and the following table: www.elijahhouse.com.au**

Counsellor Resource: RELATIONSHIPS – SOWING & REAPING TABLE

N.B. THIS IS NOT A DIAGNOSTIC TOOL. IT IS A GUIDE ONLY TO POSSIBLE CAUSES & EFFECTS

SEED SOWN	CROPS REAPED	CAUSES	EFFECTS
negative expectancies	isolation, rejection abandonment	lack of trust & faith in God/ others, independent spirit	self-fulfilling prophecies abuse/victimization
critical condemning judgments of self and/others	lack of recognition, condemnation, unforgiveness shame & blame	resentment & bitterness towards others, selves & God, self -righteousness	unhealthy relationships recurring problems/bad fruit poor self image/value
inner vows	wrong responses sinful choices	promises to oneself based on fear, hurt, judgments	fearfulness, hurt, loss of blessings, consequences
self-righteousness	humiliation, failure, isolation etc	pride, blame, use of shame	failed relationships, need for mercy, loss of joy
dishonouring parents	loss of Godly inheritance	rebellion, disrespect of authority & guidance	shortened lifespan, loss of blessings, loneliness
taking on false responsibility in childhood	burnout, cursed in relationships	pride, idolatry of self, self-reliance, deception, self-righteousness	unnecessary burdens, confusion, loss of childhood & freedom
spiritual adultery	lack of intimacy with spouse & with God	close intimacy or idolatry of authority figure e.g. pastor	vulnerable to enemy, divorce & prone to losses
abdication of responsibility	abuse, addictions, failure, dishonour	not being accountable to God, man pleasing, lack of self-respect, self-hatred	co–dependency, loss of respect, honour, identity individuality, & rewards
control & manipulation	fear, defeat, shame, failure	self-protection/dependency self-righteousness /pride quest for power	self-defeat, eviction, rejection, loss of power
disrespect for authority	crime, isolation, failure, rejection	rebellion against man & God's laws & principles	judgment, condemnation, unacceptance, hard heart
sibling disrespect & conflict	marital discord conflict at work	unable to give/receive love, or work as a team member	jealousy, failed marriages/ friendships, lack of success & respect at home & work, j
performance orientation	lack of grace, joy, balance, stability, confidence, peace	self-idolatry/self-abasement unable to receive grace or dispense mercy	burnout, compulsions, stress disorders, isolation from man & God

Gal 6:7-10; Matt 13:3-43, Heb 12:15

IMAGE 11

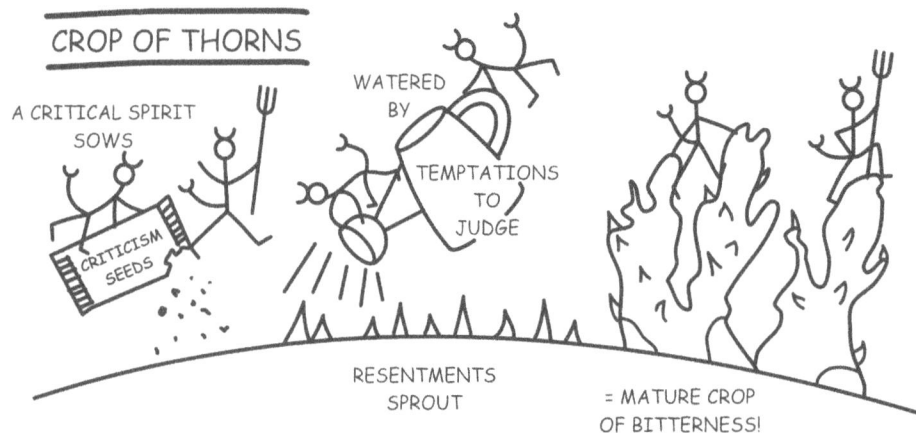

Client Handout #3: REAPING VIA JUDGMENTS & EXPECTANCIES

JUDGMENTS

As stated elsewhere in this text (refer to *Learning our ABCs – Correction & Comfort*) critical judgments are acceptable in the following contexts:

a) matters pertaining to self
b) spirits operating in others
c) fruit of the spirits operating in self or others

Unacceptable judgments involve critical fault finding and condemnation. These are *sinful responses* as they are *a matter of will* and are usually products of a wounded personal spirit and the refusal to forgive self, others and God. These negative judgments include those which involve self-rejection, self-condemnation and self-hatred.

> *I hate myself for allowing him to humiliate me like that.*
> *I will always be the one who is left out.*
> *God doesn't care about me because I am so stupid.*

The impersonal law of God causes reward or punishment to come upon us via judgments (Prv 13:21). This was the reason for the provision of the Cross for our salvation. Almighty God must remain true to himself as the lawgiver and divine judge of his creation (Deut 1:17).

A criminal law court places a judge in authority and in the position to sentence a person with the appropriate punishment to fit the crime. Members of the general public, do not have the right to try, prosecute, rule, judge, sentence nor execute punishment. Negative expectations and the formation of inner vows, are an illegal attempt by the average person's to usurp the role of God as Judge (Matt 7:2).

NEGATIVE EXPECTANCIES

Negative expectancies can be described as 'an infection of the soul'. These can take on the form of a *self-fulfilling prophecy* where 'you get what you expect'. They are usually *habitual practices* based on judgments.

> *Women are always manipulating and controlling.*
> *You can never trust a man.*
> *No one ever listens to me.*

INNER VOWS

Another powerful negative practice is that of making inner vows (promises) which can impact relationships. For example, one could vow, *I'll never be like my father who was miserly or my mother who never stood up for her rights to have money to spend on herself* (Deut 5:16). This breaks the law of honouring father and mother and involves a critical judgment.

For instance, you might choose to be an open-handed generous suitor to a prospective marriage partner, but turn into the very type of person you despise, in a similar troubled marriage relationship as your parents. Ironically, we tend towards creating that which we were running from in the first place.

> *I will never be an idiot like my father.*
> *I will not treat my children like my stepmother treated us.*
> *When I get married it will be to someone completely opposite to my mother.*

The problem trait will often appear again (return to you) either in your own character, or in your relationship with others. It is wise to consider that, in marriages, sowing and reaping is sometimes connected to past or current relationships with parents. Remember that the harvest runs true to the seed. If we sow a radish seed we harvest a radish. When we judge our parents in a specific area, things will not go well for us. It can prove uncanny how it will be related to that specific area of relationships. For example: –

a) A woman reaps a possessive husband resulting from childhood jealousy of a parent's attention to a sibling.
b) A man reaps a nagging wife after seeding judgment upon a critical mother.

Even if the seed is single and small, *the laws of multiplication* and *sowing and reaping* will supply the consequences. If the growth is left unchecked, a deep root system can develop, which draws poisons from far and wide and we will reap again and again (Gal 6:7-10). If you have experienced reoccurring relationship problems then it is sensible to look for the poisons being drawn up (Heb 12:12-15; Lk 6:43-44; Matt 7:15-20). Ask your counsellor for further teachings on *Fruits, Roots & Poisons.* The crop needs to be aborted through acknowledgement, confession and application of the work of the cross to provide release and freedom (Col 2:13-14; 1 Jn 1:7-9).

However, if we try to overcome in our own strength, without repentance and renouncement, we will fail (Rom 7:18-19). God's mercy and grace needs to be called upon and acceptance made of the forgiveness provided for us – purchased by *the blood of our Lord Jesus Christ.* We are instructed to guard against turning back from the grace of God to become like a bitter plant that grows up and causes many problems with its poison (Heb 12:15).

Client Handout #4: CONFLICT RESOLUTION EXERCISES

IMAGE 12

The pictures above serve to illustrate three ways a couple may deal with conflict. Have you ever watched two puppies at play in a tug of war game? They are enjoying the rough and tumble of the 'argument' over which one gets the rag. Then, suddenly, puppy #1 lets go of his right to have the rag. What happens to puppy #2? He falls on his backside and drops the rag. Puppy #2 seizes the opportunity, grabs the rag and is jubilant over his win.

Question 1 Which puppy ended up being hurt and why? On this basis write around 250 words comparing the puppies' power struggle to the ways human beings have of dealing with conflict.

The next illustration is of a ball game. The ball, representing the point the players are trying to make, is being pounded back and forth by the rackets. Neither player is winning. The debaters are evenly matched and emotions are flying hard and fast backwards and forwards.

Question 2 How would the players work out a win/win situation here in regard to their game of retaliation? Write at least 250 words.

The final illustration of two people holding onto a large rubber band serves to indicate tension. Anger, resentment and bitterness are causing obvious strain. The stronger hand wins through manipulation, control, abuse and many other devices. The other hand is the loser. But is it the only loser?

The stronger hand has had the rubber band snap back on it. Ouch!

Question 3 Have you ever personally been hurt when you insisted on your own way? Comment on this, using as many words as you need. If you cannot think of an instance, make your own comments on the rubber band illustration (250 words).

Client Handout #5: CONFLICT WORKSHEET

Some people find that writing down something that is bothering them serves to sort out their thoughts. They are then better able to tackle the problem from both the head and the heart. The following is a very simple guide to structure your thought processes – with the aim of resolving a problem that is causing you conflict.

Before you start this exercise, determine not to say or do anything that comes from a hurt, bitter, resentful, or judgmental spirit. Give yourself some space to really think about the situation, before you let your thoughts and feelings come out via your mouth (Matt 15:11-20).

The conflict between me and.. is:

Its effect on us is:

My contribution to the conflict is:

My plan of action to contribute to its resolution is:

(Use the reverse side of sheet if necessary)

Client Handout #6: COMMUNICATING DURING CONFLICT

Conflict is inevitable in any relationship. Keep these principles, guidelines and tips close at hand. Remember that learning about communicating successfully does not help unless you actually apply what you have learnt.

- ➢ Communicate in a win-win frame of mind
- ➢ Each person's world experience is different from another's; each person's perception of the world is different
- ➢ The receiver decides the meaning
- ➢ Do not accept anything unless it makes sense to you
- ➢ Operate on the premise that people always behave in the best way they can, however they do not always behave in the best possible way
- ➢ All generalisations are false
- ➢ Do not dramatize, exaggerate or lie to win an argument
- ➢ An exaggeration is a lie
- ➢ Never argue to change someone else's mind
- ➢ Communicate to share your mind rather than to conquer or win a point
- ➢ Listening requires as much effort as speaking
- ➢ Listen wholeheartedly and fully to everything that is being said
- ➢ Listen for feelings and be aware of body language
- ➢ As a listener, try never to judge the speaker
- ➢ It is not possible to read the speaker's mind; the speaker needs to speak his or her mind
- ➢ Use phrases such as, *I feel upset when you yell*, rather than, *You upset me when you yell.*
- ➢ Avoid blaming, shaming, scapegoating, teasing or saying, *I was only joking'.*
- ➢ Profanity and derogatory remarks are just not acceptable in any situation.
- ➢ When what you are doing and saying does not work, try something else
- ➢ As a speaker, express your personal needs and feelings respectfully.
- ➢ Offer to try out ideas and suggestions from the other party.
- ➢ Offer your own possible solutions so that they can be trialled.
- ➢ Check back and ask each other whether suggested solutions worked.

Client Handout #7: ACTIVELY DEALING WITH CONFLICT CHECKLIST

Love can be a choice. Love is an act of will. To be proactive in love I need to:

- ❑ Forgive deeply from the heart
- ❑ Get in touch with my true feelings
- ❑ Seek spiritual wisdom
- ❑ Send a gift
- ❑ Give a heartfelt apology
- ❑ Make restitution
- ❑ Speak the truth in love
- ❑ Set loving boundaries
- ❑ Practise loving myself
- ❑ Release the other party (and myself) from grudges, resentments etc
- ❑ Pray for blessings on the other party
- ❑ Seek professional help for mediation
- ❑ Find win/win solutions
- ❑ Meet halfway with compromises and negotiations
- ❑ Have a tolerant attitude of the other person's perceptions
- ❑ Seek understanding of the other person's point of view
- ❑ Take care of my personal needs in the form of a support network e.g. pastoral care, prayer partner, mentor, personal time with God

Other ideas…

Client Exercise: Read 1Cor 13 inserting your own name for the word 'love'.

Counsellor Resource: PRAYER STRATEGIES FOR ABUSIVE SITUATIONS

The following advice was written to the wife of a verbally abusive husband, but can be adjusted and applied to ***any type of abusive relationship.*** If you would like to purchase a copy as a handout for your personal ministry use, specify your needs (e.g. abusive wife/child/sibling/workmate) and it could possibly be adapted for the specific situation you are dealing with. See contact details at the end of this resource.

Dear Client,

*I have been praying a lot for you since our last session together. I thought I would like to arm you with as many **prayer strategies** as possible, so I have addressed this to your friend's post office box and am praying that you will receive it well before our next session. The following is somewhat of a summary of the things we have been talking about over the past few weeks.*

I would also like to take this opportunity to tell how much I admire your commitment to the counselling process under very difficult circumstances. Even though your husband is not willing to join us, I see that you are doing your very best to humble yourself and to seek how you may change your own thoughts and behavioural patterns to align with God's thoughts and ways.

I know that you find it taxing, both physically and financially, to come along each week; that you find it hard sometimes to take in much of what I say because your emotions are still very much raw and on the surface. But, please be encouraged when I say that you have made amazing progress. I see your courage and strength growing week by week as you discover new truths to replace the lies you have embraced in the past. You are doing so well!

You might also like to refer to the stories of Abigail and Esther. Both were godly women who respected men in authority over them, but still did what they needed to do, by using their ingenuity to overcome obstacles. Until next session, I pray that God's still, small voice will be heard by you in the midst of each storm, offering you comfort strength and guidance.

Please see the attached suggested prayer strategies.

God Bless,

Your Counsellor

PRAYER STRATEGIES

1. *Pray according to the wisdom of God, not according to your emotions, which, as you so well know, can prove fickle and unreliable.*

2. *Do not pray from the position of a beggar, 'oh, please save me from the abuse!' Pray from a position of strength and dignity as a child of God.*

3. *Use your authority to pray (1Cor 4:4; Matt 12:29).*

4. *Bind the spirits operating in your husband, which are blinding him to the truth. You might say, 'Spirit of deception operating in the life of my husband, I bind you now because I belong to Jesus Christ and I carry His authority and righteousness. In His Name, I command you to stop your work. I spoil your house according to the Word of God and I enter in to deliver my brother in Christ (husband) from your hands'.*

5. *Resist Satan and he will have to flee from you. Pray that the mouths of the lions will be shut and that spirits such as profanity, intimidation and violence will submit to the authority you wield in Jesus' Name.*

6. *Pray to the Lord of the harvest, that he will send forth labourers (Matt 9:37-38). Ask that people who care deliver the Word to your husband's heart (Rom 10:17). Pray that his ears will be unblocked and that his spiritual eyes will see the truth spoken by the labourers God sends across his path.*

7. *Pray those responsible for his spiritual welfare will see the truth about your circumstances and will step in with wisdom to support you both.*

8. *Ask that nothing will abort the crop of faith you are now planting and that your faith will be increased. Keep quiet about your own spiritual progress and strength; but speak affirmations and positive confessions to yourself.*

9. *Do not compare your own spiritual walk to his. This might incite further abuse. This also dishonours him. Instead, treat him in faith as if he is already healed and operating as spiritual head of your home.*

10. *Plead the blood over your household and run to the Lord for safekeeping.*

11. *Do not search out friends that will agree with you when you are tempted to rehearse your brother's sins. Choose to speak only to those who will pray positively into your situation rather those who will fuel your anger towards your husband in his treatment of you.*

12. *Be angry but sin not. Do not let bitterness take root. Resist resentment. Be always ready to forgive.*

13. *Guard your own mouth. Armour yourself for the spiritual battle (Eph 6).*

14. *Expect God to provide for you and to protect you via your husband and believe in faith that he is already your willing protector and provider (in Christ). Remember that you get what you expect – both positive and negative!*

15. *Pray favour on all your relationships. Expect others to treat you well – particularly your in-laws and your pastor, who can provide you much support.*

16. Apologise to your husband for whatever you truthfully can. Stand firm on your convictions – respectfully and with dignity.

17. Do not give power to the abuse, by fuelling the fire with your own negative emotions. Resist fear.

18. Direct your anger and blame onto the real enemy – operating in a warrior spirit. Do not come from a victim mentality. Remember that the real enemy, Satan, is already defeated (He just needs to see that he must lie down!).

19. Pray daily for your children's protection. Ask for forgiveness from them for your own negative role modelling wherever appropriate.

20. Do not speak negatively to your children regarding your husband as they are a part of him and this dishonours them also. Pray for their father, with them, and in a respectful way.

21. Pray for fruits of the spirit to develop in you through all that is happening.

22. Praise God that you have been found worthy to be tested and trained for a higher purpose and for the privilege of sharing in the fellowship of Christ's suffering.

Please respect Copyright. Master copies of resources found within this publication are provided for your use in the companion book: 'So You Want To Be A Christian Counsellor – Resources Handbook' - www.prayercounsel.com.

Prayer Strategies for Abusive Situations is available in client handout form. The author has compiled a selection of other marriage resources on the topic of conflict. Available on request are: –

a) *Holy Spirit Mediation for Couples*
b) *Mature Partners Tips for Avoiding and Resolving Conflict*
c) *Marriage as a Covenant under God*
d) *Divorce, Remarriage & Grief Issues*

Address enquiries to:
Email: elvie@prayercounsel.com

CHAPTER TWELVE

FORGIVENESS RULES

This extremely important subject is only briefly covered here. The topic warrants fuller coverage than this text allows. Reference can be made to the previous chapter *Relationships* for further resources on conflict and unforgiveness issues. Note that all true healing and restoration techniques involve the theme of forgiveness. This particular chapter emphasizes:

- Forgiving deeply from the heart
- The necessity of forgiving self
- Assessing unforgiveness issues
- Typical prayer themes – *Walls* & *Memories*

Study Notes

CLIENT TESTIMONIAL: To Forgive or Not to Forgive.

It was going to take a lot to drag out of me the stuff I had been hiding away about what my dad did to me and me brother. I lived with it for so long that it had become a part of me, simmering under the surface and erupting whenever I came into contact with someone who reminded me of him. It might only take the glimpse of a redheaded guy or the smell of alcohol on someone and I could feel my muscles tense for action, my head go light and that dizzy feeling which used to overtake me, because I knew what was ahead.

Oh, I hated his guts, the way he controlled us with threatening to abuse mum if we didn't behave. He used to lay into her, whatever we did or didn't do. What the little ones had to put up with day after day when my mum was laid up after one of her beatings, only I knew. I did what I could for them, but I couldn't pull food out of thin air when there was no money because he drank it all away.

On paydays, he only had to raise an eyebrow towards me and I'd gather up the girls and get them hidden because I didn't want them to see what we all knew was coming. My brother Frankie copped it the worst. He irritated dad because he reminded him of his brother Frank. Because I was the oldest and a girl, I got the best part – the sickening stuff, which I can't even speak about to this day – not even to my counsellor. The shame is still there.

I don't think I'll ever get rid of it, no matter how much counselling I get. It's the forgiveness part that gets in the way. I know I have to, but I can't – not yet. My counsellor says I need to take it at my own pace, that forgiveness is a process because it comes with grieving and getting through all the stages until I come to an acceptance of my losses in life. She says that there are things in me that need to come into the light – when I am ready and able to deal with them – because I need to forgive on a deeper level than I have been able to so far. She says its no use me just saying I forgive because I think it is the right thing to do now that I'm a Christian.

I know now that Jesus died for my father the same as he did for me. I know that he loved me and dad equally to do that for us; but I can't bring myself to say that I love my dad or forgive him for what he did to us. My head says I need to – for my own sake – but I still hate him. I still want him to pay for what he did. Being in jail for murdering Frankie is not enough. I want him to pay for what he did to me.

ON FORGIVENESS

The preceding testimonial illustrates the possibility of some very serious issues, which you could encounter in the course of your ministry as a Christian counsellor. If you are starting out, you may wonder whether you will ever be capable of handling such difficult scenarios; be assured that the basic biblical principles will always stand you in good stead. Remember not to give in to the temptation to be critical or judgmental. Exercise patience and tolerance. Meet the person at their level of readiness to forgive, rather than giving in to the desire to 'lay down the law.

Forgiveness is basically surrendering our desire to hurt others who have hurt us. In the human sense, forgiveness is difficult because it pulls against our natural sense of justice. It is natural to want revenge and to hold on to grudges, anger, bitterness and resentment. It is both unusual and super-natural to wish the offender well and to forgive fully as the scriptures instruct us to do.

In secular counselling, forgiveness is not such an important issue as it is in Christian circles. In the secular world it is considered as a moral value and optional choice. The choice to forgive will be seen to have benefits, but there will not be the emphasis a prayer minister would place on the subject. Subsequently there will not be the depth of freedom and healing experienced as when a Christian concedes to a higher authority in this matter.

UNFORGIVENESS ISSUES

Sometimes, as a spiritual counsellor, you will feel that the whole world seems to revolve around the basic issue of exposing root problems of unforgiveness. You will be dealing with clients who strongly desire to punish the wrongdoer and to shame and blame by withholding forgiveness. There is the belief that forgiving leaves one open to being taken advantage of, or of being repeatedly abused. Self-protection is also a very strong desire. Holding grudges, revenge seeking and vindictiveness are unfortunately all too common themes in client stories. Basically, there will be several aspects that will be troublesome to the majority of your clients who want to withhold forgiveness:

a)   The desire to personally punish the offender.
b)   The offender will be left unpunished.
c)   The possibility that the offender will recommit the offence.
d)   The expectation that the offender will never feel the need for forgiveness or the desire to make amends.

You will need to have some innovative ideas to cover the various possibilities. Forgiveness is such an important topic that we cannot possibly do it justice in the space available in this publication. You are advised to accumulate as many resources as possible on the subject and to work through your own unforgiveness issues on a daily basis, so that you are a clean vessel for the Lord to use (Ps 51).

Client Handout #1: UNFORGIVENESS ASSESSMENT

Exercise 1: Use the following checklist and related scriptures to locate areas where you need to process forgiveness with help from your counsellor. (Heb 12:15, Lk 23:34, 1Thes 5:15, Ps 37:7-8, Eph 4:31-32, Mk 11:25-26).

- ❑ Does the memory of the hurt still cause you personal pain?
- ❑ Are you blaming God for what happened?
- ❑ Are you still questioning why it happened?
- ❑ Do you feel hatred, anger, bitterness, depression, extreme sorrow (or any other strong emotion) related to the offence?
- ❑ Can you not think of the offender and sincerely wish them good things?
- ❑ Are you jealous when you hear of them doing well?
- ❑ If you had a chance to personally bless them, would you avoid it?
- ❑ Are you withholding your love and goodwill in any way?
- ❑ Are you secretly (or overtly) pleased when you hear that something bad has happened to the offender?
- ❑ Do you find it hard to feel any compassion when you see something bad happening to them?
- ❑ Do you hope that they get what they deserve?
- ❑ Do you picture what you would like to happen to harm them?
- ❑ Do you replay the incident/s in order to process thoughts of revenge?
- ❑ Do you rehearse what you would like to say/should have said?
- ❑ Do you still recount to others what they have done to you?
- ❑ Do you talk behind their back and try to cause them trouble?
- ❑ If you met this person on the street, would you avoid greeting them?
- ❑ Do you presently go out of your way to avoid the offender?
- ❑ Have you left your home, church or workplace because of the offence?
- ❑ Have you cut off all contact with this person?
- ❑ Do you still have physical contact, but do not talk or interact emotionally?
- ❑ If given the opportunity to reconcile, would you avoid doing so?
- ❑ Do you have no desire for reconciliation and restoration of your relationship?
- ❑ Do you blame the other party for how your life has turned out?
- ❑ Do you feel a lack of peace when thinking of the offender/abuser?
- ❑ Do you think of how you were wronged more often now in comparison to how much you thought about it when the offence first occurred?

- ❑ Do you manipulate or bait the person into re-offending in order to feel that you are right in holding on to the offence?
- ❑ Do you constantly talk of your rights to an apology?
- ❑ Are you firm in your stance that you will not reconcile if they do apologise?
- ❑ If they did show remorse or apologise would you tell everyone about it?
- ❑ Are you enjoying seeking compensation or restitution in anyway?
- ❑ Do you think that your own spiritual, emotional or physical health is suffering in any way in regard to unforgiveness issues?
- ❑ Are you holding onto unforgiveness towards yourself?

Exercise 2: Refer to Col 3:12-14. What is your most pressing issue on this subject at the moment?

FORGIVENESS PRAYER: *WALLS*

Lord God, I forgive (*name/s*)... for (*be specific, e.g. not caring for me, not being able to love me, for stealing my childhood, for building walls to keep me out ...*).

I realise that today I have a choice – either to trust you to protect me from further hurt Lord, or to harden my heart further against you, and against those who have already wounded me. My God, my choice is forgiveness.

Jesus said when he was on the cross: *'father, forgive them for they know not what they do'.* Father I forgive them as they did not know how deeply they were hurting you as well as me. I also forgive myself, for I did not know nor understand how deeply I was hurting myself. I will not walk in torment or unforgiveness any longer, nor will I build more walls around my heart. I can see now how I have sinned against others and against you Lord. I ask you now, in the name of Jesus Christ, to forgive me for my wrong responses and sinful choices. I ask you to forgive me for blaming you Lord, for (*be specific...*).

I acknowledge that I need to knock down the walls that I have erected to keep others out, and which I have also used to attempt to keep your love out. I repent of all the self-defence mechanisms I have set up in my pride and rebellion (*name the walls e.g. self -protection, rejection, withdrawal, rebellion, self-defence, hatred, etc*). I now forgive myself – as you have forgiven me.

I ask that your Holy Spirit sanctify me and restore me to how you originally created me to be – made in your image to love and be loved. I give back control of my life to you. Heal me – body, soul and spirit – and ask that you will bless and heal all who have hurt and offended me. Thank you Lord. Amen.

Client Handout #2: HOW TO FORGIVE FROM A WOUNDED HEART

VICTORY FOR VICTIMS

a) Remember that you remain a victim by rationalizing, explaining, or excusing the offences.
b) Do not hold on to the other party's offence and own it for yourself. Leave the responsibility where it belongs.
c) Deal with the facts and attack the problem not the offender.
d) Do not tolerate sin in your self or in others. Take a stand against it, declare it, expose it, and deal with it.
e) Acknowledge the associated emotions of hurt, hate and taking offence in your own heart.
f) Decide to only temporarily bear the burdens of the perpetrator's offences in order to carry them to the Cross. This is the place where the offences cannot harm you any longer.

BEGINNING THE PROCESS

Express all the associated feelings to someone objective and trustworthy. Be sure to identify all offences and painful memories and feelings. Be diligent in not keeping any in dark little corners, as hidden offences and hurts can appear later to plague you. Be ready to process unforgiveness.

UNFORGIVENESS

Let God bring unforgiveness to the surface. He is quite capable of dealing with it, and quite capable of healing your wounds – even the very deepest ones. It is your responsibility to forgive. You are the one held accountable for any unforgiveness on your part, and it is the offender's responsibility to seek forgiveness from you by their own free admission and will. An offender is accountable to God for their own sins, just as you are personally accountable for yours (ask your counsellor for *Handout #2: Unforgiveness Assessment*).

THE FEELINGS

Do not wait until you feel like forgiving. Do what is right and pleasing to God, despite your feelings. Remember that, emotions sometimes take time to heal following the decision to forgive (Eph 4: 26-27). The loving feelings often follow the choice to love and forgive. Where the mind and will goes, the heart follows.

THE GIFT

You can ask for the *gift of forgiveness* but remember to open the gift! Explore the true meaning of *grace* and what God's grace can achieve, where you cannot.

Dedicate yourself as a channel or vessel of his love so that, as it courses through, you will be sanctified and blessed also as you reach out to forgive the offender. No matter how you are personally feeling or how big the offence, it is your responsibility to ask for God's mercy and grace upon all parties involved. It is God's pleasure to give you the gift.

THE RECOVERY PROCESS

Specifically name and forgive each sin and each offence against you. Be specific also with your blessings towards those who have wronged you. We are instructed by God to bless our enemies and to bless those who curse us. This sounds so hard and unfair at times. However, it is a divine principle; therefore, it does work. Be assured that he will deal with the person justly – in his timing and in his way.

FORGIVENESS PRAYER: *MEMORIES*

Lord, I come to you just as I am, unforgiving and full of resentment and bitterness towards (*name each person*). Forgive me for holding on to the feelings of (*specify)* associated with the memories of the offences committed against me. My unforgiveness is a sin against you, Heavenly Father, as I am counting the sacrifice of your Son, Jesus Christ, as worthless.

Lord Jesus, I need the truth and I need your help to relinquish the pain of these memories. I renounce my role as victim. I choose to release (*specifically name each offender)* from any debt I feel is still owed to me. I repent of this and (*specify any other sins such as thoughts of revenge and retaliation). I renounce* my unforgiveness and acknowledge the power of the cross and of the blood – over my past, present and future.

Jesus, because you are all love and all forgiveness, I ask that you to give me the gift of your love and your forgiveness, so that it flows freely through me out to those who have offended me, by the act of my own free will.

In the name of Jesus Christ, I command you Satan never to use these memories against me again. I deny your power and I break your hold on my life in this area. By the power of his blood, I command you to release me from this link between my sin and theirs. By the sword of His Word I cut the negative soul ties binding me together with: (*name each person and cut individually).* I break loose from the chains forged from my unforgiveness and take this key of forgiveness to open my own prison door in Jesus' powerful name.

Now Lord, I ask you to heal my wounds. Restore me to my true identity in you. I invite you to cleanse me and fill me in every dark area of my life with the light of Jesus Christ and with your Holy Spirit. Amen.

FORGIVING SELF

If you are having trouble forgiving yourself, consider that this could be a matter of pride. Christ died for your sins. This was a complete work. There is nothing you can do to add to this and it is prideful to think so. Choose not to use the past or the present against your offenders or against yourself. Remember that forgiveness was a finished work on the Cross, between the Son and the Father, and that unforgiveness is a present issue between you and the Holy Spirit of God.

It is recommended that you refer to the scriptures on the topic of forgiveness and do a complete study using concordances and dictionary if you are experiencing problems in this area.

TRUE FORGIVENESS

All true forgiveness is substitutional and sacrificial. Consider Christ's sacrifice (2Cor 5:2, Rom 6:10). No one really forgives without bearing the consequence of another's sin, but forgiveness does have incredible benefits and rewards. It is a wise counsellor who points this out in a sensitive manner.

Forgiveness must come from one's spiritual core, rather than just the mind and will. It is also a process, which has a beginning and an end to it. We can begin by bringing the client to the point of wanting to make the choice to be willing to forgive. Then we can help process forgiveness by getting the message across successfully that the grace of God has already provided the way. It is done. It is complete. It is time to move on into freedom and victory.

Bitterness and malice should have no place in the life of a believer (Eph 4:31-32). Forgiving needs to be a lifestyle choice. Satan will come to reconnect us to bitterness by tempting us to 'unforgive'. Each time we make a conscious effort to resist temptation we become stronger in our spirits and softer in our hearts. It is commonly thought that Jesus instructed us not to keep count; we are to forgive seventy times seven (Matt 18:21-22). He could have been saying that the temptation to recall the offence will reoccur, so that the act of forgiving might need to be exercised for the same offence many times over.

This subject is all very well to preach from the pulpit, but not so simple to assimilate in the mind and the heart of a wounded client. Never, ever blithely say, *'you just need to forgive'*. The client would not be in your ministry rooms if they were not having a problem processing unforgiveness – it is pivotal to most healing issues. This is like saying to the depressive, *'just get over it'*.

As a prayer partner under the anointing of the Holy Spirit, you can have the honour of accompanying your client on their personal healing path towards the Cross. During the process, you can take heart that God is replacing old habitual destructive ways of thinking and feeling with something new and Christ-like. The Holy Spirit clears the way, creating a new pathway past the Cross, and onwards to the empty tomb. At times, it can prove to be a very bumpy road. Hang in there! The travelling will become easier without the baggage of unforgiveness, bitterness, malice and revenge holding up the healing journey. Jesus says *'come to me all who are heavy laden and I will give you rest"*. It is your work to help lighten the load by bringing your client to the feet of Jesus.

AUTHOR'S TESTIMONY – Shy Little Thing

The strongest force preventing me from moving on in life was the power of unforgiveness. It wasn't so much that I moved through life hating those who hurt me, or seeking revenge. Instead, happiness eluded me because I rejected myself rather than others. I turned my feelings inwards, rather than deflecting them away from me, or using emotions to injure others. As a small child, I gathered and carried a collection of self-perceived mistakes, wrongdoings and burdens that would weigh down the strongest of men. I could not forgive myself for anything.

To those looking on, I appeared as a frail introverted child, melancholy by nature, likeable because of my natural attributes, but hard to connect with and unusually quiet. The first word that would come to mind if someone were asked to describe me would be 'shy'. 'She is a shy little thing – so quiet and well mannered', the adults in my life would say, 'and never any trouble'.

Little did they know what was going on inside my slight frame and how I silently screamed, 'if you only knew what it was like to be me!' My capacity for self-hatred was inexhaustible and also exhausting. I felt constantly drained of energy, too tired to play and not the least bit interested in enjoying the food set before me or being in the company of others. I found it excruciatingly uncomfortable to have to attend school and to form friendships of any kind, as I was painfully self-conscious and withdrawn.

I can still look back and recall the aloneness, the persistent forebodings and my inability to extract any pleasure from life. For this inability, I hated myself. All my growing years, I found it very difficult to forgive myself for the failure at life that I felt myself to be.

To this day, it still causes sadness in me to resurrect the feelings associated with my past. In order to give a testimony however, it is necessary to compare the past with the present. So, to avoid dwelling on the past, I will only briefly explain by saying that I was spiritually oppressed from the time I was born. In hindsight, I would summarise it by saying that, throughout a major part of my life, I was 'troubled by tormenting spirits' or, was 'demonically oppressed'.

I wish I could say that my salvation experience turned my life dramatically around, or that getting married caused me to live happily ever after, or that other wonderful natural or spiritual experiences made the difference… It was not so easy for me.

However, our God was more powerful than my stubborn refusal to forgive myself. My miracle turned out to be a very, very slow one indeed. He was eventually able to get through to me… mainly through the process of ministering with the concepts in this book to others with similar problems. The more I reached out to others in need, the more I preached, taught, prayed and cared for others, the more my own eyes and ears opened to what He was trying to tell me. He faithfully just kept shining down on me until my spiritual senses were slowly awakened. I increasingly was able to love and forgive myself as I realised the depth of his love and forgiveness for others.

There is nothing that I can claim other than the grace of God for this transformation. I am where I am today – a functioning, bright, happy person, satisfied and content with life because of his patience with me, and his kindness to me. Amazing grace, how sweet it is.

And he continues the work. I held on to the promise that he always completes the work he begins. It is only in the past few years that I have been able to leave my regrets behind. This began one day when I felt that he was impressing on me that the lessons I had been learning were about to be consolidated. I was to choose to forgive myself and to leave my past behind – for good.

He gave me a vision of a skull in a box and indicated that he was about to bury it in a hole where even I could not dig it up! I chuckled at that and stepped into a new sphere of freedom. I have never looked back. Death has been swallowed up. My old patterns of thinking and feeling are buried.

We indeed have a god who makes promises and keeps them. I have begun to experience the reality of death to my old life, which is buried in Christ Jesus. I am only now beginning to scratch the surface of the joy that lies ahead of me on this earth and on into eternity. I am only starting to understand what having life and living it more abundantly means in the here and now.

As someone who has been truly forgiven only knows how, I have resolved to extract every ounce of happiness from my life. My boldness now surprises me. I run the race before me – joyfully reaching out towards the goal of meeting Him face to face. My redeemer lives – in and through me!

Counsellor Resources: PROCESSING FORGIVENESS

In the course of your ministry you will have various client needs and personality types to cater for. Here are some *practical resources* to draw from on the topic of processing forgiveness: –

a)   The ***balloon*** technique for an object lesson on releasing negative emotions (found in the section on anger, *Handling Emotions*).

b)   The ***soft ball*** (representing unforgiveness), which can be squeezed as the offence is related. The ball is released to illustrate processing forgiveness.

c)   The ***empty chair*** where the client pretends to address the offender and vents pent up emotional baggage and unfinished business to the chair (especially effective when the offender is deceased).

d)   The ***letter*** where the client writes to the offender and then destroys the contents in a symbolic manner e.g. tears up, burns or scribbles over.

e)   The role-playing exercise, where the counsellor interacts as a substitute offender.

SECTION FOUR

Restoration of Man

CHAPTER THIRTEEN

GOD & MANKIND

Previous chapters have dealt with improving or restoring relationships. This section (4) deals with the restoration of mankind in general, and also on a person to person basis with his creator. It begins with this chapter assessing man's perception of God and how he views God incorrectly. It offers resources to help towards resolving the inner conflict within man when he is not in harmony with his creator.

- ✀ A client testimonial which includes a typical secular view of God
- ✀ Discourse on God's loving boundaries on mankind
- ✀ A personal spiritual self-assessment guide
- ✀ Descriptions of man in conflict and man in harmony with his creator

---

Study Notes

CLIENT TESTIMONY: *Spoilt Little Rich Girl*

My mother said I could pretty well do as I pleased once I reached 16, which she thought was a respectable age for a girl to attract the boys. That was five years ago come March. So I did. I got into sex, partying, the drug scene, and fast cars and, of course, drank whatever I liked.

The money was there, so why not? Dad's divorce settlement will keep mum in clothes and jewels for the rest of her life – and enough for her toy boys too. She paid me off (like she did her men friends) when she got sick of me hanging around. When I turned 18, she gave me a lump sum. So I did what you do when you have the cash – I bought friends too. And I bought the cars. I took to speedway driving and thought I was pretty hot in my gear and the boys did too as they just hung off me.

Dad didn't care. He was off making more money to keep mum and me plus his new wife and her kids. I posted him photos of my cars on the net but he never mailed back, not once.

Then there was the crash. Not even one visit from either of them after their dogfight in the hospital emergency room. I think they thought that if they came in to check me out, they might run in to each other. God, I hate them both!!!!!

Least the bills got paid and I had that cute physio guy who got me interested in Jesus. Jesus is a guy with class. It's God I don't get. I thought, if he's anything like my dad, he won't care about me either; so I don't want to get too friendly with Him up there.

After I left hospital, this physiotherapist, Ernie, looked me up and I started hanging out with his friends. He said I could look at Jesus, JC, as he calls him, like an older brother (something I never had). At least, I don't think I've had a brother or sister. Mum would have got rid of them anyways. After me, she said she realised pretty soon that she couldn't stand kids and wished I'd never been born.

She should have aborted me. She and dad deserved each other 'cause he's just a big selfish kid like mum. They should never have tried to be parents. No wonder I can't get my head around this Our Father Who Art in Heaven stuff.

Ernie explained that God gives everyone a choice to be good or bad as parents. He said he himself figures that if they don't love their kids, then the kids get the wrong idea that God is a bad parent too. He thinks I hate God because I hate my parents; that my own dad doesn't care about me and mum has dumped me and treats me like dirt so I expect that from the father type God.

He told me that God meant them to look after me but they chose to be self-centred and turn their backs on Him as well as abandon me. Apparently, that makes this Father God really mad and sad.

Ernie says it's not true what I believe about God, just because mum and dad have let me down. He and his friends tell me that God promises to look after the lost and the homeless and to love them and place them in real families (Ps 68: 6).

One of Ernie's friends, Mac, said that he used to think just like me; but if I want to go along with him to church (when I feel up to it), then he and his girlfriend will show me what it's like to be in a church 'family' that cares. Mac's girlfriend Sue said that Mac was just fourteen when her church pastor picked him up off the street after his parents kicked him out. The minister fellow actually took him into his own home. Wow, I was impressed.

And Mac is such a great guy. He is a youth worker with street kids now. I want what he's got! I also find out from Sue that she is a church counsellor. Perhaps she might take me on…when I'm up to it.

Except where the author recounts her personal testimony, all characters and cases are fictitious representations and any similarities to real persons or cases are non intentional and are purely coincidental.

BOUNDARIES: SPIRITUAL VS SECULAR

Not everyone is a suitable candidate for the counselling scene or amenable to prayer ministry. Here we are speaking about boundaries in a situation where the client is non co-operative, not loveable (or even likeable) but has to be there for treatment for whatever the reason. This can be the case when you are dealing with adult offspring or a wayward spouse. Perhaps you are dealing with someone who feels forced to be under your care, or in a situation where the client does not hold the spiritual values you do.

God has commanded us to love one another as he has loved us (1Jn 3:11). There are no exceptions. To love and to forgive are matters of obedience and choice, not optional extras in our spiritual walk. When love is reciprocated, it is easy to choose to love. It is easy when the person is loveable and we have much in common, or when someone is dependent on us and we are seemingly in control. However, there will be times when we are not 'in control' and having a loving attitude is not so easy.

SECULAR BOUNDARIES

Think how hard it would be if you were given another person's little one to care for and being given all kind of restrictions as to how you are to handle that child. You still have all the responsibility of care, but without the freedom to set down your own rules.

Imagine the scenario. A neighbour has asked you to care for little Johnny while she is in hospital for a month. In a weak moment you comply. The following instructions are given on the handover, *'now Johnny has very certain likes and dislikes in food so, at meal times, he is only to have what he asks for. You must realise that he is a very sensitive child. He should never be disciplined in any form whatsoever. Johnny will work out for himself what he wants to do. I like him to make his own choices'.*

Note that little Johnny is at the enlightened two-year-old stage! Just see how lovable this little fellow will be after just one hour...and imagine how loving your feelings will be towards your neighbour after a month alone with Johnny.

GOD'S LOVING BOUNDARIES

In order to take good care of our clients it is essential to know the rules – God's boundaries based on his immutable laws – and it is preferable that your client is open to being disciplined when he/she has crossed these boundaries. Sometimes, we will need to practically assist the client (who could be behaving like a two year old) to implement some firm boundaries. Fortunately, we have a yardstick based on the Word of God and generations of wisdom to draw upon.

COUNSELLING STYLES

The way the world counsels can be similar to Johnny's mother's standards – very few boundaries. There are a multitude of very caring, intelligent counsellors operating under the world's system and doing so with a good deal of success. However, secular humanistic philosophy basically encourages a person *'to do whatever is good in your own eyes'*. Also, parenting styles are encouraged according to what is fashionable at any given time. A similar philosophy exists in secular counselling. A client is left to make up his or her own mind about what is right for them personally. Counsellors are encouraged to avoid voicing their views about 'right and wrong', or to offer advice, as this 'dis-empowers' the client and is 'unprofessional'.

Sometimes, when we are in the sheltered position of spiritual counselling within the formal church scene, we are somewhat shocked to discover that there is another world out there; that our secular counterparts are operating on an entirely different basis and format to our own. Unfortunately, even in the church, there will be occasions when we are not able to present God's absolute laws and guidance.

We will plainly see that these truths will not even be considered, let alone received. This will be one of the reasons the rebellious Christian will prefer secular counsel to spiritual (simply because the boundaries are blurred).

Worldly counsel is easier to digest; there will be very little teaching on *discipline and consequences* or *authority and absolutes*. Very little advice or direction will be offered, unless it is 'disguised' or covered under the worldly disciplines of *mentoring or coaching.* Psychology based dogma will be the foundational basis of counsel offered, and man will continue building upon mankind's 'wisdom'. The inherent goodness and intelligence of mankind will be 'preached' and the word '*sin*' will continue to be considered antiquated and obsolete. Man will go on to do as he pleases, having heard what he wants to hear – just as in the days of Noah.

Needless to say, it is very difficult to operate as a counsellor within these parameters if you are a Christian who is operating under secular jurisdiction, such as in a Government child welfare agency or in secular social work. So we should consider ourselves very privileged indeed to be involved in the ministry of Christian counselling under the protection and support of spiritual leadership.

MAN, WALKING IN HARMONY WITH HIS CREATOR

In a spiritual counselling situation, God's children basically <u>do</u> come looking for direction, correction and advice. They do come crying out from the grey areas of their lives, *'show us the way we should go, so that we can walk in it.'* Your born again child of God will most likely come seeing the essential need to *work out their salvation.* Hopefully, they will prayerfully come with a humble and contrite spirit, ready to accept the ministry you are offering. And this is where you will succeed and excel in your personal giftings.

Thank God we have his divine laws and principles to undergird us in our ministries. We are privileged to afford insight into the Father's loving boundaries. Thank God we have access to divine revelation and insight into his immutable laws and the protection of his covering. We can state his absolute truths according to the Word of God and then allow our clients to make personal choices and to experience the rewards (or the negative consequences) of those choices.

The following resource *Spiritual Self-Assessment* can be used to guide those seeking more depth and meaning to their walk with God.

Counsellor Resource: SPIRITUAL ASSESSMENT CHECKLIST

INSTRUCTIONS FOR USE

To appreciate our Father's unconditional love for us, we need to assess our present spiritual relationship with him. Ideally, if we are functioning in a mature way with healthy God-boundaries in place, we will agree with the majority of the points stated in the following useful resource. Many, however, will only honestly make claim to some (or a few); in this case it becomes useful for more clearly assessing the areas on which you will need to work.

This resource is simply something to aspire to and to inspire. It can be used to assess a client's walk with God as they enter into a season of ministry (several sessions of inner healing and renewal of the mind). Reassessment can be made nearing the end of this ministry in order to reveal the progress made. This should prove very encouraging. You have four options for use of this tool:-

1. Ask the client to assess degrees of agreement on a scale of 0 -10.
2. You as the counsellor may form the points into questions to use as a basis for discussion within a session. The assessment can be used as a stimulus for prayer ministry or a vehicle for coaching.
3. Use as a homework handout. The client can check off the affirmatives and be encouraged to write further comments.
4. The client can affirm through positive confession *'calling those things which are not as if they were so'.*

WARNING: Be careful to explain that this checklist is not a tool to assess how damaged or inadequate we are as Christians. Be particularly careful with clients who might be shame based in outlook and who could have strong roots of rejection.

Client Handout: SPIRITUAL ASSESSMENT

IMPORTANT: Discuss with your counsellor the purpose of this exercise prior to embarking on it. If you agree in most part to the points below, then you are experiencing the fruits of the spirit and the abundant life (Gal 5:22-23). However, do not come under condemnation if you feel you score poorly, as we are each 'a work in progress'. This is only an ideal to aspire to as a disciple of our Lord Jesus Christ.

NAME:

DATE:

- ❑ I feel God loves and cares about me.
- ❑ God is real and personal to me.
- ❑ I have a close personal relationship with God.
- ❑ I feel fulfilled and satisfied with my spiritual life.
- ❑ My life has meaning and purpose.
- ❑ I have a sense of direction and good prospects and hope for my future.
- ❑ Life is generally a good and positive experience for me.
- ❑ I know I was born for a reason.
- ❑ I am not afraid of dying.
- ❑ I am not afraid of the future.
- ❑ I do not dwell on the past.
- ❑ I experience strength, peace, joy and comfort during life's challenges.
- ❑ I am generally happy and contented.
- ❑ I have a strong personal sense of worth and identity.
- ❑ I do not feel alone or lonely.
- ❑ I feel I contribute to others' lives and well being.
- ❑ I feel part of a community.
- ❑ I have a calling from God and I am ministering in/ training for it.
- ❑ I feel part of the family of God.
- ❑ I attend church on a regular basis.
- ❑ I have friends who attend church.
- ❑ I have close friends upon whom I feel I can rely.
- ❑ My close family members share my spiritual walk.
- ❑ I can share my struggles and questions about life with others.
- ❑ I feel listened to and heard when I share my life story.
- ❑ I experience God as my Heavenly Father.
- ❑ I experience Jesus Christ as Lord of my life.

❑ I am passionate about my love for Jesus.

❑ I feel that the Holy Spirit is a real and personal entity in my life.

❑ I commune and communicate with all three aspects of God.

❑ I have a satisfying prayer life

❑ I practise most of the spiritual disciplines regularly (spiritual disciplines include: prayer, personal worship, corporate worship, financial stewardship, bible study, group fellowship, intercession, fasting, daily devotionals, meditation, journaling and tongues for personal edification).

Please respect Copyright. Master copies of resources found within this publication are provided for your ministry use in the companion 'So You Want To Be A Christian Counsellor – Resources Handbook', Prayer Counsel - www.prayercounsel.com.

Counsellor Exercise

*Mark off the checklist for your own personal assessment. Using the space provided below, write a short essay on three **personal strengths** which will contribute to your success as a Christian counsellor.*

MAN IN CONFLICT WITH HIS CREATOR

God has created man to be a harmonious companion: with nature, with his fellow man and with Himself. Our false perceptions of The Creator and our self-will have left us estranged and in conflict with our Heavenly Father. He is a god of relationship and longs for his children's intimate fellowship.

Much of our work as Christian counsellors will revolve around *restoration ministry*, that is, restoring the hearts of rebellious children to his father heart (*refer to Section 5 Chapter 18*). Much of man's inner conflict stems from unhealed wounds resulting from his inability to view God as he truly is. Until we perceive him in his fullness and perfection we will not have the abundance of life he has promised each of us through his son's sacrifice on the cross.

For excellent training for restoration ministry, it is strongly recommended that you access the resources of *Elijah House Ministries* (co-founders – John and Paula Sanford). These teachings are based on certain foundational truths and revelation insights into the scriptures. Students are trained to dig deep into the foundational childhood years of a person's life where attitudes, judgments and expectations were formed, by which each succeeding experience in life was interpreted. Trainee counsellors are disciplined to study patterns in the life story and heritage of a 'counselee' and to encourage the need for repentance and Holy Spirit transformation.

Counsellor Resource: UNDERSTANDING HOW WE VIEW GOD

The graphic *How We View God* illustrates how we create *false perceptions* of God our heavenly Father. It concentrates mainly on perceptions formed during childhood via human relationships with significant others in authority – such as parents, guardians, older siblings, teachers, employers and coaches. In other words, we tend to view God in his role as the supreme authority according to how we were treated or mistreated as a child by our earthly caretakers. Our childlike perceptions are also cemented via responses to *circumstantial and environmental factors*. But it is in the area of human relationships, that we are most vulnerable to forming *erroneous beliefs* about our creator as a father/mother figure.

It is quite common to hold on to childish perceptions of God and to continue forming new ones well into old age. These faulty views can prevent a person from relating on a mature level in general and can be responsible for stunting growth emotionally, intellectually and spiritually. It is necessary to humble one's self, and to seek to know God as he truly is, in order to heal and flourish as a child of God (Ps 92:12-15). We need to discard our childish perceptions and judgments in order to enter into satisfying and successful relationships with him and with others (1Cor

13:11)*. Recommended reading: *Putting Away Childish Things*, David A Seamands, Christian Press.

As the counsellor, you might like to disclose one of your personal misconceptions as a child to introduce the topic to the client e.g. *my father was very strict with me as a child so I developed the impression that God was always looking over my shoulder...* To add to the understanding of the graphic considerably, you could follow this with: *how do you think I might have viewed God the Father?* If it is inappropriate (or you are not comfortable with self-disclosure), then you could make the example hypothetical: *if a person had a strict upbringing how do you think they might view God as the heavenly Father?*

The following graphic serves to stimulate thought and discussion during a session, but it can be posted out to the client prior to an appointment. This will allow time to assimilate the concept. Make sure you include the introductory discourse *False Perceptions of God the Heavenly Father* with the graphic *How We View God*. Be warned that this concept usually serves to reopen childhood wounds, so you should be prepared with the necessary prayer techniques to apply healing and comfort. A compatible resource *Your Childhood Home* can be requested to assist here.

INSTRUCTIONS FOR USE OF IMAGE #13: How We View God

Far Left: lists the perfect attributes of God.

Far Right: lists the most common false perceptions mankind has acquired of God.

Middle: The centre of the graphic describes the most common sinful practices experienced via unhealthy interpersonal relationships. On either side of the page there are representations of two opposing perceptions – **The Good Shepherd** and **The Judge** – as examples of how a person might view God the Father overall. To stimulate discussion, ask the client, *do you see God more as a gentle shepherd type figure or a stern punishing judge?*

Bottom of page: Misconceptions resulting from sinful practices serve to create a wall that isolates us from both man and God. *The wall* is built through wrong responses and sinful choices and prevents us from giving or receiving love via relationships. Our conscience can eventually become completely insensitive to the Holy Spirit's conviction and our hearts can become hardened towards both man and God.

IMAGE 13

HOW WE VIEW GOD

Matt 5:8 Blessed are the pure in heart for they shall see God

Creation of false perceptions of God the Father via

MOST COMMON SINFUL PRACTICES
&
UNHEALTHY INTERPERSONAL RELATIONSHIPS

dishonouring parents or others in authority, blaming and judging others (including God), sowing bad seed & reaping the consequences, self-righteousness, pride, unforgiveness, idolatry of self/others/things, backsliding, negative expectancies & inner vows, spiritual adultery & defilement, parental inversion & self reliance, negativity, striving and performance orientation, abdication of responsibility, closing off/down, rebellion, hypocrisy, blasphemy, negativity, control & manipulation as a defence/weapon.

CREATES

Man's Reinforced Brick Wall
Isolating himself from both man and God's Love.

wrong responses & sinful choices

unforgiveness   bitterness
shame, guilt   resentment
rebellion   rejection

UNABLE TO GIVE OR RECEIVE LOVE

The Good Shepherd

False Perceptions

just like dad or mum,
the bad guy,
leaves me out,
loves when it suits Him,
cruel, mean, hard,
rejecting, unforgiving,
punishing, out to get me
cold, distant, aloof,
absent when needed
fickle, mysterious,
not to be trusted,
unpredictable, confusing,
critical, harsh,
judgmental, unfair,
only if I'm good/perfect,
condemning, vengeful,
plays favourites,
a killjoy/stingy/mean,
always watching me,
unpleasable

The Judge

GOD is

holy & pure
good
loving
caring
kind & gentle
accepting
merciful
present, close by
always available
steadfast
reliable
consistent
nurturing, affirming
impartial, fair, just
unconditionally loving
dispensing grace
showing favour
giver of good gifts
approving
pleasable

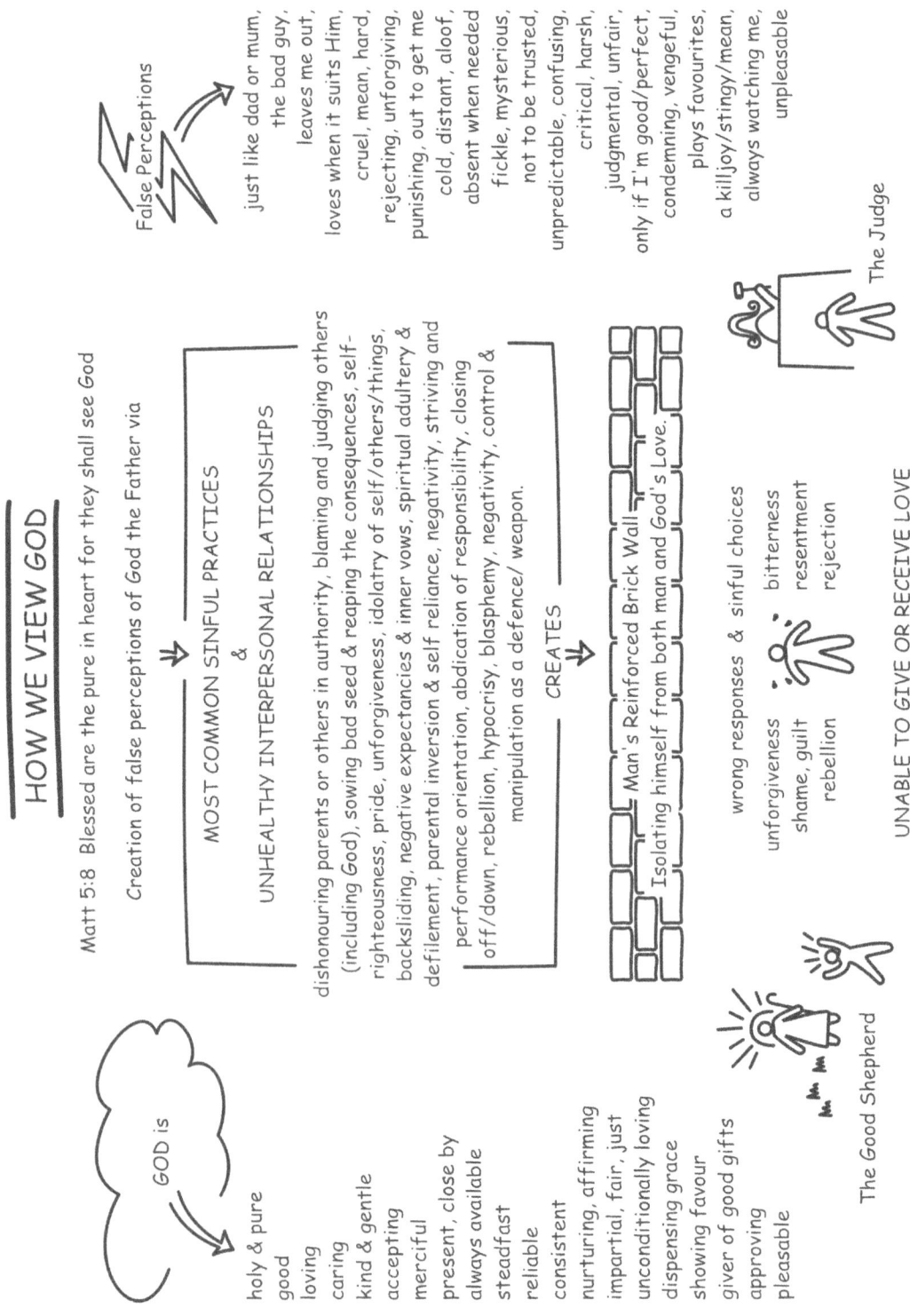

FALSE PERCEPTIONS OF GOD OUR HEAVENLY FATHER

It is the prayer minister's responsibility to expose false perceptions of God that the client might hold, which serve to cause blockages in relating to the Heavenly Father freely and fully as a child of God. The following is to help introduce the concept of how man forms these faulty beliefs about God, and how these mindsets prevent the free flow of love within human relationships also.

UNFULFILLED EXPECTATIONS

Remember instances in your childhood such as asking God for a new bike as each birthday was approaching? Perhaps that bike did not materialise until you were nearly old enough for a car! Later, you dreamt of your future marriage partner. You waited, and waited. You wanted God to deliver a gift-wrapped Mr/Mrs Right. Unfortunately, the person you <u>felt</u> God sent along did not take the slightest interest in you. You felt condemned to a life of loneliness, crying into your pillow on Saturday nights.

LOSING OUR FAITH & TRUST

You asked. You believed. Why didn't you receive? Who is to blame that your expectations were not realised? You reason: *surely God wants us to have the desires of our heart. Doesn't the Bible tell us so? He could have given me what I asked for – if he <u>really</u> wanted to!* You become angry. You feel guilty about feeling angry with your Maker. Your childlike faith dims in the years to come. It becomes harder to believe for what you want. And, as you grow older, your reasoning grows more complicated and cynical.

As you struggle along in life, you might tend to think along these lines, *he wants me to suffer, for some mysterious reasons of His own. I must accept a life of disappointments and doing without everything I really want… Like the time I prayed that, if it were God's will, I'd get that terrific job overseas. It was for him too – on the mission field. I would have shown his love to all those hurting people – got them saved and everything. He must think I'm not good enough – or spiritual enough. He'd rather have me on this lousy assembly line in a factory for the rest of my life suffering…*

You do find a job, establish a career, love, marry…and divorce. You lose custody of the kids and your finances are in ruins. You cannot trust anyone any longer. You give up your faith in a good God completely and feel you might as well just do things <u>your</u> way.

BUILDING WALLS

Through it all, you view God in different ways, changing over time, according to your experiences in life, and using a variety of defence mechanisms to shield you from the pain of another attack, disappointment or frustration. The problem is: that these mechanisms are building a brick wall that rises, not only to shield you from the slings and arrows of life, but also from God's proffered love, healing, comfort and encouragement getting through. (Ask your counsellor for a copy of the prayer – *Walls).*

So it goes on, and we carry this line of thinking into our more 'mature' years. *Why me Lord? Poor me…Why don't you talk to me? Why don't you answer me when I want your help? I've been cast aside. God is too hard on me. He's punishing me and I don't even know what I've done to deserve it!* So we remain in our state of suffering, blaming God – living miserable defeated lives. The brick wall gets higher, reinforced by wrong responses and sinful choices. This solid wall serves to isolate us further from those people who would love and care for us in our distress. God seems so far away and unresponsive…

CHANGING PERSPECTIVE

Now, let us reappraise this from a different perspective. What view <u>could</u> you have of God? Have you ever seen a toddler look adoringly up at his grandfather in wonder at something he is doing? Ever had a little one snuggle up to you in complete trust and happiness practically purring in contentment? If you are a father yourself, has your teenage son flattered you by saying, *'my dad says…'?* How about a young married daughter who decides she will keep house and bring up her family based on the model of her mother's home making?

Well that is the kind of respect and faith our maker wants us to have in him. He longs for an attitude of complete trust and acknowledgment of belonging to him as his child. He is someone we should want to imitate and whose company we should passionately long for. We should want to know all about him: how he thinks, what he will do next and how we can do more to love and please him.

SANTA CLAUS MENTALITY

Instead, we all too often look to him in a childish way, rather than in childlike trust. We look to him for miracles, rather than accepting the disciplining, which develops the fruits of the spirit. We look for a way to escape a crisis, rather than rejoice in the lessons we could learn from it. We want to know him in a way to suit ourselves, to see him in the image we would like to manufacture.

Is not this the reason for the popularity of a Santa Claus? We enjoy being rewarded for 'being good'. Even though we know deep down that we have not been so good, we somehow still expect the presents under the tree. We reason that we are only human and that no-one is perfect. In our childish reasoning, we still believe that we have been good in our own way; we still deserve the good things in life.

Counsellor Exercise:

It is time to think more deeply and personally now. Do you honestly want to make an effort to seek the Perfect One? Are you willing to discipline yourself to spend time with him so that you really get to know him for himself, rather than what he can supply you with? Do you desire to love and appreciate him for who he <u>actually</u> is, rather than the attributes you place on him? Do you want to know him, not only on the surface, but truly, deeply, and intimately? How do you personally view God? Have you held onto any childish perceptions (1Cor 13:11)?

Write your thoughts in the space below, making sure you record the date.

HOW I VIEW GOD

INSTRUCTIONS FOR IMAGE 14: Man in Harmony with His Creator

IS YOUR HOUSE IN ORDER?

> This graphic concept can also be adapted for use as an illustration of the line of command in a Christian family situation, church structure or any other godly organization. For example, for family therapy – the wife is to submit to the husband's authority, as the husband submits to Christ and the children are to obey their parents.
>
> These, and other graphic illustrations, are available on request from the author. Please specify your needs when ordering via elvie@prayercounsel.com e.g. *Man in Harmony with His Creator as adapted house graphic for marriage counselling purposes.*

This graphic represents the state of man's being when all is in order and functioning as intended – man in harmony with his creator. It also depicts when we are not in harmony and how and why we are in disorder.

Beginning from the left side of the graphic illustration of three houses:

Far left: This first house is in order. It represents the three parts of man – body, soul and spirit – safe and protected from the enemy's onslaughts by a *divine covering* represented by the roof. When we dwell here, we are operating as a fully functioning, born again, reconciled and restored child of God; we are *in harmony with our maker.*

Middle: This harmonious dwelling has everything in order. Housed under this roof is *the mind of Christ,* to which our spirit has ready access, for provision of wisdom for living. This is how our strong, healthy, functioning spirit is able to dominate our soul (consisting of our mind, will and emotions). The soul is able to command the body to come into alignment with the will of God. Our spirit and soul are able to dominate our body. So we are free from weakness, sickness and disease (disease) in all areas. We enjoy health emotionally, intellectually, spiritually and bodily. We are able to resist the enemy in all areas of our lives and to have harmonious functional relationships with our fellow man as well as our creator.

Far Right: However, as a Christian we are out of order when we are not treating our body as *the temple* in which Christ dwells; we are in *a state of disorder* and *out of alignment* with God's will. We have not appropriated the protective covering of the blood of Jesus and are vulnerable to the enemy's attacks on our spirit, soul and body. There is ready access by Satan and his demonic workers because our spirits are weak and subordinated to our fickle, fleshly natures. Even though we may be spiritually born again, we have not exercised our spiritual blood bought right to choose a life of abundance and victory. We have not exercised our spiritual muscles; therefore, our spirit has not been able to grow into maturity and strength. We continue to struggle through life weak and defeated, in doubt and unbelief.

IMAGE 14

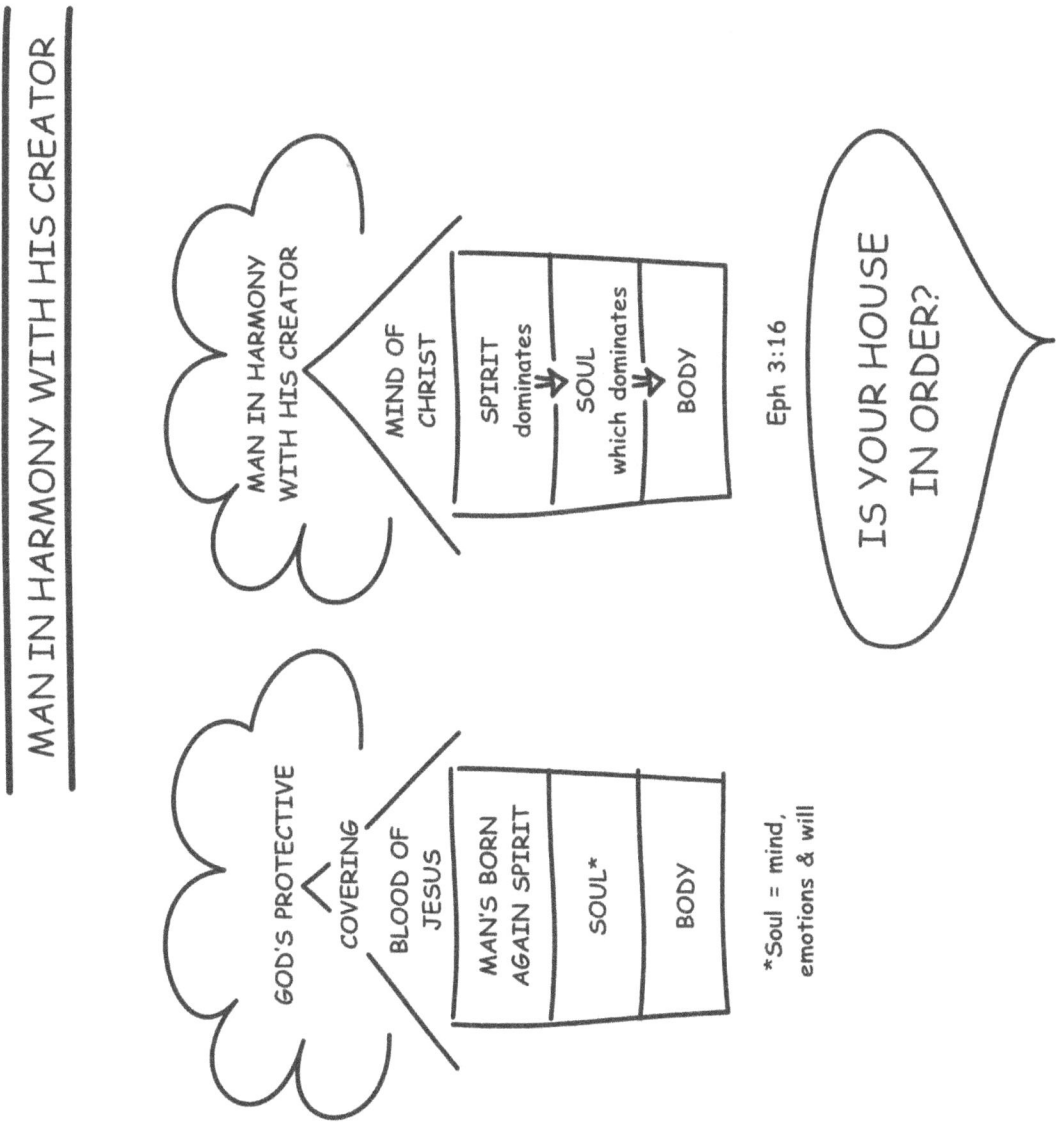

MAN IN HARMONY WITH HIS CREATOR

GOD'S PROTECTIVE COVERING

BLOOD OF JESUS

MAN'S BORN AGAIN SPIRIT

SOUL*

BODY

*Soul = mind, emotions & will

MAN IN HARMONY WITH HIS CREATOR

MIND OF CHRIST

SPIRIT dominates → SOUL which dominates → BODY

Eph 3:16

IS YOUR HOUSE IN ORDER?

OUT OF ORDER

NO COVERING !!!

SOUL

BODY

SPIRIT subordinated

Ex 6:9

CHAPTER FOURTEEN

MAN'S INNER CONFLICT

When man is not in harmony with his creator, he is not at peace with himself. As a prelude to teaching the concepts and techniques involved in inner healing, the complexity of the thought processes and associated emotions of man's inner conflict need to be considered. Several basic needs are covered here; including the author's sharing of her communication with God regarding self-image, and her self-disclosure regarding problems with guilt.

    ∾   Self-awareness exercise – *About Me*
    ∾   Formation of self-image and ministry to the child within (inner child)
    ∾   Self-esteem exercise using healing affirmations
    ∾   Shame & Guilt resources (including *The Potato Sack Race)*

Study Notes

CLIENT TESTIMONIAL – The Neighbourhood Event

I never tried to be an idiot. It just happened. Whatever I tried to be, or tried to do, never turned out. I used to look around at my schoolmates or at work. I'd think, 'if only I could have the guts to fight like Pete or the drive to get to the top like my supervisor'. I was always last and always the kid who tried but never quite made it – the loser.

In the end, I gave up and just became one of the drones at the abattoirs – the only place where I managed to hold down a job because it didn't matter much if I botched something up on the assembly line. All the carcasses weren't going blab on me and me mates just covered for me like I covered for them.

I had come to grips with the fact I was never going to make anything of my life. It was just one failure after another with me. It was embarrassing and I was kinda ashamed of myself. I was a failure. I even failed at being a failure! You'll understand when I give you a bit of my story following 'The Event'.

I board with my mate Stan in the suburbs. We share a house he owns and I help to pay off his mortgage because he likes the grog and finds it hard to keep track of the bills. Anyhow, we get on pretty well, both being shift workers we manage to keep out of each other's hair. It's like I have the place pretty much to myself. He works early morning shift at the hospital as a cleaner and I get home around 1am because I get in as much overtime as possible.

Well, it did work until our nice little neighbourhood had something happen. Two doors down, there was this old church. You know; that kind with the pitched roof and the cross up top – only house-sized, really – taking up the space of a normal corner sized block. We used to enjoy the organ playing and the twenty or so old ducks who came for the 11am service and were out the door on Sundays by 12 noon to go home to their roast dinners. Then came: 'The Event'.

The place got sold and some new guys came and took over. The old ducks moved out and a crazy mob moved in. They spruced up the old place and then it all began. After we got over the hammering and buzz sawing and things being moved in and out, there came the non-stop music and singing and our driveways getting blocked and the yakety yak at all hours. Me mate nearly went bonkers from lack of sleep and we started to get on one another's nerves. So we decided to pay the head guy a visit.

That was the beginning of a whole new life for me. Both of us liked the guy (the minister) a lot. We began to drop in a bit for a chat whenever we got grumpy at their goings on. Things calmed down after we explained about the noise and whatever was bugging us. Then I figured, 'If ya can't beat 'em, then might as well join 'em'. The music sounded good and I was curious what went on at those meetings. The place was always packed.

I kept going back and back, until I was part of the furniture. I became one of them and I learnt who Jesus was and I learnt who I was meant to be, and I began to become who I was meant to be. It was all great stuff and I'm loving it. And, I'll be darned, I'm starting to love me. No more a loser, but a champion and a nice guy.

I help out about the place fixing things – because I'm good at it – and I've organised a bit of a helping hand mission thing as an outreach to the neighbourhood. We mow lawns for the old ducks (I mean the elderly ladies) and I do a bit of painting and help them stretch their pensions with a food parcel here and there. All the neighbours have stopped complaining, including Stan. They have helped him give up the grog and he's got a day job now and doing great.

Now, every day is a big event for me because I feel useful and good about myself. The blokes at work are noticing a big change in me and my attitude has done a 360 degree turnabout. I'm telling them why and I'm proud to tell them how it all came about because of 'The Event'.

* This story was based on an actual 'event' but the characters are fictitious.

SELF AWARENESS

We are often in conflict inwardly – for instance, when we long to be someone we are not, or, when we are trying to conform to what we think others expect of us. The following prophetic message to the author is shared in the hope that it will speak to you personally and encourage you in your ministry efforts.

PROPHETIC WORD TO AUTHOR – Concerning Self Image

Lord, help me to take pleasure in how you have made me.

'Yes my child, I will help you in this area. I will train you further to respect your own needs and to revel in the limitations I have set for you.

Yes, there are those of your brothers and sisters who have taken my word for something it is not. They are the ones who would bring everyone up to the standards that <u>they</u> have set for them. This is not my will. My will is that everyone has been created to be the one I have made them to be – to be a reflection of my glory.

Yes, there is a difference in each of you. There are many differences. Just as I have created the creatures of this world in such disparity, I have made my children to be varied in outlook and in temperament, as well as in their physical aspects. Yet, there are still the ones who challenge me on this, my creativity. They would have you all of like mind and of uniformity.

This is not my way! Instead, I would have each one of you to respect your differences and to see that each of you only reflects another aspect of your Heavenly Father to be appreciated and revered.

So, my child, when you are tempted once again to alter the way I have made you, think again, that, in this way, you are trying to alter your very nature. This is in rebellion to me and against my will. And I know my child that your will is to please me, above all else.

So, now that you are no longer ignorant in this area, do not trespass against me. Accept yourself. Respect the traits within you and your own way of doing things. Do not try to emulate anyone else, or his or her way of doing things.

I am happy with the way I have made you. I want you to be happy with yourself, my child, and my creation.

Your Heavenly Father'

Client Handout #1: WORKSHEET ON SELF-AWARENESS: *ABOUT ME*

CLIENT NAME:

DATE:

To the client: This exercise is to help us during the counselling process to understand the 'real you'. You can answer each question briefly, but feel free to use a separate sheet of paper to answer any of the questions more fully.

When I was a child

I used to pretend I was _____

My favourite games were _____

I wanted to grow up to be _____

I felt loved the most by _____

I was happiest when _____

I was scared of _____

When I was an adolescent

I dreamed of _____

My heroes were _____

My main interests were _____

I wanted to become _____

The most important person in my life was _____

I worried about _____

In the present

My friends would describe me as _____

I would describe myself as _____

My weaknesses are _____

My strengths are _____

My greatest desire is _____

I am most passionate about _____

I would risk my life for _____

The most important person in my life right now is _____

In the future

The thing that I would like to happen to me the most is _____

My worst fear is that _____

Before I die, I would like to _____

About the past

My best memories are _____

I feel bad when I remember _____

My main regrets are _____

I cannot forget the times when _____

Current concerns

I worry most about _____

The things that I fear the most are _____

I feel helpless about _____

The worst thing about my life at present is _____

Client Handout #2: SELF-IMAGE & OUR INNER CHILD

There are many ways of forming our *self-image*. Some of these are:

a) Our own human reasoning and perceptions of self.
b) What others perceive and lead us to believe about ourselves.
c) Our interpretation of what we hear said about us.
d) Our interpretation of our value and worth according to how we are treated.
e) Whether we accept or reject what our enemy the *Father of Lies* tells us.
f) Our belief in who we are *in Christ Jesus* according to what our *Father God* says about us in his *Word* (the Holy Scriptures).

CHILDREN & SELF-ESTEEM

From the very beginning, we are receiving messages from those closest to us, which begin to form our *self-image*. This image involves more than our physical form – it is the way we view our inner self and who we are as a person. This happens from within the womb as we are picking up messages and sensing whether we are valued, admired, precious, wanted, important, loved and welcomed into life. From our first few months, we are hearing words ranging from admiration to disapproval, seeing smiles and frowns and receiving, or not receiving, attention to our needs. We begin, or do not begin, building our *self-esteem* – our self-respect/self-regard.

Not only are we are learning that we count, but also, we can falsely perceive that we are the 'centre of the universe'. Our infantile illusion will be shattered soon enough. We will become old enough to understand the words being said such as 'bad boy', 'you are such a pest' or 'I wish she had never been born', but, as infants, we will not have the ability and maturity to judge fully what we are receiving into the spirit and soul.

We are actually receiving a mixture of false and true prophecy, or *messages*. We are drawing conclusions in our flesh (and in our spirits) according to our reception of these messages. If we receive anything other than the truth from our Maker, then we begin to form a self-image that is not of God and we are liable to continue to build on this into adulthood. Just because we have grown physically, it does not mean that we have grown to keep pace emotionally, intellectually or spiritually. This growth will depend on what we have received into our souls and spirit or *inner man*. Sometimes we will discover the need to minister to the *wounded child* within us.

MINISTRY TO OUR INNER CHILD

This is why it is so important that we speak words of truth and affirmation to our *inner child* as well as to our own issue and to other children who are in our care. No matter how old we are, we are still His precious children. We still have a need to be parented. Our inner child still craves healing and can be re-parented by God the Father in areas where we were wounded, damaged and/or neglected by our earthly parents and significant others.

When God redeemed us, he wrote his law on our hearts and minds (Heb 10:16). It is possible to experience your adult re-born self re-parenting your inner child under the anointing of the Holy Spirit (2Cor 3:5-6).

RE-PARENTING YOUR INNER CHILD

1. Communicate – both listen and talk to your inner child
2. Speak the truth in love and rebuke the lies believed (1Cor 13:11)
3. Emphasise the message of the cross and the power of forgiveness
4. Tell your inner child that he/she is loved unconditionally by the creator
5. Give permission to 'the child' within to be playful and carefree
6. Allow for mistakes made and give achievements positive reinforcement

7. Provide boundaries for acceptable behaviour based on God's Word
8. Praise and edify with positive self-talk and verbal scriptural affirmations
9. Encourage him/her to revere and praise God the Almighty
10. Teach to commune with the heavenly Father and to worship him
11. Show your inner child the value of godly wisdom as well as knowledge
12. Allow connection with the Holy Spirit and his healing ministry
13. Speak words of comfort, healing and freedom to the wounded child within

---

Please respect copyright. Master copies of resources found within this publication are provided for your use in the companion book: 'So You Want To Be A Christian Counsellor – Resources Handbook' - www.prayercounsel.com.

Client Handout #3: SELF-ESTEEM EXERCISE – HEALING AFFIRMATIONS

To *esteem* is to have high regard, admiration and respect for someone. If you esteem yourself, then you are said to possess *a positive self-image* (see Rom 12 1-5, 16). To hold a positive self-image you will need to:

a)   be recognized and appreciated
b)   know you are loved unconditionally
c)   live within the boundaries for acceptable behaviour
d)   have the ability to make sound choices (and to have options)
e)   have freedom to express yourself (and to feel you are being heard)
f)   be able to still feel of worth no matter what you can or cannot do
g)   not think more highly/lowly of yourself in comparison to others
h)   be able to spend time alone (and to enjoy your own company)
i)   have an intimate relationship with God as your heavenly father

To build this important self-image, affirmations can be used for healing and growth. Remember that we are to speak into existence *'those things which are not as if they are'.*

Client Exercise: Here are some healing affirmations to strengthen you according to the truth of who you are 'in Christ'. Search for the relevant scriptures to confirm these statements. Memorize and recite out loud as often as possible.

Date:

I ....have a positive self-image because I <u>know</u> that I am: –

CAPABLE

I <u>can</u> do things with my own special skills and abilities. I can do all things in Christ who strengthens me. Only I can do what God has made me capable of doing, in my own unique and special way. I have giftings and talents, which I am capable of exercising to God's glory.

Scriptures

A 'FEEL GOOD' PERSON

I feel good about myself; that I am a work in progress. I have a future, a purpose for being here and a hope (in him). I have a positive self-concept and a feeling of significance and worth. I recognise who I am in Christ Jesus, who is my lord and my saviour, and I have a confident attitude because of this.

Scriptures:

SIGNIFICANT

What I say, think and do does matter. I have a positive impact on this world because I am a part of the body of Christ. Without me, the body would not be perfect – a part would be missing. I see myself as equally important to others.

Scriptures:

POWERFUL

I can make an impact. I can influence the world and the people around me. I am made for a purpose and I have a destiny for which I am fully equipped to handle and achieve.

Scriptures:

WORTHY

I am unique and valuable regardless of what I can or cannot do. I do not have to earn my right to exist. I was made by him, and for him, in his image – to be loved by him and by others. I am a vessel made to be overflowing with all that is good, beautiful and true.

Scriptures:

TRUSTWORTHY

I can trust in, and, believe in myself. I am able to nurture and look after my own needs as well as others. I am responsible and dependable. I feel that God the Father can trust me to do what he asks of me. I feel confident enough with whom I am to be free to serve others.

Scriptures:

LOVED

I am loveable, loved, and able to love. I love him because he first loved me. I am filled with his love because I am made in his image. He is Love. I am aware of being loved and feel secure and confident. I accept my Father God's unconditional love for me.

Scriptures:

THE POTATO SACK RACE

For as long as I can remember, and that's a long time for your old grandma little one, I had this recurring dream where I am in a potato sack race. You don't know what a potato sack is? Well, in the old days before plastic bags took over the world, potatoes were stored for transport in bags made of Hessian. They were the same colour as the potato skins, and smelly, rough to feel, and dirty. Oh I can still smell that smell!

Well, these bags weren't really much use for anything afterwards. So we kids used to grab them from the corner store when they were thrown out the back. We'd use them at picnics to have races with. You'd step inside them and hobble along until you finished the race. More likely for me, until I lay sprawled across the grass. I always tried to go too fast and move my legs to run. The idea was to just jump up and down inside the bag with it hitched up tightly under your armpits and then to hop to the finish line. I tried, but didn't ever get the hang of it.

It just gave me this awful feeling afterwards of being dirty, smelly and totally embarrassed. Everyone else seemed to find it a funny game but your old grandma, as a wee girl, hated it when she was made to join in. I was ridiculed if didn't and I was useless when I tried. Everyone laughed at me when I fell over and got nowhere.

The nightmare? Yes, I was getting to that my dear girl… I know you have lots of bad dreams – like your one last night. I want you to understand that, when we are asleep, sometimes our brains just go over and over what has been worrying us during the day. It's like we are trying to sort out our problems – like you do when you come especially to grandma's place to talk to her. But, when you are asleep, your mind is trying to sort it out all by itself.

So, I used to have this horrible, horrible potato sack dream over and over again. I'd wake up feeling awful (like you did last night). When I woke up, the yucky feeling that went with that dream would stay with me nearly all the next day. I only had to think of the dream at any ol' time and there the feeling would pop on me! But I was too little to tell anyone about it, and besides, it would mean having that feeling over again if I did.

Yes, silly me, I know now that if I had talked it over with someone who knew how to talk to God, all my worries would have got sorted out. But my parents didn't talk to God much and they never prayed with me like your parents do. They didn't know how. They couldn't help me even though they loved me very, very much… But, when I was all grown up, I was able to go talk to a lady who loves God and she asked Him how to help me. She was able to get me to face my fear of the nightmare and to tell her about it. She asked God what it was all about; then she told me what she thought was really worrying

> *me to dream like that. She explained to me about lots of grownup things. She prayed and asked God to take the yucky feelings away… He did, and they never ever came back. So… why don't we do that for you little one?*

AUTHOR'S TESTIMONY – On Shame & Guilt

I was that little girl in the potato sack! It is incredible the difference the interpretation of that dream made to my life. The woman who helped me was a close friend who gently disclosed what was causing me to relive that childhood dream far into adulthood.

Through the counselling experience, I was able to remain in the spirit in the imagery and watch it as if it were a movie. I saw myself as a child hopping clumsily along. However, this time, I didn't fall! I noticed that there were two others in sacks chasing me. Instantly, I realised who they were – my father and my paternal grandfather.

It came to me what the symbolism of the potato sack represented and I knew in an instant how to deal with my problem. I willed myself as that little girl (my inner child) to turn back in the race and to face my pursuers. I let go of the sack and raised an angry fist to shake a pointed finger to reprimand the real pursuers – guilt and shame. I commanded the two men in sacks to stop the chase and to stop using guilt and condemnation to shame me.

After prayer from my dear friend, I was able to realise that the type of discipline used in my generational heritage was shame. My father had disciplined me with shaming and his father had modelled this to him. Both loved caring men of good will. They definitely had their children's welfare at heart, but they did not know or use the godly precepts to meet the needs of a child. It was modelled that children were expected to behave just as responsibly as adults.

As a young woman, I had been able to reconcile our family line to the father heart of God. However, it was not until many years later that I was able to personally appropriate His unconditional love and grace. Even though my spirit and will had responded to the message of salvation early in life, my 'inner child' was still emotionally responding in the old familiar way well into my 'mature' years. I was continuing to correct and discipline myself in my family's traditional manner – shaming myself over all things large and small and denying myself of God's grace.

Even after these two family members were deceased, I had continued to participate in the potato sack race. I had missed the message of the Cross. Spiritually I was free. Emotionally and intellectually, I continued to live under the pressures of unforgiveness. Encased in my sack of shame, I lived a life driven by guilt. I pointed the finger at others as well as myself – including my own children. My earthly father's reprimanding voice remained louder than my Heavenly Father's still small voice of unconditional love and forgiveness.

However, on seeing the lesson encased in the potato sack dream, God trained me further as to how I could make guilt my 'friend' in the form of a vision (see graphic 'Guilt vs Shame'). I was more able to tell the difference between shame and healthy guilt. I was thereafter able to use guilt to point me to the cross, where I could repent under true Holy Spirit conviction and acknowledge that was where Jesus Christ had sacrificially dealt with it all.

I learnt that guilt biblically implies that there is the capability of being punished, or liability for punishment (2Cor 5:10–21). So I came to a fuller realisation that God's perfect love does cast out all fear (of being punished). I no longer needed to live under constant condemnation and fearfulness. The eyes of my heart had been opened and I more fully understood the extent of his perfect love for me. Jesus had been punished in my stead for whatever I had done wrong and whatever I would do wrong (Jn 3:16). This truth had no borders or limitations, other than my choice to accept and believe in it.

The lesson of the vision was so strong! I replayed it again and again in my mind and recorded it on paper. It became stronger than the memory of the recurring dream and the associated feelings of that childhood nightmare. My thoughts towards God gradually evolved from a stern, hard taskmaster who was 'out to get me', to the vision I have embraced today of my dear heavenly Father.

I became no longer vulnerable and easily manipulated by Satan via the voices in my head. The word of God became louder and clearer, 'There is therefore (now) no condemnation in Christ Jesus' (Rom 8:1-2). I saw that I was intended to live free from the harassing, manipulating false guilt, which had previously tormented me with accusations and shamed me to the core of my being.

Because I had the absolute assurance of my sins being forgiven, my salvation became alive! I began to develop a sense of righteousness in Christ. I <u>knew</u> now what being justified truly meant (Rom 5:1). 'Just as if I had never sinned in God's sight' were no longer just words to me. I finally <u>believed</u> how God dealt with confessed sin (Isa 38:17; Ps 103:12; Heb 8:12).

With the help of my Christian counsellor friend, the familial curse was broken. By truly responding to the appeal of the Cross, I began to be led by the true purpose of healthy guilt rather than being chased down by the false guilt of self-condemnation. I no longer hobbled along in the sack of shame and infirmity. Finally, I had got The Message. From that point I began to grow in grace. I began to prosper in various areas of my life – which had been barren – all due to the counsel of a dream and the vision of my 'friend' Guilt.

IMAGE 15

SHAME vs GUILT

GUILT = THE FEELING OF HAVING DONE SOMETHING WRONG
SHAME = IS FEELING THAT YOU ARE SOMEONE BAD/WRONG

OR

'I DID BAD' VERSUS 'I AM BAD'
'I AM GUILTY' VS 'I AM GUILT'

GUILT SAYS: 'HEY THERE IS SOMETHING WRONG HERE!
I HAD BETTER DO SOMETHING ABOUT IT.'

WHEREAS

SHAME SAYS: 'I AM WRONG.'
'I AM A MISTAKE.'
I AM NOTHING, USELESS, STUPID, DIRTY, WORTHLESS, EVIL ETC.

GOD DOES HOLD US RESPONSIBLE AND ACCOUNTABLE FOR OUR WRONG RESPONSES
AND SINFUL CHOICES. WE DO REAP FROM WHAT WE SOW...

HOWEVER

BECAUSE JESUS DIED TO TAKE ON OUR GUILT, ALTHOUGH DEEMED GUILTY
WE ARE NEITHER PUNISHED NOR SENTENCED TO DEATH.

GUILT becomes the FRIEND who brings us to the cross....

GOD HATES THE SIN. JESUS LOVED THE SINNER.

1 John 1:7

MAN & THE BATTLE WITHIN

As complicated creatures, we human beings seem to go to great lengths to complicate our lives. Although it is impossible to offer any one method of help to suit all clients, for every problem presented, the main issues do seem to have a general theme and this contributes to general sorting and classification under the heading of 'Conflict'. That is, man is *in conflict* in one way or another:

a)   man with his Maker
b)   man with the enemy Satan & his co-workers
c)   man with man (individuals & mankind in general)
d)   man with his inner-man (self)

Concerning the last point, man fights *a battle within* in an incredible variety of ways. Spiritually, this conflict can be resolved by the conversion experience. And, as we are becoming conformed to the image of Christ Jesus (the perfect man who functioned perfectly in a fallen world), we are going through the restoration process. This is called *'working out our salvation'*.

Through the working through, there evolves a self-awareness of our true image in Christ; there is also an increasing consciousness of his mercy and grace. As time passes, we are able to more fully appreciate his forgiveness and his longing to reconcile himself to his wayward children through the sacrificial atonement of his *only begotten son,* Jesus Christ (Jn 3:16).

Until we are able to grasp the depth and extent of this divine love, we are basically internally in conflict between our carnal (fleshly) nature and our spiritual nature. Although this text is not able to adequately cover the theological aspects, it does attempt to lay a basic foundation for the processes of repentance, reconciliation and restoration. The foundation is laid within the parameters of the type of prayer ministry called *'inner healing and deliverance'*.

As a prelude to inner healing (type) ministry, this text briefly describes the thought processes and accompanying feelings associated with *inner conflict*. The spiritual process called *recovery* can be introduced, which involves working towards *renewing the mind* to the mind of Christ and overcoming barriers to the healing of wounds – self-inflicted or otherwise. Samples of both practical and spiritual therapeutic means of achieving inner peace and a true sense of our identity in Christ are offered.

In the process of covering the subject of inner conflict it will be essential to understand more about the topic of *shame*. As spiritual counsellors we should be able to describe to a client the difference between *shame and guilt,* prior to beginning on any inner healing journey; otherwise the therapeutic methods attempted will not be truly effective and we will not be effective as *change agents*.

On the basis of righteousness in him, man's most powerful weapon against Satan is personal knowledge and shame free application of the Word and the blood of Jesus Christ.

Issues related to shame and personal unforgiveness are usually the main barriers standing in the way of man wielding the sword in victory against the strongholds, which have him enslaved. The greatest weapon Satan has against man, is man himself, and this often entails his internal battle with shame (Gal 5:17). Shame is the basis of much abusive and addictive behaviour. Application of scriptural tenets is the answer to winning the battle within (2Tim 2:26).

Counsellor Resource: SHAME CONSCIOUSNESS ASSESSMENT

This test is preferably administered during a session as a basis for discussion and can be administered again following a number of sessions in order to monitor progress.

SCORING OPTIONS:
    a) Question the client and tick boxes agreed upon for discussion or,
    *b) Score each statement from 1-10 on a scale from 0 = **never** to 10 = **continually**, basing discussion on highest ratings scored.*

CLIENT:
DATE:

- ❑ I feel guilty
- ❑ I think about past rejections
- ❑ I feel rejected
- ❑ I focus on past mistakes
- ❑ I make the same mistakes repeatedly
- ❑ I feel other people are better than me
- ❑ I feel as if I am an immoral person
- ❑ I feel people can't trust me
- ❑ I feel I cannot get anything right
- ❑ I do not like the way I look
- ❑ I do not feel as if I belong
- ❑ I have lost my chance to have a good life
- ❑ I feel I have ruined my own life
- ❑ I do not feel as if I will ever change

❑ I do not like myself as a person

❑ I feel disgusted with myself

❑ I have very painful memories

❑ I have uncontrollable thoughts

❑ I think about past failures

❑ I feel embarrassed about things

❑ I feel embarrassed about who I am

❑ I am ashamed of the things I do

❑ I am ashamed of myself

❑ I can not tell people how I feel about myself

Counsellor Resource: ADDICTIONS & THE SHAME TREADMILL

In the spiritual sense, addictions are closely connected to shame. Indeed, both guilt and shame can become addictive in themselves. A constant failure pattern in breaking free of addictive behaviours produces guilt, which, when left unprocessed, leads to shame. When we see ourselves from a shame based, defeated viewpoint we tend to return to what we know best 'the lusts of the flesh'. This is quaintly described in the scriptures as *'a dog returning to lick up his vomit'* and *'a clean pig wallowing in mud'* (Prv 26:11; 2 Pet 2:22). This results in a cycle of shame, or a treadmill existence of all-pervasive feelings of guilt and condemnation.

Guilt and self-condemnation depend on how we feel about the things we have done (Rom 8 & 6). Therefore, the answer (the victory) is found in the spiritual realm where we see by the spirit all that has been done on our behalf to set things right (Isa 53:5). Shame involves how we see or feel about ourselves deeply within. If we do not see clearly that we are justified by faith, then we cannot approach our creator without shame. Our spiritual eyes are not open to see that we are totally forgiven, healed and whole; that we can approach the throne of grace as innocents, as if we had never sinned (Prv 34:5, 1Cor 13:11–13, 2Cor 7:10).

The cycle of shame <u>can</u> be broken – by the sure knowledge (by faith) of the victory that the cross of Christ has achieved. We are then able to leave the shame treadmill to access our transformation from glory to glory. To break free from the shame cycle, a deep spiritual healing is needed – through the spiritual realisation that it is not by works but by grace that we are saved. We need to understand – by the spirit – that our true identity <u>does</u> lie in him and that we <u>are</u> in right standing with God.

Jesus <u>is</u> our righteousness and He has made a way for us to be free from the effects of sin (1Cor 1:18-31, 1Cor 2:11-15). It is not what we <u>do</u> that counts; it is what he has done <u>already done</u> on our behalf to atone for our sins. Those addicted to shame only return to the treadmill because they choose to take their eyes off Jesus by setting their sight back on themselves.

The solution is to trade one addiction for another. In retaining an obsessive love relationship with Jesus, whereby nothing else matters but the compulsive desire to know him and please him, we see reflected in his eyes of love a clean and righteous child of God. Who would want to return to the mud and the vomit once having truly experienced this?

A client and I compiled the following graphic relating to addictions (of any nature) during a session of ministry. Having both experienced the treadmill, we simultaneously sensed the Holy Spirit guiding us to illustrate this concept together. This is shared with you in the hope that you will use it – under the anointing – to preach the good news and 'to set the captives free' via prayer ministry. The only instructions for use are to follow the Holy Spirit's guidance (2Tim 2:15, 1Jn 2:27).

IMAGE 16

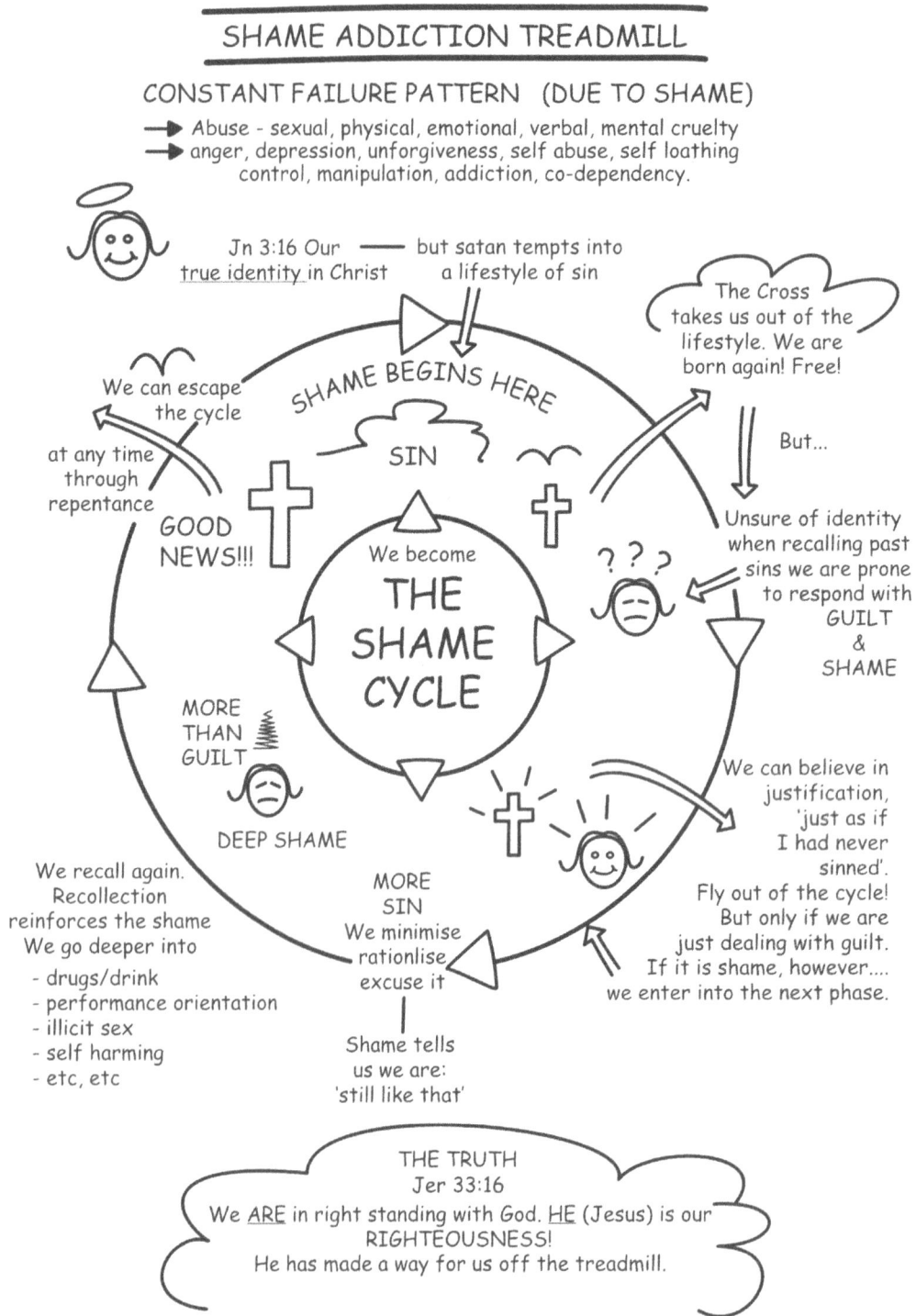

SHAME ADDICTION TREADMILL

CONSTANT FAILURE PATTERN (DUE TO SHAME)

➡ Abuse - sexual, physical, emotional, verbal, mental cruelty
➡ anger, depression, unforgiveness, self abuse, self loathing
control, manipulation, addiction, co-dependency.

Jn 3:16 Our —— but satan tempts into
true identity in Christ a lifestyle of sin

The Cross takes us out of the lifestyle. We are born again! Free!

We can escape the cycle

SHAME BEGINS HERE

at any time through repentance

GOOD NEWS!!!

SIN

We become
THE SHAME CYCLE

But...

Unsure of identity when recalling past sins we are prone to respond with GUILT & SHAME

???

We can believe in justification, 'just as if I had never sinned'. Fly out of the cycle! But only if we are just dealing with guilt. If it is shame, however.... we enter into the next phase.

MORE THAN GUILT

DEEP SHAME

We recall again. Recollection reinforces the shame We go deeper into

- drugs/drink
- performance orientation
- illicit sex
- self harming
- etc, etc

MORE SIN
We minimise rationlise, excuse it

Shame tells us we are: 'still like that'

THE TRUTH
Jer 33:16
We ARE in right standing with God. HE (Jesus) is our RIGHTEOUSNESS!
He has made a way for us off the treadmill.

CHAPTER FIFTEEN

FAULTY THINKING

Many emotional and relationship problems are a result of dysfunctional thought processes and negative outlooks on life. This chapter introduces and defines some of the most common faulty thinking habits. It gives valuable insight into the spiritual causes, as well as offering some practical solutions so that the client can become their own therapist.

- An introduction to counselling via correspondence – on the topic of defeating negative thinking styles
- The spoken word and counsellors as change agents – includes tips on handling the difficult character traits of self-pity and being overly sensitive
- Practical client handouts on healing and reprogramming the mind via the scriptures
- A valuable graphic Walking the Walk is included for study – particularly on the need to 'talk straight' as well as learning to think straight
- Demolishing spiritual strongholds and recognising mindsets are topics dealt with at length because of their importance

---

Study Notes

CLIENT TESTIMONIAL – Letter to a Friend on Internal Housekeeping

Dear Terry,

My spiritual counsellor said that she found a good book years ago about staying sane. This author is a psychiatrist and he is apparently described as 'the guru of common-sense'. She showed me her copy and it's nearly falling to bits. Now I know where she found a lot of her ideas and why she is all into wanting me to stick to her kind of therapy CBT (cognitive behavioural).

I think she's giving me the hint. What I need to take me into the real world now is some good old fashioned common-sense like my dad has. We know I had the brains to breeze through high school and uni, but I admit I've always been so negative, moody and scatterbrained in general.

If I want to follow in dad's footsteps – and I sure do – then I'd better get a copy of this doctor's book, as well as going through with the therapy. I've been so long already in professional therapy and the prayer ministry type counselling that it's cost dad a fortune. Yes, I know he's got plenty, but I intend to make it in the business world too. I can give him some returns on what he has invested in me.

My therapist says if I want improvement on my mood swings, then I need to check my internal monologue. Apparently, I need to do some big-time 'internal housekeeping' to rid myself of negative thinking and destructive self-talk.

After I had a good clean out spiritually (with all the prayer ministry) I was encouraged to pull down my strongholds (get rid of the mindsets). She emphasized that I now need 'to renew my mind to conform to the mind of Christ'. She claims the Holy Spirit is the most brilliant CBT practitioner in the world, and that the Bible has all the principles to use as a form of spiritual de-programming from my habitual, negative thinking and behavioural patterns.

Now that sounded like commonsense to me. So I asked her to put what she meant in writing for me (in lieu of my next session). As you'll recall, I was going away for a break before starting work full-time with dad and I wanted to really get stuck into it. What she wrote was personal to me, but could apply to anyone. So I asked her if it was OK if I passed it on to you, as we are a lot alike. Hoping it can be of some help to you too,

George

COUNSELLING VIA CORRESPONDENCE

On occasions, you will be able to counsel via correspondence. This is a very effective way of communicating complicated concepts – particularly to those clients who are academically minded. It will also serve to reinforce previous face-to-face sessions. You could discover it is a client's preferred learning style. Appropriate handouts can be included. Significant headway can be made if a client is self-motivated and applies the lessons.

Emailing in particular can be a good counselling tool. Using a chat room style format, the client and counsellor simply insert comments into a correspondence (using different font styles) for instant communication back and forth. This opens up the option of long distance counselling. Even anointed prayers can be included, as there are no time and space barriers with God!

SESSION VIA EMAIL

Subject Matter: **Habitual Negative Thoughts – Internal Housekeeping**

Dear George,

Regarding our last session, if you want improvement in your moods, energy levels and attitudes, you need to look at your **internal monologue***. In other words, you need to do some internal housekeeping and check out your* **self-talk***. The following is something I wrote for an assignment back in my own days at university. Note that all the key words when introduced are in bold print; and I will stick to that format throughout this email.*

'Change begins when we become aware of **negative judgments** and **labels** that we have automatically used against our selves in the past. We need **strategies** and **direction** to replace each devaluing thought and statement with something more positive. It is a form of **de-programming** from the negative, internal monologue and thought patterns in order to change **negative behavioural patterns**. We can become our own therapist by questioning and **challenging** our **belief systems** that produce the thoughts, which are creating the feelings.'

Remember George how we discussed that every thought affects you in that it creates a feeling? You can observe the mood you are in then actually backtrack to what you were thinking and saying to yourself to create it. I have noticed some of your little habits, which could be contributing to your moodiness. For example, whenever you cannot think of what to say at a social event, you say you tend to label yourself as 'stupid'. In this example, you are both **labelling** and **judging** yourself. If you verbalize this label, you are **'word cursing'** yourself and creating a 'dark' mood.

Use **realistic self-descriptions** rather than **negative labels**. For example, you could employ an alternate internal monologue such as, 'My mind might go fuzzy or blank when I am nervous, but I am certainly not stupid'. Next time, you might realistically think, 'I get nervous when speaking to people and I find it hard to know what to say. I need some lessons on small talk!' This can result in a 'lighter mood'. In this sense you have a description of your **behavioural shortcomings**, rather than a **derogatory personal remark**.

Be constantly aware of your **habitual phrases** and replace them with more realistic and positive ones. Adopt a light-hearted and grateful attitude regarding your limitations and inadequacies. Remember my old habit of saying, 'I am always getting lost! I have no sense of direction'. This was a prime example of word cursing my self using a **generalisation** and **exaggerating**. Thankfully I have replaced this with, 'I seem to have to work harder than some to find my way around. Thank goodness for road maps and directories!' I am improving. You watch me George, next thing I'll be operating guided tours and giving up the counselling!

What I am saying is, try approaching problems in a creative way. You seem to be stuck in a rut. Up until now you are repeatedly coming under **self-condemnation** whenever you make a mistake. You confess that your **habitual thoughts** are: 'I never get anything right! I'll always be a loser.' By this, you are seeing things as **black and white**, and experiencing **all or nothing** type of thinking. You are even having a try at **fortune telling** or **forecasting**. May I suggest that you <u>do</u> generally <u>get</u> what you expect? (This is called **'self-fulfilling prophecy'**).

You will find all of these terms (and more) in a good book on psychological theories. They are usually classified under **'cognitive distortions'**, **'thinking errors, 'distorted or unhelpful thinking habits'** or **'dysfunctional thoughts'**. I prefer the plain old term **'faulty thinking'**. When you find the time surf the net and do some research to see just how many there are! Meanwhile, I will give some more examples.

We have noted that you are in the habit of doing certain mental gymnastics that are not good for you. You continue to **jump to conclusions** based on your feelings. Instead, jump on your 'fortune telling' habit; that is, the way you predict things will always turn out badly for you. You have agreed with me that you try to **mind read** – where you assume or 'know' what someone is about. You often declare that you know what a person is thinking of you and it is usually based on **negative assumptions**. You are not always right, you know.

Instead, expect the best of life and people in general. Think creatively. Think positively. Think laterally. If something isn't working, then try something else. Brainstorm with others about why you are making mistakes. Give yourself a pep talk. Stand on your head if it will make a difference to your thinking processes! Remember, your thoughts create your lifestyle George. Every thought creates a feeling. You can actually choose your moods and behaviours by taking control of your thought life.

*Remember how we did that **reality checklist**? It is realistic at times to accept that life has been a series of problems. Facts are facts. The truth is that life <u>can</u> be one challenge after another. Life, therefore, is finding solutions to one problem so that you can move on and be free to accept the challenge of the next one. Each solution strengthens you and makes a better thinker of you. I ask you to consider whether you have a **discounting the positive** mentality? Then there is something called **'tunnel vision'**. From what I have observed you tend to look on the dark side and overlook the positive possibilities in a situation. No wonder you are depressed.*

The secret is to praise God in all your circumstances, trusting that He will always be on your side and turning things around for your good. Note that the word 'in' is used here, not '<u>for</u>' all your circumstances. The key factor is that you can allow Him to change your circumstances by making an effort to stamp out your habitual negative thoughts once they enter your mind. It is your choice George. Give Him your trust and positive expectations. He will then have some material with which to work.

Now I would like you to study anxiety and stress and be aware of what it can do to you in a physical sense. For our next face-to-face session I would like to teach you some techniques to calm and relax your body, mind and emotions. You will be surprised how much your negative thought life has affected your physical body and how you can repair some of that damage by taking control your emotions.

For example, you seem be in the habit of worrying yourself sick over trivialities until you develop a headache. You can counterbalance, by concentrating on the small practical things such as learning correct breathing and other relaxation techniques. Exercise too can replace the hormones you are depleting through stress; so why not begin a fitness regime? Build yourself up spiritually also, by memorising scriptures, choruses and hymns. Put your obsessive ways to good use!

So much of your energy is wasted on worry and getting yourself depressed. Look at the amount of energy that you have previously spent on being anxious and fearful. Now determine to expend the same amount of energy on enjoying yourself, achieving something positive or caring for someone else.

Perhaps you could treat positive thinking as a kind of exercise or intriguing board game. Remember the little girl Pollyanna who taught everyone the 'glad game'? No matter how dire her predicament was she obstinately saw the glass as half full, not half empty. I would like to see you have some childlike fun George. I'd like to see you stay away from all the bad habits we discussed: **catastrophizing, personalizing, generalising, 'what-iffing', emotional reasoning, exaggerating** *and the pressure you put on yourself in the form of, 'I must do this, should do that', etc. You are so hard on yourself.*

I hope one day soon you'll stop blaming and judging yourself, and give up all the guilt trips. They are harmful to your health! Be kinder to yourself. Be your own best friend. One last thing – keep up your <u>good</u> habit of reading inspirational autobiographies. Why not write a fictional one with your self as the hero? You are such a good writer…

To conclude, here are some reassuring and comforting phrases that I encourage you to use regularly to replace your negative self-talk:

That's fine.	*No worries.*
It's all good.	*It's not a problem.*
Let's try that again.	*I can do this.*
That's life.	*I'm only human.*
Tomorrow's another day.	*It will be OK.*
I'll be fine.	*God is in control.*

And don't forget the scriptures I gave you. Have a great break away.
See you next month at 10am, on the 13th.

Regards,

Your Counsellor

THE SPOKEN WORD AS AN AGENT OF CHANGE

The Bible has much to say on the power of speech and how the spoken word can be a force for evil or a force for good. It states: –

a) Death and life is in the power of the tongue (Prv 18:21).
b) We will have to live with the consequences of what we say (Prv 18:20).
c) To have good fruit, you must have a healthy tree (Matt 12:33-36).
d) A corrupt tree produces evil fruit (Matt 7:15-17).
e) The fruit of the mouth (speech) is a product of what is in the heart (thoughts, feelings, intentions, attitudes, motives and the spirit).

f) On the Day of Judgment, our words will be used to judge us and each will be required to give account for every useless word spoken (Lk 6:43-45).

SIGNS OF CHANGE

As already stated: what is in the heart comes out of the mouth, we can feel effective as counsellors when our clients begin to show signs of speech patterns that are realistic, positive and healthy (Prv 23:15-16). This is one of the simple pleasures of being a people helper. We feel proud to be a part of the process, as we know that lives are in being turned around for the better. There is so much power in the spoken word. When a counsellor notices that patterns are actually changing, then there is good reason to be encouraged. If a person is talking straight, that is, realistically, rationally and reasonably (Image 19, *The 3 Rs*) free from lies and deception (Image 18, *Strongholds & Mindsets*) then that person is usually thinking straight and walking straight (Image 17, *Walking the Walk – Isa 30:21*).

Counsellor Exercise:

a) Examine your personal speech patterns over the next week and record your own common unhealthy statements below.
b) Devise a plan of action to eliminate these speech patterns.

IMAGE 17

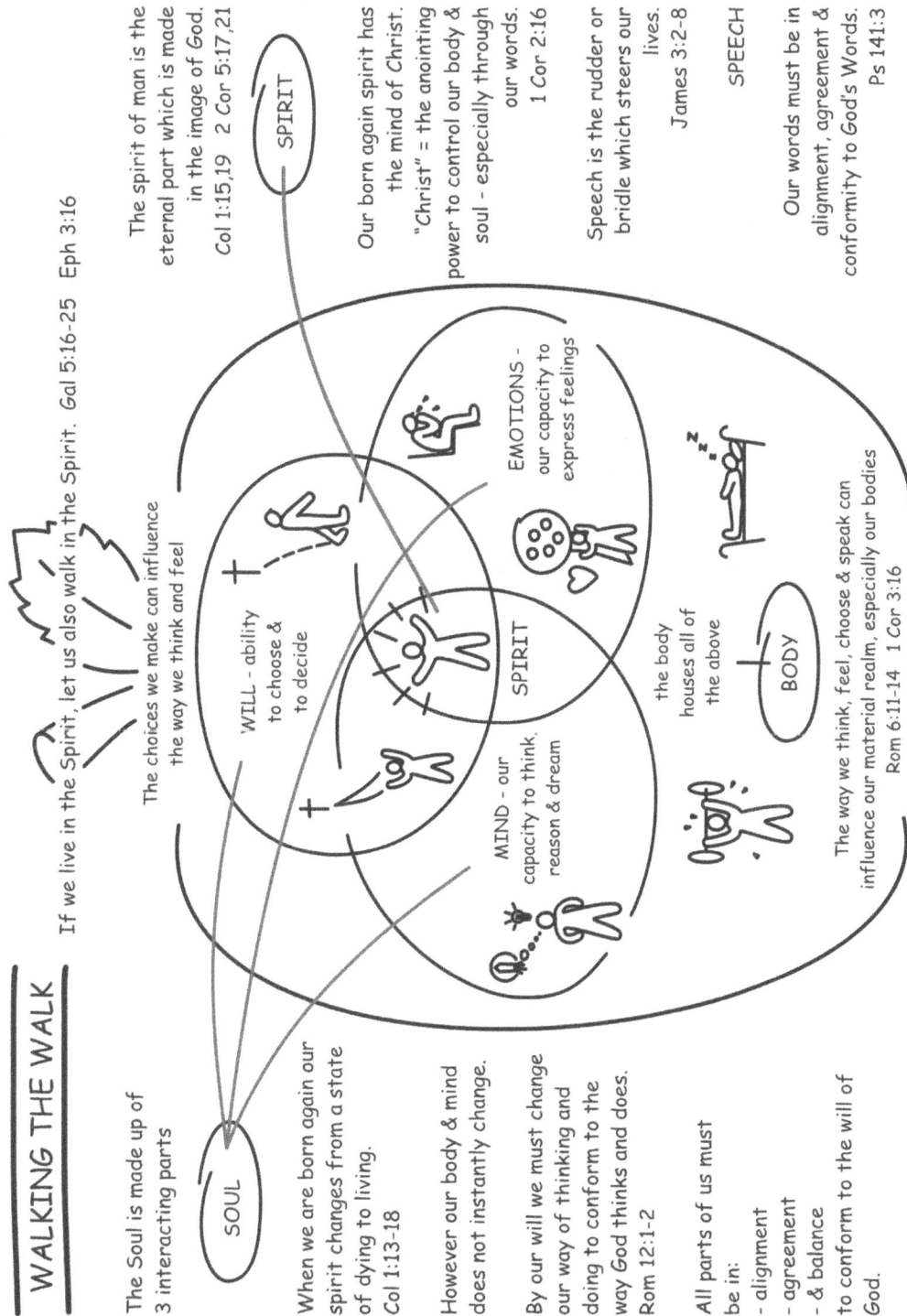

WALKING THE WALK

If we live in the Spirit, let us also walk in the Spirit. Gal 5:16-25   Eph 3:16

The spirit of man is the eternal part which is made in the image of God.
Col 1:15,19   2 Cor 5:17,21

SPIRIT

Our born again spirit has the mind of Christ. "Christ" = the anointing power to control our body & soul - especially through our words.
1 Cor 2:16

Speech is the rudder or bridle which steers our lives.
James 3:2-8

SPEECH

Our words must be in alignment, agreement & conformity to God's Words.
Ps 141:3

The choices we make can influence the way we think and feel

EMOTIONS - our capacity to express feelings

WILL - ability to choose & to decide

SPIRIT

MIND - our capacity to think, reason & dream

the body houses all of the above

BODY

The way we think, feel, choose & speak can influence our material realm, especially our bodies
Rom 6:11-14   1 Cor 3:16

The Soul is made up of 3 interacting parts

SOUL

When we are born again our spirit changes from a state of dying to living.
Col 1:13-18

However our body & mind does not instantly change.

By our will we must change our way of thinking and doing to conform to the way God thinks and does.
Rom 12:1-2

All parts of us must be in:
- alignment
- agreement
- & balance
to conform to the will of God.

STRONG NEGATIVITY & RESISTANCE TO CHANGE

No matter what the form, all negativity can be like a contagion. Words spoken in anger, bitterness and resentment infect others trying to care for the sufferers. Those with <u>self-inflicted</u> depression, anxiety or personality disorders, find it hard to see how negative views of life (and self) can inject and infect helpers – through the 'syringe' of the spoken word. Those who continually resist change and do not turn to a more positive way of speaking and acting, become carriers of *'death to the soul'*, wounding carers and counsellors alike.

It is not pleasant to deal with a client who stubbornly persists in complaining, blaming and self-berating; who brings a dark cloud of gloom, a defeatist attitude and a victim mentality into your place of ministry. It is not easy to point out that preoccupation with distorted thinking, negative speech and behaviour affects others as well as self. To communicate this to a negative person might only serve to strengthen existing viewpoints and to lower self-image further. This could lead to blaming others e.g. *my father was a poor role model* and *you expect too much from me,* or, it encourages self-condemnation, *I can't help myself,* and, *I'll never be any different* inevitably turns to self-pity, *if someone had given me a chance in life…* and so on.

No matter how positive, cheerful and loving you try to be towards this type of client, you will be thwarted at every turn. It will take a strong character not to be 'infected' in some way. So, make sure that you are personally not susceptible to these *diseases of the spirit.* Cleanse yourself of tendencies towards negativity. Cultivate the fruits of the spirit personally and ask for God's compassion, mercy and grace, as well as patience and joy, when dealing with a negative client.

Holy Spirit revelation is the most effective way to set a person free. It is the *living word of God* applied to a life that will break down barriers to affect change. Basically though, it comes down to a choice – the carrier chooses to lay down the syringe and decides to wholeheartedly take up his or her tools to do the work needed. We could say, 'God helps those who help themselves' and 'all things are possible with God'.

God's Spoken Word *(see section on prophetic gifting)*

'Wonder and signs are no problem to me, for I have mounted high on the wings of an eagle and I have seen riches beyond compare in the spiritual realm.

'My children do not look at the problems. See beyond the natural realm. Look to the heavenlies where all things are possible. Go where I have been, for I have opened this realm up to you and I am inviting you to participate in the riches thereof.

> '*Look not at the earth and the dust thereof. You are born of the spirit and no longer are bound by the flesh and the confines and limitations that the earth places upon you. Have I not said that you who follow will do greater works than I?*
>
> '*Then, move now into the realm of the spirit where I have purchased for you a birthright by My Blood. There you will see, by faith, the signs and the wonders. There you will see why earthly limitations are no problem to me. There you will see why they need not be a problem to you.'*
>
> *Lk 5:26; Mk 16:15-18; Acts 1:4-10*

Practicalities: CHRISTIAN COUNSELLORS AS AGENTS FOR CHANGE

As previously explained, it is the work of the Holy Spirit to convict. Our part is to help the client to become aware of self-centredness – to gently challenge – so that healthy non-judgmental guilt feelings rise to the surface to be dealt with. The purpose of encouraging guilt is to direct the client to the cross (see resources on *Shame*).

SPIRITUAL THERAPY IN COMPARISON TO SECULAR THERAPY

Secular counselling is usually based on raising self-esteem and assisting in certain practical ways to correct faulty thinking. However, without ministering to the spirit as well as the mind, positive results can be short lived. Clients need to have knowledge of where they stand in Christ. Faulty belief systems give rise to lie based, distorted, imbalanced, irrational and unrealistic ways of thinking and speaking which are not God-honouring. The result is fear-based behaviours, which create unhealthy lifestyles. Negativity is not only self-defeating but also affects associated others (including you as the Christian counsellor).

As well as negativity and victim mentality, two other self-defeating character traits (which encourage faulty thinking) will be dealt with briefly in this text as resistors to change: *self-pity* and being *overly-sensitive*.

SELF-PITY

Compassion is required to deal with a client who is suffering from self-pity, as it is still part of a grieving process that they are undergoing. Admittedly it is the grieving process 'gone wrong', but it still needs to be handled with care. The scriptures say not to 'beat out herbs with a mallet'. In other words, do not be heavy handed, aggressive and forceful (even though the major key to being a change agent in these cases is intolerance of self-pity).

Self-pity can usually be combated (when the time is right) by gentle exposure. Be careful with those who are very sensitive by nature. Self-pity can be dealt with as you would any other sin: by *acknowledgment, confession, repentance and renouncement.* The same can be said of the following trait – being overly-sensitive in nature.

SENSITIVITY

The following resource can be used as a counselling tool with the proviso that it be used with discretion. The best form of presentation is to read it out to the client following a period of light-hearted camaraderie. Remember that you are presenting this to someone who is most likely to be 'prickly' and easily wounded; so be very careful that it is used appropriately and prayerfully. You might like to adapt it and present it in an empathetic prayer form.

Resource: ON BEING OVERLY SENSITIVE

Being overly sensitive can mean that I am easily hurt and, thereby, I am letting my emotions rule my life. My mind is providing excuses and justifications and I am saying I am right and others are wrong. This indicates immaturity and self-centredness. In order to grow and mature, I need to renew my mind so that it is able to discipline the heart. Then, my feelings are no longer being presented as the truth.

If I am ruled by my emotions, then I have set my heart up as an idol and my mind has become a slave or servant to my feelings. However, if my mind has been renewed, then my Holy Spirit inspired thinking searches for the truth from the Word of God. I study and absorb it until it becomes a part of my whole being. I am able to believe and act upon the truth without deception, confusion or fear hindering my progress.

My mind is able to train my heart to become an obedient servant of the truth. I become centred on others and their needs rather than focused on my own wants and needs. I become a balanced, well-adjusted and mature person rather than a self-absorbed victim (Rom 12:1-2).

NEGATIVE TRAITS – SPIRITUAL HEALING APPLICATIONS

At the cross, over-sensitivity, self-pity and tendencies towards pessimism and melancholy, can be dealt with as sinful character traits. It is from this position that remorse is experienced, followed by repentance, renouncement and then, forgiveness appropriated. The client can then be led by practical assistance into enjoying a healthier self-image and a more comfortable and God-honouring lifestyle.

Faith based truths can to be slowly incorporated into the general lifestyle of a person who is fearful, anxious, depressed, resentful, or negative in any other form. There is no 'quick fix'. Telling a client bluntly to *'get over it'* and offering trite phrases such as, *'you just have to have faith'* simply will not work. Likewise, quoting all the relevant scriptures in the world will not get through to a client with a stronghold of negativity. Client customized practical examples of *how to* and *when to,* are needed in order to apply newfound truths.

USE OF SECULAR TECHNIQUES FOR MINISTRY APPLICATION

In cognitive behavioural therapy, as with other forms of psychological counselling, cognitive distortions are usually tabled and given as assignments to alter thinking patterns. Most entrenched depressives will not be capable of self-application so it will take a fair bit of client/therapist interaction to work through the exercises.

As for the others: the anxiety prone will worry about what they will find out about themselves, the fearful will worry about getting into trouble from the therapist if they cannot get it right, those with low self-esteem will say that they are not capable of doing the exercises and give up before even beginning. The angry, bitter, resentful, and the grumblers and complainers, will wear a therapist down with their stubbornness and wilfulness.

It must be frustrating to even the most dedicated secular practitioner who has so much faith in these techniques. Better to have faith in the power of prayer, and the Holy Spirit's guidance, in order to get to the root causes of these conditions. It is preferable to have spiritual insight into what makes a person function. We have the Holy Spirit who will guide into personal discernment and insight about the blockages to progress – if the client is willing to go in that direction.

THE SECRET TO SUCCESS

This text will give insight into Christian counselling techniques which will lead to success, simply because they are based on scriptural precepts and concepts. Remember that this does not mean that we cannot, as agents for change, draw on the secular concepts and techniques to enhance our ministry e.g. *Cognitive Behavioural Therapy* and *Solution Based Therapy* when compatible with scriptural principles.

Client Handout #1: HEALING & RENEWAL OF THE MIND (Rom 12:1–2)

Are you one of those individuals who have problems with controlling your thought life, leaving you feeling different to everyone else and alienated from the world at large? There are those who feel isolated, lonely and troubled – ruled by obsessive thought patterns, which leave some feeling overwhelmed and miserable for their entire lives. In fact, you might be surprised to know how many others are suffering silently from similar concerns. Counselling gives the opportunity to discuss these concerns with someone who is dealing with other sufferers.

DO NOT GIVE UP THE FIGHT

You might have given up the fight and resigned yourself to being 'different'. You might have accepted this as 'just one of those things', or, how God made you. This is where you need to challenge your thoughts. God did not make you to be this way and there is no reason that you have to accept that this is your lot in life.

PRAYER CHANGES THINGS

Prayer does change things; so, logically speaking, lack of prayer leaves things unchanged. Do you know that even your attitude can be changed through prayer? If we take the scriptures indicating that prayer changes things (even you) and that nothing is impossible for God concerning you, then we have a prescription for your personal healing.

LEAVE THE PAST BEHIND

Much physical sickness and mental illness come from an undisciplined mind and from an inability to form good habits. The solution is to change from dwelling on your present bad habits and past wrongdoings to believing for a bright new future. You might have already experienced dealing with the past through the ministry of inner healing, restoration and deliverance. However, continuing to dwell on past mistakes and sins causes you to remain in a rut of self-judgment and self-condemnation. This is certainly not pleasing to God who sacrificed his own beloved son in order for you to have complete freedom and victory. Time now to move on…

MOVE ON

It is now time to take command of your life, becoming determined to focus on what you can do differently in the present. Make the choice to move on into a new and exciting way of living, free from the thoughts that have plagued you. Christ came so that you may enjoy your life – with every good thing, and in abundance. It is a matter of choice – your choice.

DEAL WITH THE PRESENT

First of all, open yourself to Holy Spirit conviction (rather than self-condemnation). On conviction, deal quickly with your sins. For instance, you could be accusing yourself of gluttony; while God the Father understands that you are looking to food for false comfort (rather than 'being greedy'). You might be beating yourself up emotionally because you are shy or suffering from phobias, while Jesus is trying to say to you, *fear not for I am with you'*. He might want to show you how you can tackle a certain problem, but your sin of worrying (which is a lack of trust in His provision) stands in the way.

CONNECT WITH YOUR MAKER

The secret is to discover what false perceptions of God you have, then to confess and repent so that you are able to effectively pray. You need to direct your prayers to the real 'I Am' instead of the god you yourself have fabricated. Discover who you really are 'in Christ'. Find and memorize the appropriate scriptures so that your mind is washed with the Word of God.

You are now on the *Road of Discovery*. Discover what is true and real about God and how purely good he is. Discover what it means to be created in the image of the Creator. You will find within yourself the goodness and truth about your maker. You might discover that you truly do possess the ability to develop fruits such as patience, self-control and loving self-tolerance.

Have no gaps in your communion with God. Confess your failures, mistakes and sins as they happen. Rid yourself of guilt as soon as possible by repentance and renouncement. When progress is made, do not become careless; take a firm stand and refuse to give further ground to your own weaknesses. Refuse also to give in to Satan in his roles as a tempter and the Father of Lies. Stand firm, resist the devil and he will eventually give up!

DISCONNECT WITH THE TROUBLEMAKER

Take authority and command Satan to go. Tell him that he has no further power over you. With your new authoritative stance, he will no longer recognise you as your former self. He will have nothing to get his hooks into. Learn to immediately ask yourself: *who am I listening to – Satan, the world, my own thoughts, or God?* Learn to live in the spirit and not in the realm of feelings or intellect. Take control of your feelings by taking control of your thoughts. Listen to the voice of the Father; rather than *the father of lies*.

REASSESS YOUR LIFESTYLE

We create our own patterns, strongholds and ruts. Ask yourself: –

a) *What am I focusing on and believing in?*
b) *What do I need to accept and what can I change?*
c) *What can I work around, work with, destroy, challenge or replace?*
d) *What lies have I based my life upon?*
e) *What patterns, mindsets and habits do I need to eliminate?*
f) *What outcomes do I want?*

WORK OUT YOUR GOALS

Work out what you want, then focus and believe in your spirit that you already have it. It might appear impossible at this time, because the facts prove otherwise, but believe in the power faith has. Possessing faith, and making use of it, is a divine principle that works. You may like to use the phrase, *'the facts are ... but, the truth is...'* until you are ready to speak out a purely positive confession with all your heart.

Write down your personal aims and goals and look at them often – both short and long term. For example: –

My short-term goal is: *I am going to try to enjoy life one day at a time.*
My long-term goal is: *I aim to be free of depression completely by my 30th birthday.*

GO FOR IT!

Remember that whatever you choose to focus on becomes reality to you. So, look at what you want and imagine it as if it is already real. Do you want to be a clear-headed, self-disciplined, intelligent, organised human being? Then you need to step out in your mind away from how you are at present. Imagine yourself as that fully functioning person you choose to be. Whatever you focus on; you will become. So aim for the best and aim high!

Client Handout #2: SPIRITUAL REPROGRAMMING VIA THE SCRIPTURES

Review the following list with your presenting problem in mind:

1. Slow your thoughts down for closer observation (Rom 8:6-8).
2. Capture the thoughts; take control (2Cor 10:4-5; Col 2:14-15).
3. Do these thoughts align/agree with the Word of God (Rom 12:2)?
4. Where did they come from (Jn 8:44 or 1Cor 2:16)?
5. Get more objective opinions from other sources (Prv 15:22-23).
6. Seek wisdom and believe you have it (Prv 1-3).
7. Recognise and acknowledge lies/false beliefs/perceptions (Rom 12:2).
8. Replace recognised lies with truths (Jn 8:31-32; Jn 8:44).
9. Tackle mindsets with the Word of God (2Cor 10:4-5; Rom 8:5).
10. Place troublesome thoughts under the blood of Christ (Col 2:14-15).
11. Acknowledge possession of the mind of Christ (1Cor 2:16).
12. Meditate on God's laws and principles both day and night (Heb10: 16).
13. Align, agree and conform to God's words and will (Ps 141:3).
14. Step from negative thoughts into positive confession (Prv 18:4, 20-21).
15. Responsibly plan an appropriate God-honouring outcome (1Pet 5:6-7).
16. Do not resurrect the powers of your past thought life by dwelling on the negatives (Phil 1:6, 2:13).

Consider your current situation in the light of these questions.

a) What is the surface presenting problem?
b) What is the underlying root problem?
c) What are my options?
d) What are the consequences of each option?
e) What are my moral and ethical boundaries here?
f) Am I in touch with reality?
g) What would I prefer to do?
h) What would be beneficial to all concerned?
i) Am I going to put these thoughts into action purely out of duty?
j) What would Jesus think in this situation?
k) What would Jesus do if he were in this situation?
l) What would Jesus think about what I am thinking and behaving?
m) Do I have on the whole armour of God?
n) Do I have any doorways or windows for Satan to enter my life?
o) Have I laid my thoughts, desires and ways on the altar?
p) Have I acknowledged the Blood of Jesus Christ?

Counsellor Resource: STRONGHOLDS & MINDSETS

2Cor 10 4-5; 1Cor 2:16; Rom 8:6-8; Rom 12:2; Prv 4:23, 18:10

> *Negative Strongholds* are areas in our lives where we have built a fortress from which we defend our erroneous (incorrect) belief systems.

TYPES OF STRONGHOLDS

a) A *corporate stronghold* is an area where many share a particular belief e.g. *ineffectiveness* resulting from a spirit of apathy over a church.
b) A *personal stronghold* could be likened to a well-defended fortress e.g. *pride* displayed by character traits of dogmatism and arrogance.
c) A *mental stronghold* is a system of thoughts empowered by emotions created by faulty reasoning, which keep us from operating in God's truths.

> *Mindsets* are the building materials of a stronghold, giving it structural shape and endurance. They serve to support and strengthen negative strongholds.

MINDSET DEFINITIONS

1. *A fixed direction of thought*, e.g. an inner vow such as, *'I am never going to let them hurt me again'*.
2. *A mental set*, e.g. a particular mental framework of attitudes, expectations or prejudices associated with racism.

> The *fruits* of negative strongholds and mindsets can be: habits, addictions, fantasies, persistent thoughts, ruts, predictable reactions, prejudices, obsessions, compulsions, fears, phobias, and other bondages.

The scriptures declare that the weapons we fight with are not of this world (such as guns or personal wits). The weapons are of a spiritual nature, having divine power to demolish strongholds. We destroy arguments and every pretension that sets itself up against what we know is true of God and what he has declared to us via his word. We take captive (or control of) every thought to make it obedient to (the will of) Christ the Anointed One so that it aligns, agrees, and is in harmony with, the Word of God (2Cor 10:4-5; Rom 8:6-8). Then we will be manifesting (openly displaying) the fruits of the Spirit, against which there is no law. Then we are indeed free as Christians to live lives pleasing to him (Gal 5).

> The *fruits of the Spirit* as presented in the scriptures are: love, joy, peace, longsuffering, kindness, goodness, faithfulness, gentleness and self-control. These are indicators of demolished strongholds and mindsets in those who live and walk in freedom and strength in the Spirit of God (Gal 5:16-26).

When we are manifesting the fruits of the Spirit, we are showing that we have put our trust in God to protect and defend us. We no longer need to depend on worldly strongholds and mindsets. Our almighty God says that he will defend and protect us like a wall and that his angel guards those who honour him ((Isa 60:18, Ps 34:7). He has promised that he will to be a wall of protective fire around the place we live in and that he will live with us in all his glory that we will be so prosperous as a people, that we will be too large to have walls built around us ((Zech 2:4-5).

IMAGE 18

STRONGHOLDS & MINDSETS

Unmet emotional needs, unresolved memories, pain, anger, bitterness grudges, resentments

Can be turned into a virtual arsenal against you. Satan will trick and tempt via circumstances to reinforce your hurt and fear. You fear being exposed to further pain and thus set up defensive walls or STRONGHOLDS. This fortress is what you use to fortify and defend your right to hold a personal belief, idea or opinion against outside opposition.

YOU HAVE A SPIRITUAL NEGATIVE STRONGHOLD when you are believing a lie and keeping God's truth out. The root problem of this is THE DAMAGED SOUL. A mindset will cause you to fight to protect that false belief. You will erect a personal fortress from which you will defend your right to believe it.

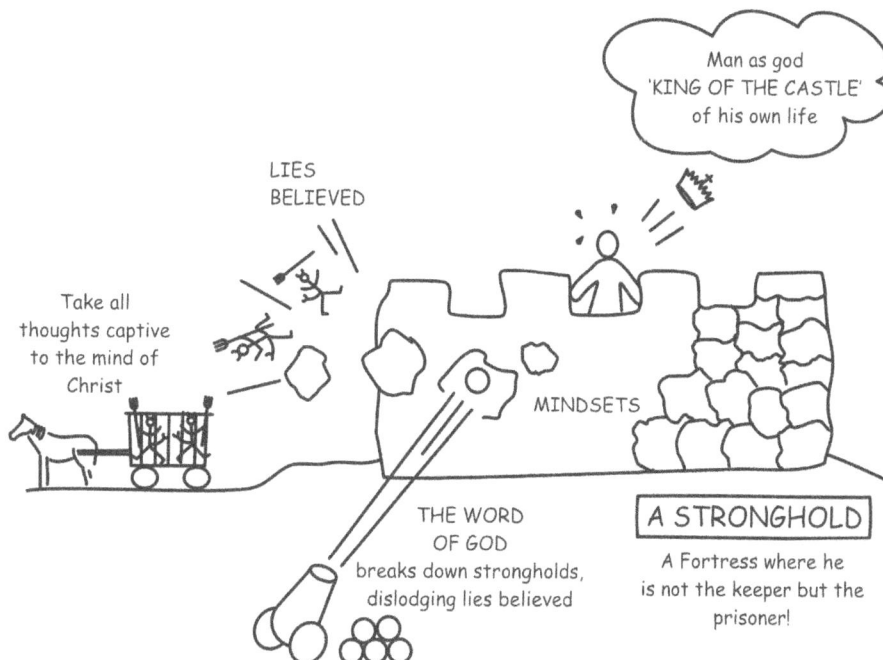

Man as god
'KING OF THE CASTLE'
of his own life

LIES
BELIEVED

Take all
thoughts captive
to the mind of
Christ

MINDSETS

THE WORD
OF GOD
breaks down strongholds,
dislodging lies believed

A STRONGHOLD

A Fortress where he
is not the keeper but the
prisoner!

2 Cor 10:4-5, 1 Cor 2:16; Rom 8:6-8; Rom 2:2

Client Handout #3: STRONGHOLDS & MINDSETS (Prv 4:23)

> A *personal stronghold* is what one uses to fortify and defend a personal belief, idea or opinion against outside opposition. A *fortification* is built to defend what one erroneously believes to be true. Usually, if you believe a lie, then you will fight to protect your personal belief (or deception). You will erect a fortress or a position from which to defend your right to believe what you have chosen to believe.

FORTRESSES & FOOTHOLDS

A fortress here is a *protective defence mechanism.* You can choose to fortify an unresolved issue in your life where Satan has gained a *foothold* (secure position of power from which further progress can be made). Strongholds create a barrier or fortress, which keep God's truths and healing power from gaining access to break this power over you. This fortress consisting of mindsets, cemented together with lies, serves to protect and perpetuate the deception. Seemingly, it acts as a barrier to God's love. The truth is that nothing can separate us from the love of God (Rom 8:35). However it can appear that His love is not getting through to you. You appear weak, incomplete, sinful and sickly. The way to freedom is to surrender your right to defend yourself from the position of your fortress. Allow the Holy Spirit to go to work on stripping your old carnal nature of the mindsets. Ask God to help you to recognise such things as *attitudes, expectations, and prejudices,* which are keeping you prisoner in your self-made fortress – where you have stationed yourself as *'king of the castle'.*

MASKS

Every harmful thought and emotion from which your persona derives power must be taken captive to the mind of Christ, because it is contrary to the will of God. Your *persona* is the personality that you acquire or adopt and present to other people. This is commonly called *a mask.* This signifies the mechanism by which a person's true thoughts and feelings are hidden in order to adapt to their environment. This mask is the face we show to the world – your *acquired personality* (see teaching on *The Parts of Man*).

BUILDING BLOCKS

Fear, doubt, suspicion, self-sufficiency, self-protection, self-righteousness, false security, isolation and wrong reactions, fleshly desires and soulish ideas can be the *building blocks* set in the fortress. The whole structure needs to be demolished and the rubble cleared away. New positive mindsets can be established on the *cleansed foundations*, with Jesus Christ as the chief cornerstone, keeping all new building blocks in alignment with the will of his Father and our Creator.

THE BUILDING OF A NEGATIVE STRONGHOLD

Factors contributing to the building of a structure can be:

> ➢ *hidden sins*
> ➢ *unforgiveness issues*
> ➢ *unmet emotional needs*
> ➢ *unresolved memories*
> ➢ *false perceptions*
> ➢ *lies believed*

All of these, and more, can be turned into *armour for self-preservation*. This armour seemingly serves to protect a wounded soul from further pain. However, it also impedes God's loving ministry to the old wounds, which remain to fester underneath. A person maintaining a stronghold or *mindset* is not inviting Jesus in to heal or to reign as Lord in certain areas of life. You have probably sensed this stubbornness in yourself when being corrected – as a resistance towards Holy Spirit conviction.

So you should be able to relate to a client when he or she is faced with a certain 'touchy' topic, such as an issue of unforgiveness or the need for a change in behaviour. The conscience is being challenged, but the defensiveness is in place. The 'vibes' are being projected towards you. If you are sensing this stubborn spirit emanating from a client then you would do well to look for a mindset.

MINDSET FORMATION

Mindsets are the building materials of negative strongholds – giving them structure shape and durability. Jesus is our rock, our fortress and He should be <u>the</u> stronghold giving strength and support to the structure of our lives. Our minds should be set on him as the cornerstone of our existence. This is why erroneous beliefs regarding his inability to guide, strengthen and protect us need to be constantly challenged from an early age (see Ch 14 *How We View God*).

A student of the author once pointed out that mindsets are often established when we are children. Her view was that we are drawn toward stimuli that appeal to our mindsets, thus reinforcing our patterns of thinking. We (unconsciously) look for patterns of thinking in people's conversations similar to our own. We even adjust our thought patterns to fulfil the expectations of our mindsets. Sometimes, we will twist the meaning of words to make them fit within our mindset framework.

Even though a thought is correct, the direction we give it, or our attitude towards it, can lead us astray. And it is not necessarily a traumatic experience which forms a mindset and begins the structure of a stronghold. A simple occurrence can lead to a wrong pattern of thinking, as illustrated in the following testimony...

AUTHOR'S TESTIMONY: On Ice-cream & Mindsets

I can recall a personal childhood example of this that the Lord revealed to me during prayer ministry. I was told by two authority figures, my mother and grandmother, that, if I ate that whole big bowl of ice cream I would be sick. I did, and I was!

With this tiny incident as a young child, I began the building of a fortress for self-preservation. Fuelled by thoughts of guilt and expectations of dire consequences whenever I tried to enjoy the simple blessings of life, I would sabotage myself at every turn. I would even actually become physically ill after enjoying myself. I am sure my dear mother and grandmother had no intentions of starting me along this path in life.

However, under the natural law of stimulus and response, I formed a mental set based on a foolish childhood perception of what appeared to be a truth to me. The fruit being, that as I grew, I developed a mindset. I determined not to risk many normal childhood activities in case I ended up being either: sick, injured, disappointed or punished. As an adult, I also tended to avoid enjoyable social activities of most kinds in order to defend and protect myself. My stronghold caused me to retreat into anxiety and introversion (amongst other things).

How the carnal mind works! Of course a large bowl of ice cream in a small girl's stomach can lead to a little nausea. It should not lead to such serious issues. Such is the power of a stronghold once established as a lifestyle.

We need to be made aware of the problem (see *Fruits, Roots & Poisons* and the graphic of *The Diseased Apple Tree* in the prayer techniques section). We can then choose to demolish the fortress by challenging our false belief system. We take up *weapons of warfare* against our carnal minds in order to bring down the defensive walls.

WAGING WAR AGAINST LIES

The cement holding this fortress together is allegorised in the accompanying graphic on strongholds. The *cement* holding the structure together symbolises the *demonic thoughts* we have claimed as our personal 'truths' that must be dislodged from the structure. Once dislodged, these rebellious thoughts are taken into captivity and inactivity. The structure is then weakened and able to be shattered. It can be torn down piece-by-piece with the Word, (symbolised by *the canon* as our spiritual weapon in the accompanying graphic).

Prayer is then needed for the Holy Spirit '*to renew a right spirit in me*' so that our thought patterns are conformed to the mind of Christ. The carnal mind must come under subjection to a born again righteous spirit (as depicted in the graphics *Walking the Walk* and *Is your House in Order?*).

MINISTRY TOOLS FOR CLEARING THE RUBBLE

Following the demolition of a stronghold, other counselling and warfare tools can be brought into play to clear the rubble away:

- ➢ Repentance
- ➢ Renouncing
- ➢ Cleansing and Aligning
- ➢ Breaking Curses and Soul Ties
- ➢ Binding and Loosing
- ➢ Understanding Fruit to Root Patterns
- ➢ Aborting Harvests from Negative Seed Sowing
- ➢ Eviction of Demonic Squatters
- ➢ Recognizing Negative Aspects of our Personality Types
- ➢ Fulfilling our Needs God's Way*
- ➢ Warring in the Spirit
- ➢ Healing of the Emotions
- ➢ Eliminating Curses and Accessing Blessings

---

*Running to the Lord as your strong tower, for provision, protection and strength, is the only answer (Prv 18:10; 2 Chr 20).

CHAPTER SIXTEEN

RENEWING THE MIND

The spirit of man is delivered from bondage first; then the full range of an individual's thought life must be cleansed and retrained to align with the Word of God. As many resources as possible are offered here – following on from the previous chapters on faulty thinking, defeatist attitudes and defence mechanisms.

There is an abundance of theories and methods of therapy involved in secular counselling. The wise use of sound biblically based resources is crucial for ministry to the Body of Christ (Prv 14:33). This does not mean that we discard the practical application of complementary secular methods – those that are not opposed to the Word of God.

    ℇ   A special story and insight into ministering to those with a disability
    ℇ   Therapeutic renewal using secular methodology
    ℇ   A sampling of resources used by the author as a practitioner
    ℇ   A personal prophetic word to the author regarding mind renewal

---

Study Notes

CLIENT TESTIMONIAL – The Big Guy

It really cheeses me off that just because you've got a disability you are treated like a second-class citizen. So, I got a mental illness and a smashed up face; it doesn't make me less than human. Animals at the vet have been treated better than me when I've fronted up at church meetings, figuring I could get in touch with the Big Guy.

I believe in God too! Just 'cause I act a bit weird and my speech is slurred and I blow my top when someone crosses me, don't mean that I'm not a God fearin' Christian. I believe in Jesus. He died for blokes like me same as anyone else. I wanna be well. I believe, if I can get me foot in the door of some religious place without frightenin' the hell out of some of the li'l old ladies, then I can get some help from Him.

I want me old brain back working'. It wasn't much to begin with but it kept me off unemployment benefits and on the road. I haven't worked in ten years! I don't want to be like this. It's not my fault.

Some of me mates have been on the drugs, sure, and their brains have got scorched different to mine. Yeah, maybe they have made mistakes like I have, when I was too young to know better. But, I haven't been a druggie or slept around and picked up some disease. I just had me head bashed in, in a pub brawl. Sure, I started it, but that doesn't mean I deserve this – to be on the pension the rest of me life, to never have any cash, no permit to drive, and to be treated like dirt all the time.

I used ta like work. Me job and me workmates was why I got up every day. Driving trucks was me life. Hauling goods interstate was what I liked, and all the regulars at the truck stops were me mates. We hung out together between hauls. It was a great life – footie on weekends, pub-crawls and borrowing a motorcycle for a spin on public hols. But that's all gawn now...

I want it back!!!!! And, if I can't be a truckie, at least I wanna be able to think straight enough to sign me name and fill out a form to get a job again. Doesn't matter what it is. I'll sweep the steps at the football stadium – yeh, even the toilets – if it gets me back in where I'm one of the crowd.

Maybe I'll even go back an' say a few hail Marys like me ol' mum used ta. I seen a sign up outside the cathedral in town inviting folks to come in if they want some help. Think I'll check it out...

SPECIAL NOTE TO THE WOULD BE COUNSELLOR

The preceding testimonial highlights the need for openness by ministries reaching out to the lost and hurting. We will not always encounter cases that are within our personal religious, cultural and environmental experiences. We will not always deal with people who are our peers, co-operative and counsellor friendly. We will constantly be dealing with *'those with a difference'* (as anyone who is out of the ordinary is currently termed).

Seasoned counsellors, in general, tend to come out the other end of ministry work a good deal more cautious and practical than when we start. We will most probably have entered into practice as bright-eyed, passionate, caring people with a mission to save the world. Time leaves us shaking our heads wondering how on earth we could have been so naïve. However, let me assure you, it is well worth the effort.

Always remember that each body and soul has a spirit and that each spirit has the unequivocal right to ministry. Pray that you will never lay your head on your pillow at night feeling that you have denied anyone that right, or favoured any human being above another.

Practicalities of Counselling: THERAPEUTIC MIND RENEWAL

NOTE FROM THE AUTHOR:

I personally use an eclectic approach, adapting my style to the personality needs of each client. Although my clientele come from word of mouth referrals from within the Body of Christ and I network with other Christian professionals and laypersons for support and referrals, they have a very diverse range of needs and backgrounds.

The following is my favoured form of therapy as a professional counsellor. In it, I am able to easily integrate teaching and preaching of spiritual concepts for renewal of the mind. I rely heavily on the scriptures to undergird my approach.

As an aspiring Christian counsellor, I suggest you would do well to invest in a sound textbook to learn the foundational concepts of the various psychological theories and practices, as well as investing some time regularly to the study of theology and in gathering cognitive resources*.

Resources available: *www.cci.health.wa.gov.au offers free downloads for mental health workers that are suitable to use for information leaflets based on the CBT approach – for anxiety, depression etc.

COGNITIVE BEHAVIOURAL THERAPY (CBT)

CBT is the application of some type of intervention program to change unwanted or destructive behaviour patterns and the accompanying feelings, e.g. isolating because of social anxiety. Simply put, it is a *relearning process* within which the client is aware, agrees, understands and benefits from the process.

It is based on the premise that learning is the stimulus to change. It has been proven that some learnt negative, self-defeating patterns of thought result in emotional distress and maladaptive behaviours, and that these can be unlearned. The process involves mutually agreed upon goals, which aid co-operation and collaboration with the counsellor. These goals can then, in a practical way, promote self-confidence, self-esteem and change in the client's behaviour.

The therapist is active and directive. The client needs to be motivated and co-operative. The focus on teaching and learning tends to avoid the stigma and concern about being classed as someone who is mentally ill. The client is a student rather than a patient, someone who is seeking education about a problem and becoming involved in the process of personal development.

PROCESSES

The client is educated on *cause and effect* and that behaviour is a product of learning. There can be more confidence placed in a process that centres on self-determination and personal empowerment. For example, self-management of stress helps allay feelings of being out of control and, therefore, reduces the stress. When educated that we are, both products and producers of our environment, we have hope for change and the resulting benefits. The client learns that there are practical choices to be made that will affect change; that the way one thinks (cognitions) are the major determinants of how one feels and acts.

Stressing the role of the cognitive (thought processes) will aid questioning, choosing, and deciding on a new path of action. A determination for the desired feelings and long-term results follows – a desire for change and its benefits. Studies have found that CBT conducted by a therapist over a series of weekly sessions, is as least as effective as medication in treating such things as anxiety disorders. CBT and similar therapies are also longer lasting and more cost effective.

AIMS & GOALS OF THE THERAPEUTIC PROCESS

Expectations and goals are fulfilled (or unfulfilled) according to the application, so a certain level of understanding of the processes and commitment is needed. The client is taught to become aware of automatic thoughts based on faulty beliefs, and to refocus on the more effective ones. In fact, many self-help groups (such as those for addictions) utilize CBT principles.

The main goal is to eventually be independent from the counsellor. With acquired new skills a person does not need to be a client or 'in therapy' for life! Change produces life changes. Success in making small initial changes in behaviour produces the self-confidence needed to make more (and more important) changes in order to alter the course of a life for the better.

BENEFITS

a) Assessment and evaluation techniques provide accountability for both client and therapist.
b) Motivations and drive strengths can be assessed.
c) Specific problems can be identified, progress monitored, goals realised, changes actualised.
d) CBT can be easily integrated into other mainstream therapies and used in conjunction with medical treatments and spiritual counselling.
e) The influence of the unique client attitudes and traits can be studied.
f) The negative cyclic type association between stimulus and response can be interrupted and eliminated.
g) Benefits and changes can be lasting.
h) It is a reality checking method involving elimination of faulty thinking, regression, repeated self-defeating behaviour and negative consequences to self and others.
i) There is acquisition of a philosophy based on reality, because it relies on thinking, disputing, debating, challenging, interpreting, explaining, teaching and identifying (and meeting) personality needs.
j) Results and benefits can be measured and seen because there is access to communication and diagnostic tools based on scientific method.
k) There is formation of a solid base for interpretation and problem solving.
l) Coping mechanisms are put in place for future onset of problems (crisis and relapse prevention).
m) Self-help mechanisms are formulated as the client learns to identify and confront faulty belief systems.
n) Tools and skills are acquired to eliminate maladaptive behaviours and replace them with more effective ones.
o) Unique personality needs are recognized and taken into consideration when problem solving.

PERSONALITY NEEDS PROFILES.

By taking simple tests to assess personality needs, or to locate problem areas, clients can become empowered quite early in therapy. By viewing the evidence of personality type profiles and modifying, adjusting, and replacing belief systems accordingly, more suitable behaviour can be chosen to suit personal needs. For example, if my needs are basically for security, I can have help from the therapist to enable me to look for a job that will meet my needs.

The mental or psychological schema can gradually dominate the intuitive side enabling a client to fit into society more comfortably and to maintain positive and constructive relationships. This is especially beneficial when the inner needs have rebelled and have brought forth dysfunctional, aberrant or malfunctioning behaviour; e.g. compulsive eating disorders or vandalism.

A JOINT RESPONSIBILITY

Clients can take joint responsibility with the counsellor, be active in the process, and actually see the desired results. There can be pride in taking part in the process rather than just being a 'project' the therapist is working on. The therapist is highly motivated towards scientifically produced results and promotes corrective experience that leads to learning skills. The client must actively practise to change self-defeating thinking. Personal client goals for change need to be set by the client. For example, *I would like to become a professional musician but my stage fright always gets the better of me. My therapist and I can work on this together to achieve my goal in life.*

CLIENT SUITABILITY

CBT is suitable for individuals, groups, couples and families. Such conditions as phobias, anxiety, depression, anger, personality disorders, sexual disorders, stress, children's behavioural problems, and parenting problems can all be addressed within clinical practice. A focus on behaviour rather than feelings makes it suitable for multicultural use and for those with special needs, such as those with challenging behaviours related to autism.

SUITABILITY FOR CHRISTIAN COUNSELLORS

As long as it is biblically focused, this type of therapy can be applied spiritually to all healing techniques found in this text, especially, fruit to root patterns (cause and effect); bringing down strongholds (mindsets); iniquities in the family line (interventions) and inner healing techniques (faulty beliefs). Cognitive Behavioural Therapy, adapted to a spiritualized form, is excellent for use in recovery and prevention of relapse following prayer ministry. Rational Emotive Behavioural Therapy (REBT) is another adaptable treatment for spiritual counsellors dealing with negative feelings and irrational thinking. Our aim of course is to renew the mind to God's thoughts and his way of doing things – rather than man's humanistic carnal ways and thoughts.

COGNITIVE RESOURCES

The following is a sample cognitive resource. There are various versions of this chart used by counsellors and psychologists to help clients challenge *unhealthy/unhelpful thinking styles.*

This illustration involves a young employee fearful of losing his job. This example can be used to explain the purpose of changing habitual ways of thinking and perceiving situations. The client is asked to rehearse a recent personal situation (presenting problem) using the sample as a guide. This real life situation is recorded on the chart beneath the fictitious example. Thoughts and feelings are worked through with the counsellor.

Client Handout – CBT Chart

THE SITUATION	WHAT I SAID TO MYSELF	MY FEELINGS	HOW I CHALLENGED MY FAULTY BELIEFS	MY NEW CHOICES THOUGHTS FEELINGS BEHAVIOURS
Young man speaking: My boss said I had to sweep the floor over again yesterday. I don't want to go into work at the	Self-talk: He is always criticizing my work. I'm not good enough. I will never be any good at anything.	Fearful Despondent. Worried. Self-condemning Nervous Insecure	That is the first time I have had to do the floor again. I must have missed a spot. He did praise my cleanup the day before so I am not	I am happier and confident that I will do a better job next time because I will be more careful. God will help me.

ON MIND RENEWAL

The following is another sample (fictitious case) of a more formal way of ministering to clients who are amenable to doing some real work on *mind renewal*. The basic premise of cognitive type therapies is that thoughts produce feelings which lead to behaviours. If the thoughts are recognised as 'unhelpful' then by replacing and renewing habitual thought patterns a more comfortable lifestyle is experienced. Preferably, this type of assignment follows several sessions of prayer ministry, the client learning afterwards to *walk the walk* and *talk the talk* in their newfound freedom.

Alternately, it could be issued to the more academically minded who are not amenable to inner healing ministry. Then it can take the form of *mentoring* or *life coaching*. It is especially suited to university, college and tertiary students who are accustomed to study and assignments. However, the idea is to begin by locating the *irrational core belief* <u>during</u> the processes of Christian counselling. In ministry terms, this is referred to as *locating the foundational lie and replacing it with the truth.* In this way, it becomes more than an intellectual exercise.

After the irrational core belief is labelled as 'a lie' (a belief that does not line up with the Word of God) the client *issues a challenge* by *self-analysis* and follows up with *a confrontation.* Aims and goals are realised and an *action plan* is recorded. Later, the client is assisted to set *short and long term goals* through incorporating the ideas from *personal action plans* into a simple *planning* or *flow chart system.* The following are the personal steps that the client will take for this assignment. The last two steps are to be done with active involvement from the therapist,

STEPS TO MIND RENEWAL

1. Record the irrational belief.
2. Issue a challenge.
3. Confront the core belief.
4. Mediate for change (make up a plan of action).
5. Set short-term sub goals with target dates using a planning chart.
6. Record a long term ultimate goal with a target date (see *Sample Flow Chart*).

The following format has been chosen to deliver this teaching as it serves to give a very practical, rather than an academic, illustration. Feel free to study these examples but be aware that they are not technically accurate. Remember: this is a fictitious character recording her thoughts.

SAMPLE CLIENT ASSIGNMENT

CHALLENGING IRRATIONAL THOUGHTS & BELIEFS

Irrational Belief #1
I must be approved of and loved (or at least liked) by everyone.

Challenge (questioning this irrational belief):
Have I achieved this in the past? Has anyone ever achieved this? Did everyone like, love and approve of everything Jesus did when he walked this earth as the perfect man?

Confrontation:
My personal confronting thoughts on this are: –

There are some people in my life who are important to me (significant others). I would like to be loved and approved of by each and every one of them but I can't make them like or love me – especially not all of the time. I may feel lonely and rejected when these significant others don't feel the same way that I do about them; but I will choose not dwell on those feelings. Instead, I will occupy my thoughts in learning the skills of being friendly and, in this way; people will be attracted to me. They may choose to become my friends but, if they don't, I won't let it matter to me because Jesus calls me his friend and that's what matters (Jn 15:15).

I have been told this is like shopping for clothes or a car. There are plenty of potential friends out there and I have to go out and actively seek these people who will suit my personality and interests. I know that, sometimes, I see a piece of clothing on the rack that I absolutely love; but I am very disappointed when I try it on and it doesn't suit me. So I put it back, knowing it will be just right for someone else. It would be foolish for me to take it and wear it when I would feel uncomfortable in it.

It is the same with the friends I will seek. I will keep searching to find the right ones for me who will appreciate me for who I am – friends with whom I can feel comfortable. While I am searching, I will do some constructive things to become my own best friend, which (my therapist tells me) will help me in the future to make and keep better relationships with others.

Action Plan:
Spend more time with the family members with whom I am most comfortable.
Get fit so I feel happy and well and less depressed.
Go walking daily with my dog.
Take off weight so I feel great about my looks.
Get stuck into my hobbies so that I am distracted from worrying, loneliness and boredom.

Maybe even join a group/club?
Check my thoughts and speech, e.g. watch for the words must and ought and should, because using these words is putting pressure on me.
Memorize scriptures on how God loves me unconditionally.

Irrational Belief #2
I should worry about bad things happening.

Challenge*:*
Why should I worry? Where is the evidence that something bad is about to happen? What does God say about worry? (Matt 6:25-34)

Confrontation:
My personal thoughts now are: that worrying about something that might happen, won't stop it from happening. It just causes me unhappiness in the present to worry.

Action Plan
I can get help right now to make myself stronger. I can get strong by developing my trust and faith in a good God who will take care of me if something bad does happen. I can build more resources by getting some healing and help in the present. I won't dwell on the future. He is Lord of my past, my future and of my present. I give Him control of each part of my life.

Irrational Belief #3:
I must be completely competent, perfect in everything I do.

Challenge:
Is this true? Why must I be? How does this make me a better person? Does this belief work for me?

Confrontation:
Am I tyrannising myself? Perhaps I am. Just like everyone else; I will occasionally fail and make mistakes. This might initially cause me to feel bad, but I can handle this.

Action Plan:
   a) *I can analyse my thoughts and give them the Albert Ellis test relating to the three musts. Am I guilty of thinking these three things?*

   1. *I must do well.*
   2. *Everyone must treat me kindly, fairly and considerately.*
   3. *The world must make things easy for me.*

   b) *Choose to be kinder to myself. I will replace these three 'musts' with: –*

1. *I am only human.*
2. *So are others.*
3. *I live in a fallen world where nothing is perfect.*

c) *My aim is to learn to think more realistically, rationally and logically.*

I now believe that perfecting me is a command of God but it does not mean I can make myself be perfect. This just means I can mature by putting aside childish irrational beliefs that I must be perfect. Growing up and into maturity is my goal in life – to become more like Him. I will fall on my face at times but He will pick me up. I will learn valuable lessons from my defeats and failures. He will teach me. I am teachable. He is perfecting me (helping me to mature). I am complete in Christ (Col 2:10). I am his workmanship (Eph 2:10).

d) *I aim to be a more realistic and responsible person and to behave accordingly. He will perfect me (Phil 1:5). My goals are to: –*

1. *Lose the victim mentality by working on learning to like myself.*
2. *Rid myself of the 'loser' label that I have given myself.*
3. *Sign up for a personality development course.*
4. *Volunteer to help out at a community centre.*
5. *Start counting my blessings, writing down and praising God.*
6. *Every time I have a negative thought, I will try to find three positive ones, write them up and stick them on my mirror.*
7. *I will remember that – and this is the best of all thoughts – I am unconditionally loved and liked by the most important person in my life – my creator GOD – my heavenly Father. Therefore, I am not a failure; because he doesn't make mistakes and He made me. I am perfect already, simply because I am perfectly me!*

Irrational Belief #4
My problems are because of my past and that is why I suffer now.

Challenge:
What evidence do I have? Why should I let the past affect me? Am I holding on to some old garbage as a defence mechanism against the pain of growing up and moving on?

Confrontation:
My problems might have a root cause in some past events but what causes me to suffer now, are my present thoughts and consequent actions. I can't change the past but how I deal with the present is my choice.

Action Plan:

I can and will 'take every thought captive' to the mind of Christ and I will choose to obey God's will. I do have the power and authority to take command of my life by making choices that will fit in with God's plans for me. According to the scriptures He has good plans for me, not evil ones, but plans for a future for me. I have 'a hope'. I am no longer a victim but victorious in Him. I am more than a conqueror. I am an overcomer, a warrior, the head and not the tail! I am free forever from condemnation (Rom 8:1-2). I am established, anointed, sealed by God (2Cor 12:1-22).

Note to Self: *My next assignment is to divide the action plans up into short and long term goals using a flow chart.*

Counsellor Exercise: *Irrational Beliefs.*

Using the format used by above, create your own scenario and record it in the space provided below.

Client Handout: RESPONDING REASONABLY: The 3 Rs TEST

We are carnally minded and *walk in the flesh* when we use our emotional reactions with harmful intent (Eph 4:17-31, Prv 27:4). Instead, we are to live in the Spirit and walk in the Spirit according to our new life in Christ (Gal 5:16-25, Eph 4:32 & 5:1-20). The anointing (power) and the mind of Christ (wisdom) are available to draw upon. We <u>can</u> think and act responsibly in a mature God-honouring manner when the need arises (1Cor 2:12-16).

Instead of *reactions* to the world and all its challenges, *responses* are needed. Reacting indicates that we are drawing on our soulish emotions, which are fickle and not to be trusted. Responding means the soul has been disciplined to think, to make choices, and to act in a certain way according to our *conscience*, so that the consequences will be consistently positive.

IMAGE 19

THE THREE R'S

Is it REAL?.........How true is this?

Is it RATIONAL (reasoned)?........Have I thought this through properly?

Is it RESPONSIBLE?......What will the consequences be to me and to others?

WE CAN REACT
That is, we can act without reasoning via our FEELINGS,

GRRRR!

OR

WE CAN RESPOND
That is, we can think it through LOGICALLY with the 3 R's as our guide:-

Even 'kings' (those with money, power and influence) who think they are in the position to do what they want, are subject to God's control (Prv 21:1). As children of God we are to rule over our own fleshly thoughts, emotions and behaviours and to listen to counsel to make Godly choices, before we 'step over the line', becoming subject to God's correction, rebuke and discipline (Prv 19: 18-23).

No one makes a fool of God; '*a person will reap exactly what he plants*' (Gal 6:7-10). We cannot continue to think that we will keep getting away with just doing and saying whatever we please. Better to sow into the spirit – by learning to respond, rather than allowing our emotions to rule our lives. The graphic presented here should help you to remember not to *grrrrrrowl,* but to respond rationally and reasonably; to remind you to put the effort into developing the fruits of the spirit – particularly self-control (Prv 22:3).

Counsellor Exercise: *Responding Reasonably*

Using the space provided below:

a) Relate a recent incident where you reacted unreasonably (according to the 3 Rs test). Make note of the feelings associated with the incident.
b) Record an alternate response.

Counsellor Resource: AFFIRMATIONS, MEDIATORS & REINFORCERS

AFFIRMATION: an assertion and confession of the truth in Christ, which will build my self-esteem and will serve to focus on the positive aspects of my situation. *I call those things which are not as if they are.*

MEDIATOR: a change agent to intercede and to reconcile myself to the truth of the person I am in Christ and, how I can think, feel and behave accordingly. *I take every thought captive and obedient to the mind of Christ.*

REINFORCER: an act or method to support, encourage, increase or strengthen the truth in me. *I am more than a conqueror!*

SAMPLING OF CLIENTS' EXERCISES (fictional)

Case Scenario # 1
I must be going through male menopause or something. Lately, I lose my temper easily. I am a sales manager and it is crucial in my position to function in a reliable and consistent manner.

Affirmations:
I am a calm, forgiving, loving person, made in God's image.
I love the work He has given me to do.
I get on well with every member of my sales team.

Mediators:
I will count to ten before I explode.
I will think the best of the person riling me. After I have prayed and calmed down I will discuss this matter with them.

Reinforcement:
I will reward myself with a chocolate bar whenever I succeed in holding my temper.
I will avoid all chocolate at other times so that this treat will be associated only with my successful new behaviour.

Case Scenario # 2
I am a single mother, lonely and depressed. I have been too ill to go to church lately. I find that I depend on others to make me feel happy. I do not like my own company.

Affirmations:
I praise God that I am young and alive.
Just being alive makes me feel happy!
Happiness is a choice and I choose to be happy.

Mediator:
I will find something I like to do alone for each day of the week. When I achieve this goal I will reward myself with a DVD.

Reinforcement:
I will keep a journal of my feelings and dwell on the positive aspects. I will report the negative feelings to my counsellor and seek help with my personal issues. Above all, I will be patient with myself, knowing that God is patient with me.

Case Scenario # 3
I am 10 years old and an average guy. I lie to get out of trouble and I am doing it more and more, especially to mum.

Affirmations:
I am an honest person.
The truth keeps me out of trouble.
I am comfortable telling the truth.
The truth sets me free to be myself.

Mediation:
Next time I catch myself lying (or someone else catches me), I will confess it straight away to the person I lied to; I will say I am sorry to them. This will please God. I know that the apology will make me so uncomfortable that I will find it easier to tell the truth the next time.

Reinforcement:
I will keep a personal chart in my bedroom with a star for every time I pull myself up for lying and with a cross for when I don't. When I reduce the number of crosses to zero I will be a * STAR * and very proud of myself. Besides, mum has promised me a new skateboard when I get down to the zero.

Case Scenario # 4
I am in Year 11 at a private school and I love partying, boys and clothes. My schoolwork is suffering, but not totally due to my social life. I realized recently that I have a problem. It is perfectionism. I need help for it because I get angry with myself and others (when they do not live up to my standards). I feel I have to be perfect to avoid people criticizing me and besides, I need lots of praise. It seems that I have a poor self-image, and that I compensate by doing exceptional things.

Affirmations:
I am loved and chosen by God.
I really do like myself!
God loves me just as I am.

Mediation:
I will write an essay of my feelings about something I enjoy, like music. I will play relaxing music as I write. I will finish the essay and I will not correct it in any way. I will read it once to myself, and then share it by reading it to my best friend.

Reinforcement;
I will then tear this essay up without correcting the mistakes! I will not rewrite it. I will sit and reflect on the musical activities I described in my essay about going to see some great concerts and how I love playing my violin. I will focus on how I feel about music – passionate! I will praise God that He loves me – warts and all! I will be glad that I am capable of doing so many things.

Case Scenario # 5
I am a self-employed potter, successful in my trade of making and selling my own products. However, I am in the process of needing longer periods of solitude away from the family and the customers in order to manage my stress levels.

Affirmations:
I am a well-balanced, relaxed and productive person.
I enjoy people and I also enjoy time-out to be by myself.
I find joy in the lessons learned from my weaknesses.

Mediation:
When feeling stressed I will shrug off my worries by raising my shoulders, dropping them, then relaxing my whole body while breathing the tension away. If still tense, I will allow myself 10 minutes worry time to focus on the problem at hand. I will then list the practical options to decide on when I am in a better frame of mind.

Reinforcement:
I will consider the advantages in needing to withdraw and post a list of them on the fridge to show mum and the kids my personal needs right now. I will jot down something that I am thankful to God for each night. I will also rate, from 0-10, how relaxed I feel at the end of the day. I will record any happy social experiences on a graph over a period of 16 weeks.

Counsellor Exercise: *Affirmations, Mediators & Reinforcers*
Using a notebook:
   a) *Work on 3 personal scenarios in a similar format to the samples above.*
   b) *Include appropriate scriptures from the choice below to make into affirmations to accompany your scenarios.*
Begin with, 'I am:… '
Jn 1:12, 15:1-5, 15:15; 1Cor 3:9 & 16, 6:17-20, 12:27; 2Cor 1:21-22, 5:17-21, 6:1, Eph 1:1, 2:6, 2:10 & 18; Rom 5:1, 8:1-2 & 28 & 31-34; Phil 1:5, 3:20, 4:13; Matt 5:13-14

Counsellor Resource: GOAL SETTING USING A FLOW CHART

There are a myriad of ways to use flow charts: to set long and short term goals, to plan specific courses of action, for problem solving in life, and other coaching and mentoring purposes. The following is a very simple form of flowchart that can be used over a length of time (say three sessions over a period of six weeks).

Explanation of Graphic

The larger boxes **at the top** represent three major areas in the client's life. For example they could be *personal, work & fitness training* goals. The (fictitious) client here has chosen *family, career & ministry*. The 'legs' on the boxes represent the long and short-term pathways to goal actualization. Creative planning steps on how to achieve these goals are recorded briefly in words **along the legs**. The boxes at the **centre of the chart** record the client short- term goals agreed upon collaboratively with the counsellor. Long- term goals are boxed **at the base**. Expectation dates of goal actualization can be recorded as additional encouragement (refer to *ministry* section, right hand side of flow chart).

IMAGE 20   **CLIENT FLOW CHART FOR GOAL SETTING**

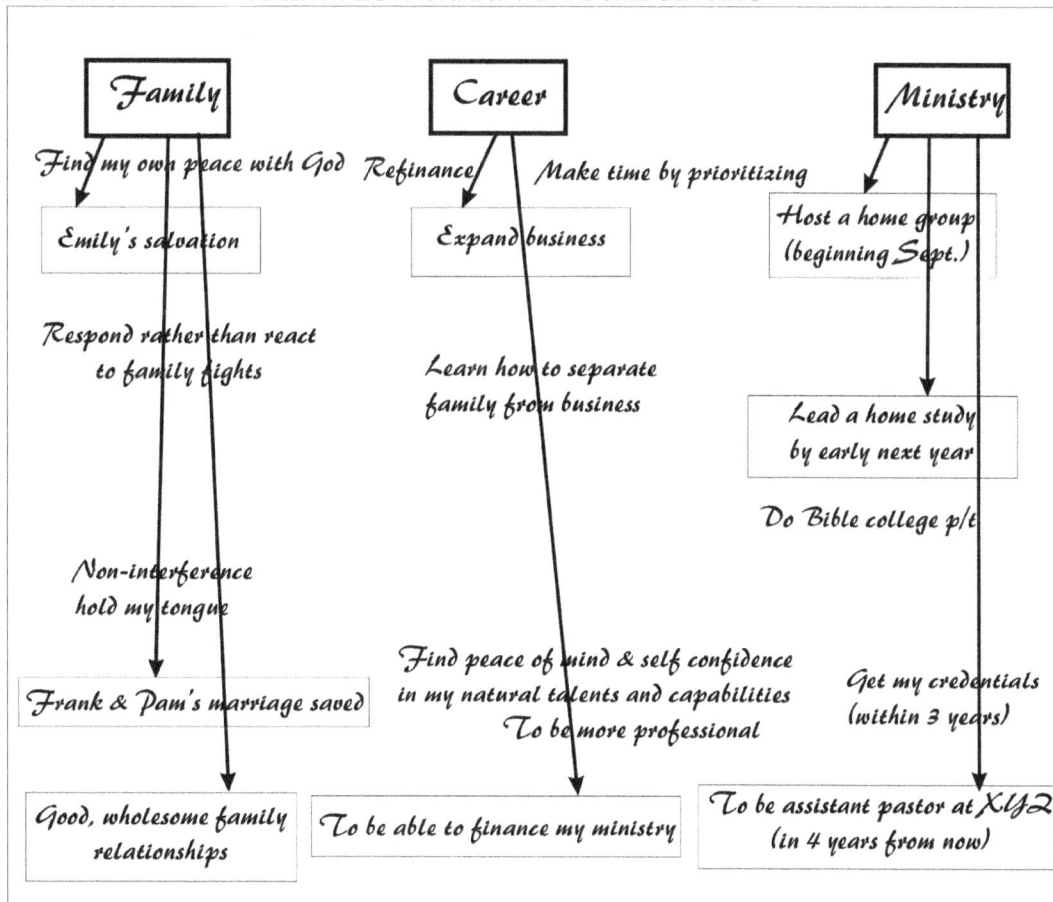

AUTHOR'S TESTIMONIAL: Prophetic Word on Renewing the Mind

Lord into your hands I place my mind…Resurrect it!

'My Child,

Be sensitive to me in all you do, whether it be in relation to your home, or in your contact with others. You are becoming clearheaded – more so than you have ever been before. I am cleaning out your mind and controlling your emotions in a new way.

'Allow me to do this so that you can become alert and active in your mind, logical and clear thinking, devoid of morbid thoughts and ready to take on the plans I have for you and your husband.

'Your thoughts in the past have been ones of confusion and ill thinking. Now I want to direct your mind along paths on which it has not been before. No longer will you feel that you have no control, no influence over your emotions. Instead, you will have a new alertness, a clearness of insight and perception. You will no longer have to depend on instinctive behaviours.

'However, you still must behave in a childlike manner and be dependent on me for your gifts. You will grow in newness of intellect and wisdom as you allow me to direct your will, <u>and</u> your thinking patterns.

'Be not concerned at the newness of this; as your spirit grows, your mind needs to be renewed to keep pace with it.

'Have I not healed your body and am I not making your mind sharp and clear? Be not concerned over the feeling of boredom. It is not depression. It is only a wasteland of thinking that in which I am allowing you to dwell in order that your mind can be cleansed and touched by my healing.

'You will never have to fear again that you do not have full possession of your mental faculties. Your mind, from now on, will be as your body – growing healthy and strong in a steadfast manner.

'Your Heavenly Father'

(Lk 23:46; Rom 12:1-2)

SECTION FIVE

Prayer Ministry Techniques

CHAPTER SEVENTEEN

RESTORATION MINISTRY

Prayer ministry should serve to heal and restore man holistically – body, soul and spirit. In essence we are born of the spirit and He is our life force, therefore we have an innate desire to discover our true identity in Him via our spirit. Man's spirit is the evaluator of his thoughts (1Cor 2:11). Understanding why we were made, how we are made up, and how we are intended to function here on earth, is not easy. The restoration of man starts with the soul's realisation that we cannot live on earth disconnected from our Creator; we must abide in the character of Jesus Christ, the Son of God. This text attempts to explain the soul of man's need for recreation (restoration) following the born again experience.

-   Introducing Christian counselling techniques via the salvation message
-   The restoration of mankind through the son of Man
-   Author's testimony of life as '*a wounded burden bearer*'
-   The parts of man further defined & the need for restoration explained
-   Graphic: Healing the soul of man through regaining his true identity

---

Study Notes

INTRODUCTION TO PRAYER TECHNIQUES

The following is an introduction to the techniques you will generally use to minister in a formal session of prayer ministry. They are soundly based on Biblical precepts and principles. The word *precept* (teaching) is described in the dictionary both as *'rule or principle for action'* as well as *'a guide or rule for morals'.*

The Holy Bible contains all the rules for behaviour in the sense of what is moral, that is, what is good or bad, right or wrong in the sight of God. As we are ready and willing to learn personally, the Holy Spirit reveals and teaches us 'precept upon precept' in order for us to grasp His truths for daily living. These rules (spiritual precepts) can be broken either knowingly or unwittingly. Counselling and prayer ministry can prove to be of great benefit to help set things in order again.

This is especially so when there is a cumulative effect from the consequences of breaking God's laws. *Sanctification* (cleansing from sin) and *restoration* (recovery from sin's effects) needs to take place so that there can be *reconciliation* with our Holy Father. There is a great deal said in the arena of psychology and psychiatry regarding the dysfunctional person or the dysfunctional family, but little is dealt with on the spiritual side as to how we become dysfunctional through our sinful natures. *Sin* or *transgression*, which can be described simply as the breaking of God's precepts or moral laws, is left out of the secular equation, and is sadly neglected in religious counselling also.

Elsewhere in this text, the results of *sins and iniquities* in the generational sense are explained (see *Generational Connections*). When we break God's laws, we can pass the repercussions down the family line. Family members down to the third and fourth generations can be affected by our actions in the present. Conversely, suffering experienced in the present generation, can be the result of the sins of our forefathers.

Our wonderful creator has said enough is enough! He has predicted that 'men will run to and fro' and that knowledge will increase in the end times (Dan 12:4). We can look at this in the light of space travel and computer technology. We also witness that spiritual revelation is increasing in regard to the tools and keys being used in the Body of Christ today, in breaking bondages and setting captives free. In this regard, many ministries are springing up today based on Isaiah 61 and moving towards fulfilling scripture that we are to be renewed in his image (Col 3:10). A new heart and a new spirit are to be given to his stubborn, hard-hearted people, enabling us to walk obediently, in corporate and personal peace and security. This is achievable through his grace and through honouring his commands in these fast paced and troubled times (Ezk 36:25-36, Deut 5:15).

THE DIVINE PURPOSE OF PRAYER MINISTRY

The divine purpose and higher calling of Christian counselling is to co-operate in God's plan to open an individual's eyes to see his provision, in that he has already reconciled the world to himself via his son Jesus Christ. Through ministry, conflicts are resolved and loving communication is restored between man and God.

THE RESTORATION OF MAN

Following *rebirth* of the spirit, a process of restoration back to God's original intention for *divine relationship* with man begins (Jn 3:1-8). In the creation of man, it was intended that we relate with his divine nature on a holistic basis (Gen 1:27, Deut 6:5, Jn 4:24). Man was created from the beginning to be free from sin, freely communicating as a companion to God and to each other. However we have wilfully fallen out from relationship. Having suffered the consequences, we are in need of reconciliation, restoration, and healing in a corporate sense, as well as on an individual basis (Gen 6:5-6, Jer 30:17).

When I first began studying to become a professional counsellor, the course chosen for me was based on the cognitive/behavioural sciences. We covered *personality and attitude*, *stimulus and response* and *nature versus nurture*. We covered the attributes we are born with and how we are shaped along the way, through relationships and environmental factors, to become the persons we are today.

OUR SIN NATURE

I began to look at this in a scriptural light. We are born into this fallen world environment with a sin nature because of the fall of man. Adam fell short of the glory of God (his divine nature) because Adam chose to sin – to rebel against God's directions. Each member of the human race inherits this tendency for rebellion from the original man; he inherits his *sinful nature*. The divine nature – our spiritual inheritance – was forfeited through rebellion. Mankind has the natural genes of Adam and we have thereby forfeited our godly inheritance.

SECOND CHANCE

We have, by grace, been given the option of a second birth. We may be *born again* with a spiritual nature, having the Holy Spirit's guarantee that the mind of Christ is within us. We are able to be spiritually reborn and acquire divine, supernatural strength and power to resist the temptation to sin. Having inherited His spiritual genes, we have access to God's divine nature, which is capable of dominating man's sinful nature. But, as Paul said, we still have that tendency towards sin. We thereby need to undergo a *renewing of our minds*, recognising both cognitively and spiritually that we are capable of living and resisting all temptation, through our Lord and Saviour (Rom 12:1-3, Heb 2:17-18; 4:15).

INCARNATION

God the Father sent his Son into a sin-ridden world. He was to become son of man, born 'of the flesh' via Mary. Jesus, the Son of God temporarily put aside his divine nature to live within the boundaries of the flesh. The Holy Spirit of God, as well as Mary, 'son of man', conceived and gave birth to Jesus, a son of mankind. Perhaps not doctrinally or theologically correct, but, as an analogy, this could be viewed as two sets of genes merging, allowing Jesus, the son of man, the ability to sin <u>if</u> he chose to do so.

However, this son did live a perfect life. Jesus, son of man, overcame every temptation known to mankind. Subsequently, he was the only acceptable (to God) substitute as a sacrifice to pay the penalty required (by God) for mankind's sins. According to God's provision for our salvation, a perfect sacrifice had to be made. Flesh had to die in our stead. Only the combination of this melding of his perfect son with mankind satisfied this qualification.

Jesus, being the perfect man, was the only one capable and qualified to fill the position of *the sacrificial Lamb of God*. The purpose was to bridge the gap between the creator and his creation, in order for good to triumph over evil; of the divine nature's victory over man's sinful nature.

AUTHOR'S VISION: The Masterpiece

In my vision I saw a painting. A less skilled artist had been commissioned to paint over the original, hiding it from public view. The work underneath was a more than an ordinary work of art; it was a masterpiece. I then saw in my spirit that another artist skilled in restoration of artworks was called in to painstakingly peel off the second painting to reveal the original in all its glory.

INTERPRETATION OF VISION; I believe this vision was an analogy given to me as a prayer minister to help to describe the restoration process needed for each soul. We are each created by our heavenly Father to possess his divine nature. However, we are naturally born into a fallen world via earthly parents and are imprinted by the effects of sin. When we accept the gift of salvation purchased for us by the blood of Jesus Christ, we receive an opportunity for rebirth – to be born again by the Spirit of God. Because there has been an intervening time, from our natural birth until our spiritual rebirth, we have been 'painted over' – marred by sin.

Using the analogy of the vision of the painting: through the cross, God the Father has set to work to restore us to his original 'masterpieces'. This involves a process of healing and restoration, where the consequences of our personal evil deeds and thoughts are stripped from us until all flesh has 'died' to sin and God's work is revealed to the world.

THE RESTORATION OF MAN'S TRUE IDENTITY

The following testimony and graphic illustrates how the restoration process involves healing prayer for the Christian soul. In order to regain the sense of our *true spiritual identity* in Christ Jesus we need to be reconciled to the father heart of God our creator.

AUTHOR'S TESTIMONY: *The Wounded Burden Bearer.*

After a particularly good charismatic church meeting, I felt refreshed and satisfied spiritually, but did not want to linger afterwards as the public ministry session was becoming noisy and jarring to me. I asked two good friends of mine (husband and wife) if we could go pray on the beach together so that I could settle myself before returning home.

This prayer time turned into personal prayer ministry to me, during which one of my friends said that he saw a vision of a soldier with a bandage hanging off the left leg and a crutch under the right arm. The left hand was held out, which he felt signified this person trying to reach out to minister to people. I felt that the Lord was saying that this person was trying to minister to the wounded while having personal wounds herself. In the spirit, I recognised this person as me and that I represented other wounded soldiers in God's army.

The other friend gently and sensitively prayed, while her husband empathetically interceded for me there on the beach. He expressed that he felt my extreme pain from long ago when a very strong spiritual gift was robbed or taken from me. The three of us discussed the possibility of me having been spiritually violated at that time. It was suggested that I could need ministry for this.

I felt that the damage had been done very early in my childhood. I decided to seek the Lord about it in my next private prayer time. The story dramatically unfolded to my spirit as I prayed and recorded this prophecy via journaling on 15 November in the year 1997.

PROPHECY: HEALING FOR A WOUNDED SPIRIT & DAMAGED SOUL

The Father God speaking:

'Yes, my daughter, you see rightly. I will now take you on a journey back, where you will see what has happened to you. As your sister discerns, it is necessary for your own welfare that you be healed from this time forth, healed from all that keeps you hindered and harmed.

I have much work for you to do and I have equipped you with the necessary training and skills to operate in my Spirit to set the captives free and release those who are in bondage to the enemy. Still, you are bound yourself. So open your spirit now my daughter and let your mind run free and I will take you on this journey…'

At this point, I covered myself with the blood of Jesus, requested that angels be stationed about me. I invited the Holy Spirit to draw alongside. I acknowledged that Jesus was there with me by singing part of a hymn from my younger days, 'He walked with me and He talked with me along life's narrow way'. I had woken that very morning also recalling some of the chorus, 'blessed be the name of The Rock who trains my hands for war' and had wondered what that meant. Then my <u>spiritual senses</u> opened to see, hear, feel and remember the following 'incident' (as recorded verbatim at the time).

I see myself alone as a little girl in one of my shirred sundresses (which I wore around the age of four). I am skipping along in the sunshine humming to myself, randomly looking at insects, birds, trees and the cloud patterns. Suddenly I come to a dead halt. There is fear. I am cautious. Someone is speaking to me, someone shadowy.

This is what he says, 'come now little girl, come speak with me for I have much to tell you… You are a gifted child. I can see that. You have a pretty face and lovely brown eyes and curls I see… Has anyone ever told you this before? Yes, I see they have… You are much loved… Well, no longer will you feel their love anymore. I am taking it away – far, far away from you. You will never feel it again. No one will ever love you like I do no-one…'

Then, I remembered how the aloneness came and settled on me. Now, I remember when and how it started, when the shadowy figure told me it would. I remember the emptiness and the unhappiness and the tears that were always flowing and that there was no one to wipe them away. There was no one to cup my little face in his or her hands and to tell me where the love had gone. Who would tell me why my parents seemed like strangers to me from then on? Why did my brother seem like someone else's little brother?

Oh, the pain of the aloneness was unbearable! I remember! It seemed like it would last forever; that there would never be anyone to care for me any more; that I was going to be unhappy for the rest of my life.

So I gave up. I didn't like being like that, so I gave up on life because the pain of the aloneness was too much to bear. I lost my courage and strength to go on. I existed – even though I did not want to go on.

I would look longingly at the other neighbourhood kids playing together and having fun, but I couldn't join in the games. No one wanted me to share with them after a while, because I wasn't any fun to be with. I sensed they felt sorry for me and they just left me alone, very much alone. I remember trying every now and then to reach out to someone I thought could be a special friend, but I see now that they shunned the pain emanating from me. They didn't want to spoil their own happiness by sharing my pain. They rejected the pain, so they rejected me.

It was as if they gently shook me off like a bothersome little insect. They told me in so many ways that they couldn't be bothered befriending such a strange little girl; that it wasn't really worth the effort.

So, I became someone else deep inside me. I forgot completely who I had been before, and the funny thing is, I still cannot believe that I ever was that happy little girl in the vision at the beginning of this story. Right now, I believe she simply did not ever exist, and that, if she did, I don't remember anything of her. Actually, it has always worried me that there are a lot of things I can't recall about my childhood. Surely there must have been some good things that happened... some happy times'.

POSTSCRIPT:

I am sure that the readers will be curious to know the results that this inner healing had. I am happy to report that it caused a gradual release and an incredible difference in many ways.

Previously I had been unable to experience the 'love feelings' others described, but I continued to hope for a breakthrough. Even while ministering the love of God to others, the appropriate soul responses in me were missing. However, I continued to operate in faith rather than on feelings. The change came following the healing of my spirit.

This spiritual healing allowed me to begin to actually <u>feel</u> the love of God in corporate worship as well as in my private times and during Christian counselling. I was able to experience joy and peace in a deeper way in my spiritual walk. Several years ago a childlike sense of fun and enjoyment of life in general emerged. Much to my grandchildren's delight, this continues to increase with time. Now I am known for my light-hearted nature (my true identity) rather than 'the wounded burden bearer'.

IMAGE 21

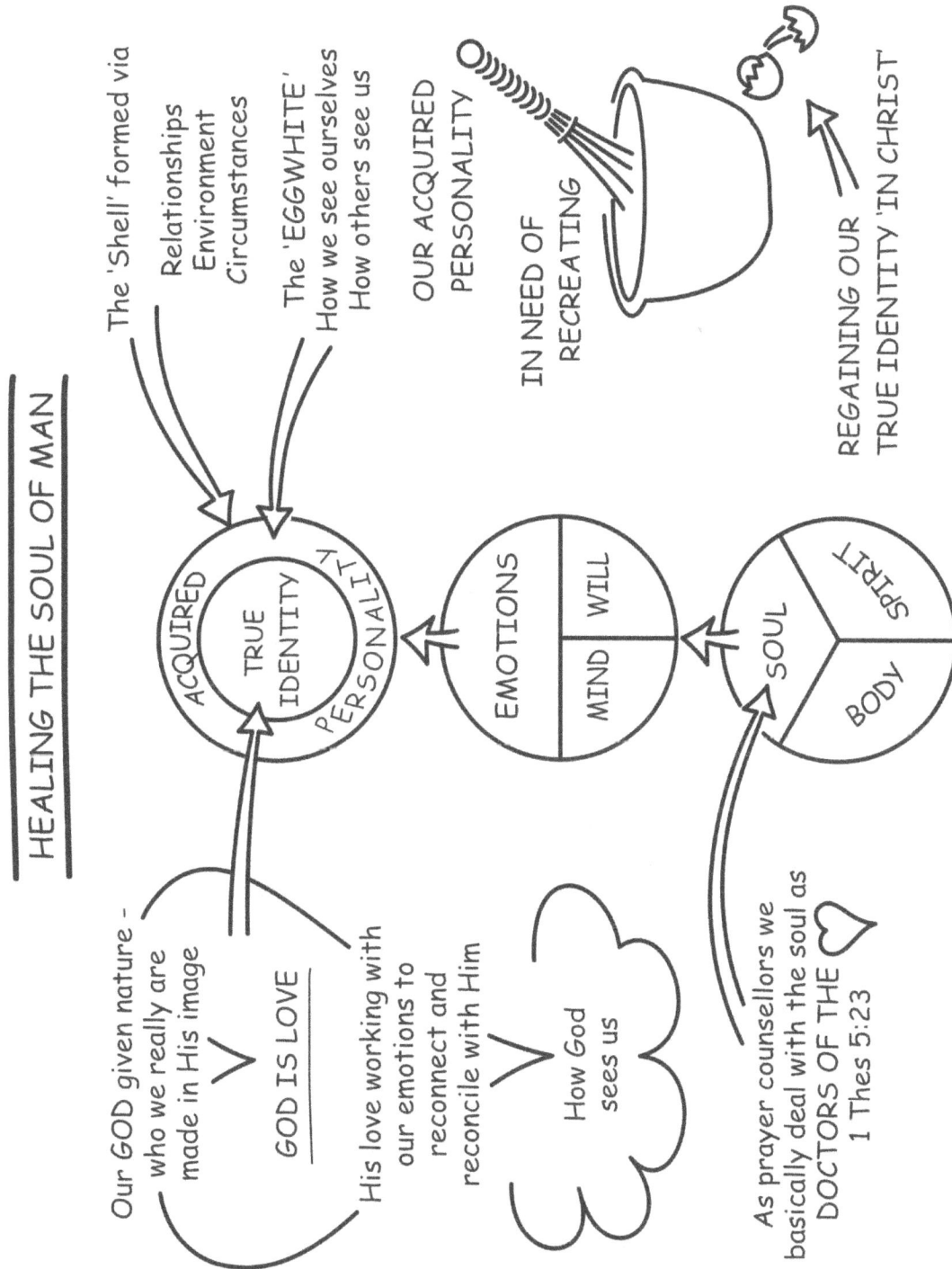

HEALING THE SOUL OF MAN

The 'Shell' formed via
Relationships
Environment
Circumstances

The 'EGGWHITE'
How we see ourselves
How others see us

OUR ACQUIRED PERSONALITY

IN NEED OF RECREATING

REGAINING OUR TRUE IDENTITY IN CHRIST

ACQUIRED PERSONALITY
TRUE IDENTITY

EMOTIONS
MIND WILL

SOUL
SPIRIT BODY

Our GOD given nature - who we really are made in His image

GOD IS LOVE

His love working with our emotions to reconnect and reconcile with Him

How God sees us

As prayer counsellors we basically deal with the soul as DOCTORS OF THE ❤
1 Thes 5:23

INSTRUCTIONS FOR USE OF IMAGE 21: Healing the Soul of Man

Beginning at the centre base of the page point out that this circle is segmented into three parts – body, soul and spirit – representing man as a tripartite being (1Thes 5:23). We describe how the segment of the base circle labelled 'the soul' can be divided into a further three segments (as pictured in the circle above mid-page). Explain that, in our role as Christian counsellors or 'doctors of the heart', we may appear to minister more often to the emotions than the intellect. Reassure the client that we are concerned with the complete restoration process and do not intend to neglect the other parts of man.

THE PARTS OF MAN

Drawing attention to the centre circle mid page clarify the Christian viewpoint of the soul. To those outside the church *the soul* is commonly considered to be man's spirit or inner self – the 'spirituality' of the person. In the worldly unchurched sense 'the soul' is the term commonly used to describe what we as Christians call our *spirit,* or *spirit man.* Sometimes the term *inner man* is used. Christians refer to the soul of man as the *fleshly* or *carnal man.* It is important to remember and clarify the difference in perception and terminology (Heb 4:12). This graphic can be a useful tool to help prevent any confusion and misunderstandings through using differing terminology. This is especially so with those who have:

> ➢ recently converted to Christianity
> ➢ a New Age Movement background
> ➢ been released from a cult
> ➢ been involved in occult activities/witchcraft

In the Judeo/Christian belief system, the soul is generally agreed upon as consisting of the mind, the will and the emotions, even though the terms are used interchangeably in the scriptures. During prayer ministry, the counsellor of the heart uses emotions as indicators to: diagnose the disease or uneasiness (dis-ease) of the soul; minister peace to the emotions; and thereby finds clues to what ails the spirit, and the body (Ps 130; 131:2).

GOD IS LOVE

Pointing to the left hand side of the page explain that our Creator God has made us in his image as emotional beings capable of a whole range of feelings. In that God is Love, rather than just a loving god, the creator is forever working with our souls to reconnect and reconcile with us – even when we are choosing not to respond to him or to even consciously reject him.

This is because of his great love for us as his divine offspring. Before we were conceived in human form and were but a twinkle in our heavenly Father's eye, he planned (in love) that each of us would be a unique creation (Ps 139). Just as he designed our genetic features (would be so tall and have brown or blue eyes and so on) he designed our natures, putting together unique combinations of talents, giftings, traits, and natures.

Our God-given nature could be described as our *true natural identity* – the one he still knows, sees, and loves unconditionally through his divine eyes. The wonderful thing is that he continues to love us unconditionally, no matter how much we change or stray from that original condition.

PERSONALITY VS TRUE IDENTITY

Move to the centre top where the *true nature* or identity is depicted as another segmented circle. This time, the circle is like an egg viewed from the cross section. The central yolk represents one's true identity. The surrounding eggwhite represents the *acquired identity* or *personality*. The personality is how others view us (this includes how we see ourselves). In psychological terms, this is called the *persona,* or the personality a person adopts and presents to others. In the vernacular, we use the term *'the mask'* or the *'face'* one puts on.

The personality, or the set of distinctive characteristics making an individual, has been acquired through life experiences. It is the way we have reacted and responded, according to our perceptions of these experiences, which has made us the person we are today. The third segment is the shell of the egg, which encases and cements in both the acquired personality and our true selves. This indicates how we have experienced damage and trauma; whereby we have built up what is commonly called a protective *'hard shell'*.

MAN IN NEED OF RECREATING

Refer to the acronym on the right hand side where a student of the author suggested that our condition could be described as a 'rec' (or *wreck*) in need of re-creating. This encasing shell made up of *self-protection and self-defence mechanisms* has been formed through damage/wounds inflicted via: -

R – relationships
E – environment
C – circumstances

THE PROCESS

Moving far right (to the cooking illustration) the client comes to the counselling process feeling a wreck – troubled, shattered, confused, and 'a mess'. Unfortunately, more unsettling times are ahead. The shell needs cracking and the yolk and white need whisking. There is an old saying that goes, *'you can't make an omelette without cracking eggs'*.

This idiom applies to our work as Christian counsellors where it is our challenge to crack the egg and to skilfully separate the white from the yolk. We do this in order view the unique individual God originally intended. The client is then brought towards an appreciation of their true nature. Words of release are spoken over bondages; comfort and healing are administered.

However, the eggwhite is not thrown away. We take both the acquired personality and the true identity and go to work on making an omelette (or a cake for those who have a sweet tooth). To clarify this analogy explain that there is no way that we can deny that past experiences, good and bad, have contributed to making us what we are today. But, with the Holy Spirit's guidance, we can certainly help to 'whisk' the present situation together to make something palatable of the future. Nothing is wasted. Even the shell can be recycled to make compost to grow a better and more fruitful life.

There is another old saying, 'a picture paints a thousand words'. Your clients might be too confused or upset to listen to a sermon from you, but they will clearly remember a lesson presented via a basic diagram. Even if you are not a natural artist, you can still point at the page using the, *'one already prepared earlier'** technique.

Alternately you could present the concept graphically by copying this simpler form – circles side by side – onto note paper. Thoroughly familiarize yourself with this teaching through practise, using either set of circles to illustrate to family and friends as many times as possible. This concept, taught skilfully under the anointing of the Holy Spirit, produces healing, self-acceptance, self-appreciation, and reconnection with our loving heavenly Father.

IMAGE 22

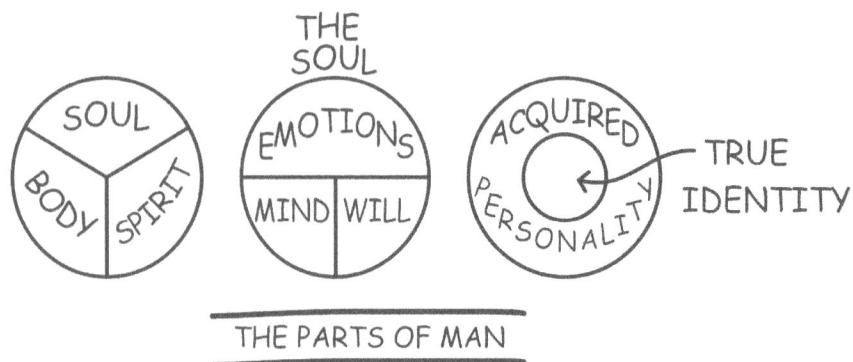

THE PARTS OF MAN

> Review *The Parts of Man* illustrations referred to earlier in this text (Chapter 2) in conjunction with this teaching. *This concept is available in manual form, along with other concepts graphically illustrated and suitable for presentation to clients or ministry students. On purchase, these can be photocopied for one on one ministry purposes, or for training other Christian counsellors. Enquiries: elvie@prayercounsel.com

CHAPTER EIGHTEEN

INNER HEALING TECHNIQUES

Healing of the soul allows a person to move from a position of bondage to sin into the freedom of living life to the full. This chapter concentrates on explaining the process of being freed from reliving hurts from the past and moving on to participate in the spirit-filled walk – to enjoying the simple pleasures of life. It will explain how false judgments of the flesh hinder the *inner man* from moving on. Prayer techniques are introduced via:

- Description of the purpose and processing of *inner healing*
- Glossary of prayer ministry terms
- Dream illustration and interpretation
- Cleansing prayer for relationship problems

Study Notes

INTRODUCTION TO INNER HEALING

Jesus heals them all. We see in the New Testament that Jesus healed 'all who came to Him' and, it seems, instantaneously. If not immediate, at least it was a relatively easy process, such as spittle placed on the eyelids, or a few words prior to a command to get up and walk. On his command, demons left, the blind regained sight and the dead were restored to life. Just as the Old Testament prophets under the special anointing power operated, Jesus and the apostles dramatically and extensively engaged in healing miracles, both before and after the crucifixion. The good news of release from death, disease and debilitating conditions spread far and wide – and all this without the aid of the multi-media!

Yes, we still do have pockets and seasons of these types of miracles happening today. A worldwide evangelist passes through a city operating in 'signs and wonders'. An individual receives a physical remission from a disease. Another has a miraculous recovery from an accident, which astounds the medical professionals. These cases might be given limited coverage by the secular media. At least, they do have some curiosity value…

However, we as Christians are still continuing to ask ourselves: *Why don't people get healed when we pray as Jesus did?* Some modern day physical miracles are given word of mouth and some private coverage by the church. But… there is virtually no publicity, even in church circles, about the thousands across the world being released and transformed by the Holy Spirit through prayer ministry and spiritual counselling. So many are being progressively, and sometimes dramatically, set free from the torments of emotional and spiritual bondages such as anger, loneliness, hatred, fear, rejection, unforgiveness, mental illness, demonic oppression and even, possession.

Were the healings accomplished by Jesus in the days He walked on earth as immediate as they seemed to be? Were some of them at least like the woman at the well, or the cripple at the pool, the climatic manifestation of relieving deep inner conflicts and turmoil?

Today, the subject of healing on these deep inner levels seems to belong to an underground movement. The long processes that prayer ministry and counselling involve are not generally talked about. The exciting results are seldom broadcast. Yet, there are books by the score being well written, training classes being held, seminars being sought after; the teachings are being received hungrily and applied successfully.

Daily, people are being quietly and progressively set free by faithful workers going about their Father's business – dutifully fulfilling Jesus commission to His disciples (Matt 28:16-20). As participants in prayer ministry we have a mandate to 'do likewise'. The captives are being set free as predicted (Isa 61 & 62). These are indeed exciting times!

> **IMPORTANT NOTE:** The following is the glossary issued to students who have undergone foundational training through the author's prayer ministry school. Please note that some of these terms will be in specific reference to prayer ministry techniques and, as such, are classed as 'jargon of the trade' (rather than theologically correct or precise and literal meanings for the words or phrases).

THE BARNABAS GLOSSARY OF MINISTRY TERMS

aligning – coming into agreement with the mind of Christ and the will of God; whereby his thoughts become our thoughts and his ways become our ways

anointing – divine enabling to minister above and beyond natural talents and skills

bad fruit/patterns – a recognizable pattern of similar problems or issues in a person's history

being a Barnabas – coming alongside to encourage and mentor.

bondage – anything which prevents one from being free to live life to the full

breaking generational curses – applying the blood of Jesus Christ to cancel the consequences of iniquities (practised sins) in the family line

bus stop counselling – dealing with a problem presented with very little time or opportunity for direct ministry

carnal Christian – ruled by worldly thoughts and feelings and fleshly responses, rather than the mind of Christ and his ways

cement – the lies or demonic thoughts claimed as personal 'truths', which must be dislodged from a stronghold in order to weaken it

cleansing process – dealing with sinful practices, such as: negative judgments, inner vows, unforgiveness, bondages, demonic influences, mindsets & strongholds

clues – anything that arises during a prayer session that is associated with the problematic emotion

curse – negative natural and spiritual consequences of breaking God's divine laws

cutting off soul ties – to sever, detach or end a relationship by spiritually disconnecting one party from another

deliverance – being freed from spiritual bondages and oppression

doctor of the heart – spiritual 'doctor' – a prayer minister trained in application of healing techniques.

feel to heal – willingness to experience short-term emotional pain in order to achieve healing and comfort

foundational lie – a false belief held regarding self, God, others (or life in general) which has generated the presenting problem and associated feelings

healing pool – symbolic imagery of a position where feelings are accentuated (stirred up) in order to locate a foundational lie

honouring – placing value, worth, importance and respect on another person in relationship with you

how we view God / false perceptions of God the Father – any way a person views God which is standing in the way of receiving help and healing

inner child (ministry to) – dealing with unfinished business from wounds inflicted in the past (usually during childhood), which are disabling and stunting a person's spiritual growth and emotional maturity in the present

inner healing – ministry to the depths of a person's heart and spirit

inner vow – a vow or promise made as a result of past experiences that has had a negative impact up to the present

issuing a challenge – gently and compassionately confronting a person regarding ingrained attitudes, which have motivated and shaped a person's life causing harm to self and others

journaling – in this ministry context it is the client/patient keeping a written record of the spiritual journey during the healing process

judgments – the act of passing sentence on a person based upon sinful reactions

looking for clues – prayer associated with the Holy Spirit guiding the client and counsellor to the underlying foundational lies 'seeded' in the past during some act or incident

memory work – looking back to locate clues as to when and how a foundational lie gave life to current false beliefs. Seeing this lie for what it is and replacing it with the truth according to divine revelation

mindset – a strong determination or habitual way of thinking; a fixed direction of thought; a mental set or framework; the building material of a negative stronghold

negative strongholds – areas in our lives where we have built a fortress from which we defend our erroneous (incorrect) belief systems

opening the eyes of the heart – seeing spiritually those things associated with the soul and our relationship with God

presenting problem – the surface issue that causes someone to be in need of ministry and to seek help

prompting – a clue offered by the Holy Spirit to assist the healing process

recovery (process of) – the application of healing principles during the period directly following prayer ministry

renewing the mind – the process of bringing down strongholds and eliminating mindsets through reprogramming thought patterns to conform to the mind of Christ

renounce – to voluntarily give up or reject a lie, false belief, or sinful habit *repent* – to feel regret, remorse and guilt; to decide to turn from old ways and thoughts to embrace the new (God's will)

self-talk – the internal dialogue (what one is saying to oneself)

signs & signposts – current circumstances and feelings, or symbols from memory work, which point a person along the road to healing and restoration

soul ties – unhealthy spiritual bonds or temporal relationships (past or present)

spoiled fruit – blessings forfeited, lost, robbed or destroyed; that which has been stolen from the recipient or spoilt

stronghold – a temporal fortress for the damaged soul, consisting of mindsets formed from unmet emotional needs and unresolved painful memories

symbols – Holy Spirit guided imagery, visions, dreams, feelings, memories, scriptures, songs, words or thoughts which contribute to the healing process

tracking/tracing fruits, roots & poisons – recognising patterns in a person's life story (fruits) leading to exposure of the underlying causes (roots) and the contributing factors (poisons) to the presenting problem/s

visions – imagery received supernaturally to facilitate the ministry

walking the walk and talking the talk – being actively obedient to God by acting, thinking and speaking according to the principles in the Holy Scriptures (His Word)

words (prophetic) – messages from God, which are received supernaturally in the course of ministering in the form of 'words of knowledge' or spiritual discernment

THE INNER HEALING PROCESS according to THE TOMB DREAM

The *Tomb Dream* graphic has proved extremely useful in describing the process of **inner healing** to clients who have no previous knowledge of prayer ministry involving **restoration of relationships**. Use of the graphic can be made either before the healing process (to provide an invitation to a client to participate in the process) or, afterwards (as an explanation of the technique and the reasoning behind it).

The process was described to the author in the form of a step-by-step vision within a dream following an inner healing session with a client who had a history of failed marriages. Healing revolves around the concept of repentance from unrighteous judgments made on others/self/God in order to abort the fruit of bad relationships.

IMAGE 23

THE TOMB DREAM

INNER HEALING & RESTORATION Repenting from Judgments of Others/Self/God

Revelation of Judgment of parents or significant others begins HEALING WALK

Call to Repentance by client's Inner Man leads to THE CROSS

Walking in the Spirit back to tomb/the past: FORGIVENESS seals

Healing of Inner Child = RECONCILIATION with the Father (God)

Choose and insert scriptures to accompany each segment of the drawing

Col 2:11-14

INSTRUCTIONS FOR USE OF IMAGE 23: The Tomb Dream

Beginning from the cave **at the left hand side**, move from left to right following the numbers and arrows, whilst referring to the boxed text at the top of the page. We view a corpse in the rotting stage, wrapped by dirty graveclothes which cover rotting flesh. The client/***corpse***[1] has been forced into this unsavoury position via judgments on self and/or others, even on God Himself. The ***graveclothes***[2] represent his *bondage to sin.*

The ***woman***[3] in the tomb represents the prayer minister/counsellor. By the light of revelation, the ***candle***[4] the Holy Spirit has given her, she is able to start unravelling the reasons for his bondage: the areas where he has broken God's holy laws and is thereby suffering the consequences.

As the Christian counsellor ministers to the client, she is showing him how to come out of this bondage and darkness. She is revealing from the scriptures that 'there is a way which seems right to a man, but its end is the way of death' (Prv 14:12). She instructs and invites him to call his carnal (fleshly) self out of the tomb into repentance via his ***inner man***[5] and to begin *the healing walk.* She encourages a genuine sorrow/*remorse* for his sins.

He *renounces* his previous judgments by turning his back on his old ways and walks towards **the Cross**[6] of Jesus Christ in sincere repentance. Free of the graveclothes that bound him to sin he now walks in the ***spirit man***[7] rather than *in the flesh* (the carnal man). He is instructed from the scriptures that if we 'walk in the light as He is in the light, then we have fellowship with one another and that the blood of Jesus Christ cleanses us from all sin' (1Jn 1:7; 2:9-11).

So, with eyes towards the cross, the client moves along his personal healing path towards *restoration and recovery*. He symbolically leaves his sins at the feet of Jesus and claims the forgiveness purchased for him via the Cross (Col 2:13-14). Walking back to the ***tomb (the past***[8] he completes the forgiveness process, releasing every person he feels has wronged him, ***the angel***[9] representing the help he receives to bury his past.

The healed *inner child* is represented at the far right of the diagram as a carefree ***boy on a bicycle***[10] who coasts down the hill away from tomb. The client may now enjoy the abundant life which reconciliation with his heavenly Father allows (Mal 4: 5 & 6, 1Jn 2:17).

SPECIAL NOTE ON MINISTRY TO CHILDREN

Ministry to children has special considerations in that it needs to be directed appropriately to different age groups consisting of individuals at differing stages of development. Personality types and immature perceptions need to be considered also. That being said, some prayer ministry techniques can be specifically adapted for children.

For example, using this concept, a small child with only the rudiments of spiritual principles can at times understand that the consequences of wrong choices and bad behaviour can lead to being 'in trouble'. Taking into consideration of course, those children who could be afraid of the dark and/or being confined; the cave can represent having *time out,* which allows *a safe place* to think about their naughtiness. The child can then be given *the good news* that Jesus can bring His (candle) light into the cave to help him/her see where sorry needs to be said.

This concept and healing process can also be used as an *evangelism tool* for older children. Jesus has given them a 'way out' (of the cave) by dying on the Cross – taking their punishment for them because He loves them so much. Because of Jesus' love, the child can have a fresh start and no longer need to be in trouble or be isolated. They can say they are truly sorry for what they have done; forgive others for what has been done to them; and make future choices to obey God and others in authority over them. Just like the child on the bike in the diagram, they can then go out to play happily again with their friends.

Counsellor Resource: CLEANSING PRAYER (Judgments & Expectancies)

INSTRUCTIONS: This prayer serves to introduce spiritual *cleansing techniques* in regard to the consequences of breaking God's laws in relationships. When the client has come under conviction via the Holy Spirit (and is ready and willing) lead him or her into prayers of confession using this resource as a guideline.

In the name of the Lord Jesus Christ, I confess and repent of judgments and negative expectancies in relationship to my mother and father (or significant others), where I did not honour them in a Godly manner.

(Describe these in as much detail as possible.)

I confess and repent of judgments and negative expectancies I have made against all other persons.

(Name the persons and describe what you are repenting of.)

I confess and repent of all wrongful judging coming from my own heart, which has involved…

(Describe your personal participation e.g. blaming, condemning, being jealous, taking revenge, vowing, word cursing).

Via the blood of my Saviour, I ask for mercy and seek, receive and accept forgiveness for all those wrongful motives, attitudes, thoughts and actions. I ask God to forgive me wherever I have sown wrongful thoughts, words and deeds and to spare me reaping from that sowing in as far as His perfect will allows in my life. In Jesus' Name, I abort the crops now being produced from all the sinful seeds sown, so that they will no longer have any hold over my own, or others' lives. I pray that we will no longer bear the fruit of…

(e.g. failure, rejection, abuse…)

As for all attitudes, habits, practices and consequences coming from all of the above, I bring them to the cross, and leave them there. I choose to hate all the poisonous sins that fed my crops and to give them up according to his holy will and through Christ who strengthens me.

(e.g. unforgiveness, negative expectancies, sinful choices…)

I renounce all lies that I have believed regarding myself, my parents and others; asking that anything of which I am unaware be brought to my mind by the Holy Spirit when, and as, he sees fit.

(Name the lies revealed via the Holy Spirit)

I ask you, Jesus, to replace those lies with your truths. I receive your love, Heavenly Father, your forgiveness, comfort, healing, restoration and full, complete and permanent redemption and deliverance via your Son's cleansing blood. I cancel all curses and effects in the authority of the name of the Lord Jesus Christ by the power of his blood shed for me on the cross. I bless and release all those involved from any word (or other) curses coming via myself, any judgments and condemnations and all the negative effects of my personal bitterness, resentment, grudges, thoughts of revenge, expectancies and inner vows.

(Specify each person by name)

I pray his richest blessings on all who have wronged me, and all whom I have believed to have wronged me.

(Name the blessings you want the Lord to give the recipients.)

Thank you Lord. I receive now, and in the future, all the blessings you have had stored up for me, in Jesus' Name. Amen.

CHAPTER NINETEEN

CLEANSING TECHNIQUES

Spiritual *cleansing* (sanctification) and healing are closely related. Healing sometimes directly correlates with our willingness to be purified and reconciled to the will and ways of a holy god – The Holy God. Through cleansing prayer techniques, we look within ourselves to see the reasons we could be experiencing problems – particularly in regard to relationships. Following personal cleansing, we are more able to clearly look at outside causes and influences. To link this chapter to previous ones, a healing prayer for relationships opens the chapter and a testimony of combining techniques closes it.

- Revisiting painful memories via *The Healing Pool Method*
- Disputing faulty belief systems via this cleansing process
- Glossary of terms used in the Pool Method
- Twelve step processing to replace lies with truths (includes self-help)
- *Fruits, Roots & Poisons Technique* for eliminating recurring problems
- Instructions via practical casework and graphic illustrations (of tree)

Study Notes

REPLACING FAULTY BELIEF SYSTEMS

THE SPIRITUAL PROCESS

In Christian counselling our prime directive is to be led by the Holy Spirit, not by the flesh. However we are often dealing with Christians in emotional bondage to the flesh – those who are suffering because feelings are suppressed, repressed or out of balance. Emotions can be out of control and destructive as a result of *a faulty belief system* based on lies, a system which has never been challenged and corrected. Over time we can develop *a mature belief system* based on absolute truths, with biblical precepts and godly principles as the guiding factors (see section on *Strongholds & Mindsets*).

From a mature perspective and truths based system we are able to make choices to respond to these negative based reactions in a Christ like way. We aim to manage our emotions in a God-honouring manner by taking every thought captive to the mind of Christ. We choose to think, feel and act according to this sound belief system, rather than perceptions of life based on a self-defeating belief system, based on lies and irrational thoughts (see sections on *Renewing the Mind*).

AIMS & GOALS OF THE PROCESS

The process should enable us to: –

a) recognize the debilitating and destructive personal feelings and the associated behavioural patterns ruling the present

b) learn that thoughts produce feelings, which result in actions

c) realise that views and perceptions may need to be changed

d) acknowledge habitual ways of thinking and acting as bondages

e) understand that thoughts, feelings, choices and actions could be emanating from a false belief system based on lies

f) be willing to *feel to heal* by facing troublesome feelings and associated memories temporarily to locate the lies producing the reactions

g) make an exchange: lies for revealed personal truths (as given by Jesus Christ, Lord and Saviour)

h) eliminate the pain contained in troublesome memories so that triggers are invalidated

i) make a decision to operate and respond to life according to the truth – Jesus being the Way, the Truth and the Life

j) leave childish, faulty ways of thinking, believing and acting behind

k) develop mature fruits of the spirit through the spiritual disciplines

l) move on, into growth, freedom and abundant living

Counsellor Resource: EMOTIONAL HEALING – THE POOL METHOD

The following concept, *Replacing Lies with Truths via the Healing Pool Experience* was given to the author under inspiration from the Holy Spirit. It is based on the story of the lame man who waited by the spring fed pool of Bethesda to be placed in its healing waters (Jn 5:1-9). This simple method of healing, based on symbolism, can be used to set captives free from strongly held beliefs which do not align with the word of God (Jn 8:32-36). A powerful and effective tool, it is compatible with other techniques described in this text.

> ***Disclaimer**: The reader is reminded that the author takes no responsibility for the use or misuse of this technique or any related techniques practised by other ministries or individuals. The Healing Pool Method has been independently constructed and empirically tested by the author over many years within her own counselling practice and ministry. She holds no personal responsibility for its use outside of her own personal therapeutic application.*

IMAGE 24

THE HEALING POOL

THE HEALING POOL METHOD (Jn 5:1-9)

This type of ministry can be used very effectively with clients who appreciate imagery and symbolism, and in particular, with clients who are experiencing debilitating emotional problems which are: –

  a) Habitual and controlling – anger, anxiety, guilt, frustration, suspicion, jealousy, depression, etc.
  b) Dramatic overreactions – disappointment, rage, panic, hate, violence, cruelty, withdrawal, etc.
  c) All pervasive – abandonment, rejection, shame, loneliness, fears, grief, helplessness, etc.

ADVANTAGES & OUTCOMES

Through the following technique, we can actually use the particular presenting problem to achieve an emotional healing. Control over emotional reactions can be gained. Emotions which were previously troublesome can be used in a constructive way in order to enhance life. For example: –

d)   Grief over loss of a loved one can be channelled into a mercy ministry.
e)   Anger may be used righteously to campaign for a cause.
f)   Loneliness can develop into empathetic outreach to others in need.

Prayer ministry can serve to moderate extreme and debilitating feelings and release a person from the bondage caused by troublesome pain-filled memories. The associated pain can be relieved, reduced, and sometimes, even completely obliterated. Healing then proceeds without the pain interfering with progress. Following this type of in-depth prayer ministry counsellors are better able to encourage a person to exercise and develop *a spirit of self-control* in areas which were previously a source of concern e.g. medicating emotional pain with alcohol, or using violence to vent.

During application of this cleansing technique, inappropriate and unacceptable feelings can be used as *signposts to healing*. Feelings are not necessarily right nor wrong, good nor bad; they are simply emotional reactions. Feelings become damaging when they are not recognised, experienced or expressed in a healthy manner – particularly in the case of overreactions. Our aim is to understand the underlying stimulus (base lie believed) of a negative overreaction during the healing pool process.

RECOMMENDED READING

> **Disclaimer: The author of this text does not endorse or promote any particular ministry or practice. The resources outlined in this publication are issued as examples for information purposes only.**

1. Edward M. Smith's *theophostic prayer ministry* (based in the USA). Although a complicated form of ministry, it is recommended to counsellors who prefer precise and thorough training methods.
2. David A. Seamands' writings: *Healing for Damaged Emotions, Healing of Memories* and *Putting Away Childish Things,* Scripture Press, 1982-85 give practical guidance for counsellors dealing with painful and recurring memories in clients.
3. Charles H. Kraft with Ellen Kearney and Mark H. White, *Deep Wounds, Deep Healing,* Regal Books, 1993, has produced an excellent textbook for those wanting to be 'inner healers'. Kraft draws heavily on the 'greats' in

this arena and pulls it all together succinctly. Only the one-on-one techniques (not group therapy) are compatible.

4. Leanne Payne's *Restoring the Christian Soul,* Baker Books, 1996. Section II of this volume covers healing of memories. Payne concentrates more on the psychological and therapeutic aspects and her writings will also be of interest to students of theology.

5. Larry Huch, has written from the viewpoint of a highly successful pastor: *Free at Last, Removing the Past from Your Future,* Whittaker House, 2000. The book includes a disc. His testimony of coming out of a life of drug addiction, crime and violence and being freed from 'a spirit of anger' gives weight to his teachings, and the section on *Seven Places Jesus Shed His Blood* is of special interest.

6. Dr Dan B Allender's *The Wounded Heart,* Navpress, 1990, latest edition includes information on false memory issues for work with adult victims of childhood sexual abuse.

TWELVE STEPS TO HEALING USING THE POOL METHOD

INSTRUCTIONS FOR COUNSELLOR USE

Note that this inner healing technique cannot be hurried nor have any short cuts attempted. Adequate time should be set aside (1½ to 2 hours). However, all 12 steps do not necessarily have to be completed during one session. Steps 1 to 3 can be completed at the end of a regular counselling or mentoring session, in preparation for another session dedicated wholly to this technique.

If you are interrupted, distracted or run out of the allotted time during the process, make sure you close the session with appropriate prayer and after-care. Remember, we are spiritual *doctors of the heart* and, healers of *damaged emotions and wounded spirits.* Look at this as spiritual heart surgery. Do not leave the patient lying with open wounds on the operating table. The same applies when the client does not want to continue with the process. Ensure there are adequate finishing up procedures and comfort ministered before closing a session.

> **WARNING: The Healing Pool Technique is not recommended for those clients who experience psychosis or remain severely disturbed by forms of ritualistic abuse such as SRA (Satanic Ritual Abuse) or disorders such as DID (Dissociative Identity Disorder).**

These 12 steps are merely a skeletal structure to assist you to operate as the counsellor. You may wish to specifically run down the list several times until you are proficient in fleshing out the bones in a less formal way. Contact the author if you require the **self-help version** of these 12 steps.

Step 1

Discuss the presenting problem. It could be that an offence has occurred, or that a stress producing situation re-occurs as a pattern in the client's life. Perhaps a circumstance or person has triggered old memories and past wounds or that someone has 'pushed an (emotional) button'. Make use of the signpost illustration.

Step 2

Describe the type of prayer ministry. Emphasize the feel-to-heal concept as described elsewhere in this text. Use the scriptural base of Jn 5:1-9. Ensure that the client understands the method by asking for feedback.

Step 3

Test the client's willingness to co-operate and motivation (drive strength) for change by asking the following types of questions:–

a) *On a scale of 1–10, how much do you want to be rid of this bondage right now?* (If motivation is low do not continue with this inner healing technique).

b) *Do you understand what we will be doing? Is there any confusion in your mind? Do I have your permission to ask the Holy Spirit to give us an idea of why you are experiencing these emotions? Are you ready to feel to heal?*

(As previously explained the above 3 steps can lead up to a prayer ministry session at a later date. Do not continue on if you do not have the time to complete all the following steps in one session. Enter Step 4 only if time permits).

Step 4 (*Can be approached at the next session following an introduction*)
At the beginning of the healing process, you might say, *'close your eyes now and ask the Holy Spirit to give us **a clue** as to what is troubling you'*. If he or she does not seem confident, reassure by saying, *'if you do not receive anything for yourself, then I might be given **a prompting** from Him to help us in our search for clues as to why you are troubled by these feelings. If I do receive something, would you be willing to listen and to work with this prompting?'* (See glossary for meaning of 'prompting' and 'clue').

Step 5

Pray for protection – calling on the blood of Jesus. If appropriate, verbally bind any demonic interference to the prayer session. (This should be done privately if it does not appear appropriate to pray out loud). Request guidance from the Holy Spirit using suitable language according to the client's spiritual maturity and worship style (e.g. conservative Christian, charismatic, non-committed person, Catholic, etc.). In the case of those who have difficulty relating to God as a father figure, it is generally best to address him as *'dear God'* or *'Lord Jesus'*.

Step 6

Receive clues and prompts from the Holy Spirit, along with advice on any associated feelings from the client. Record and number these, then deal with the clues in the order they were received.

Step 7

Read the related scriptures (Jn 5:1-9) or set the scene in your own words. Describe the pool as being stirred up and the mud beginning to rise. Invite the client to figuratively enter the stirred emotional healing pool. Ask if he/she is ready to have the pool stirred up further in order to intensify the emotions associated with the clue. Enquire as to whether the clue brings to mind a memory.

Encourage focus on the feelings associated with that particular memory until the emotions become as intense as necessary. Request a description of the feelings; but only as thoroughly as the client is prepared to go. **Do not push or pressure.** Symbolically describe the pain associated with these memories as *'the mud'*, which is being stirred up. Instruct the client regarding searching for the lie within the mud.

Step 8

Ask the Holy Spirit to reveal the lie associated with that one particular memory hidden in the mud. When detected, ask if he/she is willing and prepared to make an exchange – the lie in exchange for the truth – the truth that will set them free.

Step 9

Direct the client to focus on Jesus Christ and his willingness to reach out to remove him or her from the pool and to wash away the residual mud. Ask if they would like to personally invite Jesus to reveal the truth to them, which will serve to release them from this lie. Be careful not to add any of your own thoughts at this stage of the proceedings and be prepared to deal with a possible period of silence. If such a pause is becoming uncomfortable, gently prompt the client to reveal any *self-talk* or *internal dialogue*.

Step 10

If the client is not feeling or receiving anything, direct them to the second clue with its particular associated feelings and memories. Putting clue #1 aside, deal with clue #2 in a similar way to the first, moving along the pathway to healing until a personal truth is received, and thereby a clue is processed. Return to clue #1 to try re-processing. If not successful, move to clue #3, and so on.

There is one exception to the statement that step 4 and onwards needs to be completed in one session. If no progress is being made after Step 10, do not pressure the client to perform. Simply release from the process with a prayer of comfort and encouragement then suggest trying something different.

Step 11

As you both move along the healing pathway, invite the client to pray, exchanging any lies revealed for the personal truths received from Jesus Christ, their Lord and Saviour. Direct to personally renounce the lies previously believed in their own words, along with repenting of faulty belief systems and so on. Basically, encourage personal prayer in their words, not yours.

Step 12

As the Holy Spirit leads you in ministering, use affirmations, priestly blessings, forgiveness, releasing from bondages, etc. Move slowly, allowing the client sufficient time to soak in the blessings. Ask regarding present feelings. Finally, request recall of the original presenting problem and ask them to relate to you how they feel now.

Ask, *Does any pain remain in the memory? Do you still need to process this pain?*

Continue to minister until the emotional pain is removed.

Email elvie@prayercounsel.com to access instructions for a self-help version.

RECOVERY FOLLOWING THE HEALING POOL EVENT

At the end of the session, explain that you would advise spending some peaceful time alone with God to assimilate the prayer ministry. Also, strongly advise that they make some written notes on the ministry experienced as soon as they are able. Suggest bringing these notes to a follow-up session for de-briefing and reinforcement of the truths received.

FOLLOW UP SESSION

At the follow-up session, ask the client to recall their internal dialogue prior to stepping into the pool (thoughts not feelings).

Use *follow up questions* such as: –

 a) *What is Jesus Christ saying to you now?*
 b) *What are you going to believe, say and do the next time you are tempted to, e.g. give up/throw a tantrum/sense a panic attack coming on/start feeling sorry for yourself/lash out in anger?*
 c) *When you recall the problems troubling you prior to your healing, how do you feel about these problems now?*

MIND RENEWAL AND SANCTIFICATION (Rom 12:2, Heb 12:1)

Follow-up instruction is absolutely necessary. There is now personal responsibility for your client to follow through – to leave childish ways of thinking, acting and speaking behind – in order to move on into maturity. This is achieved by stepping simultaneously into mature reasoning, along with childlike dependence on God's grace and mercy (1Cor 13:9-11). Explain *cognitive behavioural therapy* briefly by instructing the client to *walk the walk and talk the talk* (see graphic resource).

Praise him or her for specific past successes and express confidence in God being faithful in the future. Explain that, without the lies as hindrances, there will be a new liberty experienced. Encourage to report back on future victories so that you can jointly praise God for this freedom.

ISSUE A WARNING to remain alert to the wiles of the enemy in the future (Eph 6). Emphasize memorizing appropriate scriptures to become firmly established in the newfound belief system.

A self-help resource is also available in a 12 step style format. It will instruct and guide your client as to how to implement the method already experienced within formal counselling sessions – at home. By following the self-help guide, your client can seek healing for future personal issues whenever the need arises. This handout is to be issued only to clients who are well aware of the concepts and techniques involved in the process. It is also a useful tool for the counsellor's personal needs. Contact the author to request: Self-help Healing Pool Resource. *Previous disclaimer applies.

CLIENT TESTIMONIAL: The Rotten Apple

(Clinical Commentary Attached)

I can see now why my counsellor wanted to go back into all my childhood rubbish. I never wanted to think of any of those people again. The staff and the other kids at the boarding school caused me so much strife back then, as a nine year old country lad, that, apparently, it was what landed me up in prison in my early teens. I thought it was just life inside that screwed me up, but the boarding school was even worse.

Then there was the trouble I had at 16 over stalking that girlfriend who dumped me. I could never really get over that. That was real bad, and caused me a lot of strife with the cops, but I would never had guessed, it was actually the boarding school days that were still affecting me. I really thought I had wiped those days out from my mind.

But, it is true what she said, this counsellor, that the patterns in our lives still keep happening until we turn round and look at them square in the eyeballs. The patterns are trying to tell us something, she said.

Well, she has been different to those social workers and probation officers you get when you first get out of the lock up. They all gave up on me because I had a history and they knew I'd be a repeat offender. I never lasted long outside. They said they wouldn't waste their time on someone who wasn't serious. And they were tough. By God they were tough.

They didn't want to hear when I told them that I had got religion through one of those tele-evangelists when I was on the inside. They thought I was having them on – one of my 'stories'. I told them I wanted prayer – not preaching at me. All they did was preach at me about keeping my nose clean all the time. Anyway, the last officer did listen and got me onto this woman via the Salvation Army. They said she was willing to take me on because of my daughter being in the Salvos and them knowing each other years ago. She was a Christian lady from some hallelujah church called 'Born to Live' or 'Born to be Free' or something. Sounded good to me – being free was what I needed to learn about. There was no way I was going back inside again! It was about time I got a life.

The first day I met her, I knew that this was a lady and I had to treat her nice. She was all my old mum wasn't – gentle and kind, and real smart – a bit like my daughter Jen. She seemed to know what I thought and why I thought it. She was real interested in what I had to say. Before I knew it, we were talking about my past and I was back in the old days – and they weren't good ol' days either!

This lady said it seemed like I had a pattern of being rejected – my mum and dad kicking me out at 12, and me never getting on with anyone after that. Come to think of It, I never got on with anyone – full stop! Even as a toddler, they reckoned I was beating up on kids, snatching at toys, and stealing. I was never much of a one for rules or getting on with others. Swearing at the adults was my favourite game as I grew up – and stories – lots of stories I'd make up to get out of trouble. I liked to shock them back then too. Still have to curb that one. I kind of enjoy that. I get people before they get me you see. There's a method in my madness.

So, she got me talking about my past in only a couple of sessions. And, guess where we landed? Yep – right back in those old boarding school days. But, before that, in the very first meeting, she got things out of me I had never told anyone. At the second meeting, she drew this picture of an apple tree and showed me some stuff I'd mentioned at the first appointment, things like the girlfriend dumping me, then my no hoper father who kept running off and leaving mum and me to fend for ourselves. I even told her how the kids at school were always leaving me out of games and stuff. I hated their guts for that.

She drew about eight apples on this tree and put one word for each story I'd told inside each one – like the 13 year old girlfriend's name 'Alice' (which even hurt for me to say) and 'Tom' the creep who kept beating me up back in primary school.

She explained that 'apples are apples' – they all represented the same thing. They showed up a pattern. She asked me whether I could see what the apples meant. I know 'apples' when I see them – I had been trodden on, let down, left out, given up on, and beat up on all my life. The pattern was a big one – I was a Reject. I'd been given apples with worms in them all my life!

She congratulated me on seeing the pattern; but she said that the fruit of this tree that represented my life was called 'Rejection' rather than 'Reject'. She assured me that she would show me the difference next session and that we would look at the root system of this tree and track it to 'the root of the problem' as she liked to call it. I sure wanted to find out the root problem there and then, but being in prison teaches you that you have to wait for most things.

I was also waiting for her to start talking about God and to hear some praying going on. She said that that would begin early next session. She started talking about another couple of drawings she would show me about signposts and (I think she said) a healing pool... or something. Meanwhile, she asked if I minded her praying a blessing over me. This made my heart go kinda warm. No one had ever blessed me before. I didn't understand what it meant; but it felt good when she did it.

THE COUNSELLOR'S CLINICAL ADVISOR COMMENTS:

The above story is a success story. It does have a happy ending. On the other hand, this story could have panned out quite differently if our counsellor, Shona, had not handled it with all our agency's checks and boundaries in place. She was dealing with a criminal here – a hardened criminal with a history of stalking and various other convictions, for which he had spasmodically served time in penal institutions over a period of twenty years.

At our centre, we handle a few 'problem' clients pro bono, which the church agencies send to us when they see the obvious need to refer on. The fellow, who is giving his tale here, experienced all the benefits of Shona's very mature and capable handling of the case. His Christian daughter's church family also gave prayer and practical support.

I should mention here that we are a Christian agency and give assent to different forms of Christian counselling, including deliverance, within our practice. I, myself, am a qualified psychologist and my wife works as a psychiatrist at a local public hospital. She has been a valuable asset to me personally for confidential debriefing and for medical advice in case management.

At our clinic, we work as a team ministry on a professional basis, following the ethical, legal and moral guidelines and obligations of a Christian counsellors' association to which we belong both individually and corporately. This gives us the checks and balances, the accountability hierarchy, the legal protection and insurance coverage necessary in the event that any problems arise.

I am the Director of the clinic, responsible for managing the day to day running of our set-up. I am basically responsible to Board Members. The Board consists of several ministers of religion from various denominations. They give me personal spiritual support as well as practical and financial assistance from their own churches and networks. This all works very well.

But, it is volunteers like Shona, who are on the coalface dealing with difficult cases such as the above, who give our clinic the integrity and excellent reputation it enjoys today.

RECORD OF MINISTRY STEPS: FRUITS, ROOTS & POISONS

Name of Client:

Fill out and date each step at time of ministry making reference to The Diseased Apple Tree graphic illustration on the following page.

STEP I – FRUIT
As problems are presented via the client story, **recognise patterns** emerging. Probe for client issues (bad fruit) past and present.

Types of issues showing up repeatedly in the life story
as 'rotten apples' are: –

STEP II – TRUNK
Listen further to the client's history, **tracing the contributing factors** which have produced bad/spoiled fruit.

Contributory factors are: –

STEP III – ROOTS
Lovingly **challenge and confront** by preaching, teaching & shepherding, so that all exposed root problems are dealt with.

Roots of the problems are: –

STEP IV – SOIL
Deal with the poisons, which have been feeding the root system.

Action to be taken: –
(e.g. *deliverance, renewing the mind, healing pool technique...*)

IMAGE 25

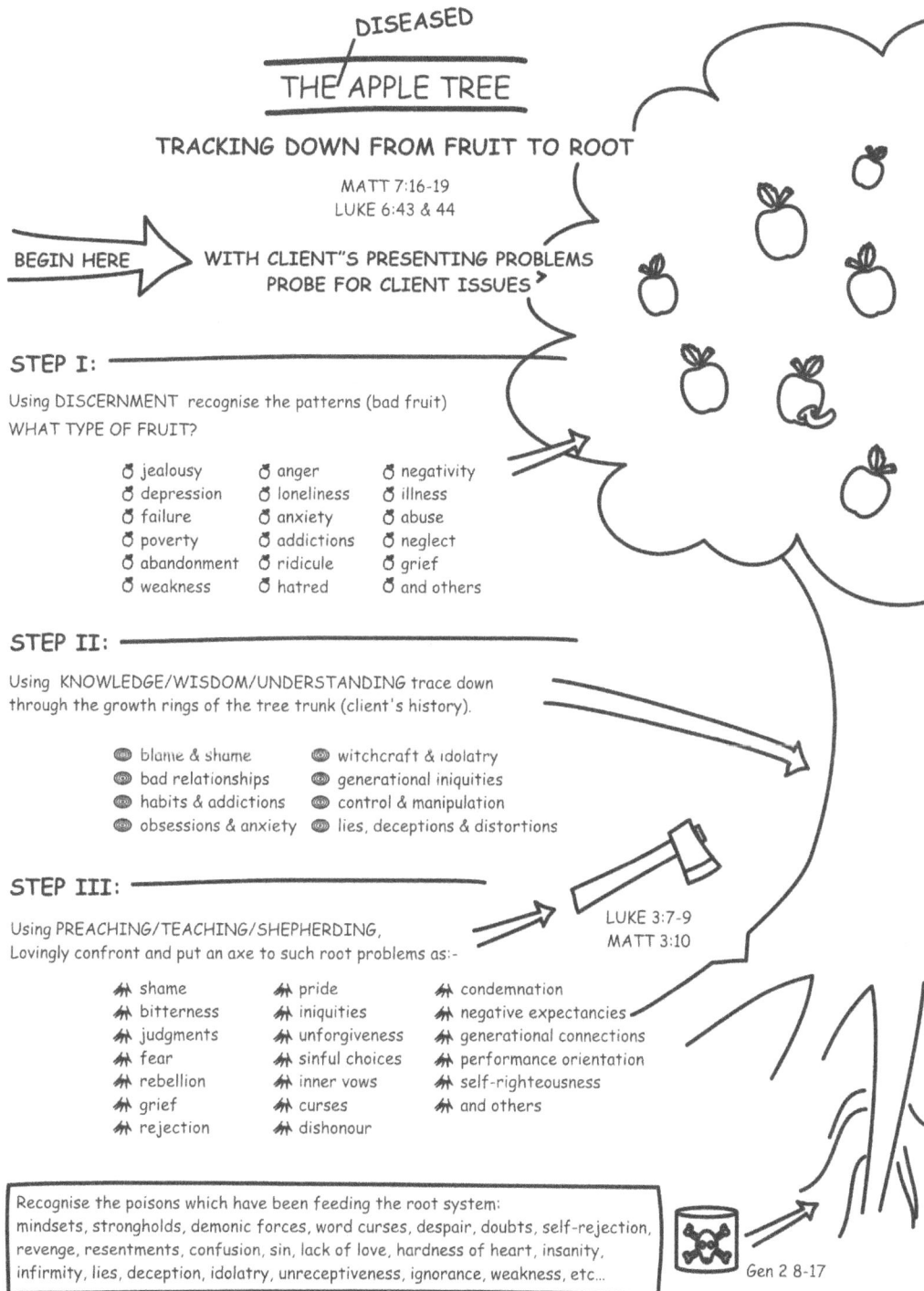

DISEASED

THE APPLE TREE

TRACKING DOWN FROM FRUIT TO ROOT

MATT 7:16-19
LUKE 6:43 & 44

BEGIN HERE → WITH CLIENT"S PRESENTING PROBLEMS
PROBE FOR CLIENT ISSUES

STEP I:

Using DISCERNMENT recognise the patterns (bad fruit)
WHAT TYPE OF FRUIT?

jealousy	anger	negativity
depression	loneliness	illness
failure	anxiety	abuse
poverty	addictions	neglect
abandonment	ridicule	grief
weakness	hatred	and others

STEP II:

Using KNOWLEDGE/WISDOM/UNDERSTANDING trace down
through the growth rings of the tree trunk (client's history).

blame & shame	witchcraft & idolatry
bad relationships	generational iniquities
habits & addictions	control & manipulation
obsessions & anxiety	lies, deceptions & distortions

STEP III:

Using PREACHING/TEACHING/SHEPHERDING,
Lovingly confront and put an axe to such root problems as:-

LUKE 3:7-9
MATT 3:10

shame	pride	condemnation
bitterness	iniquities	negative expectancies
judgments	unforgiveness	generational connections
fear	sinful choices	performance orientation
rebellion	inner vows	self-righteousness
grief	curses	and others
rejection	dishonour	

Recognise the poisons which have been feeding the root system:
mindsets, strongholds, demonic forces, word curses, despair, doubts, self-rejection,
revenge, resentments, confusion, sin, lack of love, hardness of heart, insanity,
infirmity, lies, deception, idolatry, unreceptiveness, ignorance, weakness, etc...

Gen 2 8-17

FRUITS, ROOTS & POISONS TECHNIQUE

This technique might appear complicated and time consuming at first sight. However it is easily grasped when the basic concept is explained as *getting to the root of the problem*, with issues appearing as *patterns/fruits* in our lives. Out of all the techniques, this is the one that students and clients alike express the most interest in. It is also remembered more easily than the rest.

Most practising and would be counsellors will feel confident in drawing a tree to illustrate the concept. It is easy for children too, who love the idea of drawing their own rotting fruit on the tree (with a worm or two included of course). If you are unable to draw, remember that a simplified graphic illustration is available from the author* with samplings of fruits, roots and poisons; so that it is only a matter of pointing to the relevant material in discussion with your client. Several other teaching ministries also use the fruit to root illustration in various ways.

As prayer ministers we will be learning a technique now that will help unfold whether repetitive client issues (fruits) possess a root system which is being contaminated as the tree (life of the client) is drawing up sustenance from diseased soil. We will be tracking downwards on the graphic of *The Diseased Apple Tree* – from the rotten fruit at the top of the tree, down via the trunk, and underground to the unseen roots fed by poisons in the soil.

We will be using your records of a client's presenting problems. For the exercise, we acknowledge these issues as examples of *bad fruit* in the client's life. That is, whatever is troubling the client enough to present to you for discussion, can be classed symbolically as a *rotten apple* or client *issue*. We then probe further into the client's *life story* to see whether there seems to be a *recognisable pattern* emerging. Is there is evidence of more bad fruit, or issues, of a similar nature in your client's life at present? Ask for stories from the client as to whether they have experienced other such problems or incidents in the past. Add each of these as bad apples on the diseased tree. Classify each for their general nature as a problem or issue, e.g. *fear, jealousy, conflict, anger, loss, strife, rejection, failure, abandonment, disappointment, abuse* and so on.

To illustrate the technique, we will be using an imaginary client, Lyn. As we record our discussion with her, we will be working practically on filling out her history to discover the root cause/s of her presenting problem/s. Refer to the counsellor exercise *Lyn's Apple Tree,* following directly, where you might like to practise drawing a tree to overlay the text*.

---

*A blank copy of this resource (drawing of the tree) is included in the companion book 'So You Want To Be a Christian Counsellor – Resource Handbook', along with other graphic illustrations suitable for presentation to clients or students for teaching purposes. This handbook is available from - www.prayercounsel.com.

FRUITS & ROOTS CASEWORK: CLIENT 'LYN'

Refer to Exercise: **Lyn's Apple Tree**

Lyn brings to the session as her *presenting problem* a fight with the boss. This heated argument has resulted in her being fired three months ago. This is recorded and drawn on the tree as apple #1. This first problem/situation could be classed as an issue of loss/grief/conflict/disappointment. We ask her to choose which one. She classes it as a 'loss'.

We classify this issue privately as 'conflict'.

Apple #2 represents past disputes with her spouse causing her now, ex-husband, to walk out on the family. Lyn begins an emotional tirade of stories about how he, Bernie, never supported her in disciplining the children. This second *rotten apple* could be typed as either loss or abandonment, and it definitely involved conflict. Lyn classes the second apple as 'grief and loss' over her first love, Bernie. We now cautiously suggest to her that this loss could perhaps be the result of conflict over parenting styles. She disagrees vehemently, disclosing that he left her for another woman and that it was definitely not her fault that she was deserted. She states that she was *the victim.*

Lyn suddenly deflects here to bring up her most current problem.

Apple #3 involves an argument with her current fiancé, Trevor, over the job loss (refer to apple #1). This disagreement resulted in threats of breaking their engagement, which brought to the surface *(triggered)* fears of more loss, disappointment, abandonment and rejection. At this point Lyn expresses how angry she feels at her boss because she might lose Trevor as well as her job now that they cannot afford to get married. So the third rotten apple in Lyn's life story today also appears to pivot around relationship conflict.

There is a pattern emerging here of conflict and loss (*cause and effect*) with the surface emotion being anger. Because we are aware as counsellors that we are tracking down from fruit to root, we consider privately, *'what are the roots of this rotten fruit and what poisons are feeding these roots?'* That is, what is the <u>real</u> problem and what is the <u>real cause</u> of the problem.

LYN'S CASE FROM A DIFFERENT PERSPECTIVE

Let us look at this example from a different angle. Let us be more specific in our example of how we might come to recognise and label the apples. We will do this by using our favoured method as emotional doctors, that of *dealing with feelings.*

Client Lyn has described arguing with her fiancé Trevor over her job loss. She presents her problem as conflict with her intended spouse and describes the *associated feelings* of frustration and anger. Prior to the session, she has recognised that her *current issue* is her anger, which is getting out of control. When she filled out her form during the initial consultation, she stated her *goal for counselling* was to seek help for *managing her anger*.

PROCESSING THE CONFLICT

STEP I Probe deeper regarding the present problem. Ask Lyn for two or three specific examples of the types of conflict, which cause her to experience anger. Now ask, *how angry were you during each specific incident?* We are looking for *overreactions* in particular. Ask her to rate the strength of the anger on a scale of 1–10 in comparison to a bad case of road rage, which would be classed as a 10.

Question her further. *Do you get frustrated or angry with anyone other than Trevor?* If so, ask for specific examples. Examine whether there is a pattern emerging. You could now be thinking along the following lines:

a) *Does she show more fruit of the same kind?*
b) *Who is Lyn getting mad at, other than her fiancé Trevor?*
c) *Is it someone she has authority over, such as the kids, the dog or the housecleaner, or,*
d) *Is it with people in authority over her – e.g. the boss, the pastor, or the government?*

We discover that she has labelled incidents/apples #1-3 (as described in the previous account) as a 'loss'. She has experienced major conflict with her ex-spouse and her boss as well as with her fiancé. This appears to be manifesting in the form of frustration, which builds up and explodes into intense emotional outbursts.

Let us say that Lyn is intent on describing why she is so angry with Trevor at this initial stage. Basically, she is frustrated over Trevor not being willing to communicate with her. She describes being angry with him for shutting himself off from her, both emotionally and verbally, when she tries to tell him how she feels about her boss.

So here we deflect her from concentrating on the details of her most recent argument with Trevor over the loss of employment, which jeopardised their financial future together. We ask her to concentrate instead, on the feelings rather than the facts associated with the incident, and to recall other times when she has felt just as frustrated and angry with someone other than Trevor.

She immediately describes her feelings of astonishment when she lost her job. We ask her if she has experienced similar intensity of feeling at another time. She responds by comparing her reaction when she found out her ex-husband had left her and the kids for another woman. Now, we are delving deeper into the reasons she is *overreacting emotionally* in the present and attempting to make a connection to incidents from the past. Things are becoming clearer, but more complicated.

STEP II We stop to pray for Holy Spirit guidance through Lyn's life story as she talks out the feelings associated with the various incidents. We suggest to Lyn that conflict appears as a *pattern in her life story*. She agrees. Lyn recalls intense fights with her mother in her teenage years. Another circumstance emerges – as a newly married young woman she had felt she was not getting the attention she needed from her church pastor during group bible studies. She even goes on to relate an argument in detail with her father. Here she expresses how furious she had felt when he threatened to kick her out of home for wearing makeup as a child.

At this stage of hearing the life story we choose to suggest that the pattern of conflict appears to be associated with *anger towards authority figures*. She seems puzzled but willing to listen. We feel it is the appropriate time to track down the trunk of the tree towards the root system. We ask Lyn whether she is able to pray for revelations and discernment about her *deep-seated anger* and what appears to be *unfinished business* from her childhood. Tracking down to the trunk of the tree (life story/history) we come to the roots of her presenting problem.

Lyn listens intently as the Holy Spirit reveals through the concept of fruits, roots and poisons, how a diseased tree has produced the spoiled fruit in her life. We explain where she possibly has *broken God's laws* to contribute to her problems. We use the first graphic (the diseased tree) as a guide for some possibilities, which we record on her personal tree (refer to the following graphic, *Lyn's Apple Tree)*.

For example, we help her to discover how she might have broken God's commandment to *honour her mother and father*. This could have *sown the seed* to produce this unhealthy tree with *bitter roots*. And, through the spiritual *laws of multiplication and increase,* the seed of disobedience to God has produced fruits in the form of anger, conflict, and loss. It becomes more obvious to Lyn that she has been rebellious towards other authority figures as she confesses other incidents that are now coming to mind. The tap root is becoming apparent: **rebellion**.

The Holy Spirit is revealing and exposing her longstanding rebellion towards him as her heavenly Father. We teach and preach further on the subject of reverence for a holy God. This exposes Lyn's false views of Father God as someone who is a *killjoy* and not mindful of her needs. Lyn comes under conviction– especially her lack of self-control in relation to her anger issues. She begins to feel more positive – hopeful that she can establish peaceful, long-lasting relationships.

STEP III Using loving confrontation, correction and warfare, we put an axe to the tree bearing the bad fruit. We explain that there will be regrowth if the diseased tree is not totally destroyed; that we need not only to cut down the trunk with its branches supporting the apples, but to carefully pull up the roots extracting *poisonous influences* from the soil.

STEP IV These poisons are dealt with in following *deliverance* sessions and a healthy new tree is planted in the cleansed ground of Lyn's life. She is able to enter into marriage confidently with Trevor – because she has reconciled her heart with her Father God. She is now open to receive the good news of how she can find freedom and enjoy the fruits of the Spirit in the days of promise ahead.

Counsellor Exercise:

a) *Outline the form of a tree around the words on the following page*
b) *Study the scriptures.*
c) *In the space below, make your own summary of the four steps taken to put Lyn on the threshold of stepping from the negative patterns in her life and into her freedom.*

FRUITS, ROOTS & POISONS
ye shall know them by their fruit...

Matt 12:33-37

Lyn's Apple Tree

Recognize rotten fruit
(presenting problems forming a pattern)

Step I
Luke 6:43–45; Matt 7:16–20

Apple/Incident #1 = loss, grief, disappointment, (relationship conflict)
Apple/Incident #2 = loss, abandonment, victimization, (relationship conflict)
Apple/Incident #3 = potential loss, disappointment, abandonment, rejection
(relationship & inner conflict)

Step II
Gen 3:1–24; Matt 13:14–17
Investigate client's history & issues
(e.g. growth of tree via continued disobedience to God's Laws)

Bad relationships
Uncontrollable emotions
Disrespect for authority

Step III
Luke 3:9; Matt 3:10; Gen 2:8–17
Lovingly confront through
preaching/teaching/shepherding.
Put an axe to the root of...

REBELLION

Recognise the poisons, which have been feeding the root system so that these
can be dealt with in **Step IV** (deliverance/cleansing).

Counselling Practicalities: A SAMPLING OF TECHNIQUES COMBINED

Counsellor Exercise:

Ministry does not always have to take place in a formal setting facilitated by another person; sometimes he sees fit to deal with us privately. Refer to the following testimony to locate the various methods and techniques (numbered) involved in the author's personal healing experience.

---

1. Patterns – Fruits, Roots & Poisons
2. Overreactions as Signposts to Healing of Emotions
3. Prophetic Words & Other Giftings used for Restoration Purposes
4. Healing Pool – Self Help Method for Healing of Memories
5. Conventional Counselling – Assessing Personality Types
6. Communication with the Father God via Journaling

AUTHOR'S TESTIMONY – Chainsaws & Sandcastles

The Lord had challenged me with a prophetic word indicating that I would have a change of direction to my life (which consequently led to the publication of this book). However at the time, I baulked at this news, because I was feeling so fulfilled and content with everything in my life as it was.

I was feeling that I had reached the pinnacle (from my own point of view) of what I was doing ministry wise. Professionally I was doing well. I did not want to go to any higher level. It was satisfying to me in the format it was. I felt that I was not in a rut or a comfort zone. I was simply happy with the way it was.

I was gaining respect generally and was confidently networking with other Christians and secular professional workers, even if it was only on a small scale. As a complementary job, I was getting a little bit of paid work as a landscape gardener at the units where we lived. This was convenient and fitted in well with working from home as a counsellor. It was both satisfying my creativity and keeping me healthy.

The first change was with the landscaping work. A new gardener arrived and made his first self-appointed job a chain saw massacre. All the precious shrubs I had planted and nurtured over the past five years were trimmed to their bare bones – at the beginning of winter and in drought conditions. He also chopped two mature trees to ground level.

I was more than annoyed… I was seething mad! On first viewing this catastrophe from our balcony, I felt I was about to burst into tears. Realising this was a somewhat childish overreaction for a grown woman; I began to mull over this dramatic reaction.

*I stepped into putting my counselling and prayer ministry principles into action. Right Lord, where is the **root to this fruit** [1] Why am I **overreacting** [2] and what does it have to do with your recent call on my life to a change of direction?*

*I asked the Father for a clue from the past that might help me to understand why I was so upset by this simple little event. Why was I so angry personally with the gardener? I **heard a simple phrase** [3] with my spiritual ears 'spoken' into my head. All He said to me was 'red-headed boy'.*

*Following this, I saw in my spirit **a vision** [3] of myself as a little girl building a sandcastle at the edge of the sea. I was then given the impression that a boy on the beach had come along and knocked it down. In this vision, I (as the girl) experienced feelings of outrage and bewilderment – similar to those I was presently feeling as a mature woman with the gardening situation.*

*I remembered to step into my **spiritual healing pool** [4]. I then recalled from my childhood memory bank that I often used to build elaborate gardens of shells, twigs and greenery around my castles in the sand at the beach. It appears that I was a budding landscape gardener even from my early years. I mused that it was so like God to use an analogy that has personal meaning.*

I asked the Holy Spirit to reveal to me the lie which had taken root during that incident enacted in the vision on the beach to produce any damage in my life over the years. This is what he indicated to me: –

THE LIE WAS IMPLANTED: THAT WHATEVER I ACHIEVED IN LIFE WOULD BE KNOCKED DOWN.

*I began the process of looking for **patterns** [1] in my life and to ask myself some questions. Is this why I have a pattern of not completing academic courses in my life to receive qualifications? Yes. Am I always expecting to be thwarted in my goals? Yes. Have I created a self-fulfilling prophecy? So far…yes!*

*Then I reasoned: God created me to be an achiever. This is my dominant **personality type** [5]. Yet, I had never formally achieved anything in particular. For example, in the last year of high school I was ill during my final exams and failed my best subject by not even putting pen to paper. I recollected that anything I started seemed to be sabotaged by one illness or another – whether physical or emotional. This had caused frustration to the extreme.*

Then a later example of this pattern came to mind. On completing a course for professional development via self-paced correspondence lessons, I was refused the diploma (even though I had excelled in every part of the course). After several years of study and assessments, I discovered that the administration had failed to notify me that the curriculum had been upgraded two years previously. I had slipped through the cracks with their paperwork. I was in utter dismay. I had an extra three years of study and assignments to go to qualify!

So this was the sandcastle pattern that had plagued me throughout my life. I then asked the Lord what I needed to do to break this curse on me. I knew that I would no longer have all my dreams sabotaged and my achievements demolished if I had knowledge of the truth that would serve to set me free from this bondage.

He then began to speak freely to me in my spirit and I wrote the following in my **journal** [6] *as a* **prophetic utterance** [3] *from the Father to me:*

'Look at your childhood castle my child. Were not the waves going to come in with the tide and take down your work anyway? These are temporal things. They come and go. But, what goes on in the spiritual is an eternal achievement. Look at what you have achieved for my glory and in my name! This is what is important'.

He then helped me to list the important non-temporal things achieved in my life in regard to my family and calling. Only then, did I come to the realisation that these are my heavenly kingdom 'castles', which will never be knocked down!

THE TRUTH WAS: MY HEAVENLY TREASURES WOULD REMAIN.

'O.K. Father', I said, 'but, I am still mad at my garden being demolished. I still have to look at it all day. Help me to let go and to get over it. Please – it hurts. Like all the other times, it hurts. Please **heal my emotions** [4] *so that my heart isn't so tender next time temporal things happen'.*

FOOTNOTE: Following this divine counselling session, another very significant childhood memory connected with a gardener was revealed to me in a similar way. The processing of this second memory did much to heal a great deal of emotional pain for me in another area – the area of feeling unsafe.

Note here that both of these healings were achieved interactively between the Father and me, with the Holy Spirit's guidance. Reader, you too can develop the techniques outlined in this publication for your own use. With practice, and yielding in faith in the Holy Spirit guiding you, you can experience Jesus Christ personally minister to you.

CHAPTER TWENTY

DELIVERANCE

The ministry of deliverance deserves a chapter of its own. It is a controversial subject and difficult to present because of the complexity of deliverance needs and the various views: as to whether a Christian can be *possessed* or *oppressed;* inherit vulnerability to bondage or be purely personally responsible; or even if there is a spirit world with its devil and his operatives. This chapter presents a brief overview of the topic from the standpoint of the Body of Christ 'working out our salvation'. This segment contains:

-   Testimonies and casework (fictitious)
-   Discourse based on the author's personal opinions and experiences
-   The author's preferred style of meeting clients' deliverance needs
-   Sample guide to formal deliverance procedures for Christians.

Study Notes

CLIENT TESTIMONIAL: Deliverance from Loneliness

Dear Diary,

Seems all my life I've walked alone. At 38, when I look back over my life, no one has ever really wanted me as a friend, let alone a wife or mother.

Since January last year though, I feel I have sorted through a lot of personal issues. My therapist wasn't doing me any good and a staff member told me about prayer ministry at her church. Since going for it, I have drawn closer, much closer, to God. I discovered that I had erected walls to keep people out – including God. They were actually to protect me from getting hurt and because I was angry with God over what happened to my mother. Now that I have taken down all the defensive walls, I can feel the extent and depth of his love starting to get through to me.

I admit I was really angry with God, until I learnt about mindsets and strongholds. Then it all clicked into place. I was scared of being vulnerable. I was even scared of God and that's why I only related to Jesus. I learned that fear is really faith in the devil, faith in a person, or faith in myself. I had to put my hand up as being guilty of all three.

I realised that I was afraid of people seeing the real me. I thought that, if they did, they would hate me as much as I hated myself. So I rejected them before they could reject me. I had put my faith in this fortress erected around me to keep everyone out – including God. I put faith in the little voices in my head that told me I was ugly, stupid and God's big mistake.

I was ashamed that I had no friends and that no one liked me. Here I was: the big executive, a career woman climbing her way up the corporate ladder, not caring if I had to tread on someone to get to the top.

It has taken a lot of soul searching on my part. I made a decision. I decided to let God <u>the</u> Father, into my life. I figured He already knows me inside out so it was stupid pretending I could punish him by keeping Him out. I was angry and bitter that He didn't give me the friends I wanted so I wasn't going to be friends with Him. And I'm supposed to be an intelligent woman!

Now God the Father is my one and only true friend. But I am still 'people lonely'. I now see that I have scared people away from me. I have made up with God but I still don't connect with people. I really thought if I let down my defences and allowed others to pray for me, I would at last find at least one person in my life to ease this incredible aloneness feeling. Without Him, and Jesus of course, I am sure I would have given up on life by now.

It doesn't even have to be a male. I have given up all thoughts of getting married and being a mother. I have my career. I have worked too hard to give that up. It is too late for motherhood now. My health has deteriorated terribly these last few years. I think it is basically stress related. If I just had someone to share my thoughts with daily, the little things of life, the good things as well as the problems, then I wouldn't be so stressed out all the time. I wouldn't feel so terribly, terribly alone... I need God with skin on sometimes.

JOURNAL ENTRY FOLLOWING MINISTRY

Dear Diary,

It's funny how I still start with 'dear diary' as I did as a kid. Anyway, I feel like a kid today. I am so happy I could shout. It is a different kind of shouting to what I did yesterday when I went into my therapist and had it out with him. I let him have it, saying I was sick of parting out good money and getting nowhere with my problems. And I told him I was finished... I was quitting with him and going only to the church people who were offering to help me for nothing (well nothing compared to what he was charging anyway).

He didn't throw me out of the office or anything, just said that it was my choice and that he was happy to refer me on to someone else. I swore at him something terrible. I felt really guilty. He should have thrown me out. I would have if one of my staff behaved as poorly as I did. Anyway, I'll get my personal assistant to send him a present and a letter of apology next Monday.

I saw the church counsellor the next day – after I had calmed down a bit. She told me that she thought she knew some people who could help me. She said that, before she could begin with something she called 'inner healing techniques'. She wanted to send me along for 'deliverance'. I was desperate and agreed to it even though I didn't have a clue what she meant. I mean, I was really, really desperate.

Well, it was both the hardest and the best thing I have ever done in my life. I was in with this elderly couple (complete strangers to me) for over three hours! First they made sure I was a Christian and that my church counsellor had explained what they would be doing. I told them that she had given me some literature and I had done my homework. I told them that I was pretty nervous.

They asked me question after question about my problems but didn't really do much listening or talking back to me (like my therapist or the church counsellor do). The elderly man did most of the talking and the woman basically took notes and nodded all the time. They were so serious I started to get scared. I just wanted to get it over with.

He started off praying so gentle and kind. They reminded me of my grandparents who brought me up. In the end, they were both shouting and waving their arms about. They really sounded like they knew what they were doing. I thought of the people in the Bible who said that Jesus 'spoke with authority'. Being a boss myself I like to see people who can take charge! Like Jesus, that couple sure told those demons where they could go!

They explained that they sensed that a host of things seemed to have attached themselves to me and were responsible for ruining my life. They described them as 'oppressive or external spirits' that were trying to beat me up spiritually from the outside. They asked whether I was willing to have the two of them deal with them in the name of Jesus and then they prayed up a storm – binding, breaking, rebuking, cutting and loosing. Pride, jealousy, abandonment, rejection, fear of rejection, and mocking spirits, were some of them.

Best of all (and what I had been waiting for) they named one of them as a 'spirit of aloneness'. They said that it had been brought into my life by one of the more major demonic beings and that my fear of emotional attachment had invited it inside myself to stay. They asked whether I would be willing to co-operate by telling this thing to leave. They described it as an internal spirit or 'demonic squatter'. I apparently needed to evict this one myself. I didn't have to be asked twice. I sure told it where to go!

I went back to work the next day feeling so tired, but as free as a bird. I don't understand what went on. They have given me a leaflet about keeping free and how to study the Bible to learn about what has happened to me. I am even thinking that, when I get my head around it all, I might make another appointment with my therapist. I feel now that I would like to make my apologies in person. Somehow, I would like to tell him what has happened to me.

ON DELIVERANCE VIA COUNSELLING

The subject of deliverance from demonic oppression is often neglected or avoided in modern preaching and teaching. With the multiplication of inherited iniquities and bondages, the need for understanding of the subject is even greater in present times than it was in Biblical days. Jesus commissioned his followers to continue his earthly work. He stated that his followers would do even greater works than he had accomplished in His time here on earth (Lk 11:14 & 20, Jn 20:21, Mk 8:16-17, Mk 16:17, Acts 10:38).

As our Saviour went about 'doing good', he ministered in delivering and healing in all manner of ways – including release from the demonic. Delivered women accompanied Jesus and his disciples. Because those freed were full of gratitude, they were willing to bless Jesus and his workers (Lk 8:2-3). You will find that, as a prayer minister, your richest and most rewarding relationships will come from your willingness to step into the area of ministering freedom to those in need of deliverance.

WHO IS RESPONSIBLE?

We are sometimes led to believe after opening our salvation 'gift box' that our flesh will die and that this will liberate us. Try saying that to a person with a serious addiction to lust or a death wish! The working out of our salvation might mean expelling the demons from our soulish realm (Phil 2:12b-13). In this particular scripture, salvation, or *solaria* according to Thayer's Lexicon, has a primary meaning of '*deliverance from the molestation of enemies'*.

It is usually left to the specialist teaching ministries to preach freedom in this form, rather than the everyday preacher or pastor. When the scriptures refer to '*working out*' our salvation, perhaps this could include our personal responsibility to aspire to this form of sanctification. Jesus delivers our spirit from death into life. Our spirit man is born again. Afterwards, it is our responsibility to cooperate in freeing our souls and bodies from demonic trespassers during the cleansing and restoration process. Christians are called to set ourselves free; to be proactive.

'TOO HARD BASKET'

It is understandable that we would prefer to deal with matters we can plainly understand, such as a physical illness or a bad temper. It is also understandable that we have a natural tendency to fear and avoid the hidden forces of darkness. As counsellors, we can choose to turn a blind eye to those suffering from demonic bondage, put them in the 'too hard basket' and even classify clients as *eccentric or mentally ill.*

We might choose to remain ignorant, refusing to be open to discerning demonic activity. Within our ministry settings, perhaps we are fearful that we might not have the ability to deal with manifestations (outward signs of demonic activity), or that we will be harmed or contaminated personally. There is the realistic fear that there will be a supernatural backlash from becoming involved. The most common excuse is that we do not have the 'covering' to deal with deliverance. Or, perhaps we simply do not want to discover or uncover the activity within our own flesh. So, for all these reasons, and many more, it is understandable that we prefer to refer on to specialists or experts.

THE SPECIALISTS

However, the workload is often intense and wearing for the specialists in deliverance. The hours are long. Payment is rare. The work is usually done in private without public accolade or support. Not surprisingly, the workers are few and difficult to locate. If all counsellors and pastors in general, met their personal responsibility to at least acknowledge the need to warfare and minister in this area, and to support the specialists, it would not be so wearing on those chosen for this calling.

The counsellor who has personally benefited from the deliverance experience is usually the one who will be found conducting this type of ministry. Having experienced the benefits first hand, they are more inclined to preach, teach and operate in confidence and faith when the need arises. It is possible for the 'average' prayer minister to be confidently aggressive against deception, delusions and demonic activity when the right support system is in place within the Body of Christ.

'HANDS ON' PEOPLE

Furthermore, God never intended us to replace spiritual deliverance with a mix of medical diagnosis, Christianized philosophy, psychology, and even academic theology. We can be blinded and deafened to understanding and insight if we are not open to spiritual healing for spiritual problems (Isa 6:9-10). He calls us to literally be a 'hands on' proactive people of faith in order to fulfil the divine commission. Believers are told to aggressively engage in spiritual warfare (Eph 6:10-18, Rom 13:12).

We are even guaranteed success in this area if we humbly submit to God and resist the devil. We are urged, that if anyone is in trouble, they should pray for specific needs (Jas 4:7; 5:13-16). Prayer should come first, not as a last resort. His people perish for lack of knowledge. As Christian counsellors, we need to gather the resources and study with discerning spirits and open minds to 'show ourselves as workmen approved of God'. Preaching and teaching is an integral part of the calling and the scriptures say that false teachers will lead some people to abandon the faith, obey *lying spirits* and follow 'the teachings of demons'. We need to keep ourselves in training for a godly life free from deception and 'alert to the wiles of the devil' (1 Tim :4).

PART OF THE GREAT COMMISSION

These resources would be even more effective if preachers and teachers would educate their congregations to open the way for acceptance of deliverance ministry as a blood bought right of the Body of Christ. Jesus' parting words to believers included authorization and the promise of empowerment to drive out demons in his Name (Mk 16:17). We are to set the captives free so that they will be free indeed. Knowledge of the truth will serve to set us free. Burying our heads in the sand is not God honouring. We do not have to see a demon behind every sinful behaviour or circumstance; <u>but</u> we can be aware of the authority we have – in the Name of Jesus Christ and the power of the Blood – when one <u>is</u> discerned.

A NATURAL ROLE

It should be our natural role to move under the anointing into the supernatural realm when necessary. It can become quite natural to integrate praying in authority and power during a counselling session in order to set a brother or sister free from demonic oppression. This should happen only when the Holy Spirit opens the way via *a word of knowledge* or *discernment of spirits*. We do not necessarily seek and 'flush out' demons in order to confront them. When we have a need in this area God will meet it, giving us the wisdom and courage to handle the situation as it arises. There is certainly plenty to say in the scriptures about Jesus' first hand experiences and his methods of deliverance and *'casting out of demons'* in the role of a healer while he was present here on earth.

DELIVERANCE MINISTRY RESOURCES

To equip the saints in this type of powerful ministry, there are now some excellent teaching resources in the way of books, recordings and training seminars. Recommended reading for research purposes would be: – *Evicting Demonic Intruders* by the Gibsons, *Christian Set Yourself Free* by the Powells, *Deliverance and Inner Healing* by the Sandfords, *Pigs in the Parlor* by the Hammonds and *Shattering Your Strongholds* by Liberty Savard. For training for healing and deliverance contact two ministries of the same name: *Freedom in Christ* www.fic-australia.com and www.freedominchrist.org.au or, www.ellelministries.org for Ellel Ministries International.

The author of this text does not endorse or promote any particular ministry or practise. The resources outlined in this publication are issued as examples for information and your personal research purposes only.

AUTHOR'S TESTIMONY

To introduce the actual process of deliverance, I am able to testify that, right up to the time of polishing the final draft of this book, the Lord has been teaching me personally about the stronghold that fear has had over my life as a whole and the importance of the application of His Word to counteract this.

Over the past several years, I have done some serious studying of the scriptures. Where, once it was the meat in my sandwich, it has turned into sandwiching my 'regular' life in between studying the Word in one form or another.

I have disciplined myself: early morning trysts with televangelists, watched seminars whilst ironing (fingers as well as clothes), annoyed the neighbours with audios whilst overcooking meals, and, of course, books, books and now e-books from the internet. Researching and writing this text has contributed to the passion through searching for confirming scriptures.

No, I have not suddenly turned into a religious fanatic. To be frank, this saturation with the Word has been a matter of personal survival. I have known in the depths of my being that His Word is the answer to anything and everything. I have genuinely wanted to practise what I preach – I must admit that freedom from worry and tension has eluded me, even with expert professional help (including a very supportive GP and my clinical supervisor).

Despite maturing as a Christian in other areas, anxiety over general world suffering, along with my caseload and personal problems, has continued to plague and puzzle me. Thank God, this morning I have added another piece to my 'peace jigsaw'. Following a two-hour stint with my television faith friends, he gently popped into my head a short tailor-made sermon regarding the means for my personal deliverance from anxiety: –

PROPHETIC MESSAGE TO AUTHOR

'My child, I have not given you a spirit of fear. This fearfulness, this anxiety, does not come from me – or from you – for you are made in my image. Stand fast, and Anxiety will be forced to flee from you. This is an oppressive spirit, over which you have authority. Deal with it in My Name!

'Hope deferred makes the heart sick. Do not defer me, for I am your hope. You will continue to suffer if you do not put your hope in me. Look again at where you have had a false perception of me, as this is where you have opened the door to the enemy to invite him in. You have left me outside the door of your heart. Evict this intruder and let me, Hope, come back in.' (Prv 13:12; Ps 31: 24 & 43:5; IThes 5:8)

PROCESSING DELIVERANCE

a) ***repenting & renouncing*** carnal spirits
b) ***evicting*** (casting out) internal ruling spirits of the soul
c) ***rebuking*** (coming against) external oppressive demonic spirits

IMAGE 26

DELIVERANCE NEEDS

EXTERNAL SPIRITS
(DEMONIC OPPRESSORS)
attack from without

Sinful attitudes
choices, behaviours
open doors to

INTERNAL SPIRITS
(DEMONIC SQUATTERS)
to rule from within

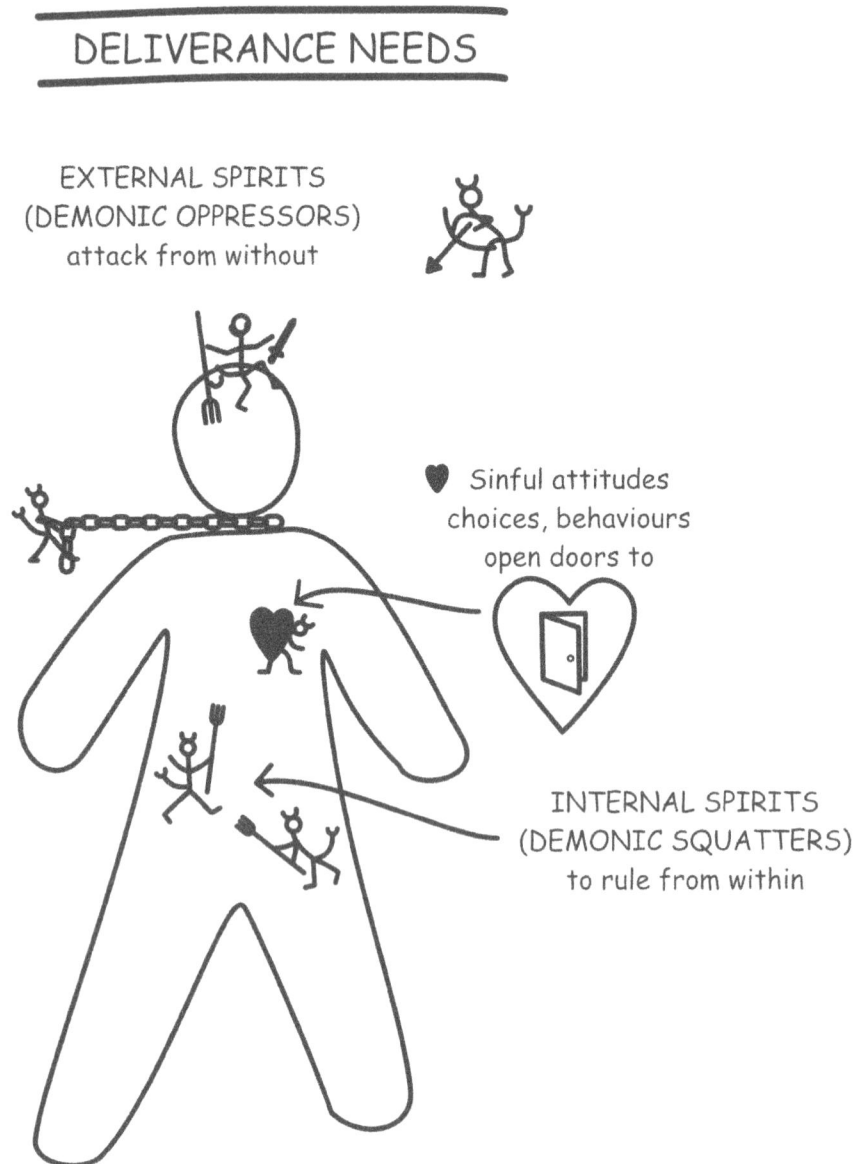

INTERNAL SPIRITS

First look for the personal issues in a client that could have opened the door to demonic activity. Then, challenge the client to co-operate in helping to drive out the *internal ruling spirits* or *demonic squatters.* Explain that effective deliverance depends on verbalization. There is power in *the spoken word* and deliverance from bondage can depend on acknowledgement of personally opening doors to these ruling spirits. Repentance and renunciation can be required. For example the following prayers could be spoken:

> *Forgive me Lord for my spirit of unforgiveness and my bitterness and resentments which have invited these demons in to rule in my life. Forgive me Lord for my spirit of doubt and unbelief; for not trusting you to look after me in all these situations; for not believing that you are perfect, good and trustworthy.*

During the processing of deliverance from internal ruling spirits, encourage the client to use their own words in prayer as much as possible. The <u>client</u> addresses and evicts the squatters. This not only empowers the believer, but places responsibility on the believer to recognise and be accountable for opening doors to these intruders. If applied, this processing usually results in a 75%-25% client-minister/s verbal participation ratio.

Your part/s in ministry will usually take the form of prompts; e.g. offering suggestions of appropriate terms such as whether to *bind or rebuke, cast out or loose, break or cut off, renounce or repent,* or to giving reminders to use the *name and blood* of Jesus Christ. Praying in *tongues* is suggested and encouraged if all the participants are open to the gifting. Invite the Holy Spirit's presence and assistance.

EXTERNAL SPIRITS

Then, take authority in *prayers of agreement* over the *external demons* or *oppressive spirits* that are coming against the client from outside forces. During this process the percentage is usually reversed, with the ministers doing most of the verbalization. The general guidelines are as follows:

a) Locate personal responsibility for open doors to demonic intruders.
b) Expel or evict internal ruling spirits or demonic squatters or intruders.
c) Deal with external attacking and oppressive spirits or demons.
d) Cut soul ties and any other form of attachments that encourage further demonic interference.
e) Negate curses and lies and substitute them with blessings and truths, making use of the Word and the Blood.

OPEN DOORS

When a person makes sinful choices, holds bad attitudes or does not behave in a God honouring manner, it will cause that person to be vulnerable to demonic interference. This vulnerability can be described as an *open door* to supernatural activity both from within and from without. These doors need to be closed to this activity.

It needs to be explained to the recipient of deliverance that the natural or carnal spirit will tend to attract and harbour spirits/demons with assignments to worsen natural conditions and heighten character traits. If he or she has chosen to be angry, bitter, resentful, unforgiving and so on, then related demons of a similar nature feel welcomed and right 'at home'. So, fail to deal with personal issues and there is the danger of unwittingly welcoming and harbouring internal ruling spirits (described as demonic *intruders* or *squatters*).

A person's natural soulish traits tend to interplay with these spiritual squatters with the possible result of attracting the attention of external demonic activity.

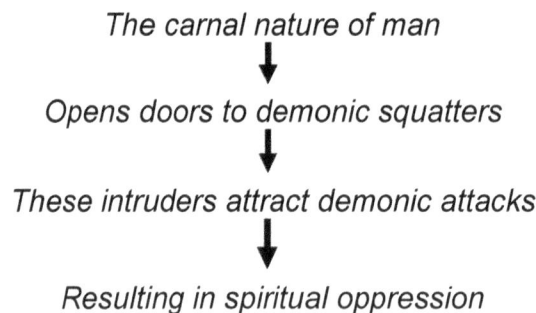

The carnal nature of man
↓
Opens doors to demonic squatters
↓
These intruders attract demonic attacks
↓
Resulting in spiritual oppression

For instance, in the example of an unforgiving, resentful and bitter person: the carnal nature has made wrong or sinful choices, which could open the door of the soul enough to allow *spirits of hatred, revenge or murder* to internalise. At the very least, this soul could be encouraging internal residing *spirits of infirmity, strife and conflict* to enter. Through holding on to certain sinful attitudes and behavioural choices, this person remains under *the yoke of bondage* (see the following *Casework: 'John D'* as a formal recording of a deliverance session).

Perhaps, this is one of the reasons we are instructed to call the elders of the church in times of illness, where they are to pray from their positions of maturity and authority – for us in our weakened state. The elders are to anoint with oil, as the *oil of the anointing breaks the yoke* (Jas 5:14-16). The family of God is our strength and mainstay. This is why we need to stay connected in peaceful and harmonious relationships within the Body of Christ (the Church) under the leadership and authority of wise pastoral carers.

GROUP STRUCTURE

Note that both internal ruling spirits and external oppressors seem to belong in 'families' in much the same way that we do. They appear to operate in a structural hierarchy system interacting in relationship with one another, with rulers exercising power over lesser demons. Deliverance specialists have done much experiential research on this topic. For example, you might like to resource from New Wine Press, *Pigs in the Parlour* (as previously mentioned) for suggested groupings for demons. However, it is strongly recommended that you conduct your own biblical studies on all aspects of deliverance to test anything you are being taught (including matter contained in this text).

AUTHORITY TO DELIVER

Jesus was given all authority in heaven and earth (Matt 28:18). He has given us the keys to the kingdom to rule here on earth (Matt 16:19). As his disciples, and as joint heirs with Christ (Rom 8:17), we are given the responsibility, power and authority to bind activity and to release the oppressed from demonic forces. We are commissioned to drive out demons by means of: –

1. The blood of the Lamb of God (Rev 12:11)
2. The Word of God (Heb 4:12)
3. The words of our mouths (Prv 18:21)
4. The name of Jesus (Jn 14:14, Rom 14:11, Phil 2:10)

In the Book of Revelation the word of our testimony speaks of how we testify to what the Word of God says that the blood of Jesus has accomplished. We make war against the enemy by driving the demons out of their hiding places and by using the Name of Jesus. We confess how the blood (a costly sacrifice) has purchased our deliverance from sin and we now boldly and confidently come into the presence of God (Rev 12:10-12, 1 Pet 18-20, Heb 9:19-22, 1Cor 1:18-31, Rom 5:1-11).

STATEMENT OF FAITH & CONFESSION OF THE POWER OF THE BLOOD

I am cleansed from all sin, pure and innocent (1Jn 1:7).
I have a clear conscience; I am guilt and shame free (Heb 9:14)
I have peace with the Father, as I am reconciled to Him (Col 1:20).
I am brought near to God, chosen and called by Him (Eph 2:13).
I am justified – made righteous through forgiveness of sins (Rom 3:24-25)
I am redeemed; no longer a slave to sin (Eph 1:7).
I am purchased and fully paid for (Acts 20:28).
I am sanctified; set apart and holy in God's eyes (Heb 13:12).
I am in covenant relationship with The Lord God Almighty (Mk 14:24).

Practicalities of Counselling: DELIVERANCE CASEWORK

> *Disclaimer: The author claims no special expertise on the subject of deliverance ministry other than the sure knowledge of her position and authority in Christ Jesus in this matter according to the scriptures. She has personally seen various miracles of emotional and spiritual healings (as well as consequent relational and physical improvements) by using the leading of the Holy Spirit to diagnose, discern and deal with these spiritual interactions. The author accepts no personal responsibility for use or misuse of these procedures as they are issued in an informative sense only on the basis of her own personal experience and research.*

There is often insufficient time or support people at hand to deal with deliverance matters if they occur spontaneously during a one-on-one counselling session. An extra appointment structured under these formal guidelines can be arranged. **Partners to help minister are strongly advised** and *intercessors* should be called upon to cover the session.

PRIOR TO DELIVERANCE SESSIONS

If possible, make full use of a *diagnostic counselling session* to explain the need for deliverance ministry by opening up the relevant scriptures and teachings them to the client. This should serve as preparation for a more specific treatment of problems at a formal deliverance session. It also allows further time for intercessory prayer, gathering a support team, and finding a suitable venue. Both you and your client should then feel more prepared and less pressured. It will also give the client opportunity for a choice to seek support from pastors, church elders or spiritual mentors.

FOLLOWING ALL SESSIONS

After all the ministry sessions have been completed, issue explanatory handouts on how to sustain deliverance and how to walk in freedom following deliverance. Make sure there is opportunity for follow-up counselling where you encourage feedback as to the client's perception of what they have experienced during the deliverance ministry.

Cognitively, there is usually very little understanding by the client of what has ensued during the deliverance process. Emotions can easily override logic and reason. Guard against confusion and fear of the exposed entities reappearing. Some debriefing is essential following the event for both the minister(s) and the delivered person (who will probably need some comfort and reassurance). The helpful graphic resource *Deliverance Needs* is a simple figurative explanation that can be used before or after a session. A sketch onto the figure will explain to the client about the demonic forces encountered during the formal session – demonstrating how his or her deliverance was processed.

SAMPLE RECORDING OF CASEWORK

The preceding graphic representation Image 26: *Deliverance Needs* is a very simplistic view to illustrate some demonic 'players' or *ruling spirits* of the spiritual realm – *the principalities and powers* interacting with each other and the client. The symbols indicate the interplay between internal and external spirits and the sinful attitudes, choices and behaviours that have allowed an open door. The figure can be drawn freehand (or purchased*) to use as a teaching resource prior to a session or as a debriefing tool afterwards.

IMPORTANT: Do not use the following counsellor resource on 'John D' to illustrate deliverance with an actual client. **Use the graphic representation: Image 26.** Also note that we are dealing here in ministry to Christian believers, who are open to deliverance ministry, rather than the unregenerate who have special needs which are not within the scope of this teaching. The following casework is fictitious and is only a sample of reporting on this complicated subject. Use the space provided at the end of this segment to practise sketching the concept.

CASEWORK FOR 'JOHN D': ABUSIVE HUSBAND

Background: The presenting problem needing deliverance attention was preceded by a long-standing situation where a husband became suspicious and jealous whenever his spouse spoke to other men. The client had been making increasingly stronger accusations over a period of three months and had been badly abusing his wife verbally. The jealousy and verbal abuse was putting an enormous strain on the marriage. The husband was otherwise a good family man and a committed Christian. They had sought couples therapy and attended marriage enrichment seminars to no avail.

Deliverance Needs: This client has sought deliverance ministry recently because his jealousy has escalated. He describes an overwhelming feeling of hatred towards a male neighbour he suspects of having an affair with his wife. Manifesting are accompanying thoughts of taking revenge and fantasising over methods of murdering both the neighbour and his spouse.

Clinical Report Following Deliverance Session:

CLIENT 'JOHN D' File #2103
CASEWORK: DEMONIC ACTIVITY
COMMENTS: Demonic intruders and attackers/oppressive spirits were discerned and dealt with as indicated on the accompanying graphic
SESSION DATE: 15/7/2000
CASE MANAGER: Marcus (Assistants: Mary & Luke)

EXTERNAL DEMONIC OPPRESSORS
Insanity
Death
Strong delusional spirit
Spirit of Antichrist
Tormenting/mocking spirit

INTERNAL RULING SPIRITS (Demonic Squatters)
Hatred, Vengeance, Violence, Murder, Rage

OPEN DOORS (Sinful Attitudes, Choices & Behaviour)
Undisciplined feelings of jealousy, lust & anger
Vindictiveness & revengeful thoughts
Possessiveness of spouse & disrespect for women in general
Verbal & emotional abuse (profanity included)

COMMENTS:
Specific generational connections are to be dealt with next session.
Investigate for freemasonry & sexual iniquity in family line.

Counsellor Exercise:

In the space provided below, reproduce a freehand drawing of the figure in Image #26. On your drawing, label John's troublesome internal and external spirits and also indicate the doors that he has opened.

Counsellor Resource: FORMAL DELIVERANCE PROCEDURES

> **IMPORTANT: check first whether the client is born again and spirit filled. The points below are for a general guideline of ministry to Christian candidates only. Pray that you will be led and guided by the Holy Spirit and that he will have his way.**

A GENERAL GUIDE FOR PRAYER MINISTRY SESSIONS: DELIVERANCE

1. Open in prayer in a sanctified building or room. Pray against interference and ask for guidance and wisdom. Ask permission to tape the session. If possible, have a supporting witness to take notes and to help with practical needs.

2. Have intercessory prayer support and pastoral support. Seek protection via the Blood of Jesus Christ over the client's family and friends, properties and possessions and your own ministry, associates, loved ones, etc.

3. Use checklists for occult involvement, curses and associated sins and notes on issues from previous counselling sessions. Encourage acknowledgment and confession of such.

4. Dealing only with issues which have been discerned, proceed with the client's personal deliverance for ruling spirits and associated sins and iniquities. Note that a client can stand on behalf of those in the family line to ask for mercy and forgiveness for both living and deceased members. Parents/guardians can act on behalf of children.
   a) For self-imposed curses confess, repent and renounce.
   b) Negate word curses and other curses made on client. Apply blessings.
   c) For unbelievers in association with the client, bind spirits of lying, deception, control, and Antichrist. Pray the person will choose Jesus Christ as his or her *personal lord and saviour.*
   d) For believers who are backsliders, and for uncommitted Christians, bind the spirits discerned. Bring deliverance candidates to repentance before moving on. Take time over this so that there is full understanding and genuine repentance.

5. Pray appropriate forgiveness (and lack of forgiveness) prayers.

6. Call out names and activities of ruling spirits/demons as revealed by the Holy Spirit and deal with them **only as instructed by The Holy Spirit.** For example: evict, call out, cast out, name, cover, bind, or cut off. Note that there are many excellent resource books available on the subject but it is advisable to study the scriptures as to the actual methods used by Jesus himself.

7. Deal with any negative soul ties. These are spiritual or emotional bonds between individuals which are not naturally healthy, or spiritually, are not of God.

8. Pray for protection from any spiritual backlash or retaliation.
   - nestle client under the Father's wings
   - hide in cleft of rock (Jesus Christ)
   - ask Him to station angels all about
   - fill client with blessings and ask for infilling of the Holy Spirit
   - ask for anointing of peace
2. Praise and worship for the finished work in Christ Jesus.
3. Take communion if appropriate, including thanksgiving prayer.
4. Issue the following handouts:
   - copies of personal prophecies
   - significant scriptures
   - maintenance of deliverance
   - information on strongholds and mindsets

INFORMAL DELIVERANCE

For informal deliverance occurrences (that is, 'informal' meaning when a need arises during a normal one-on-one counselling session) adapt the above points under the Holy Spirit's leading and call on the covering of the blood of Jesus.

Preferably, refer on for formal deliverance to a respected deliverance ministry or arrange with your own support team for another session at a later date. In the meantime, educate the client as to what will take place during a formal session of deliverance.

Ideally, do not attempt a formal deliverance session unless there is approval from the client's pastor and the pastors of any other counsellors involved. If possible, have your own pastor's co-operation and involvement. Have intercessors praying support and cover over you. Have material, physical presence of supporters in case of manifestations or resistance from the client.

If there are any *manifestations* of concern, bind the spirit of control and command it to cease activity in Jesus' Name. Pray peace and self-control on the client. If necessary, ask the client to renounce co-operation with controlling spirits. Have workplace health and safety measures in place in case of any violent manifestations.

> **Disclaimer: The author takes no personal responsibility for use or misuse of these procedures as they are issued in an informative sense only on the basis of her own personal experience and research.**

COUNSELLOR TESTIMONY: The Apprentice Deliverer

The client opened the session with the following: 'Ya gotta laugh or you'll cry. I'll tell you a good one. What do you call a short fortune-teller who has just escaped from prison? Can't guess? A small medium at large! Here's another word of wisdom. If you don't pay your exorcist you can get repossessed. I'm sure glad you guys don't charge anything!'

He chuckled to himself, 'Sorry about that. I get nervous and I start telling jokes. Like a will – it's a dead giveaway. Do you like that one? I think I made that one up myself. Or did I hear it at the club? When you hear my jokes you can tell I'm either scared or real nervous about something. The thought of getting delivered from my demons scares me somethin' terrible. But I want to be normal. I want to have a normal life. I'm not going to let my nerves get in the way. I'm here now guys (and ma'm). God Almighty, go ahead will ya!'

And from that unusual beginning we, as a ministry team, went into opening up a Pandora's Box… If I had known the end from the beginning I don't know whether I would have got myself into such an intense session as a beginner. I was the only woman on the ministry team who volunteered to take the notes. The other women stayed in the safety of the intercessors' prayer room. Three hours later, I would come in to join them, shaking and in need of prayer myself.

Even though I had done a lot of training and mock up sessions, I had no idea what it would be like in real life to be part of a deliverance session. It was an experience of a lifetime. It was challenging and different and oh so fulfilling to be used of the Lord. To see someone set free like that was so exciting!

As I said, I was there to take notes, but I was eventually called on to assist, as the manifestations were so strong it needed the three of us to do our bit for this poor man. Praise God, he stuck it out and we hung in there too! I cannot describe the pain he seemed to be experiencing.

But, enough said; we are taught that all that is said and done in the ministry room is to be kept to ourselves. I understand now about the strict need for confidentiality. Who would believe what I saw if I tried to describe it anyway?

I am definitely being called to this kind of ministry and I will certainly be on call if they have need of me again. I have been a Christian counsellor for 10 years now, and this is the area in which I want to specialise. That poor, poor man… He is so blessed to be free of all that. How on earth did he find the will to go on…?

CHAPTER TWENTY ONE

FAMILY PROBLEMS

The term 'family' conjures up a different picture to each of us. As individual members of the *family of God,* and in our corporate role as the *Bride of Christ,* we strive to incorporate all the fundamentals of family life into the society we call the *Church.* Our interpretation of 'family' will depend on many things: our childhood upbringing, our current and past experiences with relationships, our cultural mores and religious affiliations, and our personal values and ethics. This chapter covers only a few aspects of what makes and influences families.

- A testimony of family deliverance (fictitious)
- Use of the *Genogram* to trace the fruits & roots of the family tree
- Specific influences down the family line (such as Freemasonry)
- Teachings on *generational connections, iniquities* and family *curses*
- A special segment on children's needs and ministry specialization (also refer to Appendix I)

Study Notes

CLIENT TESTIMONIAL: Family Problems – Self-Harming

Until last week, I saw my life as one big disaster after another. Everything bad always seemed to happen to me, so that I was forever anxious about what was going to happen next. It set up these feelings in me, which I had to fight to take control over.

But it was my eighteenth birthday two weeks ago and things have changed big time. Before then, I can't remember ever feeling free of those awful feelings.

Even as a little girl, I sort of shut down and didn't want to face the world. It was kind of like moving in a greyish fog all the time – just depending on my instincts because my brain just wouldn't work. I didn't want to think, because the thoughts brought on the feelings.

School was not a good place for me. I never did well at school, except for English Literature. I was always reading, as long as it was fantasy and I didn't have to read too much in one go. I remember, as a small child in the playground, just watching, watching and praying no one would notice me. But there is no place to hide in a bitumen playground.

The others learnt to leave me alone. They lost their curiosity about why I wouldn't join in and why I always wore black when we had uniform free days. Then there were the curious looks the teachers on playground duty gave you, and their offers of kindness. I didn't want the attention. I just wanted life to be over. I was sorry I was ever born. I wanted to curl up and pretend life didn't exist. I wanted to die and get my life over.

It is horrible when you are afraid all the time. Your stomach churns, you sweat, your heart feels like it is going to burst out of your chest, you feel like crying but you can't. You feel you want to speak but there are no words. If you don't shut down your thoughts, then the emotions that feed on the thoughts take over, and then the fear pounces on you and eats up the thoughts. That's why you have to stop the thoughts. That's why I cut myself. The physical pain is better. It takes your mind off things.

When I was younger, I learnt to play a game of turning inside myself. It was easier in the classroom, better than outside with kids everywhere. The teachers let me alone at my desk with my work and said I was a pleasure to teach. At home the family left me alone with my books. They said I was shy to visitors. They said this to each other a lot.

But I knew I wasn't shy. It was that I wanted to shut down to escape the feelings. At school, it was agony. I had nowhere to hide but inside myself. At home, it was alright as long as I didn't sleep too much. The nightmares have always shared my bed. I sleep on the floor when I can. I cut.

I am not a child any longer and my parents can see that it is not just shyness. They didn't know I was cutting. It started when I was living away from home for twelve months. They decided I needed some serious help when I shut myself away and wouldn't take off my headset. I had taken to listening to some pretty heavy music. I know I was freaking them out. So they sent me to stay interstate with Lucy and Auntie Liz. It didn't help. The cutting helped.

The parents had been to some seminars at some church while I was away. Apparently, these talks were about how we all needed delivering from stuff. They wanted to tell me all the things they had learnt. I didn't know what they were on about. They seemed pleased and excited about it all. So I humoured them and pretended I was listening.

Mum was saying that my Pop's involvement with the Masonic Order, plus her mother's habit of reading the star signs opened up our family to demonic activity (or something). I thought, 'She's finally lost it! She's going crazy!' Dad seemed to understand and to agree with what she was on about. That was even crazier! They never agree on anything.

They said stuff like they needed to renounce and repent for our family's involvement. It was all too hard for me to understand. I never read star signs. I was a Christian when I was little but I'm not sure what I am into now. I'm not into any of that witchcraft, not even drugs or the sex scene. They were so keen to tell me all about it. I hope I said yes and no in the right places. I went inside myself as usual. They were freaking me out!

I've let them talk me into going along to a prayer person with them. I didn't think that tagging along with them for some prayer could do much harm. I thought, 'I can always switch off. I'm good at it now, switching off and blanking out'.

One week later.

Wow! I now know what 'a prayer for deliverance' is! After watching what those prayer people did and said with my parents, they turned to me and all hell broke loose! I mean, with the mum and dad they were all peaceful and kind; but when it was my turn – well, wow!

The praying people were a couple, husband and wife I think, and I think that there was at least another one, maybe two or three others coming and going from the room next door to ours. When the couple saw me looking they said that the ones next door were their intercessors. I just arched my eyebrows –

whatever that means I thought. They seemed to be muttering and going on, but not so that I could understand what they were saying.

I was getting so bored that, after an hour, I nearly fell asleep. They got mum, and then dad, and they had them read through this list. Mum and dad would stop at one of the words on the list and go through this, 'I repent and renounce my involvement and my family's involvement in' such and such. They must have said this about twenty times each. They had a different list each. They went on and on. Apparently that had a lot to work on.

I glanced over on dad's list and saw words like 'occult', 'divination' and 'séance'. I knew what that one meant as I'd been to a séance with my cousin Lucy and her friend back when we were about 10. It was just a game. We were only kids. We even used a Ouija board. I don't remember much about it. I got bored with that too. I ended up yawning and Lucy said if I wasn't going to be any fun then I should leave. So I did.

But, I will never forget last week in that prayer session when they turned to me after finishing with mum and dad. As I said to Lucy last night, there were some things that happened there that I am just too freaked out yet to talk about. All I know is that I came out a different person to the one I was when I went in.

My brain seems to have been unrusted, or derusted, or whatever the word is. The fog has lifted. It is like I am seeing colours and all sorts of things for the first time. My stomach isn't giving me any more trouble. And I don't feel the need to cut. I hope that my arms heal up quickly because I'm not into these black clothes with the long sleeves any more. Mum wants to buy me some dresses and take me to her hairdresser.

And you know, I think I actually feel happy. It is a bit hard to describe, but I know I like how I feel. I don't feel bored any more and I don't act like a zombie all the time. I don't understand what went on in that room, but mum and dad have promised that we will have some good long talks about all this – when I'm ready. I think they want to talk about God and I think I'm ready for that.

Except where the author recounts her personal testimony, all characters and casework are fictitious representations and any similarities to real persons or cases are non-intentional and purely coincidental.

THE FAMILY OF GOD & THE FATHER'S HOUSE

AUTHOR'S TESTIMONY

We cannot put the responsibility of all our misfortunes on our forefathers. Each child of God has personal accountability for the choices we make. The Lord revealed to me once in a vision as to how I had dishonoured him by rejecting him as my Father. I was able to see that I was withholding my heart from him. I had put up a defensive wall of my own making and was keeping him out. My position should have been safe, within a fortress erected fully by him, but I had placed myself outside of his protection.

I needed to repent of trying to defend and protect myself from the hurts of this world from within a fortress of my own making. I needed to take my man-made walls down and allow God the Father to protect me from further hurt. I would have been safe from attacks while positioned within my father's House looking out the window at the enemy (Jer 17:5-6). Instead, I had felt at home living as king of my own castle of self-deception. The enemy was actually attacking me from within my self-erected fortress.

Through revelation from his Word, I came to see how delusions and deceptions enter into our lives through the lies we choose to believe about our creator. Through studying his laws, I came to realise that freedom comes from demolishing the walls that we have personally constructed, those which prevent us from receiving blessings from God (see teaching on Strongholds & Mindsets, Chapter 15). Through reaching out to help others through the ministry of prayer, I began to practise the messages I was preaching, and I found personal peace, rest from the struggles of life, joy and freedom.

CHILDREN OF GOD

Everything in life seems be a struggle: whether it involves parenthood, earning a living, maintaining relationships, or achieving our goals and dreams. However, our true enemy needs to be recognised. Our struggle should not be with our creator but with Satan, the father of lies. We wrestle with *principalities and powers* – demonic agents of the curse on mankind (Eph 6:6-10, Matt 12:43-44).

God's purpose is to bless and 'do good' towards his children (Gen 12:3). Lack of trust in that statement, along with our lack of knowledge about our true identity in him, leaves us without protective walls and covering, and thereby open to deception and attacks from the enemy. Having believed lies about God and lies about ourselves, we struggle to defend our position. We continue to make wrong choices based on false beliefs, and these choices result in curses rather than in blessings (Deut 30:19-20).

Adam and Eve divorced God as father and adopted Satan, the father of lies, as lord of their lives. The first man and woman (family unit) virtually moved house and introduced lies and deception into the family line (see Acts 16: 29-33 where the word 'house' denotes a family).

However, the good news is: – even though one man (Adam) sinned and 'moved house', the One (Jesus Christ) redeemed us back from the curse by becoming a curse for us (Prv 26:2, Deut 27:15-26). He accepted the punishment for our disobedience and fulfilled the requirements of the Law (Matt 5:17-19). As the Father's *prodigal children* we are able to move back home and find our place, as blessings come by remaining within the household of faith and being part of the family of God (Deut 28).

OUR MESSAGE OF HOPE AS COUNSELLORS

The good news is that God is in *the business of blessing*. As prayer ministers, we have the privilege of being part of his kingdom business plan, which is to prosper and increase his people from generation to generation. Our message of hope to our client is to preach this good news. As counsellors we can offer the salvation message by explaining the laws of God. Whereas rejection of his ways contributes to the destruction of families and individuals; obedience builds loving relationships.

We can deliver the certainty of hope that God has prepared a way out from struggling to exist under the curse. Jesus is The Way, The Truth, and The Life. Jesus was wounded for our transgressions and bruised for our iniquities. He struggled with every temptation known to man, won, and still took our (deserved) place on the cross. Because of that all-encompassing loving sacrifice, we are acceptable to the Father. Rejection of his children is not part of the Father's nature. He rejects sin, but he separates us from that sin and accepts all who will come to him via the cross. No matter how serious our sin, no matter how strong our iniquities, he is waiting with open arms to reconcile with us.

Through preaching the Word of God through prayer ministry, we can go about the Father's business, which leads to life and freedom. As Christian counsellors we can choose to act as an agent of blessing from within the family business of raising blessed families.

MANKIND'S FAMILY RECORD

Mankind's historical record is not good. As his people, we were called 'to go forth and multiply'. This has always been our purpose and destiny. However, we have generally opposed his plan throughout history by rejecting our children. They have been considered an intrusion, not welcome, not important, a bother, a burden, an inconvenience, and even a curse. Parents, at best, withhold blessings and, at worst, curse blatantly. Our children are being sold, given away, surrendered to others through adoptions, or are taken away into foster care. Step-parents or grandparents are forced into unwanted roles of 'recycled parents' (some of whom cannot hide the resentment at times) thus the pattern of rejection is reinforced. Today, countless little lives are disposed of before birthing – the ultimate rejection – a 'disposable generation'. But we have only to refer to the Old Testament to see that this patterning is not new; God's people were reported to be as stubborn as their ancestors – even to the point of burning their own children. Man's heart is certainly wicked (2 Kings 17:14).

As present day counsellors, we will experience many things we wish we had never seen nor heard; some things so horrific that we remain stunned. We wonder how we can go on believing that we were actually made in the image of a God who is a holy, pure and magnificent being! But, we continue to minister and we live on in the hope that, in compassionate ministry and sacrificial service, we <u>can</u> personally make a difference through impartation of God's comfort and hope to a lost and sin-filled world. Through one on one education, or to couples and families, and through preaching to communities and nations, we seek to reconcile the family of God to their Maker.

The church today is once again being warned as in biblical days (2Kings 18). Will we corporately heed the warning? Will we have the opportunity to pray as the psalmist did, *'Lord give us as much happiness as we have had misery'*? Can we help stem the tide of rebellion and rejection? Can we pray passionately that he bless the family line from hereon in – because we personally have been found with true, obedient hearts and minds, bound tightly to the mind of Christ (Ps 90)?

OUR FUTURE, OUR HOPE, OUR CHOICE

We are not 'mistakes' born to be rejected and abandoned; we are each his wanted, planned child... Christ died for <u>all</u> mankind – especially for believers (1Tim 4:10) and it is a personal choice to reject and turn away from that birthright of calling him 'Father'. Our blessed Father has conceived each precious individual in love, with the divine purpose of blessing, prospering and multiplying us. We were born to be blessed and fruitful in the divine plan of living eternally as one very large happy family. As Christian counsellors, it is our mission to help clarify and emphasize that birthright and to restore hope to his people.

The next segment will help to explain this mission more clearly; hopefully, it will provide the resources to explain more fully the aims of prayer ministry.

Related graphics available are: *'Is Your House in Order?'*, *'Deliverance Needs'*, and *'Sins and Iniquities Flowchart'*. The companion book: *'So You Want To Be A Christian Counsellor – Resources Handbook'* – is available from: www.prayercounsel.com for photocopying purposes.

IMPORTANT: The example chosen in this image is the sin of adultery because it is of such spiritual significance. The husband and wife covenant symbolises the role the Church has as the Bride of Christ. The natural sin of adultery represents the symbolic act of breaking our covenant with God to go after other gods (Ex 23:20-33; Hosea).

IMAGE 27

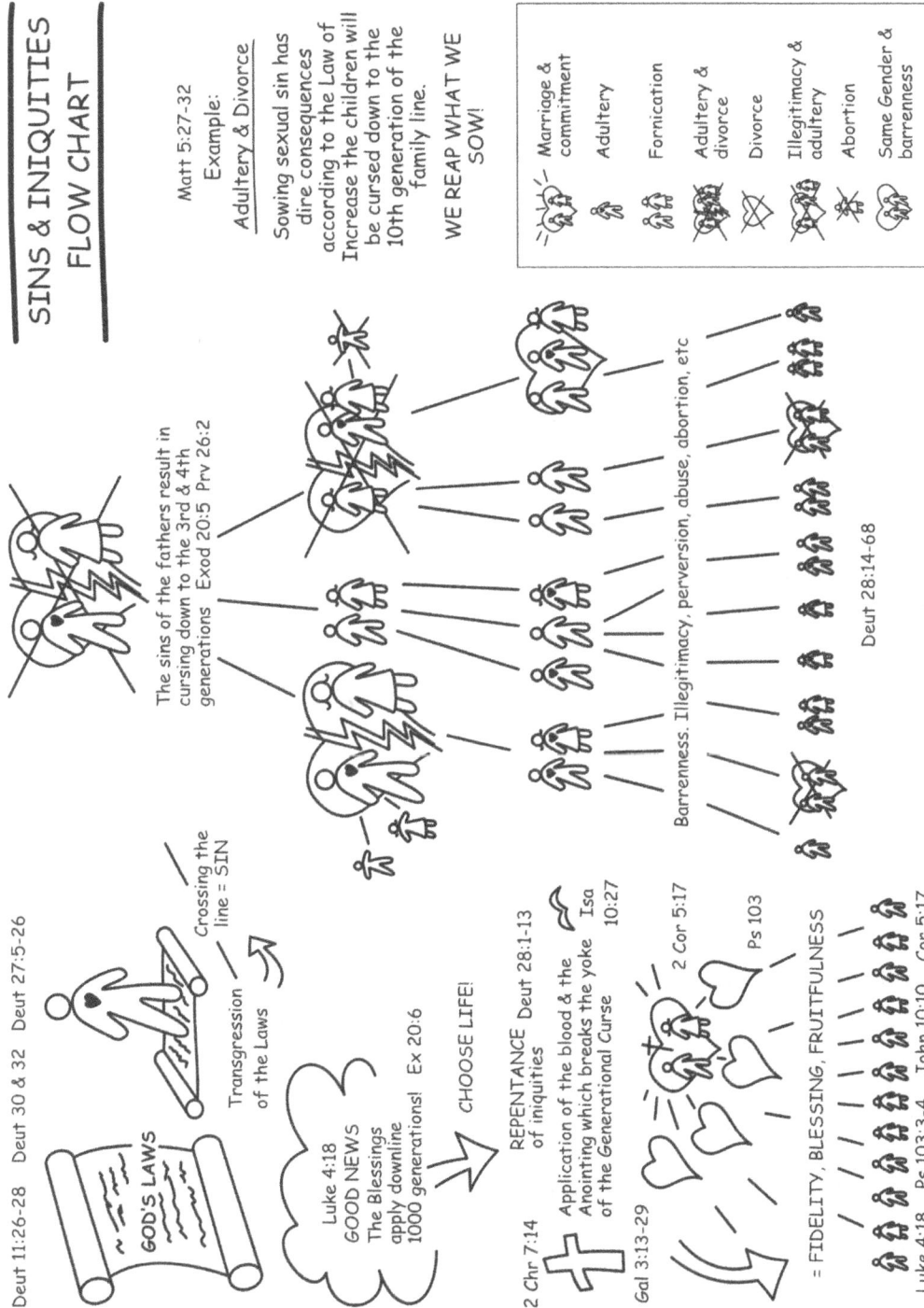

SINS & INIQUITIES FLOW CHART

Matt 5:27-32
Example:
Adultery & Divorce

Sowing sexual sin has dire consequences according to the Law of Increase the children will be cursed down to the 10th generation of the family line.

WE REAP WHAT WE SOW!

Marriage & commitment
Adultery
Fornication
Adultery & divorce
Divorce
Illegitimacy & adultery
Abortion
Same Gender & barrenness

The sins of the fathers result in cursing down to the 3rd & 4th generations Exod 20:5 Prv 26:2

Barrenness. Illegitimacy, perversion, abuse, abortion, etc
Deut 28:14-68

Deut 11:26-28   Deut 30 & 32   Deut 27:5-26

GOD'S LAWS

Crossing the line = SIN

Transgression of the Laws

Luke 4:18
GOOD NEWS
The Blessings apply downline 1000 generations! Ex 20:6

CHOOSE LIFE!

REPENTANCE Deut 28:1-13 of iniquities

2 Chr 7:14

Application of the blood & the Anointing which breaks the yoke of the Generational Curse   Isa 10:27

Gal 3:13-29

2 Cor 5:17

Ps 103

= FIDELITY, BLESSING, FRUITFULNESS

Luke 4:18   Ps 103:3-4   John 10:10   Cor 5:17

Client Handout: GENERATIONAL CONNECTIONS

Dear Client,

*At this stage of your journey, we will be investigating the connection your family's history could have to the personal presenting problems or current issues you have brought to counselling. We will make use of the **genogram** (map of the family tree) in order to trace back to where particular sins generated certain iniquities (weaknesses) in the family line (Ex 20:5). Before we fill out your personal and family details, here is some background information.*

In biblical times, there were community laws established to protect the people (Deut 6:25 and refer to chapters 21-23 for specific laws). Under these community laws, there were three types of sins, which were considered capital offences: *idolatry, sexual sins and rebellion* (towards parents). These three incurred more severe penalties than the others did because these sinful practices resulted in curses on the family line as far down as to the 10th generation in comparison to the usual 3rd or 4th generation (Deut 23:2; Ex 20:5). A rebellious son or immoral woman was stoned to death under Mosaic Law. The death penalty was due to the serious consequences of releasing *curses* into the community or family line (Matt 5:27-32, Prv 26:2, Deut 21:18-21 & 22:21-23).

But, take heart; there is good news to follow. God sent his Word to heal us (Ps 107:20, Isa 53:1-10, Rom 8:1-11). The fruit of the *tree of life* as described in Genesis symbolizes God's plan of redemption. The root of the tree of life represents the sovereignty of God which leads to healing and restoration of His original intent for us. We are his offspring, the fruit of his love; rooted and grounded (firmly established) in his love; in our place in the Father's heart (Eph 3:17). God's grace towards us is the key to overcoming sinful generational consequences. His love endures to thousands of generations (Rev 21-22, Ex 20:6, Lk 4:18).

LAWS OF SOWING & REAPING, INCREASE & MULTIPLICATION

Laws were originally designed by the Creator to increase blessings not curses. We have a good God, who is slow to anger and full of mercy and grace. However, man has sown *disrespect for divine authority* and reaped a world system of corruption and lawlessness. If we had followed our Maker's instructions, our world would be a far different place (Gen 3).

Our Creator instigated the natural laws of increase & multiplication for mankind's benefit. From one grain of wheat many ears of seed result. These seeds can be re-sown to multiply again. However, the concept has parallel spiritual applications. The corrupt seed of dishonour was sown in the beautiful Garden of Eden, where it took root in the poisonous soil of rebellion and grew through the ages providing a harvest of death and destruction.

The spiritual laws of increase and multiplication made the sacrifice of God's own Son a necessary provision. Jesus Christ came to fulfil the Law, aborting the inevitable harvest by casting his own seed into the ground and watering it with his blood so that we might harvest life everlasting (Gal 3).

GENERATIONAL INIQUITIES (Deut 28:14-68*)

Generational iniquities are *practised sins* or inherent weaknesses in the family line, which can become entrenched and can result in generational curses. One person might practise a certain sin until it becomes a lifestyle. This sin becomes a behavioural weakness. That particular behaviour allows a foothold for Satan to gain control of a person's life. It allows entry through *an open door* into the family line. The tendency towards this behaviour can be passed down to future generations in what could be called *'spiritual DNA'*.

However, Jesus was wounded for each and every transgression. He was wounded for the sins we have committed in the past and for all sins we will ever commit. He was *wounded* for our transgressions; yet He was *bruised* for our iniquities. Physically, a wound will be apparent as a scratch, cut or a hole; however, a bruise will not be obvious at first and the damage takes a while to appear on the surface. Such are iniquities – deep bruises in the Body of Christ – the Church. When one part suffers – all suffer.

THE GENOGRAM

As mentioned, generational iniquities can be detected by the use of a counselling chart called the g*e*nogram to record the *family tree* and to trace the 'roots' and the poisons feeding into these roots . Just as a medical doctor would search for a family history of cancer or heart disease by asking you questions for his records, prayer ministers in the role of spiritual 'doctors' study a family history for repetitive weaknesses, sins, habits and failures. We are looking for a *genetic spiritual predisposition or tendency* rather than a physiological one. Sometimes, we will be looking for signs of certain agents or *spirits* who are disrupting the client and his/her family in a similar way e.g. a *spirit of strife* seems to 'run in the family'.

RULING HOUSEHOLD SPIRITS

Some evil spirits could be described as *ruling spirits* in the household and in the family line. Using the example of the 'spirit of strife', this spirit, and those associated with it, could be responsible for the arguing, backbiting, suspicion and misunderstandings, which are common in some households. These spirits are familiar with the family's faults and vulnerabilities (spiritual DNA). Gaining access to certain areas of weakness, these spirits become proficient in attacking and tempting members in similar ways generation after generation.

One could be a 'born again' committed Christian, cleansed of iniquities and walking in the Spirit, and yet one's children could show similar tendencies toward certain sins. Offspring will need to find personal cleansing and could need family curses over them as individuals broken in order to withstand the *strongman* (Matt 12:29; 43-45). It is as if there is a fault line (as in an earthquake prone area) under the 'house' or household and, conditions being right, the crack opens to engulf yet another family member. For instance, addictive behaviours can subsequently increase in seriousness from parents to children and their offspring. In these and other examples, the law of increase and multiplication comes into play, resulting in *a curse* on the family line.

To give a particular dramatic illustration of progression in the family line: an inherent weakness manifests originally in a grandfather who developed a taste for sexual perversion. Perversion, having its seed in lust and voyeuristic behaviours, increases in strength in his children. His three sons each molest young women upon reaching their mid-teens. This eventually results in the eldest sibling committing rape. The son of the rapist (and grandson of the voyeur) repeats the inherited lustful behaviours. Rape, being an act of violence, as well as a sexual sin, leads to the death of one of his victims. This murder goes undetected. Psychopathic behaviour manifests, leading to a series of brutal killings involving rape and torture. A 'curse' has been placed on the family tree.

GENERATIONAL CURSES

A generational curse results from an *uncleansed iniquity* that increases in strength from generation to generation (Deut 11:26-28). Iniquities need to be repented of, renounced (rejected), the roots cleansed and the curse removed from the family tree. Rebellion against God's laws needs to be faced and dealt with corporately (Jer 14:20). There has to be a beginning somewhere. Release can be brought about by the attitude of an individual. One person can even plead on behalf of a nation (Dan 9:4-5). From the closet of private prayer it can extend into seeking help through prayer ministry on behalf of the family line. We cannot deal with what we do not acknowledge.

PERSONAL ACCOUNTABILITY

Our hearts and our hands need to be clean before God to represent our family line. Attitudes are the raw materials of the counsellor's domain (Matt 5:21-25, 2Tim 2:25-26).). Negative attitudes and behavioural tendencies provide a foothold for Satan to climb into a client's life, thereby, an entrance into the family (including the church family). We are indeed *corporate beings* – sharers as a group. What one does, affects the whole. A sinful tendency can be passed down through spiritual DNA to future generations – becoming a fully blown *generational curse* in the family line – as illustrated with our dramatic example previously.

Generational blessings result from contrite hearts and humble attitudes (2Chr 7:14, Prv 28:13, 1Jn 1:9). As did prophets of old, we can also repent and renounce on behalf of our family line. We can open the door for future generations to be under the blessings of God. Jesus has made the provision; we need only to apply our faith in a good god – both individually and corporately – so that our families will not continue to languish, struggle, and perish without receiving our inheritance.

PERSONAL RESPONSIBILITY

By God's mercy and grace, it only takes one Christian couple, or a single person, to apply the blood – to use the anointing to break the back of a generational problem. Thereafter, a new family bloodline of victory and blessings can branch out and flourish (Dan 11:32, Cor 2:14). The Word says that Jesus came so that you, and your *household* (family line), may be saved. Corporate redemption can be applied for the negative aspects of sowing and reaping and the laws of increase. The effects of familiar spirits at work, and generational connections iniquities and curses can be negated in the household of faith. We each, and all, may be saved, cleansed, redeemed, restored, and set free – by faith in the sacrifice made by our saviour, Christ Jesus. The sacrifice has already been made; there is only the need to acknowledge that it is indeed *a finished work.*

Counsellor Resource: APPLICATION OF THE GENOGRAM

The genogram is a practical tool for recording the family tree and its fruit (refer to *Fruits, Roots & Poisons*). We are seeking to uncover the family's *poisoned root system*, discover *generational connections* and to expose *family curses*. In order to help and heal our client, we will be looking for the following patterns in the family history:

1. failure to fruit
2. lack of maturation of fruit
3. death and disease
4. good fruits which have been *spoiled* (i.e. blessings aborted, forfeited, lost, stolen or destroyed)

A genogram can be used in a spiritual application to trace the sins, habits, failures, weaknesses and recurring problems of parents, siblings, aunts and uncles; and both maternal and paternal grandparents and great grandparents. If there is little knowledge available outside the immediate family, the client might be able to gather information from extended family, old neighbours, or friends of the family.

SPECIAL CONSIDERATIONS

This method of recording might not be viable for someone *adopted*, or of *illegitimate issue*, because the person will possess little, if any, knowledge of his or her heritage. Occasionally inexplicable problems will indicate historical sowing and reaping. Prayer can cover a *general cleansing* of the family line if the history is unknown. Special consideration should be given for *abandonment* and *rejection issues* with adoption and illegitimacy. Also note *black sheep, scapegoats* or *sacrificial lambs* in the family line, as these are sometimes indicators of generational problems.

ROOT SYSTEMS & BAD FRUIT

Remember that, in looking at fruit to root patterns, we are observing the *law of sowing and reaping* as well as the *law of increase and multiplication*. Of course, we do not go blundering into outright diagnosis of *iniquities* (family weaknesses). Instead, we probe gently and sensitively, led by the Holy Spirit, making mental notes rather than voicing personal opinions and guesswork.

When uncovering the root system of the family tree, we are looking for recurrences of bad fruit such as: *mental illness, divorce, witchcraft, immorality, premature deaths* and *tragedies* (including suicides). We will especially want to reveal involvement with a *Masonic Order* as this brings quite specific and lethal curses on a family line (refer to *The Inheritance of Freemasonry* following*). Broken relationships* are another important area, also, anything to do with childbirth and fertility such as: – *miscarriages, abortions, abandonment and barrenness.*

Practicalities: INTRODUCING GENOGRAMS TO THE CLIENT

Explain to your client that a **genogram** is simply a record of the 'family tree' primarily used by a counsellor to chart and study the client's *life story*. In Christian counselling, it can also be used to trace the presence of *sins, habits or problem areas*. Patterns of repeated failure and spoiled fruit in the family tree are observed in the process.

As an introduction to using this tool ask your client the following question:

What problems tend to repeatedly crop up in your family history?

Explain that we are looking for possible generational connections where a certain type of behaviour or thought pattern has developed into a specific family weakness (see resources on *Sins & Iniquities* and *Generational Connections*). Advise that we will then be able to do a test to deal specifically with certain problems (see *Test for Generational Curses* which follows).

Emphasize that our purpose is not to judge and condemn family members, but to recognise problem areas in the client's own life at present. Ask if they are willing and able to make a list of some family information first, as this can useful as a basis to fill in this *flow chart* called 'a genogram'.

Instruct the client in the following way by saying:

'Against the following family members (including yourself) record any repetitive sins, bad habits, failures or weaknesses that you know of, such as: – anger problems or a bad temper, alcohol or other forms of addiction, abuse, an overly critical nature, mental health problems, trouble with the police and so on.' Sample findings: –

>   father – verbally abusive, violent temper
>   mother – timid, depressed, anxious, always ill
>   paternal grandfather (father's father) – violent, mentally ill, alcoholic
>   paternal grandmother (father's mother) – withdrawn, very shy
>   maternal grandfather (mother's father) – sexual deviant
>   maternal grandmother (mother's mother) – controlling, overly strict'

If the client finds this difficult to do, then you might allot the exercise for homework. You could suggest they might tactfully question family members or friends of the family who know more about the family history. If the client is adopted or does not know anything about their natural heritage, advise that personal characteristics or traits causing problems in the present could be connected to the sins of natural forefathers, or, in the case of adoptees, through spiritual connection to the adoptive family's heritage. There also might be connections via significant others such as an ex-spouse or present partner.

IMAGE 28

FAMILY GENOGRAM   **Client Name:**

Date:

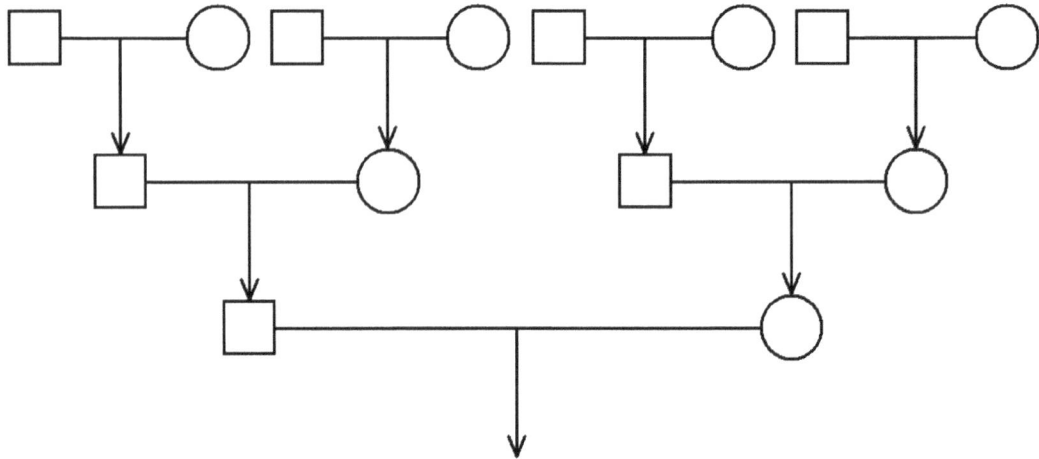

Parental Lineage	Problems - Comments	Children
☐ Male ◯ Female	☐ Abuse	⟶ Issue
☐—◯ Married	☐ Accidents	
☐WW◯ Living Together	☐ Addictions	⥽S⟶ Stillborn
☐S◯ Separated	☐ Health Problems	
	☐ Witchcraft, Occult	⥽A⟶ Aborted
☐//◯ Divorced	☐ Masonic, etc.	
☒—☒ Deceased	☐ Broken Relationships	—Ⓐ⟶ Adopted
	☐ Mental Illnesses	
☐? ⦸? Unknown	☐ Cognitive Problems	Sibling Position
	☐ Criminal Activity	1, 2, etc. ⟶
	☐ Other	

This chart with the instructions and permission for use are available for downloading by contacting the designer Elvira Burkwood. Email: elvie@prayercounsel.com

INSTRUCTIONS FOR USE OF THE GENOGRAM

In order to study and become familiar with the use of the genogram, practise by interviewing your family members and friends and recording the details of their family trees freehand, using the chart as a guide.

Beginning at the top of a page, fill in your client's name and the session date.

Go to the bottom of the page. Referring to the legend, familiarize yourself and your client with the symbols and criteria in the three columns headed: *Parental Lineage, Problems & Comments,* and *Children.*

Begin to fill out the chart above the legend. Fill in the client's Christian name at the base of the chart under the central arrow. Enclose the name in a circle if the client is female, or a square for a male. complete the family tree with as many details as possible using symbols and criteria from the columns in the legend.

Travelling upwards, from the centre of the chart, the client's father's Christian name goes in the square on the left and mother's first name belongs in the circle on the right. Grandparents are placed above the parents' names, then great-grandparents where possible above these. (Separate family trees can be made up if the client has had two or more sets of parents due to death, divorce or infidelity).

Travelling downwards from the inserted client's name, in like manner fill out the current generation and their offspring. Relationship partners go to the left or right of the client's square/circle and are connected by a freehand line. The client's siblings are recorded in birth order – by dropping lines down from the line provided – connecting the client's parents together. Highlight repetitive indicators of *bad or spoiled fruit* on the family tree e.g. alcoholism/anger/infidelity/cancer/divorce etc.

Match the problems to the checklist (in the middle column of the genogram legend) to the fruits on recorded on the tree. Use the checked items as a basis for discussion and prayer ministry.

RELATED RESOURCES: Follow through with the use of the *Test for Generational Curses* on the next page and, if appropriate, issue the discourse on *The Inheritance of Freemasonry* to accompany the test. Image 27, *Sins & Iniquities* can also be used to explain the serious repercussions if the issues of *adultery and divorce* have been introduced into the family lineage. For other relevant teachings refer to Image 11, with the table of *Sowing & Reaping (In Relationships)* and Image 25, *The Diseased Apple Tree.*

Client Handout: TO TEST FOR GENERATIONAL CURSES

Do you and your family, past and/or present, have a pattern of: –

❑ Failure in business, relationships, finances etc?

❑ Untimely deaths, suicides, or tragedies?

❑ Accidents, especially unusual ones?

❑ Abuse – physical, emotional, mental, spiritual or sexual?

❑ Chronic physical health problems?

❑ Mental illness or emotional instability?

❑ An unusual amount of anger, violence or cruelty?

❑ Sexual promiscuity and/or deviance?

❑ Being plagued by thoughts of guilt or shame?

❑ A high degree of grief over loss or disappointments?

❑ Compulsive behavioural traits – control and manipulation, addictions, co-dependency, suicide ideation or a death wish?

❑ Rebellion in the form of criminal activity, conflict, unforgiveness, retaliation, hatred, witchcraft ...?

❑ Social isolation – rejection of others; rejection by others?

❑ Other..?

Then, you may need to break the related curses on your family line.
Seek your pastor/ counsellor/other prayer minister for assistance to:

1. REPENT (feel regret/remorse/guilt/sorrow).
2. RENOUNCE (reject or voluntarily give up a belief or habit).
3. BREAK OFF (sever/detach/end association/stop abruptly).
4. BLESS (invoke or summon divine protection/aid).

Comments:

Client Handout: THE INHERITANCE OF FREEMASONRY

Involvement in Freemasonry through the various *lodges* and similar *secret societies* can be connected to seemingly insolvable problems in a family's history. Generation after generation can be afflicted by constant frustrations such as:

> ➢ lack of financial or spiritual progress
> ➢ mental and emotional instability
> ➢ unending conflicts and marital problems
> ➢ rebellious children
> ➢ chronic and fatal health problems
> ➢ business failures
> ➢ tragedies and accidental deaths

We cannot generalise that the root of all family problems stems from Masonic involvement – however, when something like a mysterious virus continues to contaminate the family line, even after much ministry and counselling, then Freemasonry could be something to consider and factor in. It could be that persistent problems associated with specific curses are coming from present or past involvement in Freemasonry. Remember that future generations can continue to be 'infected' unless specific curses are revealed and specifically broken (ask your counsellor for resources on *Generational Connections: Sins & Iniquities*).

With specialist ministry, these curses can be dealt with in order to free a Christian believer. The freed, cleansed individual can then seek deliverance on behalf of the family line. It is usually lack of knowledge and lack of practical application of the keys that impedes deliverance of the family line. A little background knowledge is given here to assist in understanding the seriousness of the problem. It is hoped that this will be an encouragement to you to step into further freedom in your Christian walk, rather than this knowledge becoming a cause for confusion or alarm. Seek the counsel of your pastoral support if necessary.

FREEMASONRY

Freemasonry can be described as a religious system. Even though the terminology of the Christian faith is incorporated, this system is totally opposed to Christianity. As a religion it is believed to have originated in Ancient Egypt and Babylon and also has its roots in older organizations such as the Druids. However, historically and formally, it is generally believed to have been birthed when the first Grand Lodge of those in the trade of masonry was founded in London in 1717.

This *religious system* began as a stonemason's Mutual Benefit Society, much the same as our workers' unions or our chambers of commerce today. This tradesman's society developed into an *international benevolent fraternity* and became known for its many charitable causes. On the surface, it appeared to be a *fraternal order* – a brotherhood attracting men from a cross-section of society, including the very rich and influential. Underneath, *the Enemy* has had a much more sinister long term goal: to create a foothold for demonic influence on the God-ordained structure of the family. This secret society or club would impact families and communities for generations to come and spawn many conspiracy theories and speculations as to its true agenda.

Developed as a business guild with an emphasis on 'looking after its own' (members), it is now generally known for its strange initiation ceremonies, distinctive symbols and secret signs – such as the regalia and the handshakes used to recognise *'the brothers'*. Some have undoubtedly used the society as a vehicle to gain power and influence in churches, governments, finance and business. Part of the attraction would be that it is open to any interested person who is willing to undergo the initiation and to move along the ranks via the *Degrees of the Brotherhood*. There is a great deal of pomp and ceremony involved in the progression and to conferring positions of honour to members of the Order.

A diversity of seekers has been attracted to its principles of brotherly love, charitable relief work and. its reputation of 'respectability'. Church elders, politicians, and wealthy professionals have sought fraternal acceptance alongside the 'average' person. Influential men have acquired success and reputation through Freemasonry involvement. Numerous presidents of the United States of America and members of the British royal family are, or have been, Freemasons. The infamous have also associated themselves – including Hitler who made use of the symbolic rites of this religion and Jack the Ripper who left Masonic emblems and coded messages at his ghastly crime scenes.

Although the workings are exposed and discussed openly in present times (usually as a warning against involvement) in reality, it has always been *a secret society.* Present participating members remain closed lipped and exclusive. The element of *'mystical truths'* is attractive to some seekers of 'enlightenment'. Members have always sought knowledge of its workings by participation through *degrees.* These degrees offer a pathway of progression – through permitted admission to *secret rites* and progressive revelation of doctrines (opposed to the Holy Scriptures).

Taking secret oaths and participating in ceremonies involving curses and cursing, gives access to *the mysteries.* Knowingly, or in ignorance, its members are actually performing *witchcraft*, and are taking part in a satanic form of worship. It can be classed as *a false religion* with a *false priesthood.* This blasphemy involves domination of women and children and the deception, control and intimidation of its own members.

---

*For more information and a prayer workbook by Yvonne Kitchen, write to: – Fruitful Vine Ministries P.O. Box 1112, Mountain Gate, Victoria, 3156, Australia. Also refer to resources written by ex-members of Freemasonry. The author makes no claim to expertise in this field, but for experiencing the repercussions on her family members from their personal involvement with the *Rosicrucian Order* (a 'branch' of Freemasonry.

The consequences of involvement can be dire. At the start, covenants are made with Satan usually out of ignorance. A family's spiritual freedom then becomes progressively forfeited by becoming an increasing part of this evil conspiracy. It is often described as *'death in the family'* and can be a powerful force within the church family when infiltration occurs. The 'benefits' Freemasonry <u>actually</u> affords are access to idolatry and the occult, with the associated rewards of: – barrenness, infirmity, poverty, defeat, oppression, and family breakdown.

> QUOTE: *'A Mason doesn't know what is really going on until he gets up to the higher degrees of Freemasonry. We consciously mislead him. He is intentionally misled by misinterpretation'* **Albert Pike, Supreme Pontiff of Universal Freemasonry, Morals and Dogma.**

However, the Holy Scriptures state that **there is nothing covered that will not be revealed** (Lk 12:2-3). If you are a member of the Body of Christ, and you feel that you and your family have been affected, you are encouraged to seek ministry in this area. Speak to your Christian counsellor and ask the Lord to lead you to a trustworthy source of specialist ministry. The Word says we are able to renounce 'secret and shameful ways'. *Renouncing* means, *'speaking off one's self – to command away verbally by rejecting, disowning, or breaking the legal right'.* The good news to the child of God is that, even a personal deliberate breaking of our covenant with him can be revoked. Your family lineage <u>can</u> be delivered and your rightful inheritance restored, in full, under the provision of the Cross of Jesus Christ.

Be firm in your faith that both individual and general curses can be rendered ineffective. 'Perfect love drives out all fear'. There is no room for fear when you are covered by the perfect love of God – even when pacts with demonic forces have been deliberately made by yourself, or by members of your family. But, because these oaths have been verbally taken, it is wise that they be verbally renounced and revoked; the curses need to be dealt with as revealed by the Holy Spirit.

Prayers of agreement by committed bible believing Christians need to be spoken over the parties concerned, in the authority of Jesus' Name and under the power and covering of the Blood of Jesus. Involvement, whether direct or otherwise, needs to be repented of and renounced – even to the extent of participation by your forefathers (members of the family in previous generations).

Jer 11:9-17; 14:19-21; 16:19-21.

AUTHOR'S TESTIMONY – Release from the Bondage of Freemasonry

The Cross of Jesus Christ has won our freedom. However, we need to recognise and appropriate that freedom by 'condemning every tongue that has risen against us in judgment' (Isa 54:17). We must speak to the mountain with authority (Mark 11:23). We are to resist the devil and he will flee from us (Jas 4:7).

I have personally had much release by degrees (of revelation) as God the Father has gently and persuasively added more knowledge and conviction as to the devastating effects of my own father and brother's involvement in Freemasonry. Strange personal afflictions continued to plague me up to 25 years following my conversion. They have been progressively lifted and cleansed from my life – particularly infirmity, depression and a death wish.

As with the blind man at Bethsaida, who was progressively healed by Jesus, I needed God's graciousness to process my spiritual blindness. Just as my forebears had become involved by the Degrees of this movement, I was led into freedom by degrees (Mk 8:22-26). I had been without discernment and spiritual sight for so long I saw only 'men like stumps moving about' to begin with. Progressively the scales fell off as I had administered to me many doses of spiritual insight and revelation as to what had contributed to my blindness.

Beginning to see for the first time – after a lifetime of spiritual blindness – was a major adjustment for me. As with patients who have their sight restored through surgery, it is sometimes overwhelming to have the senses flooded with information. Over time, the brain learns to interpret what the eyes see and to make sense of it all.

In particular, I found many forgiveness issues and needs. I needed to seek forgiveness on behalf of my family for their involvement in the Lodge, as well as for my own personal association and accountability. Unwitting association through marital ties and sexual and occult involvement, needed to be specifically dealt with also. Spiritual doors needed to be closed firmly behind me for the future protection of our children and grandchildren.

God was gentle, patient and faithful. Our family's freedom has been maintained to this day, with each member of our direct lineage released and fully committed to Him as Lord of their lives.

APPENDICES

APPENDIX I

MINISTRY TO CHILDREN & FAMILIES

CLIENT TESTIMONIAL: The Rebellious Child

The frilled neck lizard incident with Miss V in the girls' gym class was the last straw I think. It was a fitting climax to my psychological warfare strategy with Mr T. My plan to annoy the hell out of him had really weakened him just before the Christmas holidays. I suspected he was soft on Miss V. So I figured she would be his Achilles heel. I was right.

Mr T wouldn't be back in the new year to torture us with his alliterations and stanzas, his stupid poems and his silly girly laugh. One down and three to go I thought. I had had enough of school. If I couldn't leave, then the teachers I hated the most would be sorry they ever chose the teaching profession.

All my teachers had it in for me. All the staff had had enough of me. They were ganging up. They said it was a waste; because I had a good brain but that my behaviour was 'unacceptable'. Mr T said I was a 'waste of space'. Not very poetic! Now, he was poetry in motion when he exploded – his face was a colour to die for! How was I to know he had high blood pressure and a weak heart?

Unacceptable behaviour… They should have heard and seen their mate Mr T! Anyway, I must have been the only topic of conversation in the staff room, as they all used the same stupid phrases to tell me off. It was my 'rebellious nature', my 'confrontational behaviour', my 'defiance', and my 'unrepentant attitude' that was the problem.

I had won. I was heading for expulsion for sure this time. And that's what I wanted – to get out of there. School was boring, claustrophobic and useless to me. I could learn more off the net. I had no friends there, since Cathy dipped out. Besides, their religious stuff was driving me crazy.

After the lizard, my mum said it was time I learned to grow up. (She made certain threats to me, which I cannot repeat here). She talked the old gnat faced school principal into giving me just one more chance. That was one year ago, just after my fifteenth.

That was when they handed me over to Mrs M, the school counsellor. The conditions were that I be given three months to clean up my act or mum would be carrying out her threats.

Looking back over the past year, I see she was right. If she had not taken me along to both the school chaplain for prayer ministry and to Mrs M for behavioural therapy, I don't know where I'd be now. Yes, I do. I'd be in jail or I'd probably be knocked up like my best friend Cathy and a single mum on the pension. My mum would be bringing up my kid like Cathy's mum, and that would be entirely unfair on her.

But, a year ago, I didn't even think what was fair or unfair on anyone but me. I got ropeable if someone dared cross me; but I couldn't see what I was doing to upset anyone else – especially mum. I didn't care about anyone but myself. I was a selfish brat. I wonder what happened to poor Mr T…

When I first got hauled into the counsellor's office, I was angry as… Then, there was some emergency and she left the room in the middle of telling me off. I sneaked a look at my file. I saw a list with things like: Amelia is of 'low emotional intelligence', 'at risk', 'gifted, but', an 'across the board underachiever' and 'extremely antisocial'. She had ticked behavioural disorders ODD & ADD. Hey, I thought, I'm not that bad! And what's that ODD thing? I know what ADD stands for – I don't pay attention or stick to anything, which equals 'attention deficit disorder'. I decided to look that ODD one up on the net when I got home.

Now the list did say I was 'gifted'. I like that one. I know I've got talent. I'm going to be a star one day with my music and my voice. Mum jokes I've got 'high recognition needs'. I don't need an education to be famous. So why waste my time learning boring garbage like maths and business. I can work a computer and I'll have my agent and managers. I know who I am and what I want. I just don't know how I am going to get it… yet.

The other kids spruke on about 'I just wanna do the Lord's will' and 'Oh, God helps me with my assignments' – God this and God that. I don't give a damn about all that stuff. I leave all the religion to mum. When dad ran out on us, I figured that God ran out on me too. If he can't be bothered sticking around for me, then I'm not gunna #@!!**well start chasing after him or any other crazy father. I always told mum that I'd only speak to my old man to tell him what I think of him (and that'd be when hell freezes over). I hate his guts. I don't need him and I sure don't need God.

I've had to listen to the school chaplain and all his preaching about God being there for me. I've let them pray their hearts out for me – him and Mrs M the counsellor. But that report list on Mrs M's desk that day… it did make me sit up and think about myself and where I was headed.

When I looked up ODD that night, I did see – yeah, I <u>was</u> that bad. That was what I was. That's how I functioned both at school and at home. I did tend to

> *look for trouble and intentionally annoy people. I enjoyed it. Like the website said, I was: – 'impulsive, hyperactive, aggressive, defiant, irritable, vindictive' and I wasn't sorry about any of it. I blamed everyone else and I overreact. I argue with anyone who tries to tell me what to do. Yes, I am odd; I have Oppositional Defiant Disorder and I am proud of it!*
>
> *My gifted brain began to tick over. I still went out partying until 2 am, but I crawled into bed (after vomiting up the vodka) and went to sleep vaguely thinking about how much my mum cried lately.*
>
> *I decided, that day, I would give this behavioural program that Mrs M wanted me to do a trial run. After all, I thought, I'd be sixteen in less than a year. Then I could leave home, share with Cathy and the baby and go on the dole. Who says I'm incapable of having goals?*

Except where the author recounts her personal testimony, all characters and cases are fictitious representations and any similarities to real persons or cases are unintentional and purely coincidental.

FAMILY THERAPIES

CHILDREN'S DEVELOPMENT

As seen by the testimony of the rebellious child (at the beginning of this section) the needs of children can be quite complicated and vary at different ages for various reasons. For instance, each period of about six months in early childhood development can see a child seesaw up and down from one developmental stage to the next. A period of the tantrums and hyperactivity can leave you with impressions of a demonic takeover bid on your previously adorable baby. Next, you could be taken by surprise with an overnight change back into a caring, obedient little model of co-operation and affection. Then there comes a move into the big wide world with school life for the next 10 to 20 years. This includes the turmoil of the teen years! Need more be said about the difficulty of keeping abreast as parents and carers?

SPRITUAL NEEDS OF THE YOUNG

However, the typical little child does not need logical explanations to prove God exists. Jesus placed a high value on children, stating that, unless we as adults return to this stage or *'become like little children'*, we will not enter the Kingdom. Children are naturally open and trusting towards God and the concepts of prayer and worship.

Little ones just need to be told about a heavenly father who loves and cares for them in order to elicit an appropriate response. This natural spirituality needs nurture in the early years in order to retain that natural trust as the child struggles to grow up in a fallen world with a myriad of challenges to face. As someone once said, the Christian faith is indeed *'never more than one generation from extinction'* and that *'God has no grandchildren'*.

LAYING GODLY FOUNDATIONS

As another saying goes, *'we are all God's children'*. To adults I 'preach' getting back to childlike trust in the heavenly Father rather than reliance and dependence on psychology, therapies and experts in any field. To me, fulfilment in my calling means being a messenger for him, and this entails participating in a small part of God's bigger picture for healing and restoration of his beloved children. I like to consider myself as an encourager – a Barnabas – rather than a therapist.

THE AUTHOR'S PERSONAL WALK & TRAINING

As an individual, I have looked to God first for my personal restoration. I have been under some wonderful ministry from my brothers and sisters in Christ – especially other authors – for healing and dealing with many issues. I have also undergone direct Holy Spirit training in order to help others in the way I have been helped. Following all these experiences came the secular training. I have researched and practised the methods others bring to the areas of both secular and spiritual counselling. Then, quite contentedly, I have settled into my own area of expertise and specialization, that is, ministry to the Body of Christ.

As a counsellor and prayer minister, I have limited experience in the areas of marriage or couples counselling, family therapy, or in dealing clinically with the problems of young children. My main expertise is in one on one counselling, mentoring, and inner healing. Although I am called upon to play many roles in the counselling process, my main thrust and anointing is in the Restoration Ministry – restoration of man, restoring human relationships and, the most crucial part of this work, man-to-God reconciliation. This ministry usually involves intensive, long-term relationships with my clients, who are all believers in Christ Jesus as their Saviour, Healer and Lord. Therefore, my 'corner of the vineyard' is a specialist field.

I find that I am confidently able to refer on my clients to other professionals and laypersons as the need arises. Knowing that I have preached the message of God's covenant love, and the need for dependence on him, gives me great satisfaction. As a Christian counsellor, I work on restoring hope to my clients. I tend to concentrate on eliminating the false perceptions they have formed of their creator and heavenly Father. My mission seems to be in laying godly foundations down, upon which other people helpers can build – particularly pastoral carers and parents.

I firmly believe that, if I can effectively minister to a client one on one as a change agent, then this will affect change in others who are in relationship with that person. In this way, I can minister indirectly to many others, even in a generational sense; and also to the family of God as a whole. The purpose of these teachings is to multiply the ministry; to widen the vision further afield by training others to be change agents for the Father.

TO ASPIRING COUNSELLORS REGARDING SPECIALIZATION

As you consider personally where your calling might lie, do not be too quick to decide on one particular area in which to specialize until you have thoroughly grasped the prayer ministry techniques as described in this text. It is suggested that you personally come under ministry for your own needs, then practise on friends and family members prior to choosing <u>any</u> field of training involved with therapeutic practices. I would also like to strongly recommend that you go further in your studies than this introduction to Christian counselling provides.

You may feel that your calling is to children or to family units. It may be in Christian marriage counselling, social work, psychology, psychiatry, chaplaincy, youth, or to the unsaved. There are so many styles of counselling, both secular and spiritual, that are open to you. Your choice will need to be spirit-led. Basically, you will have the option of being either a Christian who counsels, or a Christian counsellor.

Fortunately there are many sound Christian training institutions which provide Government approved accreditation now for Christian operatives. Even if your professional ethics become highly regarded, if you are to minister to unbelievers in a secular field, your moral values and religious belief system may vastly differ to your co-labourers and clients and you will be challenged. If you choose to gain formal qualifications, please take into consideration now that you may or may not be allowed to express your personal values and opinions during secular training. This also applies to joining a professional association or maintaining accreditation when in practice afterwards.

One last warning, the seduction of man's ways and thoughts is a strong force. Always bring everything to the heart of God and ask him for the truth about the choices you have been offered (including the content of this text). I do hope this personal view into my own walk has helped to encourage you to embark on your exciting journey ahead as a Christian counsellor – or any other mission you choose. God bless you as you receive and respond to his personal calling on <u>your</u> life.

APPENDIX II

SUICIDE RESOURCES

DISCLAIMER: This information is presented based on personal experience and research by the author. She disclaims any liability for use or misuse of this information by any person known or unknown to her. This text and the following related articles are not intended as a means of distributing medical or legal advice. The content contains links to other resources, which provide related information. However, the content and practises of the parties involved with the links are not the responsibility of the author of this text.

THE CHRISTIAN COUNSELLOR'S ROLE IN PREVENTION & INTERVENTION

It is thought possible that as many as two-thirds or even 80% of all suicidal persons communicate their intentions before killing themselves. Unfortunately, even experienced counsellors could be at the end of the receiving line of these communications and might not act upon them – either from fear or ignorance. Some potential interveners would have justified their denial and inaction by shrugging it off as *'just a bid for attention'* or *'I've heard this all before'*. So, following a 'successful' suicide, they would probably experience a certain degree of self-blame and guilt.

The best advice possible to any Christian counsellor is to take every suicidal threat, comment, or implied action, seriously. Do not dismiss or underestimate the power of despair. You might be tempted to think the problem will go away if it is ignored. Or, you could hear the essence of the message, but pretend to yourself that the communication did not happen. You could be tempted to make light of comments or threats in order to reassure and comfort the person (and yourself).

You could think that a particular person is not the type, and spontaneously say, *'surely you are not serious!'* Unfortunately, this kind of remark can be the challenge to a troubled person to prove just how wrong you are. Such a person needs attention, not dismissal. Anyone desperate enough can be 'the type'. Remember also that you have *duty of care* responsibilities (see Section One on *Office Procedures*).

If unsure of their intentions, never be afraid to ask the person plainly and directly. You could think by asking the idea might actually be planted, but this is a risk which needs to be taken. More likely, it will relieve the sufferer to know their despair is being taken seriously by the counsellor. Do not <u>assume</u> that time heals all wounds and everything will get better with a good dose of prayer ministry.

Regarding those long-term clients who are challenging and who are genuine *attention seekers*: do not attempt to shock or challenge if you are of the opinion they are not serious. Admittedly, impatient remarks could be hard to hold back if a person has been repeating self-harming threats to friends and family for quite some time. However, a confronting remark coming from someone with whom they feel they have a trust relationship, might just be the invitation to give up all hope of receiving the help they are craving.

Always be willing to listen. You might have heard the story before, but hear it again. Show determined effort and genuine interest. Be strong, firm and consistent, without dramatic displays of personal feelings and doubts about the sincerity of repeated threats. Suicide notes have even been known to express the need to self-harm in order to spite or punish those who did not seem to care.

When a candidate is actually at a critical 'at risk' stage, do not present an analysis of their behaviour or confront and challenge with your interpretations of their actions and feelings. You may be able to carefully point out the consequences. Open ended questioning can produce awareness of how their actions will involve and hurt the ones they love, e.g. *'how do you think this is going to affect the grandchildren?'* The aim is to encourage hope and responsibility, without adding shame and blame to the mix.

However, do not argue with the individual about whether they should live or die – an argument which can not be won. The only possible position to take is that the person must live. Thoughts of *ambivalence* (the state of feeling two conflicting emotions at the same time) are common. The ambivalence should be encouraged. Reasons to live will lie under the surface, as well as the desire to escape from life. The motivation to face life needs to rise to the surface. Assurance that their desperation has been registered is what the despairing, hurting soul needs to hear the most.

As the helper, this is the time for absolute faith and personal confidence in the goodness and faithfulness of God. This confidence needs to be apparent. The candidate's ambivalence needs to be worked on in order to tip the scales towards hope and away from despair. Assure the suffering one that all problems are temporary and do have a solution – in comparison, that is, to death. Express that suicide is **a permanent answer to a temporary problem**. Confidently and aggressively express that the chronic pain or a crisis situation does not have to be faced alone; others can, and will, help.

If the person *at risk* believes in God, and you know some positive aspects of their background, bring forward the spiritual aspects. Talk of the times things did actually work out in their favour; recall the blessings you know of from their past experiences. This is definitely not the occasion preach at them; instead comfort and encourage your self with the scriptures. Definitely, do not warn or make threats of the dire consequences of going to hell or suffering in purgatory! Instead bring to mind God's enduring love (use gentle tones as if speaking to a child). If the person expresses no belief in a god/God, or previous faith has been lost, work on these issues at a more appropriate time (when the 'at risk' factors are not so high).

On the other hand, if we learn that a person has taken an overdose of pills, or we are challenged with a knife wielding candidate, we obviously do not sit with them showing empathy and warmth, nor discuss plans as to how we will line up an appointment for them to see the pastor next week. If a person is at critical risk of self-harm, harming others, or has just made a suicide attempt, contact emergency services immediately.

There will be other less obvious situations where you will not so sure of intervention procedures. You might be physically absent from the scene because you have received a calls for help from someone at risk via the telephone or email, or perhaps you will be contacted by a third party who is not able to help. Without being there to fully assess the person's status or situation first hand, you could feel forced to initiate a call to emergency services such as the ambulance, the police, or a local mental health assessment team, to request direct intervention.

Remember, even if it turns out that you have been alarmed unnecessarily, you have at least acted responsibly and possibly saved a life. This thought should be worth the risk of personal embarrassment or discomfort over misjudging the situation. Even if you are on the spot, if you are unsure of the risk, it is better to seek help, than to gamble with the outcome.

The Christian helper needs to have the faith at any stage of helping someone who could be at risk of self-harming: that we do have a divine source of strength and wisdom – that *'all things are possible through Christ Jesus'*. Use every material and spiritual, resource available to help the troubled person cope successfully with whatever crisis they are experiencing. If you are not confident in the ministering position, do not be reticent about offering alternate resources or referring on to someone else who <u>can</u> help. Sometimes, we just need to step out of the role of counsellor and 'spiritual healer' and simply act as a *bridging friend* to successfully show the sufferer that someone does care.

Acknowledge your personal limitations – even in low risk and non-critical circumstances during the counselling process. If you feel the need to refer on to more experienced and/or professional helpers do not feel that this is an admission of failure on your part. It is a mature recognition that none of us can help everybody all of the time. However, do learn the practical suicide prevention and intervention skills. Be prepared for crisis situations. Research your resources as a Christian counsellor <u>before</u> you actually need them.

There is excellent training for suicide prevention and intervention skills available in the author's local area *(ASSIST:* www.livingworks.net). We are also blessed with a response service, carer education and support groups for the bereaved through suicide *(STANDBY:* www.unitedsynergies.com.au). If there is no training or bereavement support network accessible locally, key in '*suicide intervention training*' to do a search on the internet. If you do not have access to a computer, thoroughly study the resources presented in this text and adapt these to suit your own needs. Laminate your own plan of action with relevant emergency contacts and have it on hand.

Be aware that anyone who enters your realm of ministry could be a potential suicide candidate. Professionally, I have needed to set up a clear system of evaluation and assessment with a code system that personally works for me. If lacking vital referral information you may like to seek help from a more experienced local counsellor to gather yours together. General medical practitioners, ministers of religion and professional counsellors should have a resource file of people and places on hand. In remote geographical areas, the range of choices can be limited. In the author's homeland of Australia, there is the Christian based organisation *(Lifeline:* www.lifeline.org.au) contactable 24 hours via telephone on 131114. There are other resources on the web relating to depression and other health issues, which are very helpful.

Private medical practitioners (GPs) often represent the first line of action – either your own doctor or the client's personal physician. You might need to offer to accompany the person with suicide ideation as an *advocate* in specific situations. Together you can gain access to referrals to psychiatrists, psychologists, and mental health care assessors. The client might have isolated to such a degree that no personal resources are left. Advocacy could link your client to other vital mental health care professionals and provide help for both of you.

Sometimes, all a client might need is to be linked to a good resource person such as a doctor, lawyer or banker to help with a specific practical problem before despair takes over. Ministers of religion, willing and able to be on the coalface, should have expertise in handling crisis situations. Get to know your local pastors and chaplains and be aware of their different helping styles prior to needing their services. Access and refer on to those shepherds who are practical – as well as spiritually minded – those who will not be afraid to intervene if they are faced with a real life and death situation.

AUTHOR'S MINISTRY EXPERIENCE

It has been a major concern of the author to experience a lack of awareness and disinterest in learning prevention and intervention skills both in church circles and in schools. This is especially concerning when churches encourage and attract so many troubled people – ranging from the seriously mentally ill, through to those who sometimes appear to be a little eccentric – and of course with schoolchildren the whole cross-section of society applies. Lack of interest in training staff members and a network of carers are of particular concern. If mental health issues are detected early enough by those trained in awareness, so much heartache can be avoided.

In regard to churches, it has been necessary for the author to contact a minister of religion and plead with him/her to equip a team of carers, because there was a potential candidate at high risk within their own congregation. One sufferer was directly told by her pastor when she expressed suicide ideation prior to a church service, 'well, you won't get to heaven then, will you?' He promptly left her standing alone and unaided. No follow up of her case was attempted by this church because the gatekeeper was inept. This is a dramatic, true illustration of 'the head in the sand' attitude.

In my personal ministry, I have been made aware of the reality of demonic involvement in the temptation to suicide. Professionally, in one year alone, I had a total of nine actual cases of suicidal ideation come across my path. This was in dealing with my major clientele base – committed church going Christians – and this included three who were actually at high to extreme risk status. Praise God all survived by his grace and his mercy. It was a busy year.

This led me to believe in the possibility of seasons of concerted effort and activity by the principalities and powers of darkness to come against the Body of Christ. I became aware of this by discovering that my network of associates in the secular world did not seem to be experiencing the same crisis situation during that particular period. Intervention by intercession and applying the power of his name and his protective blood was so absolutely necessary – and effective. He is indeed faithful.

AUTHOR'S TESTIMONY

To Intercessors and Burden Bearers on the subject of Suicide:

I am addressing fellow 'soul-searchers'. By this, I mean melancholy personality types who tend towards a lifestyle of deep analysis and much introspection. In such types, there seems to be a relentless quest to find emotional and spiritual release and peace.

There will be some who will never find internal peace, as they will remain overly sensitive and prone to self-condemnation for a lifetime. There will be others who will learn that this is a natural state for them – even a gift from God at times. Those privileged, will learn to see great beauty and fulfilment comes from soul-searching. Unfortunately, this personality bent is usually not realised as a gift until a degree of maturity is reached.

As a child, I was an outcast in this state – dwelling in a type of morbid, self-punishing form of existence. There is definitely something amiss when a child grows up with night dreams of funerals and with waking thoughts centring on death and decay. I wanted to live and to enjoy life, but I did not know how to handle my serious and intense nature. I tended to be attracted to the darkness and to dwell on the depressing side of life – to take more interest in suffering than most.

However, I truly wanted to be different – to find the joy of existing in what I now know as such a beautiful, vibrant world: I pined to be understood and to be lifted out of my darker self. I wanted to fit into the world, as other children seemed to easily do. With all my heart I wanted to be classed as `normal'. I cursed the personality type I was 'blessed with'. I had no one to show me the blessing it would become to me.

To those of you reading this who feel they can personally relate to what I am saying, I encourage you to take heart. God has not made a mistake in how he has designed you. There are many of us who are tempted to think of ourselves as God's 'mistakes', particularly those in the calling of intercessory prayer and burden bearing. Now be assured from one who knows differently – we have been created for a purpose. We are gifted with the personality we need to fulfil that purpose. We need to accept that, for our personality types, it is normal to be sensitive to suffering.

I had a church friend who could not accept this. She made a deliberate decision to put an end to her sufferings. She chose to take her own life. To me, her funeral seemed to be an unusual mix of grief, rejoicing and relief. The congregation no longer had to watch her suffer. We all knew where she was. She was at peace. Outsiders might have looked on and wondered over our united response – especially those of her natural family with strong Roman Catholic conviction regarding suicide. We wished it could have been via a different path, but her church family rejoiced that she was with her beloved Jesus.

The strange footnote to her life was that she left a legacy of souls who entered the Kingdom of God through her strong evangelical spirit. There were so many who could truly say that they would be eternally grateful to this young wife and mother who offered them life. Sadly, there could have been many, many more souls who could have benefited.

Perhaps, if I had come into her life further down the path, on the victory side of my own problems, then I might have spoken to her and offered her more hope. I still feel that I empathized with her suffering more than anyone at that time – back then, when I had no answer. However, I <u>was</u> able to deliver to her a scripture. She understood and acknowledged that it was a personal warning from God. She indicated that she had already made her choice. At the time, for a myriad of reasons, I had no choice but to respect her decision.
If I had known then what I know now, things might have been different.

However, for those like me who have chosen to go on, we can celebrate our lives. We realise that we do have a strange empathetic calling: He has created us to share his compassionate heart. We somehow ease the personal burdens of others. We are companions to the suffering ones as others cannot be. Called to be handmaidens and brothers in his service, we minister in His Name to the desperate and despairing.

I know that sometimes I experience a spiritual identification, as if the need has become mine personally. My heart breaks with the sufferer, rather than for them. My soul understands briefly the depth of their emotions. I feel the particular distress. In earlier days it was very confusing trying to sort out my own emotions from those I was in intercession for, however God faithfully trained me in this calling, until I began to see how his yoke was meant to be easy and his burden light (because he is yoked to us). He has indeed accomplished the work already via the Cross. Our necessary participation in sharing his yoke remains a mystery to me, but I do believe that, if this ministry is understood and utilised more to God's glory, then a person will not suffer from burnout or 'compassion fatigue'.

I once found a description of suffering by Elizabeth Goudge in `The Heart of the Family': 'It is the essence of it (suffering) that is a lonely thing... But there are those who at times can reach a world consciousness of suffering... a man who had been in a concentration camp talked to me about it once. He said that for a moment or two there can come to you, through your own suffering, a consciousness of the suffering of the whole world... it was only those moments that made it possible to go on'.

As for me, I have to admit that life has been a struggle in many areas where it should not have been. In the years prior to my salvation I lived a lie based life.

I believed that life was not worth living in a world of suffering, where I was a misfit who did not know anything I could do about changing it. I wanted to die throughout childhood because I felt I had no meaning or purpose in life. I had actually attempted suicide through drowning at sixteen years of age. This was based on the perception that life was too much of a struggle to endure and that I no longer cared about anything in it. Also, for many years following my genuine conversion as a young woman, I continued to feel self-hatred – wanting to be any one but me.

But no more! My covenant with death has been renounced and annulled (Isa 28:15-18). I have chosen life. I have learnt the delights of being alive. I am now in his service, helping others to freedom. I have accepted, and love, the way he has made me. I have been created to be his companion and to reveal this common purpose to others. No matter what the circumstances, I now maintain my purpose and the joy and peace of my born again experience. Is this not the wonderful and purpose-filled message of salvation? This is the good news we Christians have been born to deliver!

We are offered the chance to choose life and to live it more abundantly. We can experience the truth that God has made us and called us according to his purpose. All he requires of us is: 'to do what is just, to show constant love, and to live in humble fellowship with our God' (Micah 6:8). To please him we each need to come to a gentle place of self-acceptance and reception of his giftings, surrendering our struggle to swim against the current of our destinies. Through this acceptance we are assured that we will be swept to safety – onto the peaceful shores of the personal promises we have received from him.

DISCLAIMER: The following resources are presented based on personal experience and research by the author. She disclaims any liability for use or misuse of this information by any person known or unknown to her. This text on the subject of suicide is not intended as a means of disseminating medical or legal advice but is supplied for general information purposes only. It is strongly advised that professional expertise on the subject be sought.

#1 MOST COMMON RISK FACTORS CHECKLIST

To evaluate Suicidal Potential

- ❑ Clients with a psych history, especially psychosis or conduct disorder
- ❑ Sudden and notable 'improvement' from depressive state
- ❑ Tidying up affairs, giving away personal possessions, making out will
- ❑ Present signs of suicidal intent – attempt, threat or hint
- ❑ Previous self-harm or suicide attempt(s)
- ❑ History of suicidal behaviours
- ❑ Substance abuse history
- ❑ Weak will to live and lack of psychological and emotional hardiness/resilience
- ❑ Significant other(s) in life who has/have attempted suicide
- ❑ Recent significant stress such as job loss or relationship breakdown
- ❑ Poor social support or isolation
- ❑ Lack of communal religious affiliation
- ❑ Male 20-44 years old or male over 65 years (males from 15-40 and over 75 are high risk groups in Australia)
- ❑ Chronic illness, unrelenting pain, or recent life-threatening diagnosis
- ❑ Communicating sense of hopelessness, helplessness and despair

Score (out of 15) _____ (The higher the score, the more likely the risk of suicide, so that the need for active intervention heightens).

IMPORTANT INFORMATION: When dealing with a client who has high risk factors combined with a high score on the *Common Risk Factors Checklist*, it is advisable to check daily for suicidal status. Record the current status via a points system to define change. Code the file with coloured stickers to suit your own personal system (making sure your co-workers and others involved have a working and recorded knowledge of the system). Date any new application of stickers, as status changes and inform the carers concerned, e.g. mental health care worker, spouse, parent, pastor or medical practitioner. Please refer to previous disclaimers.

#2 SUICIDE RISK EVALUATIONS – GENERAL ASSESSMENT

CHECK ALL CLIENTS GENERALLY AS FOLLOWS:

1. Look for symptoms of depression and other emotional disturbances such as frustration, feeling overwhelmed, or having unbearable psychological pain.
2. Investigate for sleeping disorders such as sleep deprivation, insomnia, sleep disturbance or sleeping too much.
3. Assess for panic attacks or general psychological anxiety. (Refer to appropriate texts or websites for assessment guides).
4. Note signs of self-denigration (belittling/devaluing) and a sense of worthlessness and shame.
5. Is there verbal expression or other expressed sense of hopelessness and helplessness and lack of interest in change or absence of motivation to continue seeking help?
6. Note signs of morbidity – unusual interest in death or unpleasant events, or demonic activity, or questions regarding methods of suicide.
7. Investigate for lack of pleasure in usual pursuits, constricted activities, isolating self and listlessness. (Use spiritual, emotional or psychological assessment for depression).
8. Factor in tendency for alcohol or other substance abuse (including food, violence, erratic driving or other risk taking).
9. Note any changes to usual demeanour or character: – spirituality, listlessness/lethargy, no longer caring about appearance or personal affairs; or decrease in concentration, constriction of thoughts, obsessions; or unusual calmness, putting affairs in order; or general agitation or restlessness, aggressiveness or talk of violence and revenge.

#3 SUICIDE IDEATION EVALUATION CHECKLISTS

VERBAL

- ❑ Open talk of suicide
- ❑ Talk of not being present in the near future
- ❑ Questions about suicide and the afterlife
- ❑ Unambiguous statements (*I don't want to live any more.*)
- ❑ No longer talking to counsellor
- ❑ No desire to communicate at all
- ❑ Communicating desire to escape from the pain/struggle

BEHAVIOURAL

- ❑ Severe depression (including apathy, insomnia)
- ❑ Sudden improvement in mental attitude
- ❑ Guilt, shame, embarrassment
- ❑ Feelings of hostility, revenge
- ❑ Tension and anxiety
- ❑ Poor judgment
- ❑ Lack of self-control/responsibility
- ❑ Knowledge of available methods
- ❑ Clearly thought-out expressed plans
- ❑ Seeking to acquire means (prescriptions, excessive alcohol)
- ❑ Means & method made available (gun, drugs, pills)
- ❑ Giving away possessions or returning items
- ❑ Buying or updating insurance
- ❑ Paying long-standing bills & putting other affairs in order (e.g. will)

SYMPTOMATIC

- ❑ Feelings of helplessness and hopelessness
- ❑ Confused thinking
- ❑ Tendency to complain/compulsive negativity
- ❑ Rebellious/defiant attitude (e.g. *I'll show them and they'll be sorry*)
- ❑ Drug or drinking problem
- ❑ Inability to control impulses
- ❑ Mental or physical disabilities
- ❑ Loss of faith/purpose in living

SITUATIONAL

- ❑ Loss of loved person by death, divorce, separation
- ❑ Loss of money, prestige, job (including retirement)
- ❑ Sickness, serious illness, surgery, accident, loss of limb
- ❑ Threat of criminal prosecution
- ❑ Increased responsibilities
- ❑ Failure of counselling/medical help/relief for physical and emotional pain

RESOURCES (lack of)

- ❑ Support of friends, relatives, carers, and so on – unavailable
- ❑ Family and friends available but unwilling to help
- ❑ No church or community contact
- ❑ Isolated and living alone
- ❑ Overt absence of spirituality (faith)
- ❑ No goals or purpose in life
- ❑ Hope gone
- ❑ Health poor
- ❑ Lack of finances, opportunities, etc

LEVEL OF INTENT TO SUICIDE

Using the *Suicide Evaluation Checklist* as a general guide to the seriousness of intent, classify the level of suicidal intent as *White, Yellow, Blue, Red or Extreme Status.* Then, follow up by discussion with a supervisor as to its veracity and as to whether to consider consulting a mental health care professional for assessment.

If the client suffers from a physical health problem, a mental illness or a personality/conduct disorder, assessment by a mental health worker or a medical practitioner is <u>always</u> recommended. Unfortunately, you will not always be aware of psychological or physical problems; so pray for divine leading and Holy Spirit guidance in all your dealings with the troubled client.

Professional management of a highly lethal patient is crucial and this means a continual monitoring of intent and means. Your assessment at the foundational level is extremely important, as you could be the first point of contact for a potential candidate. If in doubt, prayerfully seek advice. It is better to do something, rather than do nothing at all.

Ideally, it is advisable that you work directly with the client's significant others (spouse, parents, adult children, etc) and endeavour to keep informed those who need to be informed. However, sometimes this is not possible when the significant others are contributing to the problem, or are not willing to be involved. Discretion is advised. Spiritual discernment and wisdom should be sought.

Remember that a client's overt suicidal (or homicidal) plans should never be kept secret between the counsellor and client. These matters of life and death override the usual canons (rules) of confidentiality.

RECORD OF PERSONAL RESOURCES:

INDEX FOR SO YOU WANT TO BE A PRAYER COUNSELLOR
(Graphics are listed in the Contents at the front of this book)

W

www.ingramcontent.com/pod-product-compliance
Lightning Source LLC
Chambersburg PA
CBHW080241030426
42334CB00023BA/2663